MW00904313

Pre-Exam Course Workbook

Real Estate Training Institute

ISBN: 9798580172729

Real Estate Training Institute

Name _____

Month _____

Year _____

Google Classroom Code

_____

Online Classroom Login for www.goretionline.com

Learner Support Site

Access is granted to the school's fully functional Online Website at: www.goretionline.com. You may complete your profile with pictures, "Friend" others and communicate freely. You may delete your account at any time.

Username

_____

Email used for www.goretionline.com

_____

Password Clue

_____

Notes:

Welcome to the Real Estate Training Institute

Our Mission

Our mission is to provide our adult learners with the highest quality instruction in classroom and online real estate courses to prepare them for a successful professional career in the real estate industry.

Our Vision

The Real Estate Training Institute will flourish as a distinctive Mississippi institution of learning that fosters a culture of diversity, values, and student-centered experiences. As the premier real estate licensee support system, RETI will remain dedicated to the positive development of Mississippi's real estate community.

Our Statement of Diversity

The Real Estate Training Institute is dedicated to creating an intellectual, cultural, and social climate that allows everyone the opportunity to contribute to the educational experiences at the school.

The people at the Real Estate Training Institute promote acceptance and appreciation of all individuals regardless of age, sex, race, color, marital status, familial status, physical or mental disability, religious creed, national origin or sexual preference and identity.

Our Philosophy of Education

Quality education is paramount.

Collaboration

Nurturing an environment grounded in common goals and trust enable our school members to reach beyond the jurisdictional and educational minimums. Together we search for what our adult learners need and deserve both educationally and individually and foster a safe environment where our instructors and learners become explorers and risk-takers of innovation. Removing the fear to participate begins the concrete foundation on which the Real Estate Training Institute operates. A quality education grows from a positive school environment.

Inclusiveness

Fostering social networks, friendships, and support to enhance the personal growth of our adult learners is essential. Communication between the adult learners to instructors and learner to learner provides social interaction to many learners who may not have had the opportunity of group inclusiveness unless participating in RETI's adult programs. The individual's desire to be included is respected. Our backs never turn towards our learners.

Continuous Improvement

Continuous school improvement is a necessary component of the Real Estate Training Institute's quality education. Improvements begin with our instructor's commitment to life-long learning and exploring. Participation in the Real Estate Educators Association is mandatory to foster instructor growth and development for the continuous improvement of the Real Estate Training Institute.

Open Door Policy

By opening the doors to our classrooms through both physical and virtual environments, we strive to improve real estate consumer safety and experiences with our graduates. We open our classrooms to educators not only in our schools but to schools creating a positive impact in the community.

Leadership

Leadership starts at the top. We value our instructor's expertise by focusing on their strengths first. We then help them develop in other areas to foster their leadership skills. We continuously inspire our instructors to be leaders.

Our instructors inspire our learners not to be followers but to lead. Our learners are encouraged to be leaders in their communities.

Communication

Through the school's use of Zoom, www.goretionline.com, Google Classroom, and chat, we aspire to be accessible through digital communication.

Headings; Gender

The headings in this book and all reference material and statements by representatives of the Real Estate Training Institute are for convenience of reference. Unless the context clearly indicates otherwise, each pronoun herein shall be deemed to include the masculine gender, feminine gender, neutral gender, singular gender, vice-versa and plural forms.

Locations

Biloxi 2650 Beach Blvd. #35 Biloxi, MS 39531 (across from the Edgewater Mall) (228) 35-8585	**Southaven** 728 Goodman Rd E. (The stand-alone building.) Southaven, MS 38672
Oxford The Enterprise Center 9 Industrial Park Dr. Oxford, MS 38655	**Hattiesburg** Woodall Center at Pearl River Community College 906 Sullivan Dr. Hattiesburg, MS 39401

Contact

(228) 354-8585
email: information@msrealtycourses.com

Mississippi Real Estate Commission

Mississippi Real Estate Commission
Lefleur's Bluff Tower, Ste 300 4780 I-55 North
Jackson, MS 39211
Phone: (601) 321-6970
FAX: (601) 321-6955
Email: info@mrec.state.ms.us
Web: www.mrec.ms.gov

PSI Services LLC
3210 E Tropicana
Las Vegas, NV 89121
www.psiexams.com
https://candidate.psiexams.com/

Salesperson's License Qualifications

Every applicant for a resident license as a real estate salesperson shall be age eighteen (18) years or over, shall be a bona fide resident of the State of Mississippi prior to filing his application, shall have successfully completed a minimum of sixty (60) hours in courses in real estate as hereafter specified, and shall have successfully completed the real estate salesperson's examination.

Broker's License Qualifications

Every person who applies for a resident license as a real estate broker:
(a) shall be age twenty- one (21) years or over, and have his legal domicile in the State of Mississippi at the time he applies;
(b) shall be subject to the jurisdiction of this state, subject to the income tax laws and other excise laws thereof, subject to the road and bridge privilege tax laws thereof;
(c) shall not be an elector in any other state;
(d) shall have held a license as an active real estate salesperson for twelve (12) months prior to making application for the broker's examination hereafter specified;
(e) shall have successfully completed a minimum of one hundred twenty (120) hours of courses in real estate as hereafter specified; and
(f) shall have successfully completed the real estate broker's examination as hereafter specified; and
(g) shall have successfully been cleared for licensure by the commission's background investigation; and
(h) sign a form under penalty of perjury stating that the applicant will not hire any real estate salespersons for thirty-six (36) months from the date of approval of his or her active real estate salesperson's license.

Real Estate Training Institute

The Pre-Exam Course (Pre-License)

Sixty (60) hours of courses in real estate education approved by the Mississippi Real Estate Commission.

No more than eight hours of education can be delivered within a twenty-four-hour period.

General Schedules

Day Course Schedule	Night Course Schedule
Monday - Friday 8:30 am to 4:30 pm	Monday - Friday 5:30 pm to 9:30 pm
Day School Locations	**Night School Locations**
Biloxi Hattiesburg Oxford	Southaven Biloxi

(These times and days may change.)

CONTENTS

MODULE ONE: PROPERTY OWNERSHIP

Real Property vs. Personal Property

Real Property	Personal Property
• Land and things permanently attached to the land. • When you own real estate, you own from the center of the Earth and up unto infinity.	• Personal property is movable. • Personal property – "Personality" can be called chattel. • ☐ Chattel is the French word for cattle. Cattle are movable.
Conveyed by Deed	**Conveyed by Bill of Sale**
Fructus Naturales • The natural fruit of the land. (apple tree, orange tree, olive tree)	**Emblements** • Crops cultivated yearly. (corn, cucumbers, cotton, squash, tomatoes…)
☐ Once planted, oranges, grapes, pears, figs, avocados, apple trees and other natural fruit of the land are real estate.	The orange in your hand. ☐ When an orange falls from its tree, it is personal property.
Examples of Real Property include buildings, fixtures attached to the building, fences, structures, fruit, nut, and ornamental trees and bushes. Standing timber and a vineyard are real property.	Examples of personal property include the chair you are sitting on, furniture, books, tables, paper, pens…

☐ Manufactured homes can be personal property unless permanently affixed to the land.
☐ A personal property loan document is called a **Chattel Mortgage.**
☐ Standing timber is real property.

Bundle of Legal Rights

Real property includes interests, benefits, and rights automatically included in the ownership of real estate.

The bundle of legal rights/sticks includes the rights of real estate ownership.
1. Possession
2. Control
3. Enjoyment
4. Exclusion
5. Disposition
6. Encumbrance

When property transfers from the seller to the buyer, UNLESS indicated, all real property must remain.

Fixtures vs. Trade Fixtures

Fixtures	Trade Fixtures

• A fixture is a personal property that has been attached to the land or a building.	• Owned and installed by a tenant for the tenant's use.
• Doors, water heaters, built-in air conditioners, sinks, faucets, and ceiling lamps. • Fixtures include buildings, standing timber, pear trees, apple trees, orange trees, fences, doors, faucets, plumbing fixtures, washer-less faucets, hot water heaters, fences, landscape shrubs, and in-ground swimming pools. • Fixtures are the Landlord's Property.	• An article owned by a tenant, attached to a rented space, is used in conducting business. Example (Dining booths at a restaurant) • Personal property is attached by a commercial tenant to assist in a trade or business. If the tenant does not remove trade fixtures within a reasonable time after the lease expires, they become the landlord's property. • **Accession (Trade Fixtures)** • If the tenant leaves behind a trade fixture, the landlord will acquire this property by accession. • ☐ the price of a fixture does not determine if it is real or personal.

☐ A bowling alley is the most trade fixture business.

Test for Fixtures (MARIA)

1. Method of annexation
2. Agreement between the parties
3. Relationship of the parties – lessor/lessee
4. The intention of the annexor (If ivy growing in a free-standing pot attached to the front of a building, is it real Property? NO)
5. Adaptation of the article to real estate

Real vs. Personal Property Quiz

☐ QUESTION	ANSWER
1. Real property includes: a. Fixtures. b. Cultivated annual crops. c. Leasehold interests. d. Mortgages.	a. Fixtures are annexed to real property. They become real property.
2. A standing wood fence: a. Personal b. Real	b. A standing wood fence has been annexed to real property.
3. Grapes in a bowl: a. Personal b. Real	a. Grapes in a bowl have been severed from the tree. (Personal property)
4. A Vineyard: a. Personal b. Real	b. A vineyard is real property. Planted once.
5. Real Property consists of which of the following? a. trade fixtures	b. When you own real estate, you own from the center of the earth up into infinity.

b. minerals, oil, mines, or quarries c. emblements d. chattel	
6. Cultivated annual crops are normally classified as: a. Personal property. b. Fixtures. c. Real property. d. Fructus.	a. Cultivated yearly indicates personal property.
A cornfield: a. Personal b. Real	a. Planted corn is cultivated yearly. Corn is emblements. Emblements are personal property.
7. Which of the following would be considered a part of the real estate? a. Perennials planted in a tub. b. House plants. c. Annual crops (corn, wheat). d. Perennial shrubs in the ground.	d. Perennial shrubs are planted once. They are NOT cultivated yearly.
8. All the following interests in real estate are considered real property interests EXCEPT: a. Trees. b. Leases. c. Fences. d. Water rights.	b. Leases are considered personal property. The lease (paper) can be picked up and moved.
9. An olive grove: a. Personal b. Real	b. Planted once thus real.
10. All the following would be considered fixtures EXCEPT: a. Stock-designed removable storm windows. b. Custom fitted wall-to-wall carpeting. c. Built-in kitchen stove. d. Built-in dishwasher.	a. Stock-designed removable storm windows. They are removable. Method of attachment is a consideration.
11. All the following are appurtenances EXCEPT: a. Trade fixtures. b. Water rights. c. Buildings d. Mineral rights.	a. Trade fixtures are personal property.

☐ A farmer is entitled to the fruits of his/her Labor.

☐ If a tenant farmer is evicted, he is allowed to cultivate and harvest the crops. Emblements are personal property.

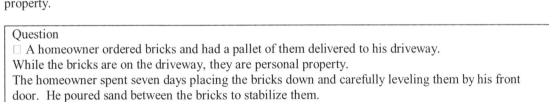

Question
☐ A homeowner ordered bricks and had a pallet of them delivered to his driveway.
While the bricks are on the driveway, they are personal property.
The homeowner spent seven days placing the bricks down and carefully leveling them by his front door. He poured sand between the bricks to stabilize them.
When that job was completed, he moved patio furniture on the completed patio. Are those bricks real or personal?

ANSWER: The bricks are real because his intention was to build a permanent patio.

Annexation	Severance
<ul><li>Personal Property can be annexed to real property.</li><li>Personal property that has been attached (annexed) to the real property becomes real property. Such as doors, windows, moldings…. They are called fixtures.</li></ul>	Real Property can be severed from real estate. A fixture severed from the real property becomes personal property. Such as doors, windows, moldings….

☐ A homeowner tore down the fence between his property and his neighbors. He put the wood on the driveway for his friend to pick up and recycle. When the fence boards are on the driveway, the fence is personal property. The fence was severed from the real property.

Appurtenances

The rights, privileges, and improvements that go with a transfer of the land, even though they may not be part of it. Examples are water rights, rights-of-way, and easements.

Surface, Subsurface, and Air Rights

Surface rights = The land. **Water Rights**	Subsurface rights = Under the land. **Mineral Rights**	Air rights/Air lots = Above the land.
Surface rights: Ownership rights in a parcel of real estate that are limited to the surface of the earth.	Subsurface rights: The rights to the natural resources below the earth's surface.	Air rights: The rights to use the space above the earth; may be sold or leased independently, provided the rights have not been limited by law.

Water Rights

Legal systems for water rights are managed by the states.
Three Types of Water Rights

Littoral Water Rights	Riparian Water Rights	Prior Appropriation
<ul><li>Littoral rights are rights concerning properties that abut stagnant water like an ocean, bay, delta, sea, or lake. Littoral rights are usually concerned with the use and enjoyment of the shore, but also may include rights to use the water.</li><li>Littoral = Navigable</li></ul>	<ul><li>Flowing Water</li><li>All landowners whose properties adjoin a body of water have the right to make reasonable use of it as it flows through or over their properties. If there is not enough water to satisfy all users, allotments are generally</li></ul>	<ul><li>The prior appropriation doctrine, or "first in time – first" in the right, was developed in the western United States in response to water scarcity in the region.</li></ul>

Waterways • Rights **cannot be lost through non-use** and are indefinite in duration.	fixed in proportion to frontage on the water source. • Riparian water rights **cannot be lost through non-use** and are indefinite in duration.	• An appropriative right **depends upon continued use** of the water and maybe lost through non-use.
These rights cannot be sold or transferred other than with the adjoining land.	These rights cannot be sold or transferred other than with the adjoining land.	These rights can generally be sold or transferred, and long-term storage is not only permissible but common.
Occur because of land ownership.	Occur because of land ownership.	An appropriative right exists without regard to the relationship between the land and water.

Littoral Water Rights

- The Mississippi River and Lake Michigan are Navigable Waterways and Littoral.
- Tidal waters ownership: The land between low water and high water is reserved for the use of the public by state law and is regulated by the state.

Riparian Water Rights

Under riparian doctrine, water rights belong to those landowners whose land physically touches a river, pond, or lake.
All states (31 states) **east of the Mississippi River** have water allocation laws based on the Riparian Doctrine.

- Flowing Water.
- Reasonable use.
- Gives all owners of land contiguous to streams, lakes, and ponds equal rights to the water, whether the request is exercised or not.
- The riparian right is **usufructuary**, meaning that the landowner does not own the water itself but instead enjoys a right to use the water and its surface.
- A landowner who owns land that physically touches a river, stream, pond, or lake has an equal right to water use from that source. The water may be used as it passes through the landowner's property, but it cannot be unreasonably detained or diverted, and it must be returned to the stream from which it was obtained. The use of riparian water rights is generally regulated by "reasonable use."
- Riparian water rights cannot be lost through non-use and are indefinite in duration. Therefore, a riparian landowner does not lose their riparian right by not putting the water to use.
- There is no "water ownership".

Prior Appropriation

- The doctrine of Prior Appropriation.
- Found in the Western United States. (West of the Mississippi River.)
- The doctrine evolved during the California gold rush when miners in California needed to divert water from the stream to locations needed to process ore.
- A simple priority rule resolved customs and principles relating to water diversion developed in

the mining camps.

Four Essential Elements

1. Intent
2. Diversion
3. Beneficial Use
4. Priority
5. Intent

Diversion

1. A point of diversion is an essential element of the consumptive use of water rights.
2. Beneficial use is the essential characteristic in defining a prior appropriation water right. Since water is a scarce resource in the west, states must determine what water uses are acceptable.

Priority

"First in time-first in right."

1. The first appropriator on a water source can use all the water in the system necessary to fulfill his water right. A junior appropriator cannot use water to satisfy his water right if it injures the senior appropriator.
2. A senior appropriator cannot change any component of the water right if it injures a junior appropriator.
3. Any change of a water right (time of use, place of use, the purpose of use, point of diversion, etc.) cannot harm another water user, regardless of priority.

Mineral Rights

- Mineral rights are property rights to exploit an area for the minerals it harbors.
- Mineral rights can be separate from land and air property ownership.
- Subsurface rights may be leased or sold.
- If a landowner wants to keep the mineral rights but sell the land he owns, the landowner must expressly reserve the mineral rights, or they will automatically pass to the buyer.
- Mineral Acres
- Acres where the mineral interests have been retained in whole or in part.

Air Rights/Air Lots

Air Rights are also known as air lots. Those ownership rights, not including surface rights or subsurface rights, allow you to use the open vertical space above a property.

Land Characteristics and Legal Descriptions

Land Characteristics

Physical Characteristics of Land	Economic Characteristics of Land
• Immobility • Indestructibility • Nonhomogeneity, or uniqueness	• Scarcity • Improvements • Permanence of Investment • Situs (Location, Location, Location)

Legal Description

A property description is more accurate than street addresses and required in contracts, deeds, or other real property transfers.
The three primary methods of legal descriptions are:
1. metes and bound
2. governmental survey systems
3. subdivisions (lot, block, and tract)

Usage of Legal Descriptions

A legal description of the real property being conveyed in a real estate deed must be present for legal transactions.

Survey

Legal descriptions are based on a survey of the property, which is performed in most states by a licensed surveyor.

Types of Legal Descriptions

Metes and Bounds	Government Survey System\Rectangular Survey System	Lot and Block Subdivision Plat Map
• The Oldest Type of Measurement • The original 13 states, the older parts of the country and Texas.	• Units are in a rectangular grid form.	• Subdivision Plat Maps will overlay either the Metes and Bounds or the Rectangular Survey System.
The areas of the country that use Metes and Bounds are the original thirteen states, the older parts of the country and Texas.	AKA: The Public Land Survey System (PLSS) Baselines and Meridians 36 Sections	

	Section 16 is set aside for schools.	
POINT OF BEGINNING (POB) The most important feature is the Point of Beginning. (POB) The surveyor begins and ends at the POINT OF BEGINNING (POB).	Measured as the Ox Plows.	

Metes and Bounds

- The boundaries are described in a running prose style, working around the parcel in sequence, from a point of beginning and returning to the same point. It may include references to other adjoining parcels (and their owners). The surveyor will always return to the POB.
- The system uses physical features of the local geography, along with directions and distances, to define and describe the boundaries of a parcel of land.

Metes	**Bounds**
The term "metes" refers to a boundary defined by the measurement of each straight run, specified by a distance between the points, and an orientation or direction.	A more general boundary description such as along a certain watercourse, a stone wall, an adjoining public roadway, or an existing building.

☐ Point of Beginning (POB)

- An Oak Tree, rock, or a human-made **monument** can be a landmark used to measure land using the "metes and bounds" approach—point of Beginning or POB.
- You may see a question that will say either "a very large oak tree" or "A large boulder. If you get that question, your answer is "metes and bounds.

Monuments

- Markers used as points of beginning or other corners in metes and bounds descriptions. It May be artificial (iron stakes or man-made) or natural (trees, river centerline) provided by nature.
- The area of the country that uses metes and bounds are the original 13 states, and the older parts of the United States, and Texas.
- A typical description for a small parcel of land would be: "beginning with a corner at the intersection of two stone walls near an apple tree on the north side of Muddy Creek road one mile above the junction of Muddy and Indian Creeks, north for 150 rods to the end of the stone wall bordering the road, then northwest along a line to a large standing rock on the corner of the property now or formerly belonging to John Smith, thence west 150 rods to the corner of a barn near a large oak tree, thence south to Muddle Creek road, thence down the side of the creek road to the starting point." (USGS)

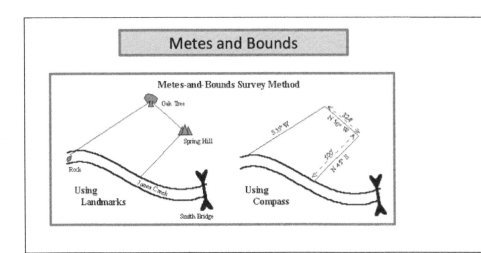

Government Survey System

☐ **The Public Land Survey System (PLSS)**

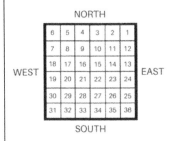

- All lands in the public domain are subject to subdivision by this rectangular system of surveys, which is regulated by the U.S. Department of the Interior, Bureau of Land Management (BLM).
- Section numbering begins at number one in the upper right northeast.
- Sections are numbered right to left and left to right down the rows until reaching the lower right southeast section.
- This wandering arrangement is based on how farmers plowed their land or "as the ox plows."
- This numbering system's benefits guarantee that a section is always adjoined by its preceding and succeeding section.
- A legal description example would be The E ½ of the NE ¼ Section 31, T6N, R6W. This would be a description of 80 acres.

divides land into **rectangles**

6	5	4	3	2	1
7	8	9	10	11	12
18	17	16	15	14	13
19	20	21	22	23	24
30	29	28	27	26	25
31	32	33	34	35	36

is referenced by degrees of **longitude and latitude**

Township

- A 6 mile-square parcel of land in the Governmental Survey System.
- A township contains 36 sections. Each section is one square mile.
- Six hundred forty acres is one square mile.

☐ Which area size is the smallest, one square mile or one acre?
ANSWER: one acre.

Section

- One square mile or 640 acres.

9

Principle Meridian	**Baselines**
The main imaginary lines that run north and south, crossing a baseline at a specific point. There are 36 principal meridians in the US.	East-west imaginary lines, crossing a principal meridian at a specific point and forming boundaries of Townships in the Government Survey System of land description.
Range	**Township lines**
A six-mile-wide strip of land or townships runs north and south of a baseline and numbered east or west of a principal meridian. They are used in the Governmental Survey System.	Run parallel to baselines.

Each square is one square mile.

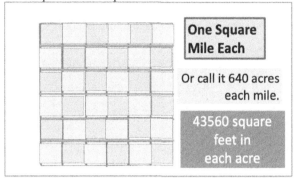

How to remember how many square feet are in each acre.
4 old ladies driving 35 in a 60

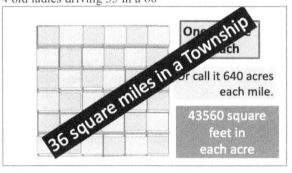

☐ If you are walking from section six to section thirty-six, what direction are you walking?
Southeast

Section 16

NOTE Section 16 is set aside for schools.

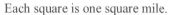

Correction Lines

- Correction lines are for the curvature of the Earth.
- There are four townships in a row north to south. (Four in a row) The fifth township shifts over. The line is called the correction line. It is for the curvature of the Earth.
- If not corrected, the township on the Baseline would contain more area than one further north.

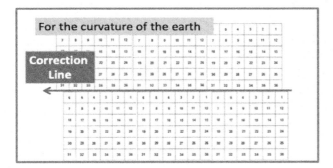

Lotting

There are various reasons why not all sections contain 640 acres, which is contrary to the above-described rectangular system.	It is common for sections along the northern tier and the western range of a regular township to be irregular and contain lots. Sections and lots are used to identify these non-aliquot parts. Lot sizes may vary from 40 acres to more than 40 acres, but they are considered subdivision units within a section.	Lotting occurs when special surveys, including mineral surveys and river and lake surveys, meander because the reduced land area surrounding them cannot be described as a whole. Lot numbers correspond to the 36 sections of a township.

Arpent

In Louisiana, parcels of land known as "arpent sections" or "French arpent land grants" also pre-date the PLSS but are considered to be PLSS sections.	The French arpent land divisions are long and narrow parcels of land typically found along navigable streams in southern Louisiana and along major waterways in other areas. French settlers started subdividing land in the 1700s, according to typical French practices at the time. Following the acquisition of Louisiana, the Spanish and American governments continued the project.	As a consequence of this land division method, each landowner had access to a river and land suitable for cultivation and habitation. Section numbers for these areas are assigned just like those assigned to standard sections, despite the fact that they are frequently higher than the normal upper limit of 36.

Lot and Block

- Subdivision Plat Map will overlay either the Metes and Bounds or the Rectangular Survey System.
- A sub-divider will break the land into lots, blocks, and street addresses. Once completed, the new legal descriptions are recorded.

- This map can overlay the main types of measurement.
- This map breaks up a large parcel of land into smaller parcels.
- A sub-divider would break down the individual lots with the Lot and Block numbers system using an engineer or surveyor.
- The new smaller lots are recorded to give constructive notice to the world.

- **The map must identify:**
  1. Individual lots.
  2. The block in which the lot is located.
  3. A reference to a platted subdivision or similar.
  4. A reference to find the cited plat map.
  5. A description of the map's place of the official recording.

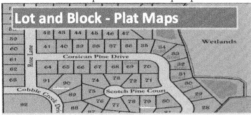

lot-and-block (recorded plat) system

Recording of Legal Descriptions

Legal Descriptions are filed in the county that the property is located.

Usage of Legal Descriptions

In a real estate deed, a legal description of the real property being conveyed is required to be present. The deed can also include a reference to the recorded map, survey, or deed containing the legal description to meet this requirement.

A Broker obtained a listing. The listing is an empty lot in the downtown area of Pretty City.
- On the right side of the building, the address is 200 Baseline.
- On the left side of the building, the address is 160 Baseline.
- Directly across the street, the address is 181 Baseline.

What address should the listing broker include on the Multiple Listing Service?
☐ Answer: The legal description.

Measuring Elevation

Datum	Benchmark
- A datum is a fixed starting point of elevation. - A point of reference for measuring elevations. - The United States Geological Survey (USGS) uses	- The term is generally applied to any item used to mark a point as an elevation reference.

the mean (average) sea level in New York Harbor. • A point, line, or surface from which a vertical height or depth is measured.	• A reference point or **marker** is placed by a surveyor and used to establish elevations and altitudes above sea level.

Measuring Land Elevation

- Topographic Maps / Contour Maps
- A topographic map showing the lay of the land of an area (works well for describing hilly terrains).

Contour MAP

Contour maps are most beneficial in a hilly area.

Measuring Livable, Usable and Rentable Area

Livable	Usable	Rentable
Measure the exterior width and length of your home.	The entire structure. Wall to wall interior.	Reports the largest space. Entire space including stairs and hallways. Includes a portion of the common areas.
Exterior	Interior	Includes common areas.

Information supplied by American National Standards Institute, Inc. (ANSI)

Source: The ANSI Standard - Short Summary.
https://accuratehomemeasuring.com/index.php/frequently-asked-questions/24-the-ansi-standard-short-summary

Measuring Structures
When reporting square footage, real estate agents should carefully follow these Guidelines or any other standards that are comparable to them, including those approved by the American National Standards Institute, Inc. (ANSI).

- Living Area Criteria Living area (sometimes referred to as "heated living area" or "heated square footage") is space that is intended for human occupancy and is:

1. Heated by a conventional heating system or systems (forced air, radiant, solar, etc.) that are

   permanently installed in the dwelling (not a portable heater) which generates heat sufficient to

   make the space suitable for year-round occupancy.

2. Finished, with walls, floors and ceilings of materials generally accepted for interior construction (e.g., painted drywall/sheet rock or paneled walls, carpeted or hardwood flooring, etc.) and with a ceiling height of at least seven feet, except under beams, ducts, etc. where the height must be at least six feet four inches [Note: In rooms with sloped ceilings (e.g., finished attics, bonus rooms, etc.) you may also include as living area the portion of the room with a ceiling height of at least five feet if at least one-half of the finished area of the room has a ceiling height of at least seven feet.]; and

3. Directly accessible from other living area (through a door or by a heated hallway or stairway). Real estate appraisers and lenders generally adhere to more detailed criteria in arriving at the living area or "gross living area" of residential dwellings. This normally includes distinguishing "above-grade" from "below-grade" area, which is also required by many multiple listing services.

- Real estate agents are permitted to report square footage of the dwelling as the total "living area" without a separate distinction between "above-grade" and "below-grade" areas.
- Living area (sometimes referred to as "heated living area" or "heated square footage") is space that is intended for human occupancy.

MEASUREMENT CONVERSION GUIDE

1 Acre = 43,560 square

1 Foot = 12 inches
1 yard = 3 feet
1 sq. yard = 9 sq. feet (3 ft x 3 ft)
1 cubic yard = 27 cubic feet (3 ft x 3 ft x 3 ft)
1 Mile = 5,280 feet
1 Mile Square = 640 acres
1 Section = 1 mile long, by 1 mile wide
1 Section = 640 acres
1 Township = 6 miles long, by 6 miles wide
1 Township = 36 sections
1 Township = 36 square miles1 Yard = 36 inches
1 Yard = 3 feet
1 Yard Square = 9 square feet

Look up, "Disney Strawman".
Define Strawman?

Encumbrances and Effects on Property Ownership

An encumbrance is a claim, charge, or liability that attaches to real estate.

Property Liens

- Liens are encumbrances.
- Liens can affect property ownership.
- A lien refers to non-possessory security interests.
- A lien is a financial encumbrance, which gives a creditor the right to foreclose on the property if the property owner doesn't repay a debt.
- The property can be sold against your will to pay off a debt.
- All liens are encumbrances, but not all encumbrances are liens.

Release of lien
When the debt is fully repaid, a release of the lien is provided by the lender.

Types of Liens

1.	2.	3.
Voluntary **or** **Involuntary**	**Statutory** **or** **Equitable**	**General** **or** **Specific**

1.

Voluntary Liens	Involuntary Liens
<ul><li>A lien voluntarily placed on a property by a property owner.</li><li>A voluntary lien is where the property owner willingly takes some action that enables the placement of a lien against the property. A mortgage is the most common example of a voluntary lien.</li><li>mortgage</li><li>trust deed</li><li>chattel mortgage</li></ul>	<ul><li>A typical example of an involuntary lien is a tax lien. A tax lien is issued by the government when taxes are owed. Suppose a property owner avoids paying income taxes or property taxes on their home, the Internal Revenue Service (IRS) will file an involuntary lien to alert creditors that they have a right to your property.</li><li>taxes</li><li>mechanics liens</li><li>judgements</li><li>Weed liens" and "Demolition liens</li><li>Homeowner Association</li></ul>

2.

Statutory	Equitable
<ul><li>A statutory lien is a lien arising solely because of a statute. It is essentially a lien that is created automatically by</li></ul>	<ul><li>These are liens that are imposed by the court to maintain a certain degree of fairness or "equity" in the situation surrounding the property. They usually</li></ul>

the operation of a statute or law (meaning it doesn't require any subsequent judicial action such as a lawsuit or court judgment).	arise when one person holds possession of the property for another person. These situations can often be quite complex and may involve multiple parties and state laws.
3.	
General	**Specific**
<ul><li>General liens could be liens on everything you own</li><li>A General lien could be a lien on several properties one person owns. It's not specific because it is of several properties, not just one.</li></ul>	<ul><li>Specific liens are liens specifically on a single property.</li><li>Property tax liens are attached to property until paid; special assessments may also be attached to pay for specific improvements that benefit a property.</li></ul>

Protection from Liens

Homestead Rights

- Homestead laws offer protection against foreclosure on judgment liens. (Unsecured liens)
- A certain amount of a property's value is protected from judgment creditors.

MORE ABOUT PROPERTY TAXES

Property taxes are liens.

Equalization

Equalization is a step-in property taxation to bring uniformity to tax assessment levels across different geographical areas or classes of properties. Equalization is usually in the form of a uniform percentage of increase or decreases to each area or class of property.

Tax rates

Property taxes are a major source of income for local and state governments and are used to fund services such as education, transportation, emergency, parks, recreation, and libraries.

Types of Taxes

Ad Valorem	Special Assessments
<ul><li>Ad valorem tax lien (ad valorem = according to value).</li><li>This is your property taxes paid once a year.</li><li>Taxes are to meet the demand of the government.</li></ul>	<ul><li>A special assessment is an added tax paid for by the people who benefit from an improvement.</li><li>A special assessment can be charged to a neighborhood to help pay for new street improvements, sewer lines, or road repairs.</li><li>Special assessment liens are considered</li></ul>

• Ad valorem is specific, involuntary, statutory liens.	improvement taxes. • ☐ Only the people who benefit from the improvement pay the special assessments.

Mechanic's lien

- These liens are afforded to laborers, contractors, or suppliers on your real property if you don't pay for the construction or materials used to improve the property.
- A mechanic's lien can be filed against real property by a person who provides labor or materials for the improvement of that property.
- When a mechanic's lien is filed for the non-payment of labor or materials used to improve a property, the effective date of the lien is the date the improvement, work or materials were furnished.

Taxes are to meet the demand of the government.

Payment Priority of Liens

- Payment of general and special assessment taxes takes priority over all other liens, regardless of when the liens were attached.
- Other than real estate tax liens, all other liens usually are paid off in the order that they were recorded in the appropriate local office of public records — the county clerk's office or some other office of public records.

First in Time, First in Right
Liens with the highest priority are typically paid off first ("first in time, first in right").

Subordination Agreements
A subordination agreement is a legal document that establishes one debt as ranking behind another in priority for collecting repayment from a debtor.

Lis pendens – lawsuit pending	Writ of Attachment
• A lawsuit has been filed. • A foreclosure can wipe out a Lis pendens. • A current lawsuit on real property is called a Lis pendens. (Litigation Pending).	• Imposed to secure payment of a judgment. • Secured on property to prevent the sale of property.

Easements

- Easements are the rights to use another's land.
- Easements are for Ingress and Egress.
- In and Exit.

Creating an Easement

- An easement is recorded and in your deed.
- By express grant in a deed from the owner of the property.
- By express reservation by the grantor in a deed of conveyance.
- By use.
- By implication.

Appurtenances to Land

- Appurtenant means "in addition to" or "belonging to".
- In every easement appurtenant, there are two parcels of land that are involved.

Easement Appurtenant

- An easement is most like a "right of way".
- Easements "run with the land", meaning that when a real estate owner sells the property, the easement automatically transfers with the property deed.
- An easement is annexed to ownership. It is a right to use another's land.

Dominant Tenement	Servient Tenement
<ul><li>The "dominant tenement" is the land owned by the holder of the easement.</li><li>The tenement that benefits from the easement.</li></ul>	<ul><li>The burdened land.</li><li>The tenement on which the easement is placed.</li><li>An easement to a servient tenement is an encumbrance.</li></ul>

The dominant tenement and the servient tenement are usually adjacent, although this is not a requirement for an easement appurtenant.

In an easement appurtenant, the two tracts of land can be contiguous or noncontiguous.

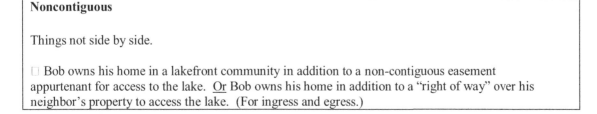

Noncontiguous
Things not side by side.   ☐ Bob owns his home in a lakefront community in addition to a non-contiguous easement appurtenant for access to the lake. Or Bob owns his home in addition to a "right of way" over his neighbor's property to access the lake. (For ingress and egress.)

Terminating an Easement

- When the purpose for which it was created no longer exists.
- MERGING OF TITLES.
- By the release of the right.
- By abandonment.
- By the non-use of a prescriptive easement by its owner.
- By adverse possession.
- By destruction.
- By court decision.
- By excessive use.

> □ A truck driver has an easement over his neighbor's property to store his large truck when he is not working.
> The easement may be terminated if the man sells his truck and retires.

Types of Easements

Easement in Gross

- Frequently for utilities Utility Company Access. There is no dominant tenement. All the homes up against a Gross Easement are Servient Tenements.
- Buried utility lines are examples.
- When a gas company wants to bury its pipes over the property of several homes, they will apply for an easement in gross.
- There is no dominant tenement in an Easement in Gross.
- A water company may lay pipes upon private Property through an easement in gross.
- BTW. The water company is a non-profit.

Party Wall Easements

- The wall on the between two townhomes (garden homes) is called a party wall.
- Party Fences or party walls.
- The fence between yards or properties.

Easement by Necessity

- An easement by necessity is essential to the landlocked property.
- □A property cannot be landlocked.
- Landlocked property. It is because owners must have ingress to and egress from their land.

Easement by Prescription – Prescriptive Easement

- Continuous usage, without the owner's approval. Its usage is visible, open, and notorious. It's based on the principles of Adverse Possession.

- It's when someone has been using another's property for a long period of time.

Meet Bob and Al
Bob was driving over the northeast corner of Al's property for 10 years.
Al knew about it but didn't like it. Al never said anything to Bob.
One day, Al decided he wanted to build a home for his daughter on that portion of land that Bob has been driving over.
Al asked Bob to stop using his property.
Bob took Al to court and was granted permission to continue to drive over Al's property.
Al's intention to build his daughter a new home on that section of land had to be abandoned.
Bob was granted a Prescriptive Easement.
Easement by Prescription is based on Adverse Possession.

Adverse Possession

- A way of taking title to another person's property by the open, continuous, notorious, and hostile use of another person's property for a statutory period.
- It can result in the possessor acquiring title to the property if the true owner does not move to evict the possessor before the period of limitations expires.

Hostile Possession

Possession that is without the consent of the owner and the assertion of which conflicts with the property ownership interests of the owner.
- the possessor must have entered the property and must have exclusive possession of the property.
- the possession must be "open and notorious".
- the possession must be adverse to the rightful owner and under a claim of right; and
- the possession must be "continuous" for the statutory period.

Encroachment

☐An encroachment is an improvement built over the property line and onto another's property.
☐The best way to find an encroachment is to hire a surveyor.
☐Bob's garage extended onto Sally's property. It is an encroachment.
☐If a homeowner is concerned that the construction project next door is encroaching on her property, she should hire a surveyor.

☐ Sharing a driveway is an encumbrance.

License

Temporary use of another person's property.
☐A revocable right.
Example: Mark allows Glen to fish from his pond in the month of August

Nuisance

A nuisance is an activity or condition that interferes with a neighboring owner's use and enjoyment of his property, including odors or noises.

Identify the Situation

1. A telephone company just installed a large telephone pole on the northeast section of Anthony's property.
a. Easement in Gross
b. Prescriptive Easement
c. Easement by Necessity
d. Adverse Possession
e. License
f. Encroachment

a. Easement in Gross
This is a utility easement.

2. Andria is allowing Terry to fish from her private pond in the month of August while Andria is on vacation.
a. Easement in Gross
b. Prescriptive Easement
c. Easement by Necessity
d. Adverse Possession
e. License
f. Encroachment

e. License
This is a revocable right. It's temporary.

3. Carlos and Mike are neighbors and friends. Mike has been driving over the north west section of Carlos' property without Carlos's agreement for over ten years. Carlos didn't like that his friend drove over the property, but his wife said not to say anything. She wanted to be a good neighbor. A more direct road to Mike's house was built by the city last year. Mike continues to drive over Carlos' property, nonetheless.
a. Easement in Gross
b. Prescriptive Easement
c. Easement by Necessity
d. Adverse Possession
e. License
f. Encroachment

b. Prescriptive Easement
Long period of time and open

4. Mark was excited to build his new patio cover. When the wood was delivered to his driveway, Mark was happy and started building that day. The patio cover is beautiful, and his partner loves it. Two months later a new buyer of the lot next door sent a letter to Mark with a copy of a survey. The letter stated that the new patio was built over Marks's property line and onto the neighbor's property by 17 inches.
a. Easement in Gross
b. Prescriptive Easement
c. Easement by Necessity

d. Adverse Possession
e. License
f. Encroachment

f. Encroachment
Encroaching on the neighbor's property.

5. Tina's neighbor allowed her to drive over a section of the neighbor's property in order to reach her landlocked property.
a. Easement in Gross
b. Prescriptive Easement
c. Easement by Necessity
d. Adverse Possession
e. License
f. Encroachment

c. Easement by Necessity
Landlocked property. A property cannot be landlocked.

6. The Peacock family noticed that a home in a desirable neighborhood has been vacant for several months. The parents decided to move their family into the home. They installed new locks, turned on the electricity, gas and trash service. The parents enrolled their two children into elementary school. They were there for over a year until they decided to repaint the outside of the house because the paint was fading. Their lawn and garden were well kept.
The family was able to stay in the house and their children lived there until they graduated college. The parents are still in the house, but they just got served a notice to vacate from a person who claims to be the owner.
a. Easement in Gross
b. Prescriptive Easement
c. Easement by Necessity
d. Adverse Possession
e. License
f. Encroachment

d. Adverse Possession
Adverse Possession. They occupied the property openly and were there for a (state mandated) statutory period of time.

Types of Ownership

Ownership in severalty/sole ownership

- One individual holds the title.
- Sole rights to ownership.
- Sole discretion to transfer part or all ownership rights to another person.
- Maybe a single individual or an artificial person, such as a corporation.

Co-ownership, a title held by two or more individuals

Tenants in Common

- Undivided Interest.
- ☐ A tenant in Common can sell their interest without the approval of the other in Common Tenants.
- You can will your interest in real estate if you own as Tenancy in Common.
- Tenancy in Common has possession as a common component.
- ☐ A husband-and-wife own property, and when the husband died, one-third of his interest went to each of his children, and one-third went to his wife. What form of ownership did he and his wife most likely have? In Common. (Unequal interests) It appears the property was transferred to the heirs because the husband had no will.
- Tenants in common have no right of survivorship, meaning that if one tenant in common dies, that tenant's interest in the property will be part of their estate and pass by to that owner's devisees heirs, either by intestate succession or will.
- Co-owners have unity of possession and the right to occupy.
- Tenancy in common is a form of concurrent estate in which each owner, referred to as a tenant in common, is regarded by the law as owning separate and distinct shares of the same property.
- This form of ownership is most common where the co-owners are not married or have contributed different amounts to purchasing the property.

Joint Tenancy with Rights of Survivorship

Four unities (PITT)

Possession	Interest	Time	Title

- A joint tenancy or joint tenancy with right of survivorship JTWROS is a type of concurrent estate in which co-owners have a right of survivorship, meaning that if one owner dies, that owner's interest in the property will pass to the surviving owner or owners by operation of law, and avoiding probate.
- The deceased owner's interest in the property evaporates and cannot be inherited by their heirs.
- Under this type of ownership, the last owner living will own all the property, and on his or her death, the property will form part of their estate.
- Joint co-owners have an equal share in the property.
- This form of ownership is common between spouses, parents, and children, and in any other situation where parties want ownership to pass immediately and automatically to the survivor.

Partition

- Partition can be brought to force division or the sale of the property.
- To terminate a joint tenancy, one of the four unities must be destroyed.
- Upon termination, a tenancy in common is formed between the third person and the remaining joint co-tenant(s).

Partition in Kind is the physical division of the land

- The court decides how to split up the land between co-tenants, so each receives a portion equal to their share. If the court cannot equitably split up the land, then partition by the sale will be used.
- In partition by sale, the court forces the sale of the property, and each co-tenant receives their share of the profits.

☐ A husband and wife took the title as joint tenants so that when one passes away, the title to the real estate will avoid probate.

Tenancy by the Entirety

- Some states.
- Husband and Wife only.
- Rights of survivorship.
- In Tenancy by the Entirety, each spouse is one-half a person. It takes at least one person to sign a listing.
- A Tenancy by the Entirety cannot be partitioned.

Termination

- Death of either spouse; survivor becomes an owner in severalty.
- Agreement between both parties.

Right of Survivorship

- A key feature of a joint tenancy whereby the deceased joint tenant's ownership rights automatically pass to the surviving joint tenant(s). It is valid for Tenancy by the Entirety.

Debts

- Tenancy by the Entirety (used to) gives protection to the other spouse's debts. When a husband-and-wife own property as Tenant by the Entirety, they both need to sign the listing agreement even if one spouse has a large amount of unpaid debt.

☐ When there is a Tenants by the Entirety ownership, a broker should get both husband and wife to sign the listing.

Community Property

- Spanish Common Law is usually found in the western states.

- Property a couple acquires after marriage is the property of both husband and wife. (Does not include inheritance.)
- Requires both signatures for the property to be conveyed.

Separate Property.
- Property owned by one of the spouses before marriage.
- ☐Inheritance or gifts.
- Property purchased with proceeds of separate property.

Surviving Spouse's Interests

A surviving spouse's right to receive a set portion of the deceased spouse's estate — usually one-third to one-half.

Dower

The life estate interest of a wife in the real property of her deceased husband.

Curtesy

The life estate interest of a husband in the real property of his deceased wife.

Statutory Share

Because discrimination based on sex is now illegal in most cases, most states have abolished dower and curtesy and generally provide the same benefits regardless of sex — and this amount is often known simply as the statutory share.

Ownership by Business Organizations

General Partnership	Limited Partnership
• A business organizational form in which all general partners actively participate in ownership and management and are liable for all debt and actions. • All partners are general partners who participate in the partnership and share full liability.	• A business organizational form in which general partner(s) are liable for all debts and actions and limited partners carries no liability beyond their investment. • Has both general and limited partners. • Limited partners do not participate in running the business.

Limited Liability Companies (LLC)

- Members have the limited liability of a corporation, plus the tax advantages of a partnership.
- ☐One person can be an LLC.
- A business organization is treated as a limited partnership from a federal tax point of view and an "S" corporation from a liability point of view.

Corporations	S corporations
<ul><li>A legal entity created under state law, consisting of an association of one or more individuals but existing separately from such individuals. Managed by its board of directors, each shareholder's liability is limited to his/her investment.</li><li>A legal entity or A person.</li><li>Exist in perpetuity (forever) until formally dissolved.</li><li>Managed and operated by the board of directors.</li><li>Provide its shareholders with limited liability.</li><li>Corporate profits are usually subject to double taxation.</li></ul>**Double Taxation** The disadvantage of a corporation is double taxation.	<ul><li>Corporations elect to pass corporate income, losses, deductions, and credits through to their shareholders for federal tax purposes.</li><li>Shareholders of S corporations report the flow-through of income and losses on their personal tax returns and are assessed tax at their individual income tax rates.</li><li>This allows S corporations to avoid double taxation on corporate income. S corporations are responsible for tax on certain built-in gains and passive income at the entity level.</li></ul>**Pass Through Taxes**

A corporation pays double taxation. An "S Corporation" is considered a pass-thru company.

Joint Venture	Syndication
THE BUSINESS<ul><li>A form of business organization in which two or more individuals come together for a business purpose and share in the venture's profits or losses.</li><li>It is treated like a partnership for tax purposes.</li></ul>	THE PEOPLE<ul><li>A process for two or more people coming together to operate an investment, such as partnerships, corporations, etc. It is not a form of ownership. "Mom and Pop Shops."</li></ul>

Real Estate Investment Trusts (R.E.I.T.S.)

- Money funds through which small investors participate in large real estate projects through ownership of certificates. REITS are created and managed by brokerage companies.
- REIT: A conglomerate of investors who pool their money to buy investments such as residential income property, high rises, malls, commercial buildings.

Common- Interest Ownership

Condominiums
<ul><li>The owner holds fee simple title to the airspace of a unit as well as an undivided share in the common elements.</li><li>Common elements are owned by condominium unit owners as tenants in common.</li><li>You own a portion of the common areas like the pool, elevators, hallways, and entryway. The</li></ul>

ownership interest in the common area is an appurtenance.
- Common elements in a condominium do not include the owner's assigned parking spot. The assigned parking space is not shared.
- In a condominium, the owners own real estate.
- A condominium complex cannot eminent domain the property adjacent to their parking lot to expand the condo's parking lot. Only the government can eminent domain.
- It is possible to have two deeds when you buy a condo. One for the unit and another as tenants in common for the common elements.
- At the close, the buyer will receive additional paperwork when buying a common elements property. CC&Rs

Co-ops - Cooperatives - Stock Ownership

- A corporation owns the real estate and the inhabitant's own stock in the corporation.
- A purchaser of stock becomes a shareholder in the corporation and receives a proprietary lease.
- The IRS treats a cooperative the same as real estate for tax purposes.
- Co-ops are personal property but has a real property condition disclosure if there are 4 or less transferring.
- In a Cooperative (Co-op) or (stock cooperative), a person owns stock in a corporation that owns the building s/he lives in. The amount of stock could identify the square footage of his unit. They look very similar to a condo.
- A Cooperative is considered personal Property because the residents own the stock and not the building. Stock is chattel.
- If a stockholder doesn't pay his mortgage, the other stockholders will have to pay his shares for the corporation to avoid loan default.

Timeshares

- Interval Ownership.
- Real Property.
- A timeshare owner owns property along with other owners.
- Timeshares are most often a vacation home.
- The use of the estate is limited to the timeshare interest.
- The title is held as Tenancy in Common. Several people own one unit.

Plan Unit Development (PUD)

- A community planned with a variety of individual ownership interests such as residential and shared interests of common recreation areas.
- Building an entire community.

How to Own Real Estate

Estate Interest

One's a legal interest in the property – either freehold or non-freehold.

Freehold	Non-freehold
<ul><li>Freehold estates involve ownership, non-freehold estates include tenants.</li><li>Freehold OWN.</li><li>Estate for an indeterminable time.</li><li>Real property ownership is for an indefinite duration. (e.g., fee simple, life estate).</li></ul>	<ul><li>Non-freehold – Less than Freehold.</li><li>Less than freehold means you are leasing or renting.</li></ul>

Fee-Simple Absolute

- Fee simple absolute is the highest form of ownership.
- People may call it Fee Simple, Fee Simple Estate, or Fee Simple Absolute.
- The most complete and absolute ownership of real property. It is freely transferable, has an indefinite duration, and may be left to heirs. All other estates are created from a fee simple estate.

Fee-Simple Defeasible

- Fee simple defeasible is a legal term and type of property ownership, where the ownership is dependent on specific conditions. If the conditions of ownership are violated, the property may be returned to the grantor or to a specified third party.
- Fee simple defeasible means the highest form of ownership with a condition. An example would be a hospital that is given Property to keep if they remain a nonprofit or a zoo that receives Property by deed and is allowed to keep it if they don't charge an admission fee.

Two Defeasible Fees Conditions are Available
1. Fee Simple Determinable
2. Condition Subsequent

1. Fee Simple Determinable	2. Condition Subsequent
Condition Violated. Fee Simple Determinable. <ul><li>"B to A and his heirs so long as the land is used for residential purposes".</li><li>It uses words of duration, such as "so long as" "while used for", and "until".</li></ul>	Condition NOT MET. Fee Simple Subject to Condition Subsequent. <ul><li>"B to A and his heirs; however, if the land is not used as a library, then it reverts back to B"</li><li>It may be cut short or divested at the transferor's election when a condition occurs.</li><li>It uses words such as "but if", "provided, however", and "on condition that".</li></ul>

Reversion to the Original Grantor upon a violation.

Remainderman
The future interest created when a grantor creates either a fee simple determinable or a fee simple subject to

condition subsequent and rather than retaining a future interest in himself, creates one instead in a third party.

How to tell who gets the property

OR OR OR is the GIVOR Ee ee ee is the gimee gimee gimee the propertee	Grantor Lessor Vendor Optionor	Grantee Lessee Vendee Optionee

Life Estate Ownership

☐ A life estate is a freehold estate. The life estate holder is responsible for the taxes. The life estate holder can collect rent if they lease the property. The lease ends when the life tenant dies.

• Remainder– remainderman • The person who gets the Property after the life estate holder dies. • Mary was granted a life estate for her life. Upon her passing, the Property will pass to her child. The type of ownership the child has is remainder. (Remainderman)	• Reversion • An example would be, "Bob gave a life estate to Sal. When Sal dies, the Property will revert back to Bob."

Pur Autre Vie Pur Autre Vie means "for the life of another." It's a life estate based on another's life.

☐ Carol had a life estate. She rented the Property to Tom for five years. In year three, Carol died.
What is the status of Tom's lease?
The lease is now void. It was only valid during the term of the life of Carol.

☐ One cannot will a life estate.

Property ownership **held in trust.**
Real estate held on behalf of another.

(BROKER) **1. Main Types of Trusts** While the basic structure of trust remains pretty much the same, there are several different types of trusts with different purposes and specifics. **2. Living Trust** This type of trust allows the trustor to benefit from the trust while alive but passes the assets and property on to a beneficiary (using a trustee) upon their death. **3. Testamentary Trust** A testamentary trust often called a will trust, is an agreement made for a beneficiary's benefit once the trustor has died and details how the assets must be endowed after their death. This type of trust is often instituted by an executor, who will manage the trust after their will and testament have been created. **4. Revocable Trust** A revocable trust is a trust that can be changed, terminated, or otherwise altered during the trustor's

lifetime by the trustor themselves. It is often set up to transfer assets outside of probate.

5. Irrevocable Trust

On the contrary, an irrevocable trust is one that a trustor (grantor) cannot change or alter during his or her lifetime or be revoked after his or her death. Because this type of trust contains assets that cannot be moved back into the possession of the trustor, irrevocable trusts are often more tax-efficient – with little to no estate taxes at all. For this reason, irrevocable trusts are often the most popular as they transfer assets completely out of the trustor's name and into the next generation or beneficiary's name.

6. Funded or Unfunded Trust

In the case of a funded trust, it means that property has been put inside for the trust. An unfunded trust is simply the trust.

7. Credit Shelter Trust

A credit shelter trust, also known as a bypass trust or a family trust, is a trust fund that allows the trustor to grant the recipients several assets or funds to the estate-tax exemption. Basically, this allows the trustor to give a spouse or family member the remainder of the estate tax-free. These kinds of trusts are often prevalent because the estate remains tax-free forever, even if it grows.

8. A Charitable Trust

is a trust that has a charity or non-profit organization as the beneficiary. In normal cases, this type of trust would be built up during the trustor's lifetime and, upon their passing, be doled out to a charity or organization of the trustor's choosing, avoiding, or reducing estate taxes or gift taxes.

9. Blind Trust

A blind trust is a trust that is handled solely by the trustees without the beneficiaries' knowledge. These trusts are often used to avoid any conflicts between the trustees and beneficiaries or between beneficiaries.

10. Land Trusts

Trusts can be used for privacy (to keep wills private) or a good way to hide ownership).

☐ A distinguishing characteristic of owning property by the land trust is that the legal owner's identity is kept confidential.

MODULE ONE: Ownership QUIZ

☐ Question	Answer
1. A very old oak tree! 1. North America 2. Metes and Bounds 3. Rectangular Survey 4. Straight Line Method	2.Metes and Bounds A very old oak tree could be used as a monument and point of beginning in the metes and bounds legal description.
2. Under a government rectangular survey, a correction line is required because of? 1. an error in legal description. 2. the curvature of the earth. 3. the monument being in the wrong place. 4. errors made by surveyors.	2.the curvature of the earth. Corrections offset the curvature of the earth.
3. Match: Real property. 1. can't be moved 2. movable 3. chattel 4. tractors	1.can't be moved Real property includes things permanently attached to the earth.
4. How many sections are there in a township? 1. Sixty-four 2. Thirty-four 3. Thirty-six. 4. Six hundred and forty.	3.Thirty-six. There are thirty-sections in each township.
5. In a township, the section north of Section 10 is? 1. Section 22 2. Section 7 3. Section 3 4. Section 12	3.Section 3
6. If you are walking from section 6 to section 36, what direction are you walking? 1. southeast 2. southwest 3. northwest 4. northeast	1.southeast Section 36 is southeast of section 6.
7. A family of four was fishing on a lake. A property owner living on the lake told the family that he could not fish within 25 feet of the property shoreline. The family told the property owner that he could fish anywhere on the lake. Which is true? 1. The family is right. The lake and the lake lands are	1.The family is right. The lake and the lake lands are public property. The waterfront property owner has the right to a beach deposited by currents and access to the lake. The government regulates access such as

public property. 2. The owner's is correct since the land is private. 3. The owner has property rights that allow him to prevent the family from fishing within thirty feet. 4. The owner's ownership is the entire lake.	piers and wharves to assure that public rights are protected. The waterfront property owner does not own the lake.
8. With a metes and bounds legal description, a surveyor begins at a starting point called the? 1. neighbor location marker 2. a Range Line 3. monument point 4. point of beginning	4.point of beginning Surveyors begin and end at the point of beginning.
9. How will a parcel be described if it does not have a lot and block number and is too irregular to be described as a fraction of a section? 1. governmental survey system 2. metes and bounds 3. subdivision plat map 4. meridian system	3.subdivision plat map In a running prose style, the boundaries are described in sequence, beginning at a beginning point and returning to the same point; compare with the oral ritual of beating the bounds. This may reference adjacent parcels (and their owners), which may be referenced in future surveys. When the description was compiled, permanent monuments may have been placed where there were no suitable natural monuments.
10. The term nonhomogeneity refers to? 1. Scarcity 2. Immobility 3. Uniqueness 4. Indestructible	3.Uniqueness No two properties are the same.
11. What is measured to determine the legal descriptions of air rights and high-rise condo apartments? 1. elevations 2. datums 3. benchmarks 4. meridians	1.elevations A surveyor uses datums and benchmarks when measuring elevation. Air rights and high rises are determined by measuring elevation.
12. The government survey system is not generally used in? 1. the northern states. 2. the southern states. 3. states west of the Mississippi River. 4. the original 13 states. (colonies)	4. the original 13 states. (colonies) Metes and Bounds description is primarily used in the original thirteen states, the older parts of the country, and Texas.
13. Which of the following is not a physical characteristic of land? 1. Shipabilit 2. Immobility 3. Nonhomogeneity 4. Indestructibility	1. Shipability Immobility, Non-homogeneity, and Indestructibility are physical characteristics of land-living.
14. In a transaction what type of legal description is used in most cases?	2. The same one used in prior transactions, verified by a surveyor.

1. The street address only. 2. The same one used in prior transactions, verified by a surveyor. 3. The metes and bounds if the property is west of the Mississippi River. 4. The one the seller guesses are correct.	If possible, use what has already been documented. Use a surveyor to verify the legal description is correct.
15. Legal property descriptions may not be based on which of the following? 1.The government survey system. 2.The rectangular survey system. 3.A street address. 4.A previous survey.	3. A street address A legal description is the formal address.
16. What section in a township is set aside for schools? 1.section 6 2.section 12 3.section 16 4.section 14	3. Section 16 Each section 16 is set aside for schools. There are cases whereas the city/county does not need the land. In that case, it is common to lease the property on long term 99-year leases.
17. The horizontal lines running at six-mile intervals parallel to the baseline in the rectangular survey system. 1.Inchoate right 2.Township lines 3.Steering 4.Tenancy in common	2. Township lines Principal Meridian Township Lines Baseline
18. MATCH: Easements created by the unrestricted use of the property over a long period of time without the consent of the owner. 1.Eminent domain 2.Reservation 3.Prescription 4.Necessity	3.Prescription A prescriptive easement is an easement upon another's real property acquired by continued use without permission of the owner for a legally defined period. State law, which varies by state, defines the time period required to acquire a prescriptive easement.
19. You have been driving over your neighbor's northwest section of his land to reach your barn quickly. You were doing this for many years. Your neighbor knew you were driving over the property but didn't say anything to you. He was trying to be a good neighbor although he didn't like what you were doing. One day the neighbor announced that you needed to stop using his property because he wanted to build a house for his daughter. Because you went to real estate school, you know that you might be able to be granted? 1.easement by prescription	1.easement by prescription Prescriptive easements also called "easements by prescription," are created when an individual continually and openly uses a portion of another person's property without the permission of the owner. This most frequently happens in rural areas, when a landowner fails to notice their property being used.

2.a license 3.easement in gross 4.easement by necessity	
20. The land that benefits from an easement is called? 1.Defeasible fee 2.Subjective property 3.Dominant tenement 4.Servient tenement	3.Dominant tenement The dominant tenement is the land that is benefitted by the easement. The servient tenement is the land that is burdened by the easement.
21. Encumbrances that automatically transfer with the land are? 1.trade fixtures currently being used and attached to the property. 2. appurtenant easements. 3.the tenant's emblements. 4.a freestanding stove, dishwasher, or refrigerator.	2.appurtenant easements. Easements transfer with the land.
22. What type of easement is usually granted to a utility company to service equipment? 1.Easement by prescription. 2.Easement by inheritance. 3.Adverse easement. 4.Easement in gross.	4.Easement in gross. An easement in gross will be used by a utility company or government.
23. It is your driveway that your neighbors use to reach their garage on their property. It is explained by your attorney that the neighbor's property includes an easement attached granting them this right. The property you own is? 1.The dominant tenement. 2.The servient tenement. 3.The leasehold interest. 4.The licensed property.	2. The servient tenement. Your driveway is on the property over which the easement runs and is the servient tenement. The adjacent property owned by the neighbors is known as the dominant tenement.
24. An easement can be created for what length of time? 1.forever. 2.any of these. 3.a term for years. 4.the lifetime of a person.	2. any of these. An easement can be forever or a time.
25. Which type of ownership is most often used for a timeshare? 1.Stock Cooperative 2.Tenancy in common 3.Tenancy in severalty 4.Joint tenancy.	2. Tenancy in common In a tenancy in common, there is usually more than one owner of property or land. ... Tenants-in-common pass their property to their estates after they die. A percentage of each independent owner may be equal or different.
26. How is title held when a person owns a cooperative? 1.Tenancy in common 2.Tenancy by the entirety 3.Joint tenancy	4. Stock A corporation owns the building, and the people living in the building own stock in that corporation. The occupants are given a

4.Stock	proprietary lease to live there.
27. In a transaction what type of legal description is used in most cases? 1.The street address only. 2.The same one used in prior transactions, verified by a surveyor. 3.The metes and bounds if the property is west of the Mississippi River. 4.The one the seller guesses are correct.	2. The same one used in prior transactions, verified by a surveyor. If possible, use what has already been documented. Use a surveyor to verify the legal description is correct.
28. What is the owner of a life estate in property entitled to? 1.Future real estate taxes. 2.Possession of the property. 3.Refunds on rent when the property passes to the remainder man. 4.A Reversionary Right.	2. Possession of the property. The life estate holder has the right of possession.
29. Three brothers own a hotel and took title as tenants in common. After many years, one brother decided to sell his interest. He may legally? 1.Sell if there is a majority vote. 2.Not sell because tenancy in common cannot be sold or willed. 3.Sell because tenancy in common has an undivided interest that is transferable. 4.Not sell because of JTWROS.	3. Sell because tenancy in common has an undivided interest that is transferable. In a Tenant in Common, the shares in the property may be of unequal size and can be freely transferred to other owners both during the owner's lifetime and via a will. Even if owners own unequal shares, all owners still have the right to occupy and use all the property.
30. Which of the following is false? 1.When a homeowner tears down an old, rotted fence and places the boards on the curb, those fence boards are then real property. 2. Trade fixtures are personal property. 3. A water heater that is installed in a home is a fixture.	1. When a homeowner tears down an old, rotted fence and places the boards on the curb, those fence boards are then real property. The fence is personal property. It has been severed from the land.
31. After purchasing a piece of landlocked property, the buyer tried unsuccessfully to obtain access to the nearest road. He would be granted access by way of. 1.Appurtenant easement 2.Easement in gross 3.Easement by necessity 4.Adverse possession	3. Easement by necessity Landlocked property must have access.
32. Which of the following is an example of an encroachment? 1.A storage shed that butt up to your neighbor's fence. 2.An easement by prescription. 3.A fence built beyond a property boundary and onto a neighbor's property. 4.A Dominant Tenement.	3. A fence built beyond a property boundary and onto a neighbor's property. Building a structure on another person's property is encroachment.
33. A woman owned a life estate. Using a standard	1. Valid only if she was living.

lease, she leased the property for 5 years. She died shortly after. What is the status of the lease? 1.Valid only if she was living. 2.Legal and valid for 5 years. 3.Not valid because a life estate cannot be leased. 4.Valid if an heir agrees to honor the lease.	The life estate holder loses all rights upon their death.
34. A pool contractor installed a pool and hot tub for the owner of a newly purchased estate. When presented with the final bill, the owner refused to pay. 30 days after the work was completed, the contractor drove by the house and saw a 'For Sale' sign in the yard. What should the contractor do? 1.File a mechanic's lien with notification of Lis Pendens. 2.Begin demolition of the pool. 3.Sue the listing agent. 4.File a formal complaint with the city.	1. File a mechanic's lien with notification of Lis Pendens. Mechanics liens, when filed, guarantee payment when the property sells.
35. Tenants in common: 1.JTWROS 2. May have unequal shares. 3.Cannot (testate) their interest in the property. 4.Ownership by severalty	2. May have unequal shares. Tenants in common may have different amounts of share and will their property.
36. An electrician rewired an entire house for a customer. To ensure he receives payment for the work, he filed a lien. The lien can be considered all the following except? 1.Mechanic's lien 2.A specific lien 3.A voluntary lien 4.An encumbrance	3. A voluntary lien A mechanics lien is an involuntary lien to the homeowner.
37. A garage was built 30 years ago. It extended 6 inches onto a neighbor's lot. This encroachment is an example of which of the following? 1.A dominant easement 2.A servient tenement 3.A license 4.Adverse possession	4. Adverse possession Adverse possession is built on time. Each state has its own time limits, but 30 years would appear sufficient.
38.Two neighbors own contiguous parcels. One has granted the other an easement appurtenant for ingress and egress. If one of the neighbors decides to sell, which of the following statements is true? 1.The dominant and servient tenement status does not change. 2.The easement appurtenant expires. 3.The buyer will have to pay and receive an additional deed for the easement. 4.The seller cannot sell if there is an easement on the property.	1. The dominant and servient tenement status does not change. Easements run with the land.
39.Bob and Steve purchased a vineyard as joint	2. In severalty

tenants. Bob died testate; how does Steve now own the property? 1.Joint tenants 2.In severalty 3.Tenancy in common with the new owner. 4.Ownership is determined by Bob's will.	The last surviving person in a joint tenancy will own the property by themselves.
40.A couple owns their house as tenants by entirety. The husband dies and his will states that all his holdings are to go to his son. What is the status of the ownership in the house? 1.The son and wife own the house together. 2.The son has sole ownership of the property. 3.The son and wife take ownership as tenants in common. 4.The son has no interest in the property.	4. The son has no interest in the property. In tenants by the entirety, rights of survivorship prevail.
41.Three sisters take title to an income producing property in unequal shares. What does this mean? 1.Common law property 2.Ownership in entirety 3.They are joint tenants. 4.They have title as tenants in common.	4. They have title as tenants in common. Tenancy in Common is the only partnership ownership that can have unequal shares.
42.Legal property descriptions may not be based on which of the following? 1.The government survey system. 2.The rectangular survey system. 3.A street address. 4.A previous survey.	3. A street address. A legal description is the formal address.
43.A land description that has a POB and ends at the POB and is based on directions, minutes and linear measurements is based on? 1.Metes and bounds 2.Benchmark metal markers 3.Datum 4.Townships	1. Metes and bounds The POB is the most important feature in a mete and bounds description. The surveyor will start and finish at the POB.
44.In the rectangular survey system, the principal meridians run? 1.East and west 2.North and South 3.Along the correction lines 4.Government survey system	2. North and South Principle meridians run north and south. Baselines run east and west.
45.You and your brother own a house. Your brother would like to sell his interest in the house to your aunt. What type of ownership do you and your brother have in the property? 1.By entirety 2.Tenancy for years 3.Tenancy in common 4.Life tenancy	3. Tenancy in common In a Tenancy in Common, each partner can disperse their property separately.
46.Tenancy by entirety can only be held by?	2. Husband and wife

1.Joint tenants 2.Husband and wife 3.A life tenant 4.Lis Pendens	Seldom used, Tenancy by the Entirety is for husband and wife only.
47.Which of the following would be considered a fixture? 1.Chattel 2.Personal property 3.A storage shed 4.A water softener	4. A water softener A water softener is attached as a fixture. A shed is not real property because they regularly sit on top of the land.
48.Within the same township if you travel from section 8 to section 26, what direction are you travelling? 1.Southwest 2.Northeast 3.North 4.Southeast	4. Southeast
49.Susan holds a life estate interest in a property. Her interest is? 1.An interest that can be sold 2.A remainderman 3.Limited to her life 4.Tenancy at will	3. Limited to her life. On the death of a life tenant, the estate either reverts to the original grantor or a remainderman will be named to be the next owner.
50.A man and wife who own their property as tenants by entirety. All the following is correct except? 1.Both have a right of survivorship. 2.The parties must be husband and wife. 3.Each can sell or will their half of the ownership. 4.Both parties must sign the deed.	3. Each can sell or will their half of the ownership. Both signatures are needed on contracts in real estate when the property is owned as Tenancy by the Entirety. Each person is considered a ½ person. It takes one person to sign a contract.
51.The county library holds title to its land and building with the condition that if it ever changes for the access to the building and books, title will revert to the original owner. This type of ownership is which of the following? 1.Fee simple 2.Defeasible fee 3.Remainderman 4.Revisionary	2. Defeasible fee Defeasible fee is ownership with a condition. If the condition is violated, the property will revert to the original grantor.
52.Which of the follow is considered personal property? 1.Subsurface rights 2.Chattels 3.Air rights 4.Water rights	2. Chattels Chattel is the French word for Cattle. It means movable objects. Personal property is movable.

53.Fee simple ownership as tenancy in common with people who don't know each other could be which of the following? 1.JTWROS 2.Time Share estate 3.Life estate 4.Fee simple defeasible	2. Time Share estate In a timeshare estate, several people own the same unit, but all the interests are uneven.
54.In a situation where state water rights are automatically conveyed with property is (*hint- best answer answer) 1.Prior appropriation 2.Prior subjective conditions 3.A condition stated on all loan documents. 4.Alluvial	2. Prior appropriation There are three water rights. Riparian, littoral, and prior appropriation. The correct an answer was the only water right mentioned.
55.Two lots owned by the same seller and of the same size were sold two days apart. The lot directly on the sand beach was sold for $100,000 more than the lot across the highway which will have a peek-a-boo look at the water. What characteristic was taking effect? 1.Permanence 2.Streetus 3.Situs 4.Situational indestructability	3. Situs Location- location - location. Situs means area preference.
56.A foremost reason for buying a condo over a luxury single family home on the ocean is 1.The back yard 2.Price 3.Loan terms 4.Discount points	2. Price As a general rule; Many condos will cost less than single family homes.
57.Ownership of common stock in a corporation 1.Can be real estate. 2.Is a deed. 3.Is considered personal property. 4.Is required to purchase a home.	3. Is considered personal property. Stock is movable.
58.A homeowner paid his neighbor $10,000 to have access to cross over the southeast portion of his property to reach a new road. This is an easement 1.By prescription 2.In gross 3.Appurtenant 4.For safety	3. Appurtenant Easements require two properties. There was no "time" factor or necessity described in the question. Because of that, you can rule out easement by prescription and easement by necessity. All easements are easements appurtenances.
59.The best example of a buffer zone is 1.A warehouse between a neighborhood and strip mall. 2.Garden homes between a single-family residential neighborhood and a shopping center. 3.An office building between a commercial strip	2. Garden homes between a single-family residential neighborhood and a shopping center. Garden homes traditionally do not have as many children as single-family residences. The garden homes put a traffic barrier between the

mall and a school. 4.All the above.	children and the mall.
60.A contour map is used for which of the following locations? 1. Flat low-lying areas 2. Desert towns 3. A very hilly location 4. They are never used	3. A very hilly location Contour maps measure land elevation.
61.A very old oak tree or a very large boulder 1. Lots and Blocks 2. Rectangular Survey System 3. Metes and Bounds	3. Metes and Bounds Reference is to the POB.
62.What is a good example of a buffer zone? 1. A large park between an office building and a single-family residence neighborhood. 2. A coffee shop between office buildings and a park. 3. A subway station between a city and the suburbs.	1. A large park between an office building and a single-family residence neighborhood. The large park with buffer traffic, people, and noise.
63.How many square feet in an acre? 1. 43,560 2. 55,000 3. 640	1. 43,560 4 old ladies driving 35 in a 60
64.Real Property includes all the following except? 1.Water rights 2.Oak trees 3.Chattel 4.Rose bushes	3. Chattel Chattel is personal property.
65.Metes and Bounds is associated with? 1.Point of beginning 2.Meridians 3.Baselines 4.Rectangles	1. Point of beginning The most important factor of metes and bounds is the POB.
66.Bob, a truck driver, has an easement where he benefits. It allows him to have a wide ingress and egress so that he can store his very large truck when he is not driving it. How could this easement be terminated? 1.The servient tenement holder rejects Bob's right for ingress and egress. 2.Bob retires from truck driving, sells his truck, and wants to end the easement. 3.When the servient tenement holder buys a bigger truck and access for Bob's truck is narrowed. 4.When Bob sells his truck.	2. Bob retires from truck driving, sells his truck, and wants to end the easement. The easement is no longer needed.
67.Corporations may take title in which of the following ways? 1.Tenants by the Entirety or Joint Tenants. 2.Joint tenants and tenants in common. 3.In Severalty or joint Tenants.	4.In Severalty. Corporations are considered a single person.

4.In Severalty.	
68.Usually takes priority over all other liens. 1.Capital gain 2.Comprehensive Loss Underwriting Exchange 3.Testate 4.Real estate taxes and special assessments	4. Real estate taxes and special assessments Taxes take priority.
69.The imposition of a tax, charge, or levy, usually according to established rates. 1.Assessment 2.Arbitrage 3.Defeasible fee 4.Attachment	1. Assessment This is your ad valorem taxes. Basically, the property taxes.
70.Highest type of interest in real estate recognized by law. The holder is entitled to all rights incident to the property. Continues for indefinite period and is inheritable by heirs of owner. 1.Fee simple 2.Regulation Z 3.Attachment 4.Abandonment	1. Fee simple Fee simple ownership is the highest form of ownership in real estate.
71.Run north and south? 1.Meridian 2.Baseline 3.Friable 4.Alluvion	1. Meridian The principal meridian runs north and south.
72.The land and the improvements there-on designated by the owners as his or her homestead. 1.Fee simple estate 2.Homestead protection 3.Accrued depreciation 4.Freehold estates	2. Homestead protection For the purposes of statutes, a homestead is the one primary residence of a person, and no other exemption can be claimed on any other property anywhere, even outside the boundaries of the jurisdiction in which the exemption is claimed.
73.An item installed by commercial tenant and removable by tenant before expiration of lease? 1.Negligence 2.Buffer zone 3.Trade fixture 4."Time of the essence"	3. Trade fixture Trade fixtures are installed to commercial property to allow the renter to conduct business.
74.Which of the following would not be a specific lien? 1.A voluntary mortgage 2.IRS judgment 3.Taxes on real estate 4.A mechanic's lien	2. IRS judgment An IRS judgment can be on several properties.
75.Usually takes priority over all other liens. 1.Capital gain 2.Comprehensive Loss Underwriting Exchange 3.Testate	4. Real estate taxes and special assessments Taxes take priority.

Real Estate Training Institute

4. Real estate taxes and special assessments	
76. Which of the following is MOST likely evidence of ownership in a cooperative? 1. Tax bill for an individual unit 2. Existence of a reverted clause 3. Mutual Funds 4. Shareholder stock	4. Shareholder stock A co-op owner has an interest or share in the entire building and a contract or lease that allows the owner to occupy a unit. While a condo owner owns a unit, a co-op owner does not own the unit. Co-ops are collectively owned and managed by their residents, who own shares in a nonprofit corporation.
77. Public land use controls include all the following except? 1. Shag carpets and marble countertops 2. Efficient heating and cooling equipment 3. Increased insulation in walls and roof 4. Energy Star® appliances	1. Shag carpets and marble countertops Shag carpets and marble countertops are decorating choices.
78. Which of the following is NOT an encumbrance on real estate? 1. property taxes 2. fixture 3. easement in gross 4. a shared driveway	2. fixture An encumbrance is any legal thing that burdens or restricts usage or transfer of a property.
79. An owner purchased an interest in a house in Beachfront. The owner is entitled to the right of possession only between July 10 and August 4 of each year. Which of the following is MOST likely the type of ownership that has been purchased? 1. Partnership 2. Time-share 3. Condominium 4. Cooperative	2. Time-share A timeshare (sometimes called vacation ownership) is a property with a divided form of ownership or use rights. These properties are typically resort condominium units, in which multiple parties hold rights to use the property, and each owner of the same accommodation is allotted their period.
80. A married couple co-owns a home and has the right of survivorship. This arrangement is MOST likely? 1. Community property 2. Severalty ownership 3. tenancy in common 4. An estate by the entirety	4. An estate by the entirety Tenancy by the entirety is a form of joint property ownership reserved for married couples. Tenancy by the entirety allows spouses to jointly own property as a single legal entity. Both spouses are equally and undivided owners of the property.
81. Which statement applies to both joint tenancy and tenancy by the entirety? 1. There is no right to file a partition suit. 2. The last survivor becomes a severalty owner. 3. A deed will not convey any interest unless signed by both spouses. 4. A deed signed by one owner will convey a fractional interest.	2. The last survivor becomes a severalty owner In both, there is a right of survivorship.
91. A license is an example of 1. An easement appurtenant	4. A personal privilege

2.An encroachment 3.A restriction 4.A personal privilege	A license is a revocable right to use someone's land for a specific purpose. It's a temporary personal privilege.
82.Which of the following refers to ownership by one person? 1.Severalty 2.Tenants by the entirety 3.Community property 4.Tenancy in common	1. Severalty Ownership in *severalty* (aka tenancy in *severalty*) is when *real estate* is owned by a single person or legal entity.
83.The four unities of possession, interest, time, and title are associated with which of the following? 1.Community property 2.Severalty ownership 3.Severalty ownership 4.Joint tenancy	4. Joint tenancy The creation of a JTWROS requires four unities: a. acquires the assets at the same time. b. must have the same title on the assets. c. each owner must have an equal share of the total assets. d. co-owners must each have the same right to possess the entirety of the asset.
84.A parcel of property was purchased by two friends. The deed they received from the seller at closing transferred the property without stipulating a form of ownership. The two friends took title as which of the following? 1.Community property owners 2.Tenants by the entirety 3.Tenants in common 4.Joint tenants	3. Tenants in common When a form of ownership is not stated, Tenants in Common will be applied.
85.Three people are joint tenants with rights of survivorship in a tract of land. One owner conveys his interest to a friend. Which statement is TRUE? 1.The other two owners remain joint tenants. 2.The new owner has severalty ownership. 3.They all become tenants in common. 4.They all become joint tenants.	1. The other two owners remain joint tenants The new "partner" did not take title at the same time as the others. The new owner holds title as Tenancy in Common.
86.A trust is a legal arrangement in which property is held for the benefit of a third party by the? 1.A trustee 2.An attorney-in-fact 3.A beneficiary 4.A trustor	1. A trustee Trustees are trusted to make decisions in the beneficiary's best interests.
87.A corporation is a legal entity, recognized as an artificial person. Property owned solely by the corporation is owned as? 1.Severalty 2.Partnership 3.Trust 4.Survivorship tenancy	1. Severalty A corporation is a one-person entity. A corporation holds title as "severalty".

88.If property is held by two or more owners as joint tenants, the interest of a deceased co-owner will be passed to 1.The state, under the law of escheat. 2.The state, under the law of frauds. 3.The heir of the deceased. 4.The surviving owner or owners.	4. The surviving owner or owners Property owned in joint tenancy automatically passes, without probate, to the surviving owner(s) when one owner dies.
89.A man owns one of 6 percent of the units in fee simple, along with an 6% ownership share in the parking facilities, recreation center, and grounds. What kind of property does he own? 1.Land trust 2.Cooperative 3.Condominium 4.Time-share	3. Condominium The condominium building structure is divided into several units that are each separately owned, surrounded by common areas that are jointly owned. Condominiums are a type of common-interest development.
90.According to some states, any real property that either spouse owns at the time of marriage remains separate property. Further, any real property acquired by either spouse during the marriage (except by gift or inheritance or with the proceeds of separate property) belongs to both equally. What is this form of ownership called? 1.Partnership 2.Joint tenancy 3.Tenancy by the entirety 4.Community property	4. Community property Any income and any real or personal property acquired by either spouse during a marriage are considered community property and thus belong to both partners of the marriage.
91A real property ownership interest that can be an estate interest or a right of use is 1.Leasehold 2.A time-share 3.A condominium 4.A cooperative	2. A time-share A timeshare (sometimes called vacation ownership) is a property with a divided form of ownership or use rights. These properties are typically resort condominium units, in which multiple parties hold rights to use the property, and each owner of the same accommodation is allotted their period.
92.Which of the following is NOT a form of co-ownership? 1.Community property 2.Tenancy by the entirety 3.Ownership in severalty 4.Tenancy in common	3. Ownership in severalty Ownership in severalty means one person owns the property.
93.The real property interest that takes the form of personal property is? 1.Condominium unit ownership 2.Single Family unit ownership 3.Cooperative unit ownership 4.Ownership in severalty	3. Cooperative unit ownership What is a co-op? Short for cooperative housing, these housing units will have a member living in a place with other residents, but instead of owning your unit, you own shares in the whole complex.

BONUS QUIZ

LAW Shelf Ownership Quiz

https://nationalparalegal.edu/
https://lawshelf.com/coursewareview

1. John conveys Blackacre to "Jim and Tim." The presumption is that Jim and Tim are...
    1.tenants-in-common in Blackacre.
    2.joint tenants in Blackacre.
    3.none of these; a conveyance to more than one person is presumptively invalid.
    4.tenants by the entirety in Blackacre.

2. Lisa owns Coalacre. Underneath Coalacre, there lies a coal mine that extends beyond the borders of Coalacre. John accesses the coal mine through another property and takes some coal from the coal mine. To whom does the coal belong?
    1.Lisa, because natural resources underneath property belongs to the owner of the property.
    2.John, because he did all the work to get the coal.
    3.John, based on the rule of capture.
    4.John, because coal is a fugitive resource.

3. Superman and Wonder Woman are joint tenants in the Hall of Justice. Superman conveys his interest in the Hall of Justice to Aquaman without Wonder Woman's permission. What is the status of the Hall of Justice?
    1.Wonder Woman and Aquaman own it as joint tenants.
    2.Wonder Woman and Aquaman own it as tenants-in-common.
    3.Wonder Woman and Superman still own it as joint tenants.
    4.Wonder Woman and Aquaman own it as tenants by the entirety.

4. Joe and Vicky are neighbors. Joe and Vicky have agreed, in writing that Joe may cross over Vicky's lawn to get to a street that is on the other side of her property. Joe sells his property to Aaron. May Joe still walk over Vicky's property if he so desires?
    1.No, because the right to the easement stays exclusively with the owner of the dominant

tenement.

2.Yes; if Joe gave Vicky consideration for the easement when it was originally transferred.

3.Yes; because Joe was the person who received the easement in the first place.

4.No; because Aaron now has the right to use Vicky's property, and so allowing Joe to do so also would widen the scope of the easement.

5. Ozzie and Harriet are husband and wife, and they live in Idaho (a community property state). Harriet inherits $100,000 from her Aunt Mabel. She then goes and uses that money to buy Whiteacre. Whiteacre is considered community property.

    1.True

    2.False

6. Ozzie and Harriet are husband and wife, and they live in Idaho (a community property state). Harriet inherits $100,000 from her Aunt Mabel. Ozzie and Harriet decide to buy Whiteacre for $500,000. As part of the payment, Harriet uses the $100,000 that she inherited from Aunt Mabel. Whiteacre is considered community property.

    1.True

    2.False

7. Jerry conveys his apartment "to George for life, so long as no wild parties are held in the apartment." Jerry regains the apartment…

    1.when George dies, but only if he had held at least one wild party in the apartment.

    2.upon the earlier of George dying or holding a wild party in the apartment.

    3.when George holds a wild party in the apartment.

    4.when George dies.

8. Anthony, Barbara, Cedric, and Debra all own property that borders a small lake. One day, Cedric installs a pump where his property meets the lake and starts pumping the water from the lake to water his crops. Because of this, the water level of the lake goes down. Anthony, Barbara, and Debra complain. Cedric claims that he may continue to use his pump. If the jurisdiction follows the riparian doctrine, who is correct?

    1.Cedric

    2.Anthony, Barbara, and Debra

9. Oscar conveys Garbageacre to Bert and Ernie, as joint tenants. In his Will, Ernie conveys his share of Garbageacre to Big Bird. Big Bird now owns a one-half interest in Garbageacre

    1.False

    2.True

10. Sam conveys Cheersacre "40% to Rebecca, 30% to Norm and 30% to Cliff". A few years later, Cliff dies. Who now owns Cheersacre?

    1.Rebecca owns 70% and Norm owns 30%.

    2.Rebecca owns 40% and Norm owns 30% and Cliff's heirs own 30%.

    3.Rebecca owns 55% and Norm owns 45%.

    4.Rebecca owns 40% and Norm owns 30% and Sam owns 30%.

11.Joker, Riddler, Penguin and Mr. Freeze own the Bat Cave as joint tenants. Mr. Freeze dies. THEN, Penguin transfers his interest in the Batcave to Archer. What is the status of Archer's ownership of the Bat Cave?

    1.He owns a one-third interest, as a tenant-in-common.

2.He owns a one-quarter interest, as a joint tenant

3.He owns a one-quarter interest, as a tenant-in-common.

4.He owns a one-third interest, as a joint tenant.

12. Roper owns an apartment building. He sells an apartment "to Jack, so long as he does not sell it to anyone without allowing Roper the chance to buy it first for its fair market value." Is this condition valid?

1.No, because a grantor can never attach conditions when he or she sells property.

2.No, because this is an unreasonable restraint on alienation.

3.Yes, because a right of first refusal is considered a reasonable restraint on alienation.

4.Yes, because it's Roper's property, so he can do whatever he wants with it.

13. Oscar conveys a one-half interest in Garbageacre to Ernie. Two weeks later, he conveys the other one-half interest to Bert and adds the language "I intend that you should be a joint tenant with Ernie and that you should each have a right of survivorship over the other's property." Is this language effective?

1.no

2.yes

14. Archie owns a 75% interest in a seaside cabin. Jughead owns a 25% interest in the same cabin. Jughead and Archie both want to use the cabin over a weekend. Archie claims that, since he owns a 75% interest, he should have first shot at use of the cabin. Is he correct?

1.No, because co- tenants share an equal right of possession, even if one owns more than a one-half interest.

2.No, neither gets first shot at using the cabin, but Jughead must pay Archie some rent money if he uses it because Archie owns most of the interest in the cabin.

3.Yes, but he must give Jughead first crack at the cabin 25% of the time.

4.Yes, because he owns 75% of the cabin; so, he always gets first shot at using the cabin.

15. The city water department owns an easement in gross that allows Larry to play golf on the Lakeside golf course any time he wishes to. Larry lives 3 blocks away from the course, which makes it very convenient for him to walk to the course whenever he wants to play. Is his house considered the dominant tenement?

1.Yes

2.No

16.Sam and Rebecca each own a one-half interest in Cheersacre as tenants-in-common. Sam sells his interest in Cheersacre to Woody without consulting Rebecca. What happens to Cheersacre?

1.Sam forfeited his interest in Cheersacre, and so Rebecca now owns the whole thing.

2.Woody and Rebecca are now tenants-in-common, each with a one-half interest.

3.Sam cannot sell his interest in Cheeracre, so the former status still stands (Sam and Rebecca each own a one-half interest in Cheersacre).

17. Oscar conveys Garbageacre, "60% to Bert and 40% to Ernie, as joint tenants with rights of survivorship." What is the status of Garbageacre?

1.Bert and Ernie each own a one-half interest in Garbageacre since Oscar obviously intended for the parties to be joint tenants.

2.Bert owns 60% and Ernie owns 40% as tenants-in-common, because only spouses can be joint tenants.

3.Bert owns 60% and Ernie owns 40% as tenants-in-common, because there cannot be a joint tenancy with the co-tenants owning unequal interests.

4.Bert owns 60% and Ernie owns 40% as joint tenants, because Oscar clearly intended for the parties to have rights of survivorship

18. Which of the following would qualify as a watercourse?
  1.A well dug deep beneath a property
  2.All of these.
  3.A stream flowing alongside a property
  4.A puddle of rainwater that collects on a property

19. Jerry conveys his apartment "to George for life, and then to Kramer for life and then to Elaine." Kramer then sells his interest in the apartment to Newman. Kramer dies while George is alive. When George dies, who will get the apartment?
  1.Jerry's heirs until Newman dies, then Elaine.
  2.Elaine.
  3.Newman, until he dies, then Elaine.
  4.George's heirs until Newman dies, then Elaine.

20. Which of the following is a non-freehold estate?
  1.leasehold for years
  2.fee simple
  3.life estate
  4.pur autrie vie

21. Joe and Vicky are neighbors. Joe and Vicky have agreed, in writing that Joe may cross over Vicky's lawn to get to a street that is on the other side of her property. What interest does Joe have in Vicky's property?
  1.An easement in gross, because it is Joe, and not Joe's property, that holds the right to walk across Vicky's lawn.
  2.An easement appurtenant, because every easement is presumed to be an easement appurtenant unless expressly agreed otherwise by the parties.
  3.An easement appurtenant, because the interest and reason that Joe obtained the interest relates to the positions of the properties.
  4.An easement in gross, because every easement is presumed to be an easement in gross unless expressly agreed otherwise by the parties.

22. Joe and Vicky are neighbors. Joe and Vicky have agreed, in writing that Joe may cross over Vicky's lawn to get to a street that is on the other side of her property. Later, Joe sells his property to Aaron. May Aaron use Vicky's property to access the street?
  1.Yes, if Joe gave Vicky consideration for the creation of the easement.
  2.Yes; because an easement appurtenant runs with the land.
  3.No; because Vicky probably did not intend for Aaron to be able to cross over her property.
  4.No; because Joe still has the right to use Vicky's property, and so allowing Aaron to do so also would widen the scope of the easement.

23. Jerry conveys his apartment "to George for life." George then conveys the apartment "to Kramer, in fee simple absolute." What interest does Kramer have in the apartment?
  1.A fee simple absolute.
  2.A life estate, with his own life as the measuring life.
  3.A life estate pur autre vie, with George as the measuring life.
  4.A life estate pur autre vie, with Jerry as the measuring life.

24. Batman orally conveys to Joker an easement that allows Joker to park his car in the Batcave. Is the oral conveyance enforceable?
> 1.Yes; because Joker could die within a year, extinguishing the easement; thus, the transfer is not for an interest in real estate for one year or more.
> 2.No, because it violates the Statute of Frauds.
> 3.Yes, because any easement is not considered an interest in property.
> 4.Yes, because an easement in gross is not considered an interest in property.

25. Sherrie and Al operate a business and are thinking of incorporating. Which type of corporation would allow them to avoid double taxation?
> 1.a professional corporation
> 2.an S corporation
> 3.a C corporation
> 4.a close corporation

26. In resolving disputes over whether a business enterprise may be characterized as a partnership, a court will look to see whether the existing business relationship involves
> 1.a sharing of profits
> 2.a sharing of losses
> 3.a sharing of losses
> 4.all of these

27. The concept of double taxation means that
> 1.government taxes both earnings and retained earnings
> 2.government taxes both management salaries and dividends to them
> 3.government taxes both earnings to the corporation and to individuals
> 4.tax rate for corporations is double that of individuals

28. Ethel conveys an apartment "to Lucy and Ricky," who are husband and wife "as joint tenants". Lucy and Ricky share the apartment as…
> 1.Tenants-in-common
> 2.Joint tenants
> 3.None of these; a conveyance to more than one person is presumptively invalid
> 4.Tenants by the entirety

29. Responsibility for the overall management of the corporation is entrusted to
> 1.corporate officers and managers.
> 2.the board of directors.
> 3.the shareholders.
> 4.the owners of the corporation.

30. Sam and Rebecca each own a one-half interest in Cheersacre as tenants-in-common. Sam writes a will, leaving his interest in Cheersacre to Woody. Sam dies. Woody now owns a one-half interest in Cheersacre.
> 1.True
> 2.False

31.Mr. Lodge is selling his house for $500,000. Jughead and Archie decide to buy it. Jughead pays Mr. Lodge $300,000 and Archie pays $200,000. Mr. Lodge conveys the house by a deed "to Archie and Jughead." Which of the following is correct?
> 1.There is a presumption that Archie and Jughead will each get a one-half interest in the house.

2.There is a presumption that Jughead will get 60% of the house and Archie will get 40% of the house.

3.Jughead will definitely get a 60% interest in the house and Archie will definitely get a 40% interest in the house.

32. Lucy and Ricky own Blackacre as tenants by the entirety. On May 1, Lucy and Ricky get divorced. On May 5, Lucy dies. In her will, Lucy leaves her interest in Blackacre to Ethel. Who owns Blackacre?
   1.Ricky
   2.Ricky and Ethel, as joint tenants
   3.Ricky and Ethel, as tenants-in-common
   4.Ethel

33. Jason and Jumana Kidd are husband and wife who live in New Jersey. Jason makes $10,000,000 in one season playing basketball. Who owns that money?
   1.Jason
   2.Both Jason and Jumana

34. A parcel of real property can be divided by…
   1.occupancy
   2.All of these.
   3.space
   4.time

ANSWER KEY

1. John conveys Blackacre to "Jim and Tim." The presumption is that Jim and Tim are…	1.tenants-in-common in Blackacre. Any conveyance of property to two or more people who are not husband and wife will be presumed to be a tenancy-in-common unless there is clear intent to the contrary by the grantor
2. Lisa owns Coalacre. Underneath Coalacre, there lies a coal mine that extends beyond the borders of Coalacre. John accesses the coal mine through another property and takes some coal from the coal mine. To whom does the coal belong?	1.Lisa, because natural resources underneath property belongs to the owner of the property. Minerals and other natural resources that are embedded in the ground beneath property inherently belong to the owner of the surface property above. Coal is solid and does not inherently flow from place to place.
3. Superman and Wonder Woman are joint tenants in the Hall of Justice. Superman conveys his interest in the Hall of Justice to Aquaman without Wonder Woman's permission. What is the status of the Hall of Justice?	2.Wonder Woman and Aquaman own it as tenants-in-common. A joint tenant has the right to convey his or her interest in the property to anyone he or she wants to. However, once this is done, the joint tenancy is destroyed with respect to the share of the property that has been transferred. The

	new transferee takes over as a tenant-in-common with the remaining interest holders in the property.
4. Joe and Vicky are neighbors. Joe and Vicky have agreed, in writing that Joe may cross over Vicky's lawn to get to a street that is on the other side of her property. Joe sells his property to Aaron. May Joe still walk over Vicky's property if he so desires?	1.No, because the right to the easement stays exclusively with the owner of the dominant tenement. The right to use an easement appurtenant always resides exclusively with the owner of the dominant tenement. Note that choice 4 is technically a true statement, but its reasoning is not necessary because the seller of a dominant tenement does not keep the right to use the easement
5. Ozzie and Harriet are husband and wife, and they live in Idaho (a community property state). Harriet inherits $100,000 from her Aunt Mabel. She then goes and uses that money to buy Whiteacre. Whiteacre is considered community property.	2.False The answer is False. Assets that are obtained or purchased by using separate property are considered separate property. Since the $100,000 is considered separate property because it came from a gift from a third party, an asset bought with that money is also considered separate property.
6. Ozzie and Harriet are husband and wife, and they live in Idaho (a community property state). Harriet inherits $100,000 from her Aunt Mabel. Ozzie and Harriet decide to buy Whiteacre for $500,000. As part of the payment, Harriet uses the $100,000 that she inherited from Aunt Mabel. Whiteacre is considered community property.	1.True If separate property is co-mingled with community property so that it is not possible to tell what the source of the purchase of a specific asset is, then the entire asset is presumed to be community property. Obviously, it is impossible to determine what part of Whiteacre has been purchased with the community property money. Since the separate property has been co-mingled with the community property, the entire asset will be presumed to be community property. Therefore, the answer is True.
7. Jerry conveys his apartment "to George for life, so long as no wild parties are held in the apartment." Jerry regains the apartment…	2.upon the earlier of George dying or holding a wild party in the apartment. Either event can force the property to revert back to the grantor.
8. Anthony, Barbara, Cedric, and Debra all own property that borders a small lake. One day, Cedric installs a pump where his property meets the lake and starts pumping the water from the lake to water his crops. Because of this, the water level of the lake goes down. Anthony, Barbara, and Debra complain. Cedric claims that he may continue to use his pump. If the	2.Anthony, Barbara, and Debra The Riparian doctrine provides that the rights to water belongs equally to all the owners of lands that border the water source. Therefore, one owner cannot use the water in a manner

jurisdiction follows the riparian doctrine, who is correct?	that would take away the usage of the water from the other riparian owners.
9. Oscar conveys Garbageacre to Bert and Ernie, as joint tenants. In his Will, Ernie conveys his share of Garbageacre to Big Bird. Big Bird now owns a one-half interest in Garbageacre	1.False A joint tenant has a "right of survivorship" on the co-tenant's interest in the property. This means that if one party dies, the other party automatically takes over the interest by operation of law. Thus, although Ernie could convey his interest to Big Bird while he was alive, as soon as he dies, his interest goes straight to Bert. Since a will only takes affect after death, it is ineffective, and Bert now owns the whole Garbageacre.
10. Sam conveys Cheersacre "40% to Rebecca, 30% to Norm and 30% to Cliff". A few years later, Cliff dies. Who now owns Cheersacre	2.Rebecca owns 40% and Norm owns 30% and Cliff's heirs own 30%. A tenant-in-common does not have a "right of survivorship" in the property. This means that when one of the tenants-in-common dies, his or her share does not automatically pass to the other tenant. Instead, the decedent's share passes with the rest of his estate to his heirs. Choice 3 is wrong because Sam gave away all his interest in Cheersacre and did not retain a future interest for himself or his heirs.
11. Joker, Riddler, Penguin and Mr. Freeze own the Bat Cave as joint tenants. Mr. Freeze dies. THEN, Penguin transfers his interest in the Batcave to Archer. What is the status of Archer's ownership of the Bat Cave?	1.He owns a one-third interest, as a tenant-in-common. This is a complicated one! When Mr. Freeze died, the rights of survivorship kicked in and so the others all then owned a one-third interest in the property. Then, when Penguin sold his interest to Archer, that broke up the joint tenancy with regard to Archer's interest. However, Archer still does get the one-third interest from Penguin, although it is now as a tenant-in-common.
12. Roper owns an apartment building. He sells an apartment "to Jack, so long as he does not sell it to anyone without allowing Roper the chance to buy it first for its fair market value." Is this condition valid?	3. Yes, because a right of first refusal is considered a reasonable condition on alienation. Although restraints on alienation are disfavored, reasonable restraints are allowed. A "right of first refusal," which allows the seller first crack at buying it back if the buyer ever wants to sell it is a valid condition.

13. Oscar conveys a one-half interest in Garbageacre to Ernie. Two weeks later, he conveys the other one-half interest to Bert and adds the language "I intend that you should be a joint tenant with Ernie and that you should each have a right of survivorship over the other's property." Is this language effective?	1.no Of the "four unities" required to form a joint tenancy, one of them is the unity of time. This means that both joint tenants must receive their interest at the same time. This did not happen in this case. Incidentally, the "unity of title" is also lacking here because the two interests must have been conveyed by different instruments if they were conveyed at different times.
14. Archie owns a 75% interest in a seaside cabin. Jughead owns a 25% interest in the same cabin. Jughead and Archie both want to use the cabin over a weekend. Archie claims that, since he owns a 75% interest, he should have first shot at use of the cabin. Is he correct?	1.No, because co- tenants share an equal right of possession, even if one owns more than a one-half interest. Every co-tenant of a concurrent estate has the equal right with all the other co-tenants of to possess and use at the same time any and all of the property. There is no greater or lesser right of possession based on ownership.
15. The city water department owns an easement in gross that allows Larry to play golf on the Lakeside golf course any time he wishes to. Larry lives 3 blocks away from the course, which makes it very convenient for him to walk to the course whenever he wants to play. Is his house considered the dominant tenement?	2.No There is no such thing as a dominant tenement of an easement in gross. A dominant tenement can only exist in relation to an easement appurtenant.
16. Sam and Rebecca each own a one-half interest in Cheersacre as tenants-in-common. Sam sells his interest in Cheersacre to Woody without consulting Rebecca. What happens to Cheersacre?	2.Woody and Rebecca are now tenants-in-common, each with a one-half interest. In a Tenancy-In-Common either party may sell or transfer his or her share of the property to any person, for any reason. If one of the tenants does sell or transfer his or her share, then the buyer takes the seller's place and becomes a tenant-in-common with the party who did not sell his or her share.
17. Oscar conveys Garbageacre, "60% to Bert and 40% to Ernie, as joint tenants with rights of survivorship." What is the status of Garbageacre?	3.Bert owns 60% and Ernie owns 40% as tenants-in-common, because there cannot be a joint tenancy with the co-tenants owning unequal interests. Of the "four unities" required to form a joint tenancy, one of them is the unity of interest. This means that each joint tenant must have an equal interest in the property. In this case, there is an unequal interest, so the joint tenancy conveyance fails. When that happens, it is replaced by a tenancy-in-common.
18. Which of the following would qualify as a watercourse?	3.A stream flowing alongside a property

	A watercourse is a source of water external to the property that can be accessed because it borders on the property Well water is ground water and rain puddles are surface water.
19. Jerry conveys his apartment "to George for life, and then to Kramer for life and then to Elaine." Kramer then sells his interest in the apartment to Newman. Kramer dies while George is alive. When George dies, who will get the apartment?	2.Elaine. Kramer could only transfer the interest that he owns in the apartment. In this case, Kramer received a remainder interest after George that was to end at his death. Thus, when Newman got the apartment from Kramer, he only received a life estate pur autre vie with Kramer as the measuring life that was only to take effect at George's death. Since Kramer died while George was alive, Kramer's interest never did vest and never will vest. Therefore, Newman never gets the property, and it goes to the holder of the remainder interest after George.
20. Which of the following is a non-freehold estate?	1.leasehold for years A leasehold is a non-freehold estate.
21. Joe and Vicky are neighbors. Joe and Vicky have agreed, in writing that Joe may cross over Vicky's lawn to get to a street that is on the other side of her property. What interest does Joe have in Vicky's property?	3.An easement appurtenant, because the interest and reason that Joe obtained the interest relates to the positions of the properties. An easement that is held by a person in his or her capacity as owner of a property is an easement appurtenant. In this case, clearly, the only reason Joe needs to cross Vicky's property is because of the relative position of her property in relation to his property. Therefore, the easement is an easement appurtenant.
22. Joe and Vicky are neighbors. Joe and Vicky have agreed, in writing that Joe may cross over Vicky's lawn to get to a street that is on the other side of her property. Later, Joe sells his property to Aaron. May Aaron use Vicky's property to access the street?	2.Yes; because an easement appurtenant runs with the land. An easement appurtenant is considered to be owned by the owner of the dominant tenement in his or her capacity as owner of that land. Therefore, if the land is sold, the easement is transferred along with the property. Choice 1 is incorrect because consideration is not a necessary element of the transferring of interests in real estate.
23. Jerry conveys his apartment "to George for life." George then conveys the apartment to Kramer, in fee simple absolute." What interest does Kramer have in the apartment?	3.A life estate pur autre vie, with George as the measuring life. George tried to convey the apartment to Kramer in the widest possible terms (fee simple absolute is the highest ownership

	interest in land that there is). However, he cannot convey more than he owns. When Jerry gave George the life estate, the estate that George got lasts until George's death. Therefore, Kramer, who steps into George's shoes, takes over as the life tenant with George remaining the measuring life.
24. Batman orally conveys to Joker an easement that allows Joker to park his car in the Batcave. Is the oral conveyance enforceable?	2.No, because it violates the Statute of Frauds. An easement is considered an interest in real property. Thus, a conveyance of an easement must be in writing to be enforceable.
25. Sherrie and Al operate a business and are thinking of incorporating. Which type of corporation would allow them to avoid double	1.a professional corporation The creation of the S Corporation business form was done to allow a middle ground between the limited liability aspects of a full corporation and the tax attributes of a partnership. As such, an S corporation adopts the characteristic of a partnership that requires the taxing authority to treat an S Corp as a 'pass through' entity where the corporation is not taxed on its profits, but the individual shareholders are taxed on the distribution that the firm makes to them.
26. In resolving disputes over whether a business enterprise may be characterized as a partnership, a court will look to see whether the existing business relationship involves:	4.all of these Trying to determine if a partnership exists can be an exceedingly complex task for a court in a situation where no formal partnership exists. As such, the court will typically look to any factor it may find helpful to answer the question.
27. The concept of double taxation means that	3.government taxes both earnings to the corporation and to individuals When a company earns money, the government taxes the corporation. When a company later distributes money to shareholders, the government taxes the distribution made to shareholders. Thus, the concept of double taxation means that any distribution from a company has already been taxed once, and on the distribution, is taxed again.
28. Ethel conveys an apartment "to Lucy and Ricky," who are husband and wife "as joint tenants". Lucy and Ricky share the apartment as…	2.Joint tenants If the intent of the donor is to create a joint tenancy or a tenancy-in-common between the husband and wife, this intent can override the presumption that a transfer to husband and wife creates a tenancy by the entirety.

29. Responsibility for the overall management of the corporation is entrusted to	2.the board of directors. Remember, while shareholders own the corporation and officers and managers have control over the daily operations of the corporation, ultimate responsibility for managing the corporation falls on the company's board of directors.
30. Sam and Rebecca each own a one-half interest in Cheersacre as tenants-in-common. Sam writes a will, leaving his interest in Cheersacre to Woody. Sam dies. Woody now owns a one-half interest in Cheersacre.	1.True A tenant-in-common does not have a "right of survivorship" in the property. Sam may give his interest in the tenancy or leave it by wll, to anyone he chooses. Therefore, the correct answer is true.
31. Mr. Lodge is selling his house for $500,000. Jughead and Archie decide to buy it. Jughead pays Mr. Lodge $300,000 and Archie pays $200,000. Mr. Lodge conveys the house by a deed "to Archie and Jughead." Which of the following is correct?	1.There is a presumption that Archie and Jughead will each get a one-half interest in the house. If property is conveyed to two or more people, the presumption will be that this conveyance is to each of the parties, in equal shares.
32. Lucy and Ricky own Blackacre as tenants by the entirety. On May 1, Lucy and Ricky get divorced. On May 5, Lucy dies. In her will, Lucy leaves her interest in Blackacre to Ethel.	3.Ricky and Ethel, as tenants-in-common A divorce automatically breaks up a tenancy by the entirety and converts it into a tenancy-in-common. So, on May 5, Lucy and Ricky were tenants-in-common on Blackacre. Thus, when Lucy died, her interest in Blackacre was transferred by her will to Ethel. Thus, Ethel takes Lucy's place and Ethel, and Ricky are now tenants-in-common on Blackacre.
33. Jason and Jumana Kidd are husband and wife who live in New Jersey. Jason makes $10,000,000 in one season playing basketball. Who owns that money?	1.Jason Mississippi is not a community property state. Under the common law, money earned by one spouse belongs to the spouse that earned the money.
34. A parcel of real property can be divided by…	2.All of these. A parcel of real property can be divided by space (physically dividing the property), occupancy (by allowing both owners to have possession of the property) and by time (by having one party own a current interest in the property and another own a future interest).

Definitions Module One

Air Rights
The property interest in the "space" above the earth's surface. Owning, or renting, land or a building

includes the right to use and develop the space above the land without interference by others.

Appurtenance
The attachment of a right or property that attaches to the property.

Arpent
French arpent land divisions are long narrow parcels of land, also called ribbon farms, usually found along the navigable streams of southern Louisiana, and found along major waterways in other areas.

Baseline
A baseline is the principal east-west line (i.e., a parallel) upon which all rectangular surveys in a defined area are based. The baseline meets its corresponding principal meridian at the point of origin, or initial point, for the land survey.

Bundle of Legal Rights
All the legal rights attached to the ownership of real property.

Common Areas
Those portions of a building, land, or improvements and amenities owned by a planned unit development (PUD) or condominium project's homeowners' association (or a cooperative project's cooperative corporation) that are used by all the unit owners, who share in the common expenses of their operation and maintenance. Common areas include swimming pools, tennis courts, and other recreational facilities, as well as common corridors of buildings, parking areas, means of ingress and egress, etc.

Condominium
A unit in a multiunit building. The owner of a condominium unit owns the unit itself and has the right, along with other owners, to use the common areas but does not own the common elements such as the exterior walls, floors and ceilings or the structural systems outside of the unit.

Cooperative (Co-op) Project
A project in which a corporation holds title to a residential property and sells shares to individual buyers, who then receive a proprietary lease as their title.

Dominant Tenement
The benefited land is called the dominant tenement The land that benefits from an easement., and the burdened land—that is, the land subject to the easement—is called the servient tenement.

Easement
The right to use another's land for a stated purpose. A nonpossessory (incorporeal) interest in landed property conveying use, but not ownership, of a portion of that property.

Easement by Necessity
A right to use the property of another. An easement by necessity is an easement that is created when the owner of a landlocked parcel has no access to a public right of way such as a street or highway.

Easement by Prescription
Prescriptive easements also called "easements by prescription," are created when an individual continually and openly uses a portion of another person's property without the permission of the owner. This most frequently happens in rural areas, when a landowner fails to notice their property being used.

Easement in Gross
An easement that attaches a particular right to an individual or entity rather than to the property itself. The easement in gross is often considered irrevocable for the life of the individual, but it can be rendered void if the individual sells the property upon which the easement request was based.

Economic Characteristics of Land

1. **Scarcity**: While land isn't considered rare, the total supply is fixed.
2. **Improvements**: Any additions or changes to the land or a building that affects the property's value is called an improvement. Improvements of a private nature (such as homes and fences) are referred to as improvements *on* the land. Improvements of a public nature (e.g., sidewalks and sewer systems) are called improvements *to* the land.
3. **Permanence of investment**: Once land is improved, the total capital and labor used to build the improvement represent a sizable, fixed investment. Even though a building can be razed, improvements like drainage, electricity, water, and sewer systems tend to be permanent because they can't be removed (or replaced) economically.
4. **Location or area preference**. Location refers to people's choices and tastes regarding a given area, based on factors like convenience, reputation, and history. Location is one of the most important economic characteristics of land (thus the saying, "location, location, location!").

Eminent Domain
The right of government to take private property for public use upon payment of just compensation. The fifth amendment of the U.S. Constitution (taking Clause) guarantees payment of just compensation upon appropriation of private property.

Encumbrance
Any claim or liability that affects or limits the title to property. An encumbrance can affect the title such as a mortgage or other lien, or it can affect the physical condition of the property such as an easement. An encumbrance cannot prevent the transfer of possession, but it does remain after the transfer.

Equitable Lien
A specific type of lien. These are liens that are imposed by the court in order to maintain a certain degree of fairness or "equity" in the situation surrounding the property. They usually arise when one person holds possession of property for another person.

Equalization
To distribute evenly or uniformly **equalize** the tax burden

Estate
A right or interest in property. Defines an owner's degree, quantity, nature and extent of interest in real property. There are many different types of estates, including freehold (Fee simple, determinable fee, and life estate).

Estate Tax Lien
When someone dies, federal estate tax liens can be imposed against his or her assets.

Fee Simple
A complete, unencumbered ownership right in a piece of property.

Fixture

A permanent part of a house or apartment. A fixture is real property and conveys with the transfer of real estate; it is not personal property. This means it will be sold with the house and the seller will not remove it before the house is transferred to the buyer.

Fructus Naturales
The natural fruits of the land on which they arise, such as the produce from old roots and uncultivated plants, and wild game.

Homeowners' Association
An organization of homeowners residing within a particular area whose principal purpose is to ensure the provision and maintenance of community facilities and services for the common benefit of the residents.

Ingress
A means of entering.

Joint Tenancy
The concurrent ownership by two or more persons with the right of survivorship.

Judgment
A court ruling that gives a creditor the right to take possession of a debtor's real or personal property if the debtor fails to fulfill his or her contractual obligations.

Judgment Lien
A lien on the property of a debtor resulting from the decree of a court.

Land
The earth's surface down to the center of the earth and upward to the airspace above, including the trees, minerals, and water.

Legal Descriptions
The written words which delineate a specific piece of real property. Also known as a "Legal Description". In the written transfer of real property, it is universally required that the instrument of conveyance include a written description of the property.

Lien
A claim or charge on property for payment of a debt. With a mortgage, the lender has the right to take the title to your property if you don't make the mortgage payments.

Littoral Rights
littoral rights are rights concerning properties that abut static water like an ocean, bay, delta, sea or lake, rather than a flowing river or stream. Navigable waters.

Mechanics Lien
A legal claim against a home or other property. Mechanic's liens are typically used by subcontractors and suppliers when they haven't received payment for improvements they made to a property. They are a way to seek payment for the work done remodeling or improving a home.

Metes and Bounds
Measurement of or boundaries of a tract of land as identified by natural landmarks, such as rivers, or by man-made structures, such as roads, or by stakes or other markers. A principal legal type of land

description in the United States, metes-and-bounds descriptions are commonly used wherever survey areas are irregular in size and shape. The land boundaries are run out by courses and distances, and monuments, natural or artificial, are fixed at the corners, or angles. A course is the direction of a line, usually with respect to a meridian but sometimes with respect to the magnetic north. Distance is the length of a course measured in some well-known unit, such as feet or chains.

Mineral Rights
Property rights to exploit an area for the minerals it harbors. Mineral rights can be separate from property ownership (see Split estate). Mineral rights can refer to sedentary minerals that do not move below the Earth's surface or fluid minerals such as oil or natural gas.

Noncontiguous
Not contiguous

Personal Property
Any property that is not real property.

Physical Characteristics of Land
1. **Immobility**. While some parts of land are removable and the topography can be altered, the geographic location of any parcel of land can never be changed.
2. **Indestructibility**. Land is durable and indestructible (permanent).
3. **Uniqueness**. No two parcels of land can be exactly the same. Even though they may share similarities, every parcel differs geographically.

Point of Beginning
is a surveyor's mark at the beginning location for the wide-scale surveying of land.
An example is the Beginning Point of the U.S. Public Land Survey that led to the opening of the Northwest Territory and is the starting point of the surveys of almost all other lands to the west, reaching all the way to the Pacific Ocean.

Planned Unit Development (PUD)
A real estate project in which individuals hold title to a residential lot and home while the common facilities are owned and maintained by a homeowners' association for the benefit and use of the individual PUD unit owners.

Prescriptive Easement
Also called "easements by prescription," are created when an individual continually and openly uses a portion of another person's property without the permission of the owner. This most frequently happens in rural areas, when a landowner fails to notice their property being used.

Principle Meridian
The principal north-south line used for survey control in a large region, and which divides townships between east and west. The meridian meets its corresponding baseline at the point of origin, or initial point, for the land survey.

Public Land Survey System
The surveying method developed and used in the United States to plat, or divide, real property for sale and settling. Also known as the Rectangular Survey System, it was created by the Land Ordinance of 1785.

Real Property

Land and anything permanently affixed thereto — including buildings, fences, trees, and minerals.

Riparian Rights
The right of the owner of land bordering a non-navigable lake or stream to the use and enjoyment of the water that flows across their land or is contiguous to it. Under the riparian rights doctrine, all owners of land underlying or abutting the water have equal rights to it. In comparison, the prior appropriation doctrine would not confer equal rights to all owners of land underlying or abutting the water.

Servient Tenement
A parcel of land that is subject to an easement. The easement may be an easement in gross, an easement that benefits an individual or other entity, or it may be an easement appurtenant, an easement that benefits another parcel of land.

Statutory Lien
A statutory lien arises automatically by statute (law).

Subsurface Rights
A landowner's right over minerals and other substances found below a property. A person acquires a subsurface right through purchase from a landowner. The assessment of subsurface rights for tax purposes is made on the production of oil and gas from the subsurface.

Surface Rights
The ownership of the surface of the land. This includes dwellings, buildings, the right to till the land for crops and even the ability to dig into the land.

Tax Liens
If you haven't paid your taxes in a while, the government can also choose to put a lien on your property until you're current on your taxes.

Tenancy in Common
An arrangement where two or more people share ownership rights in a property or parcel of land. The property may be commercial or residential.

When a tenant in common dies, the property passes to that tenant's estate.
Each independent owner may control an equal or different percentage of the total property.

Tenancy in Severalty
An exclusive and separate right of possession or ownership, unshared with others (□ "person" for legal purposes that owns the property could be a corporation). Or in simpler terms, it is the sole ownership of a property.

Topographic Map
The shape and character of the Earth's surface, and maps were among the first artifacts to record these observations.

Trade Fixtures
An article of personal property annexed or affixed to leased premises by the tenant as a necessary part of the tenant's trade or business. In other words, they are articles placed in the buildings by the tenant to help carry out a trade or business.

Voluntary Lien
A type of lien in which the owner of a property grants another party legal claim to that property as a guarantee for payment of a debt or a service rendered.

Water Rights
The right of a user to use water from a water source, e.g., a river, stream, pond or source of groundwater. In areas with plentiful water and few users, such systems are generally not complicated or contentious. In other areas, especially arid areas where irrigation is practiced, such systems are often the source of conflict, both legal and physical. Some systems treat surface water and ground water in the same manner, while others use different principles for each.

MODULE TWO: Government Controls and Rights in Land

Police Power

The rights of the government. To protect the public.

Zoning and Land Use Laws

Enabling Acts/Rights

☐ Cities and local municipalities can decide their own zoning through State Enabling Acts or Rights.
• Zoning powers are generally granted to local government pursuant to enabling acts.

Master Plan

• A comprehensive growth plan that guides the long-term zoning, use, and development of a community.
• The general purpose of a master plan is to control and accommodate social and economic growth.
• The master plan outlines.
1. Amount of growth.
2. Growth patterns.
3. Accommodating future demand.

Zoning

• ☐ Zoning implements the city's master plan.
• **Zoning is a three-phase process.**
1. Development of a master plan.
2. Administration of the plan.
3. Implementation of the plan through public control of zoning.

Zoning Laws, Planning, and Land Use	The Most Frequently Used Zoning
• Zoning includes various laws falling under police power. • Zoning is the process of dividing land into zones (e.g., residential, industrial) in which certain land uses are permitted or prohibited. • The type of zone determines whether planning /permission for a given development is granted.	1. Commercial 2. Industrial 3. Residential 4. Agricultural

☐ If a public control and a deed restriction conflict, the more restrictive of the two takes precedence.

Legal Non-Conforming Uses and Variances

- A legal nonconforming use is a use of property that was allowed under the zoning regulations at the time the use was established, but which, due to changes in local regulations, is no longer a permitted use.

Grandfather Clause

- Permission to continue doing something that was once permissible but is now not allowed. In zoning, it permits a nonconforming use. For example, an existing auto repair shop being allowed to remain in a shopping area that is being revitalized.

Conditional Uses and Special Exceptions	Zoning Variance
<ul><li>A conditional use is a zoning exception that allows the property owner to use their land in a way not otherwise permitted within the zoning district.</li><li>To obtain a conditional use permit, there must first be a public hearing.</li></ul>	<ul><li>A request for a deviation from the Zoning Code.</li><li>An example would be a homeowner allowed to build a fence closer to a lot line than the zoning allows.</li><li>A permanent exception granted to either build a new structure or conduct a new use that would not be permitted under the current zoning.</li></ul>

Application for a Variance

- If your use of land or proposed building does not entirely conform to existing zoning and land use laws, you can apply for a variance.
- Typically, the landowner must show that she will experience a substantial financial hardship if she does not receive a variance.

Planning Department

- Provides the municipality with the goals and objectives for its future development.
- Most municipalities have a specific Planning or Zoning Department that will propose zoning ordinances and oversee zoning and land use hearings.
- These departments will also make decisions regarding variances (see below), conditional use permits and other issues that may implicate a zoning or land use ordinance.
- ☐ Generally, the department will have a public hearing ☐ (first step to zoning or making a change in zoning) where the individual or group whose land is affected can present their case.
- The hearing also allows public comment on the case.

Zoning Examples

Bulk Zoning

- A method used to control density and overcrowding by restricting setbacks, building height, or ratio of open area.

Spot Zoning

- A zoning to a particular parcel of land.

Use Zoning

- Zoning for a particular use.

Density Zoning

- Ordinances restrict amounts of houses per acre that can be built within a particular subdivision.

Residential zoning regulates:
- Limits the number and size of dwelling units and lots in an area.
- Can limit the type of residences allowed.

A primary objective of residential zoning is:
- regulate rates of appreciation and depreciation of land.
- disperse intensity of usage.
- promote the value and planned land use of a neighborhood.
- eliminate nonconforming uses, variances, and special exceptions.

Buffer Zone

- Some areas adopt buffer zones to separate residential areas from commercial and industrial zones.
- A strip of land separating two parcels that are zoned differently, such as undeveloped land separating a shopping center from a residential neighborhood.
- For use in nature conservation, a buffer zone is often created to enhance the protection of areas under management for their biodiversity importance.

Downzoning	Up zoning
• Changing the zoning to **more restricted** use, such as from multi-family to single-family which will restrict the density • Rezoning of an area that would be less dense in population. An example would be a neighborhood that downzoned from multi-unit residential zoning to single-family residences only.	• A change in zoning to a **less restricted** use such as from single-family to multi-family use.

Aesthetic Zoning

- Zoning requires new structures to match an existing architectural style.

Height Districts

- Building heights are a type of land use regulation. These regulations restrict the height of buildings within any given area.

Floating Zones

- Floating zones are found where noncompliant use is permitted within a specific zoning area.

Cumulative Zoning

- Zoning permits a less restricted use as well as the designated use. For example, single-family homes may be built interspersed with multi-family use.

Conservation Zoning

- Open zoning where the intent is to keep the parcel in its natural or agricultural state.

Conservation Easement

- An area where development would not be permitted to leave the natural habitat untouched.

Holding Zones

- To restrict development in certain areas before there has been an opportunity to zone or plan it, the planning department within a municipality may temporarily zone the land for low intensity uses.

Inclusionary Zoning

- Specifies inclusions within a development, including a playground, or that a percentage of homes must be affordable for low-income families.

Exclusionary Zoning

- Exclusionary zoning is any zoning ordinance which has a purpose, effect or result of achieving a form of economic or racial segregation.
- An exclusionary zoning ordinance can cause economic segregation by restricting land usage to high-cost, low population density residential development.
- These restrictions can effectively prevent low to moderate-income families and individuals from moving into an area. In turn, minority groups with low-income levels may also be excluded from living in certain areas.

Setback

- The distance which a building or other structure is set back from a street or road, a river or other stream, a shore or flood plain, or any other place which is deemed to need protection.
- Setbacks are generally set in municipal ordinances or zoning.

Building Codes

- Standard established by local or state government to protect the public by regulating building and construction methods including plumbing, electrical and fire.
- The main purpose of building codes is to protect public health, safety, and general welfare as they relate to the construction and occupancy of buildings and structures.

Certificate of Occupancy

- Proof by the county that a structure has met building code requirement and may be occupied. Issued either when a building is new or when remodeling required a building permit.

Eminent Domain

- The government can take privately owned property for the good of the public. Acquire personally owned real estate for the benefit of the public.
- The owner is paid Just Compensation
- Compensation usually follows the court action of condemnation. (Eminent domain)
- The judicial or administrative action of eminent domain.
- Condemnation is compensation to the property owner. Known as "Just Compensation".

Reverse Condemnation

- The property owner is forcing the government to use Eminent Domain to take his/her property.
- The only person who can do Reverse Condemnation is the property owner.

☐ A county airport took several homes to expand its runway through the government power of an eminent domain.
☐ When the county took several streets through eminent domain to extend an airport runway, they left one house. The owner is experiencing extreme noise and shaking due to the expansion. The homeowner may be able to get the county to take the property through reverse condemnation.

- Under eminent domain, the government can appropriate property if they feel it is for the community's greater good. But the owner of any lands claimed under eminent domain is entitled to reasonable compensation, usually defined as the fair market value of the property. Compensation for the property is paid through the process of *condemnation*.

Inverse Condemnation

- A situation in which the government takes private property but fails to pay the compensation required by the 5th Amendment of the Constitution, so the property's owner must sue to obtain the required just compensation.

☐ Can a condo complex eminent domain three houses adjacent to its parking lot to expand their parking? NO
Only the government can eminent domain.

- **Dedication** is the voluntary transfer of ownership of land from a private party to a government.

Taxation

Property taxes can be defined as a charge on real estate which is used to pay for services provided by the government. Unpaid property taxes result in a specific lien. This means you can lose your property if you don't pay your property taxes.

Property Taxes and Special Assessments

Ad Valorem	Special Assessments
The Latin phrase ad valorem means "according to value." So, all ad valorem taxes are based on the assessed value of the item being taxed. **Assessed Value/Assessment** Assessed Value is a percentage of true value. **Assessor** An official (or sometimes the treasurer) who determines the assessed valuation of real property.	The tax is charged only to the owners of property in the neighborhood that will benefit from the project. A special assessment is a term used to designate a unique charge that government units can assess against real estate parcels for certain public projects. This charge is levied in a specific geographic area known as a special assessment district (SAD).

☐ Water and Sewer Departments are nonprofits.

Escheat

The government takes your property if you die without a will and no heirs can be found. (Or a property is abandoned.)
Land cannot be ownerless.

Controls and Rights in Land QUIZ

1. A city had the community gather to develop and give suggestions or a revised public land use control map. Public land use controls include all the following except? a. city master plan. b. environmental protection laws. c. deed restrictions. d. building regulations.	c. deed restrictions. Deed restrictions are private use restrictions.
2. A home in a residential zone is converted to an antique store. This would be an example of a. a legal variance. b. an illegal use. c. a legal nonconforming use. d. a legal conforming use.	b. an illegal use. This property would be illegal non-conforming use. The property owner may have to shut down until a variance is granted.
3. A shop was originally built in a commercial zone. The zone has since been changed to a residential zone. The Zoning authorities will permit the continued use of the shop. The shop will be zoned? a. a legal nonconforming use. b. a variance. c. a special exception. d. an illegal nonconforming use.	a. a legal nonconforming use. The property will be "grandfathered" and allowed to continue the use of the property as a shop. If the property falls, burns down or otherwise gets destroyed, the new zoning will become effective.
4. The best example of a buffer zone is? an office building between a commercial strip mall and a. a school. b. a warehouse between a neighborhood and strip mall. c. All of these. d. garden homes between a single-family residential neighborhood and a shopping center.	d. garden homes between a single-family residential neighborhood and a shopping center. The Garden home between the mall and the Single-family Residences. SFRs may have more children than a garden home complex.
5. The purpose of a building permit is a. to establish an enabling act. b. to regulate minimum construction standards. c. to regulate the volume of a market's building activity. d. to override a deed restriction.	b. to regulate minimum construction standards. Building codes are police power. They are to protect the public.

6. A property on Main Street that was formerly a retail store will become the site of a new city hall, made possible by the government's power of
a. Eminent domain
b. Taxation
c. Possibility of reverted
d. Escheat
	a. Eminent domain
	
	The four governmental powers that limit private rights on land are:
	
	PETE
	   police power
	   eminent domain
	   taxation
	   escheat

7. Inverse (Reverse) Condemnation may be brought by a. the property owner. b. the city government c. the federal government. d. the state government.	a. the property owner. Only the property can inverse or reverse condemnation
8. Escheat happens? a. when the heirs reject the property. b. because property – land cannot be ownerless. c. land reverts to the original grantor. d. land reverts to the original grantee.	b. because property – land cannot be ownerless. When a person dies intestate (without a will) and no heirs can be found, the property escheats to the state because land cannot be ownerless.
9. An escheat occurs when? a. a property owner dies. b. a property owner dies with a valid will. c. a property owner dies without a valid will. d. a property owner dies without heirs or a valid will.	d. a property owner dies without heirs or a valid will. When a person dies intestate (without a will) and no heirs can be found, the property escheats to the state because land cannot be ownerless.
10. A city will issue a building permit to? a. to establish an enabling act. b. to regulate minimum construction standards. c. to regulate the volume of a market's building activity. d. to override a deed restriction.	b. to regulate minimum construction standards. Building codes are police power. They are to protect the public.
11. A home in a residential zone is converted to an antique store. This would be an example of a. a legal variance. b. an illegal use. c. a legal nonconforming use. d. a legal conforming use.	b. an illegal use. This property would be illegal non-conforming use. The property owner may have to shut down until a variance is granted.

Regulations of Certain Land Types

Flood Zones

- FEMA has created their Flood Insurance Rate Maps (FIRMs) to show the areas of high-risk, moderate-to-low risk, and areas where the risk is undetermined.
- These high-risk areas are SPECIAL FLOOD HAZARD AREAS
- High-risk areas have at least a ☐ 1% annual chance of flooding.
- The 1% flood is also referred to as the **Base Flood**.

☐ Flood insurance is required for structures in these high-risk areas if they have a federally backed mortgage.

- FEMA's flood mapping program is called Risk Mapping, Assessment, and Planning, or Risk MAP.

Wetlands

☐ Wetlands are set aside for conservation.
Mostly always wet.
- Wetlands are the link between the land and the water.
- They are transition zones where the flow of water, the cycling of nutrients, and the energy of the sun meet to produce a unique ecosystem characterized by hydrology, soils, and vegetation—making these areas very important features of a watershed.
- Marshes are wetlands dominated by soft-stemmed vegetation, while swamps have mostly woody plants.
- Bogs are freshwater wetlands, often formed in old glacial lakes, characterized by spongy peat deposits, evergreen trees and shrubs, and a floor covered by a thick carpet of sphagnum moss.
- Fens are freshwater peat-forming wetlands covered mostly by grasses, sedges, reeds, and wildflowers.

Floodplain

- A floodplain is defined as a low-lying area near water, which floods during periods of high rain.
- It floods.
- Floodplains are the low-lying areas adjacent to rivers. Wetlands are land areas covered with water, either permanently or seasonally, and are frequently found on floodplains.

Types of Hazards

Sources for Hazards: EPA

Formaldehyde

- Formaldehyde is a colorless, pungent gas that is soluble in water and most organic solvents. It is used as a raw material in the manufacture of paints, plastics, resins, photographic materials, and in building materials such as fiberboard and some foam insulation.

Sources of Formaldehyde in the Home

- Formaldehyde is emitted from products in which formaldehyde has been used in their manufacture.
- These include composite wood products, urea-formaldehyde foam used in insulation, and curtain and upholstery textiles treated with formaldehyde resins for wrinkle resistance.
- The two most used resins are urea- formaldehyde and phenol-formaldehyde. Composite wood products used within the home include:
- particleboard, used for subflooring, shelving, and in furniture.
- hardwood and plywood paneling, used in furniture and as a wall covering.
- medium density fiberboard, used as cabinet doors, tabletops, furniture, and shelving; and, softwood plywood, for exterior use and subflooring; both are manufactured using phenol-formaldehyde resins.

How is formaldehyde harmful?

- The Office of Environmental Health Hazard Assessment has concluded that exposures to formaldehyde can cause cancer in humans.
- Exposure to airborne formaldehyde may also cause non-cancer symptoms, such as irritation to the eyes, skin and respiratory tract, coughing, sore or burning throat, nausea, and headaches.
- Reducing Indoor Formaldehyde Levels
- Immediate measures include opening windows to increase ventilation and reducing the number of new composite wood products in a home. Formaldehyde emissions increase with increasing humidity and temperature.

Lead

- Many homes and condominiums built before 1978 have lead-based paint.

Lead Found in the Home

- Many houses and apartments built before 1978 have paint that contains lead.
- In 1978, the Consumer Product Safety Commission banned paint containing high levels of lead for residential use.
- Lead-based paint that is peeling, chipping, chalking, or cracking is a hazard and needs immediate attention.
- Lead-based paint may also pose a hazard on surfaces children can chew, or in areas with heavy wear.
- These areas include windows, windowsills, doors and door frames, stairs, railings, banisters, porches, and fences.
- When painted surfaces bump or rub together they generate lead dust.
- Likewise, dry-scraping, sanding, or heating lead paint during repainting or remodeling also creates

---

huge amounts of poisonous lead dust. This lead dust can poison your family.

Soil

- ☐ can become contaminated with lead from deteriorating exterior paint, and from leaded gasoline emissions. Lead in soil can be a hazard to children who play in bare soil. It can also contaminate the home when people bring soil into the house on their shoes.
- Lead can leech into food cooked, stored, or served in certain imported dishes or handmade pottery.
- Lead can be present in drinking water of older homes that have plumbing with lead or lead solder.
- Homebuyers and renters have important rights to know about whether lead is present — before signing contracts or leases.

Homebuyers

- Federal law requires that before being obligated under a contract to buy target housing, including most buildings built before 1978, buyers must receive the following from the home seller:
- An EPA-approved information pamphlet on identifying and controlling lead-based paint hazards Protect Your Family from Lead in Your Home.
- Any known information concerning the presence of lead-based paint or lead-based paint hazards in the home or building.
- For multi-unit buildings, this requirement includes records and reports concerning common areas and other units when such information was obtained because of a building-wide evaluation.
- An attachment to the contract, or language inserted in the contract, that includes a "Lead Warning Statement" and confirms that the seller has complied with all notification requirements.

Ten Day Inspection Period

- A 10-day period to conduct a paint inspection or risk assessment for lead-based paint or lead-based paint hazards.
- Parties may mutually agree, in writing, to lengthen or shorten the time for inspection.
- Homebuyers may waive this inspection opportunity. If you have a concern about possible lead-based paint, then get a lead inspection from a certified inspector before buying.

Asbestos

- These minerals occur as bundles of strong, flexible fibers that are chemically inert, do not burn, and have good insulating properties.
- Asbestos is a good fire retardant.
- A mineral fiber that occurs in rock and soil.
- Where is asbestos found in the home?
- Asbestos has been used in many products found in the home to provide insulation, strength, and fire protection. In 1989, the U.S. Environmental Protection Agency (U.S. EPA) announced a phased ban of asbestos products to be completed by 1996. The most common items in the home that may contain asbestos are:
  1. vinyl flooring.
  2. duct wrapping on heating and air conditioning systems.
  3. insulation on hot water pipes and boilers, especially in

4. homes built from 1920 to 1972.
5. some roofing, shingles, and siding.
6. ceiling and wall insulation in some homes built or remodeled between 1945 and 1978, and in sheetrock taping compounds and some ceiling materials.

Friable

- Friable is the material that can be easily crushed or pulverized to a powder by hand pressure. Friable materials have a higher potential to release fibers.
- Asbestos fibers that are released into the air and inhaled can accumulate in the lungs and pose a health risk.
- This risk can be divided into two general categories:
  1) risk of asbestosis; and
  2) increased risk of cancer.

The U.S. EPA classifies asbestos as a known human carcinogen.

- If asbestos fibers are inhaled, the likelihood of contracting lung cancer or mesothelioma (cancer of the lining of the chest or abdomen) increases. As more asbestos is inhaled, the risk of developing cancer further increases.
- Symptoms of cancer may not develop until 10-40 years after the first exposure.

Does the law require mitigation?
- Asbestos mitigation is at the discretion of the homeowner.
- ☐ the best way to handle asbestos is to encapsulate it.

Urea-formaldehyde foam insulation (UFFI)

- Pumped Between the Walls
- Urea-formaldehyde foam insulation (UFFI) was installed in the wall cavities of some homes during the 1970's and has been used in the manufacture of mobile homes.
- Banned
- The Consumer Product Safety Commission banned the use of UFFI in homes and schools in 1982.
- Formaldehyde emissions from UFFI decline with time. Thus, in homes where UFFI was installed prior to 1982, formaldehyde concentrations are generally comparable to those in homes without UFFI.

Polychlorinated Biphenyls (PCBs)

- PCBs are a group of man-made organic chemicals consisting of carbon, hydrogen, and chlorine atoms.
- PCBs have no known taste or smell, and range in consistency from an oil to a waxy solid.
- PCBs belong to a broad family of man-made organic chemicals known as chlorinated hydrocarbons.
- PCBs were domestically manufactured from 1929 until manufacturing was banned in 1979.
- They have a range of toxicity and vary in consistency from thin, light-colored liquids to yellow or black waxy solids.

- Due to their non-flammability, chemical stability, high boiling point and electrical insulating properties, PCBs were used in hundreds of industrial and commercial applications including:
  - Electrical, heat transfer and hydraulic equipment
  - Plasticizers in paints, plastics, and rubber products
  - Pigments, dyes, and carbonless copy paper
  - Other industrial applications
  - Transformers and capacitors
  - Electrical equipment including voltage regulators, switches, re-closers, bushings, and electromagnets
  - Oil used in motors and hydraulic systems
  - Old electrical devices or appliances containing PCB capacitors
  - Fluorescent light ballasts
  - Cable insulation
  - Adhesives and tapes
  - Oil-based paint
  - Caulking
  - Plastics
  - Carbonless copy paper
  - Floor finish

1979 PCBs were banned.

Landfills

- Modern landfills are well-engineered facilities designed to receive specific kinds of waste, including municipal solid waste (MSW), construction and demolition debris (C&D) and hazardous waste.
- Landfill facilities must be designed to protect the environment from contaminants, which may be present in the solid waste disposed in the unit.

Groundwater

☐ Landfills built on the wrong type of soil can pollute groundwater,

Underground Storage Tanks (USTs)

- EPA: Approximately 544,000 underground storage tanks (USTs) nationwide store petroleum or hazardous substances.
- The greatest potential threat from a leaking UST is contamination of groundwater, the source of drinking water for nearly half of all Americans. EPA, states, territories, and tribes work in partnership with industry to protect the environment and human health from potential releases.

Leaking Underground Storage Tanks (LUST)

☐ Can pollute groundwater.

Electromagnetic Fields (EMFs)

- EMFs are caused by circulating electrical currents.
- EMFs are suspected of causing cancer.

Mold

- Molds are simple, microscopic organisms, present virtually everywhere, indoors, and outdoors.
- For molds to grow and reproduce, they need only a food source – any organic material, such as leaves wood, paper, or dirt— and moisture.
- Mold growth on surfaces can often be seen in the form of discoloration, frequently green, gray, brown, or black but also white and other colors.
- Molds release countless tiny, lightweight spores, which travel through the air.

Exposure to indoor molds

- Everyone is exposed to some mold daily without evident harm. It is common to find mold spores in the air inside homes, and most of the airborne spores found indoors come from outdoor sources.
- Mold spores primarily cause health problems when they are present in large numbers and people inhale many of them. This occurs primarily when there is active mold growth within home, office, or school where people live or work.
- People can also be exposed to mold by touching contaminated materials and by eating contaminated foods.
- Molds will grow and multiply whenever conditions are right—sufficient moisture is available and organic material is present.

The following are common sources of indoor moisture that may lead to mold problems:

  o   Flooding
  o   Leaky roofs
  o   Sprinkler spray hitting the house
  o   Plumbing leaks
  o   Overflow from sinks or sewers
  o   Damp basement or crawl space
  o   Steam from shower or cooking
  o   Humidifiers
  o   Wet clothes drying indoors or clothes dryers exhausting indoors

Indications of moisture problems

- Warping floors and discoloration of walls and ceilings can be indications of moisture problems.
- Condensation on windows or walls is also an important indication.

Mold in the home
- Mold contamination is extensive, it can cause very high and persistent airborne spore exposures.
- Persons exposed to high spore levels can become sensitized and develop allergies to the mold or other health problems.
- Mold growth can damage your furnishings, such as carpets, sofas, and cabinets.
- Clothes and shoes in damp closets can become soiled. In time, unchecked mold growth can cause serious damage to the structural elements in your home.

Symptoms Commonly Seen with Mold Exposure

- Molds produce health effects through inflammation, allergy, or infection.
- Allergic reactions (often referred to as hay fever) are most common following mold exposure.
- **Typical symptoms that mold-exposed persons report (alone or in combination) include:**
- Respiratory problems, such as wheezing, difficulty breathing, and shortness of breath
- Nasal and sinus congestion
- Eye irritation (burning, watery, or reddened eyes)
- Dry, hacking cough
- Nose or throat irritation
- Skin rashes or irritation
- Headaches, memory problems, mood swings, nosebleeds, body aches and pains, and fevers are occasionally reported in mold cases, but their cause is not understood.

Stachybotrys chartarum

- May produce compounds that have toxic properties, which are called mycotoxins.
- Mycotoxins are not always produced, and whether a mold produces mycotoxins while growing in a building depends on what the mold is growing on, conditions such as temperature, pH, humidity, or other unknown factors.
- It can grow on material with a high cellulose content, such as fiberboard, gypsum board, and paper. Growth occurs when there is moisture from water damage, water leaks, condensation, water infiltration, or flooding.
- Constant moisture is required for its growth.

Radon

Radon is a gas that has no color, odor, or taste and comes from the natural radioactive breakdown of uranium in the ground. **You can be exposed to radon by two main sources:**
1. radon in the air in your home (frequently called "radon in indoor air") and
2. radon in drinking water.

Exposure to Radon Causes Lung Cancer in Non-smokers and Smokers Alike
- Radon is the number one cause of lung cancer among non-smokers
- An inspector will measure for radon up to the third floor.

Radon in Drinking Water
- Radon is a naturally occurring radioactive gas that may cause cancer and may be found in drinking water and indoor air. Some people who are exposed to radon in drinking water may have increased risk of getting cancer over the course of their lifetime, especially lung cancer.

Radon Mitigation
- Radon is easily mitigated.

Radon and New Construction
- By building radon-resistant new homes, builders and contractors provide a public health service — helping to reduce buyers' risk of lung cancer from exposure to radon in indoor air.

- Using common materials and straightforward techniques, builders can construct new homes that are resistant to radon entry.

Environmental Hazards QUIZ

1.Radon has been found in every state a. True b. False	a. True Radon is part of building codes in 27 states. radon is found everywhere, so most states regulate it.
2. Radon a. enters the house through the basement. b. is caused by friable asbestos. c. enters the house through the roof vents. d. is nothing to be concerned about?	a. enters the house through the basement. Radon is produced when uranium, thorium, and radium, which are radioactive metals, decay in rocks, soils, and groundwater.
3.The presence of radon is suspected when a house is inspected. What action should be taken by the prospective purchaser? a. There is no need to inspect if you can't smell it. b. Hire a general contractor to remove it. c. Hire a radon inspector d. There is no need to inspect if you can't see it.	c. Hire a radon inspector The EPA recommends that all houses, regardless of what radon zone the house is located in, be tested for radon during point of sale. The most common procedure for radon testing during real estate transactions is for the potential buyer to request the radon test as part of the overall home inspection.
4.The seller's property disclosure indicates the condition of all but which of the following? a. The electrical system b. The appliances if included in the sale c. The title d. The heating and cooling system	c. The title The PCD is filled out by the sellers on any fixed property attached to the home as well as permits and naturally disaster inquiries.
5.Which of the following was once pumped as insulation and is now banned a. Radon b. Carbon Monoxide (CO) c. Lead paint d. Urea-Formaldehyde Foam	d. Urea-Formaldehyde Foam The 1982 ban on UFFI is one factor contributing to decreased levels of formaldehyde that are found.
6. Broker Green obtained a listing from Brown to sell his home. Brown told Green the electricity wiring was in and connected and signed a listing to that effect. Green believed there were no electrical installed on that street or neighborhood, so he checked with the city and found he was correct. Green showed the house to Jones, who did not ask about electrical connections, and Green made the sale without any comment. Later, Jones found that the electrical was not ran on his street. Which of the following is true? a. Jones was to blame because he could have checked with the city, "caveat emptor". b. There is no provision in the law to cover the situation c. Green may rely on the listing, even though he knew it to be incorrect.	4.Green had a duty to tell Jones, even though he did not ask. This would be a material fact which must be disclosed by the broker because the broker must treat all customer/prospects fairly and honestly.

d. Green had a duty of care to tell Jones, even though he did not ask.	
7. If a Lead-Based Paint Disclosure form is not executed at the time of the sale of a dwelling built prior to 1978, the purchaser? a. is not obligated to purchase the property under the terms of the contract. b. is entitled to an inspection paid for by the seller. c. may suffer damages as a result of caveat emptor. d. may sue the seller for damages.	a. is not obligated to purchase the property under the terms of the contract. Congress passed the Residential Lead-Based Paint Hazard Reduction Act of 1992, also known as Title X, to protect families from exposure to lead from paint, dust, and soil. Section 1018 of this law directed HUD and EPA to require the disclosure of known information on lead-based paint and lead-based paint hazards before the sale or lease of most housing built before 1978.
8. All the following characteristics can add to value in a property except? a. Radon b. Location c. Situs d. Disposition	a. Radon Radon is a hazard for real estate. Radon is easily mitigated
9. A client would like to sell his house after owning it for one year. The client let the agent know that the property was treated for termites 14 months ago. What should the agent do? a. Tell the client not to disclose the information so the agent's husband can retreat the property and make money. b. Tell the client to disclose that information. c. Tell the client that radon is nothing to be afraid of. d. Tell the client to keep his car out of the garage so as not to attract any new termites.	b. Tell the client to disclose that information. Disclose, Disclose, Disclose
10. A seller was cooking for her family when a fire broke out in the kitchen. The burned ceiling joists were treated and sealed. Will the seller have to disclose these repairs? a. Yes, known latent defects still must be disclosed. b. Only if the home inspector discovers them and lists it as a defect in the home inspection c. No since they were repaired. d. No. It doesn't affect the value.	a. Yes, known latent defects still must be disclosed. Disclose everything.
11. Private homes built before 1978 may contain potentially dangerous levels of lead. The FHA a. will not lend money on these properties. b. require the seller to remove the lead before selling. c. require testing before the property can be sold. d. require the buyer to acknowledge a disclosure of the presence of any known lead paint.	d. requires the buyer to acknowledge a disclosure of the presence of any known lead paint Homes built before 1978 require the buyer to acknowledge a disclosure of the presence of any known lead paint.
12. Which of the following is a naturally occurring radioactive gas located in soils with a concentration of	a. radon

uranium in the rock a. radon b. mold c. asbestos d. CO_2	Radon is a naturally occurring radioactive gas that can cause lung cancer. Radon gas is inert, colorless, and odorless. Radon is naturally in the atmosphere in trace amounts. Outdoors, radon disperses rapidly and, generally, is not a health issue. Most radon exposure occurs inside homes, schools, and workplaces. Radon gas becomes trapped indoors after it enters buildings through cracks and other holes in the foundation. Indoor radon can be controlled and managed with proven, cost-effective techniques.
13. The Department of Housing and Urban Development estimates that most private homes built before 1978 contain potentially dangerous levels of lead. FHA? a. requires the buyer to acknowledge disclosure of the presence of any known lead paint. b. Requires the buyer the opportunity to have the requires the paint be removed before closing. c. Nothing is required	a. requires the buyer to acknowledge disclosure of the presence of any known lead paint. most buildings built before 1978, require buyers to receive the following from the home seller: An EPA-approved information pamphlet on identifying and controlling lead-based paint hazards Protect Your Family from Lead in Your Home (PDF). Any known information concerning the presence of lead-based paint or lead-based paint hazards in the home or building.
14. What term refers to what happens to asbestos when it ages, disintegrates, and becomes airborne? a. Friable b. Sodium hydrogen carbonate c. Encapsulation d. Oxidation	a. Friable Asbestos can easily be broken. It can release inhalable asbestos fibers into the air as a result.
15. Which of the following limitations is not a basic right of the government in privately owned real estate? a. Police Power b. Escheat c. Deed Restrictions d. Ad valorem Property Taxation	c. Deed Restrictions Deed restrictions that restrict the use of a property are not the same thing as governmentally imposed restrictions discussed above. Deed restrictions are rights reserved by private persons as opposed to limitations imposed by government. In most cases, the property tax appraiser should not recognize deed restrictions when analyzing highest and best use. The rights to be assessed are the fee simple rights without encumbrances, subject only to the limitations imposed by government.
16. Private restrictions on real property can be written either as a condition or as a covenant. Which of the	b. Violation of a condition can result in penalties which are more severe, and can

following is most correct concerning such restrictions? a. All are true. b. Violation of a condition can result in penalties which are more severe and can result in loss of title. c. Violations of such restrictions are subject to criminal prosecution. d. When recorded, they become public restrictions.	result in loss of title Violation of a condition can result in loss of title, which is more severe than damages or an injunction, which result from violations of a covenant.
17. Airborne asbestos fibers are known as? a. Sodium hydrogen carbonate b. Friable c. Encapsulation d. Radon	b. Friable Asbestos is most hazardous when it is friable. The Friable asbestos can cause cancer.

Comprehensive Environmental Response, Compensation, and Liability Act

CERCLA
- A Nine Billion Dollar Fund
- Also known as Superfund
- The Comprehensive Environmental Response, Compensation, and Liability Act — otherwise known as CERCLA or Superfund — provides a Federal "Superfund" to clean up uncontrolled or abandoned hazardous-waste sites as well as accidents, spills, and other emergency releases of pollutants and contaminants into the environment.

- ☐ Liability can be several and individual.
- ☐ It can be retroactive.
- ☐ the guilty party is held responsible for the cleanup without excuse.
- This law created a ☐ tax on the chemical and petroleum industries and provided broad Federal authority to respond directly to releases or threatened releases of hazardous substances that may endanger public health or the environment.

Cleanup

- EPA's Superfund program is responsible for cleaning up some of the nation's most contaminated land and responding to environmental emergencies, oil spills and natural disasters.
- In the late 1970s, toxic waste dumps such as Love Canal and Valley of the Drums received national attention when the public learned about the risks to human health and the environment posed by contaminated sites.

Superfund's Goals

- Protect human health and the environment by cleaning up contaminated sites.
- Make responsible parties pay for cleanup work;
- Involve communities in the Superfund process; and
- Return Superfund sites to productive use.

The Love Canal environmental disaster marked what would be the genesis of the EPA's Superfund program. As a direct regulatory response to this disaster, as well as to other hazardous waste sites across the country, Congress enacted the Comprehensive Environmental Response, Compensation, and Liability Act (CERCLA) on December 11, 1980.

Superfund Cleanup Process

1. Preliminary Assessment/Site Inspection (Site Assessment)
This stage includes a review of historical information and includes visiting a site to evaluate the potential for a release of hazardous substances. EPA determines if the site poses a threat to people and the environment and whether hazards need to be addressed immediately or additional site information will be collected.

2. National Priorities List (NPL) Site Listing Process

The NPL is primarily an information resource that identifies sites that warrant cleanup. It is a list of the worst hazardous waste sites identified by Superfund. The list is largely based on the score a site receives from the Hazard Ranking System.

3. Remedial Investigation/Feasibility Study (Site Characterization)

This stage involves an evaluation of the nature and extent of contamination at a site and assessing potential threats to human health and the environment. This stage of the process also includes evaluation of the potential performance and cost of the treatment options identified for a site.

4. Records of Decision (Remedy Decisions)

The ROD explains which cleanup alternatives will be used at NPL sites. Leading up to the issuance of the ROD, the EPA recommends a preferred remedy and presents the cleanup plan in a document called a Proposed Plan for public comment. Following the public comment period, the EPA issues a final Record of Decision.

5. Remedial Design/Remedial Action

Detailed cleanup plans are developed and implemented during the remedial design/remedial action (RD/RA) stage. Remedial design includes development of engineering drawings and specifications for a site cleanup. Remedial action follows design and involves the actual construction or implementation phase of site cleanup.

6. Construction Completion

This milestone indicates all physical construction required for the cleanup of the entire site has been completed (even though final cleanup levels may not have been achieved). For example, a groundwater treatment system has been constructed though it may need to operate for several years for all contaminants to be removed from the groundwater.

7. Post Construction Completion

Activities undertaken during this phase help ensure that cleanup work at a site continues to protect human health and the environment. Work can include routine monitoring of a site; routine reviews of the site to ensure cleanup continues to be effective; and enforcing any long-term site restrictions (e.g., institutional controls)

8. National Priorities List Deletion

Once cleanup goals have been achieved and sites are fully protective of human health and the environment, EPA deletes them from the NPL.

9. Site Reuse/Redevelopment

EPA's goal is to make sure site cleanup is consistent with the likely future use of a site.

Superfund Amendments and Reauthorization Act (SARA)

The Superfund Amendments and Reauthorization Act of 1986 (SARA) reflected EPA's experience in administering the complex Superfund program during its first six years and made several important changes and additions to the program. SARA:

- stressed the importance of permanent remedies and innovative treatment technologies in cleaning up hazardous waste sites.
- required Superfund actions to consider the standards and requirements found in other State and Federal environmental laws and regulations.
- provided new enforcement authorities and settlement tools.
- increased State involvement in every phase of the Superfund program.
- increased the focus on human health problems posed by hazardous waste sites.
- encouraged greater citizen participation in making decisions on how sites should be cleaned up; and
- increased the size of the trust fund to $8.5 billion.

SARA also required EPA to revise the Hazard Ranking System to ensure that it accurately assessed the relative degree of risk to human health and the environment posed by uncontrolled hazardous waste sites that may be placed on the National Priorities List (NPL).

☐ SARA = Innocent Landowner Immunity
☐ Increased the size of Superfund fund to $8.5 billion

Brownfield Legislation

- ☐ Helps rejuvenate and resurrect derelict, toxic industrial waste sites.

Mothballed Brownfields

Mothballed brownfields are properties that owners are not willing to transfer or put to productive reuse.

Private Controls

Homeowners Association

- An organizational framework set up for self-governance by owners through adoption and enforcement of bylaws.
- Homeowner's Dues are associated with ownership for the upkeep of the buildings and common areas.
- Maintenance of common elements is funded by fees charged to each unit owner.
- Homeowner's Association are to protect property value.
- The primary purpose of land-use controls is to limit population density, noise, pollution and maintain its aesthetics.

Bylaws

- Rules and structure for administering the homeowners' association.

Deed Restriction

- A limitation on use.
- Provisions are placed in a deed to control the future use of the property.
- Violation of a deed restriction could be jail, a fine, or both.

Covenants, Conditions & Restrictions (CC&R's)

- CC&Rs is the paperwork package of disclosure that the seller must provide to the buyer.
- CC&Rs are private, voluntary rules (intended to be beneficial) used in homeowner associations and PUD's.

☐ The homeowners enforce the CC and Rs in a Neighborhood Association. (People who live in the community)
☐ Deed restrictions may not be discriminatory. Discriminatory deed restrictions are not enforced.
☐ The purpose of restrictions is to preserve the value and quality of the neighborhood.

Common Elements

- Areas in a condominium project or PUD where all owners share an undivided interest and full ownership, such as hallways, swimming pools and clubhouses.

Limited Common Elements

- These areas in a community of common interests are reserved for the exclusive use of a particular owner, including decks, storage areas or parking spaces.

Amenities

- They enhance value by a home's proximity to the amenities of the property. Examples are a bike trail, a community pool, or a beautifully shaded park.
- Amenities are community assets that increases the value of the neighborhood's property value.
- Not on the individual homeowners' land.

Features

- On the property. Enhances an individual's property owners' real estate.

Homogeneity

- Similarity: Neighborhoods with homogeneity of houses are generally stable in value.

Conformity

- A property that conforms to its surrounding properties in style, age, size, appearance tends to maximize value.

Master Deed

- Describes the physical location of the common and individual elements (units) of a condominium.

Subdivider

- One who partitions a large parcel of land for resale as individual lots.

Attractive Nuisance

- An item or property which might attract the curious (children) to their detriment, e.g., a swimming pool, construction site, abandoned appliances, etc. Owners generally have direct liability for attractive nuisances that are not secured.

QUIZ Sort: Private Controls

MODULE TWO QUIZ: Controls and Rights in Land

1. A candy store in a residential neighborhood is most like? a. a zoning variance. b. A special use property. c. a special commercial permit. d. nonconforming use.	d. nonconforming use. Nonconforming uses are more likely to create commercial uses in residential areas. When the store was built, it was following the zoning, but when the zoning was amended, it no longer was.
2. The city acquires a tract of land for a highway. What power will they exercise? a. Zoning b. Bulk Zoning c. Eminent Domain d. Restricted Covenant	c. Eminent Domain Taking private property for public use is known as eminent domain. Government may only exercise this power if it provides just compensation to property owners, as stipulated by the Fifth Amendment.
3. CERCLA authorizes two kinds of response actions a. True b. False	a. TRUE The Comprehensive Environmental Response, Compensation, and Liability Act (CERCLA or Superfund) divides response actions to hazardous substance releases into two categories: removal actions and remedial actions.
4. When a property owner dies without a will or heirs, the property? a. become at sufferance. b. is executory c. becomes the property of the closest neighbor. d. escheats to the state.	d. escheats to the state. Land cannot be ownerless.
5. Covenants, conditions and deed restrictions are examples of? a. private restrictions b. public encumbrances c. public restrictions d. deed transferable liabilities	a. private restrictions CC and Rs are private restrictions.
6. Escheat happens a. because property – land cannot be ownerless. b. when the heirs reject the property. c. land reverts to the original grantor. d. land reverts to the original grantee.	a. because property – land cannot be ownerless. Land must be always owned.
7. Carol wants to open an ice cream store on a lot that is zoned for residential. Jim, a. will need to obtain a variance or a conditional use permit. b. will need to petition the local courts to change the	b. will need to obtain a variance or a conditional use permit. Permits with special uses and variances are used along with many other methods to

zoning.	preserve the community and neighboring
c. will be able to open if the people in the neighborhood write letters to the mayor.	properties. Municipalities as well as property owners have the flexibility to allow
d. All the above can happen.	reasonable uses of the property while minimizing adverse impacts on neighbors.
8. The PRIMARY purpose of zoning ordinances is to	b. implements the city's master plan.
a. control the quality of building materials.	
b. implement the city's master plan.	Zoning implements a city/county master plan.
c. establish appropriate boards for appeal.	
d. regulate business districts.	
9. Superfund program focuses on	d. All of these are correct.
a. ensuring that people can live and work in healthy, vibrant places	Cleanup of some of the nation's most contaminated areas and response to accidents
b. making a visible and lasting difference in communities	and natural disasters are EPA's responsibilities under its Superfund program.
c. making communities healthy again	Superfund aims to make a visible and lasting difference in communities, so that people can
d. All of these are correct.	live and work in healthy places.
10. Zoning laws such as setbacks and property use are determined at a	d. local level.
a. federal level.	Zoning laws are set at the local, city, or
b. county level.	county level.
c. federal, state, and local level.	
d. local level.	
11. The purpose of laws that provide for property to escheat to the state or county when a landowner dies with no will and no heirs is to	c. prevent property from being ownerless.
a. save the cost of a judicial claims process.	Land cannot be ownerless.
b. provide an additional source of revenues to the state or county.	
c. prevent property from being ownerless.	
d. increase the amount of land available for public use.	
12. Public land use controls include all the following except	b. deed restrictions.
a. building regulations.	A deed restriction restricts only the property
b. deed restrictions.	owner.
c. environmental protection laws.	
d. city master plan.	
13. If a condition is violated in a deed what is the most severe punishment?	d. the violator can be fined and/or must go to jail.
a. the property lease will be voided.	
b. the property will revert to the original grantor.	The penalty for a violation of a deed
c. the violator will go to jail.	restriction can be a fine and / or jail.
d. the violator can be fined and/or must go to jail.	
14. MATCH: Friable asbestos	c. airborne asbestos
a. is addictive and must be avoided.	
b. is healthy air.	Asbestos is most hazardous when it is friable.
c. airborne asbestos	The term "friable" means that the asbestos is

d. airborne asbestos coupled with lead.	easily crumbled by hand, releasing fibers into the air.
15. What mineral was used for insulation on heating ducts? a. Sodium hydrogen carbonate b. Friable c. Asbestos d. Radon	c. Asbestos Until the 1980s, heating ducts contained asbestos insulation that is now known to cause cancer called mesothelioma.
16. When does a lender require flood insurance? a. When the property was flooded by a busted water line. b. When the property is in a Flood Hazard Zone. c. When the seller puts down more than 20%. d. When the buyer is using an out of state lender	b. When the property is in a Flood Hazard Zone. When purchasing in a flood zone, the lender will require flood insurance to protect their investment.
17. Banned from use in the 1970s, this material was pumped between the walls for insulation: a. Lead b. Urea-formaldehyde foam c. Encapsulation	b. Urea-formaldehyde foam UFFI was pumped between the walls as insulation. UFFI was most used in the 1970s
18. Which hazard enters the house through the basement? a. Sodium hydrogen carbonate b. Radon c. Asbestos d. Down zoning	b. Radon Radon is a naturally occurring radioactive gas that can cause lung cancer.
19. A landowner wishes to build a neighborhood grocery store on a busy street in an area zoned for residential use. Which of the following would MOST likely be used to obtain permission for this store? a. Conditional use permit. b. Conditional use permit or zoning variance. c. zoning variance. d. spot zoning.	a. Conditional use permit. A conditional use permit is a zoning exception that allows property owners to use land in such a way that is not typically permitted within the zoning district.
20. An Environmental Impact Statement is considered police power because it deals with which of the following? a. Fish b. Boats c. Health and Safety d. Pets	c. Health and Safety Environmental Impact Statement explores the safety and the environmental effects of a proposed project.
21. An Environmental Impact Statement a. projects the dollar amount of an entire project. b. summarizes the neighborhood in general terms. c. projects the impact on the environment of a proposed project. d. is used only for state projects.	c. projects the impact on the environment of a proposed project. The environmental impact statement (EIS) is a government document that outlines the impact of a proposed project on its surrounding environment.
22. Which of the following is NOT an example of governmental power?	a. Remainder

a. Remainder b. Police power c. Eminent domain d. Taxation	The four governmental powers that limit private rights on land are represented by the acronym PETE (police power, eminent domain, taxation, and escheat).
23. Use restrictions are usually contained in a document called a/an _____ a. Declaration of Covenants, Conditions, and Restrictions (CC&Rs) b. County map c. City restriction list d. Community rules	a. Declaration of Covenants, Conditions, and Restrictions (CC&Rs The rules of the HOA community are described in the Declaration of Covenants, Conditions, and Restrictions (CC&Rs)
24. A certified inspector should check around potentially wet areas such as showers, toilets, and basements for which hazard? a. Condemnation b. Mold c. UFFI d. Radon	b. Mold Homes and buildings are susceptible to mold growth. Mold grows in places where there is a lot of moisture, such as around leaky roofs, windows, pipes, or in flood-prone areas.
25. A land use that existed before a certain zoning district was established and is currently not consistent with the restrictions imposed on land uses in that district is referred to as a: a. Variance b. Nonconforming use c. Transitional use d. Planned unit development	b. Nonconforming use In zoning terms, a nonconforming use is one that is not allowed under current zoning laws but existed either before current zoning laws or as part of a conditional use permit.
26. Superfund law created a tax on? a. gasoline stations b. the public c. citizens d. chemical and petroleum industries	d. chemical and petroleum industries The potential responsible parties (PRPs) have traditionally paid roughly 70% of Superfund cleanups, reflecting the polluter pays principle. However, 30% of the time the responsible party cannot be located or cannot pay for the cleanup.
27. Zoning Ordinances primarily a. implements a city master plan. b. implement the quality of workmanship. c. control business. d. control water quality.	a. implements a city master plan. The long-term master plan drives the decision to zone.
28. Which of the following is not an example of the exercise of police power? a. Rent control. b. Building codes. c. Zoning laws. d. Deed restrictions.	d. Deed restrictions Deed restrictions are private land controls. Police powers are Government Controls in Land.
29. Which of the following is TRUE about the federal lead-based paint law? a. Buyers can opt out of lead-based paint inspections.	a. Buyers can opt out of lead-based paint inspections

b. It requires the seller to remove any known lead-based paint. c. The listing broker must give the disclosure to the buyer d. Listing brokers must disclose the information to the buyer.	Sellers must disclose lead-based paint, not brokers.
30. The best example of a buffer zone is a. a warehouse between a neighborhood and strip mall. b. garden homes between a single-family residential neighborhood and a shopping center. c. an office building between a commercial strip mall and a school. d. All the above.	b. garden homes between a single-family residential neighborhood and a shopping center. The Garden home between the mall and the Single-family Residences. SFRs may have more children than a garden home complex.
31. Radon is a. a colorless, odorless, and tasteless gas occurring naturally from the decay of substances. b. colorless, odorless, and tasteless friable asbestos. c. a lead by-product. d. a black mold infestation that has become airborne.	a. a colorless, odorless, and tasteless gas occurring naturally from the decay of substances. Radon is a radioactive gas that forms naturally when uranium, thorium, or radium, which are radioactive metals break down in rocks, soil, and groundwater.
32. Which of the following is a substance which causes cancer in human beings? a. Brownfield b. Carcinogen c. Superfund d. Hazard	b. Carcinogen Carcinogens are substances, radionuclides, or radiation that cause cancer.
33. MATCH: A naturally occurring mineral composite that once was used extensively as insulation in residential and commercial buildings, in brake pads, and in fire-retardant products, such as furniture. a. asbestos b. UFFI c. lead d. radon	a. asbestos Fibers of asbestos are naturally occurring fibrous minerals. Mesothelioma and asbestosis are cancers and diseases caused by asbestos exposure.
34. Ground water contamination could come from the following except? a. Underground gas storage tanks b. Waste disposal sites c. Cement d. Sodium hydrogen carbonate	c. Cement Groundwater contamination happens when substances like gasoline, oil, road salts, and chemicals get into the groundwater and contaminate it, making it unfit for use by humans.
35. Which of the following is a naturally occurring radioactive gas located in soils with a concentration of uranium in the rock a. radon b. mold c. asbestos	a. Radon Radon is a naturally occurring radioactive gas that can cause lung cancer. Radon gas is inert,

d. lead	colorless, and odorless. Radon is easily mitigated.
36. Bike trails and dog parks that enhance value are known as? a. Amenities b. Addendums c. Features d. Amendments	a. Amenities Amenities refer to things that are designed to provide comfort and enjoyment to a community.
37. Use restrictions are usually contained in a document called a _____ a. Declaration of Covenants, Conditions, and Restrictions (CC&Rs) b. Community rules c. County map d. City restriction list	a. Declaration of Covenants, Conditions, and Restrictions (CC&Rs) CC&Rs are the document outlining the community use restrictions.
38. EPA's Superfund program is responsible for? a. pick up trash. b. Responding to private pool spills. c. cleaning up some of the nation's most contaminated land. d. responding to wildlife emergencies.	c. cleaning up some of the nation's most contaminated land. Superfund is responsible for cleaning up some of the nation's most contaminated land
39. Superfund program focuses on? a. making communities healthy again. b. ensuring that people can live and work in healthy, vibrant places. c. All of these are correct. d. making a visible and lasting difference in communities.	c. All of these are correct. Superfund tries to bring the property back to a healthy community

Definitions Module Two

Aesthetic Zoning
Aesthetic zoning means a zoning in which, zoning regulations such as conformity to architectural and landscaping requirements are imposed to preserve the aesthetic features or values of an area.

Amenities
They enhance value by a home's proximity to the amenities of the property. Examples are a bike trail, a community pool, or a beautifully shaded park.
Amenities are community assets that increases the value of the neighborhood's property value.
Not on the individual homeowners' land.

Asbestos
A toxic material that was once used in housing insulation and fireproofing. Because some forms of asbestos have been linked to certain lung diseases, it is no longer used in new homes. However, some older homes may still have asbestos in these materials.

Assessor
Tax assessment, or assessment, is the job of determining the value, and sometimes determining the use, of property, usually to calculate a property tax. This is usually done by an office called the assessor or tax assessor. Governments need to collect taxes in order to function.

Attractive Nuisance
An item or property which might attract the curious (children) to their detriment, e.g., a swimming pool, construction site, abandoned appliances, etc. Owners generally have direct liability for attractive nuisances that are not secured.

Brownfield
the term "brownfield site" means real property, the expansion, redevelopment, or reuse of which may be complicated by the presence or potential presence of a hazardous substance, pollutant, or contaminant. Cleaning up and reinvesting in these properties protects the environment, reduces blight, and takes development pressures off greenspaces and working lands.

Buffer Zone
A buffer zone is a neutral zonal area that lies between two or more bodies of land, usually pertaining to countries. Depending on the type of buffer zone, it may serve to separate regions or conjoin them.

Building Codes
A set of building construction requirements developed and administered by national and local bodies to ensure that buildings meet certain minimum standards for structural integrity, safety, design, and durability.

Bylaws
A by-law is a rule or law established by an organization or community to regulate itself.

Commercial Building
Any building other than a residential or government building, including any building constructed for industrial, retail, business, or public purposes.

Comprehensive Environmental Response, Compensation, and Liability Act (CERCLA or Superfund)

The Comprehensive Environmental Response, Compensation, and Liability Act (CERCLA) created a tax on the chemical and petroleum industries and provided broad federal authority to respond directly to releases or threatened releases of hazardous substances that may endanger public health or the environment.

Conformity
A property that conforms to its surrounding properties in style, age, size, appearance tends to maximize value.

Conservation Zoning
Also known as **conservation design**, is a controlled-growth land use development that adopts the principle for allowing limited sustainable development while protecting the area's natural environmental features in perpetuity, including preserving open space landscape and vista, protecting farmland or natural habitats for wildlife, and maintaining the character of rural communities.

Covenants
In planned communities[edit]. In contemporary practice in the United States, a *covenant* typically refers to restrictions set on contracts like deeds of sale. "

Density
The average number of dwelling units or persons per gross acre of land, usually expressed in units per acre, excluding any area of a street bordering the outside perimeter of a development site

Downzoning
A change in zoning classification of land to a less intensive or more restrictive district such as from commercial district to residential district.

Eminent Domain
The right of government to take private property for public use upon payment of just compensation. The fifth amendment of the U.S. Constitution (taking Clause) guarantees payment of just compensation upon appropriation of private property.

Environmental impact statement (EIS)
For government projects, an environmental impact statement will be done. And EIS is done to determine that effect of a project on the community. The report include the detail description of the proposed project.

Exclusionary Zoning
Exclusionary zoning is done to safeguard the individual's property value, reduce traffic congestion, and exclude unalike groups. Exclusionary land-use policies exacerbate social segregation by deterring any racial and economic integration, decrease the total housing supply of a region and raise housing prices.

Features
On the property. Enhances an individual's property owners' real estate.
On their property.

FEMA Map
a Flood zone map created by the Federal Emergency Management Agency
(FEMA) sometimes called a FIRM or Flood Insurance Rate Map.

Flood Insurance
Insurance that compensates for physical property damage resulting from flooding. It is required for

properties located in federally designated flood hazard zones.

Grandfather Clause
A provision in which an old rule continues to apply to some existing situations while a new rule will apply to all future cases. Those exempt from the new rule are said to have grandfather rights or acquired rights, or to have been grandfathered in.

Hazard Insurance
Insurance coverage that compensates for physical damage to a property from fire, wind, vandalism, or other covered hazards or natural disasters.

Homeowner's Association
A homeowner association (or homeowners' association, abbreviated HOA, is a owners' association or a Property Owner's Association - POA) property is a private association often formed by a real estate developer for the purpose of marketing, managing, and selling homes and lots in a residential subdivision.

Typically, the developer will transfer control of the association to the homeowners after selling a predetermined number of lots.

Incentive Zoning
The use of bonuses in the form of increased project density or other benefits to a developer in return for the developer providing certain features, design elements, uses, services, or amenities desired by the locality, including but not limited to, site design incorporating principles of new urbanism and traditional neighborhood development, environmentally sustainable and energy-efficient building design, affordable housing creation and preservation, and historical preservation, as part of the development.

Inverse condemnation
A situation in which the government takes private property but fails to pay the compensation required by the 5th Amendment of the Constitution, so the property's owner has to sue to obtain the required just compensation.

Landfills
Modern landfills are well-engineered facilities designed to receive specific kinds of waste. Landfill facilities must be designed to protect the environment from contaminants, which may be present in the solid waste disposed in the unit.
☐ Landfills built on the wrong type of soil can pollute ground water.

Lead-based Paint
Many homes and condominiums built before 1978 have lead-based paint. Paint that has chipped or is deteriorating, or on surfaces that rub together such as windows and doors, creates lead dust which can pose serious health hazards to occupants and visitors. Homebuyers and renters have important rights to know about whether lead is present — before signing contracts or leases.

Legal Non-Conforming Use
A type of zoning variance where a parcel of land may be given an exception from current zoning ordinances due to improvements made by a prior owner or before the current zoning ordinances made the desired use non-conforming under local law.

Master Plan
Comprehensive planning is a process that determines community goals and aspirations in terms of

community development. The result is called a comprehensive plan or general plan, and both expresses and regulates public policies on transportation, utilities, land use, recreation, and housing.

Mold
Molds are part of the natural environment and can be found everywhere, indoors and outdoors. Mold is not usually a problem unless it begins growing indoors. The best way to control mold growth is to control moisture. Molds can have a big impact on indoor air quality.

Opportunity Zones
Opportunity Zones are economically distressed communities, defined by individual census tract, nominated by America's governors, and certified by the U.S. Secretary of the Treasury via his delegation of that authority to the Internal Revenue Service. Under certain conditions, new investments in Opportunity Zones may be eligible for preferential tax treatment. There are 8,764 (August 2021) Opportunity Zones in the United States, many of which have experienced a lack of investment for decades.

Police Power
Police power is the capacity of the states to regulate behavior and enforce order within their territory for the betterment of the health, safety, morals, and general welfare of their inhabitants.

Polychlorinated Biphenyls (PCBs)
A group of man-made organic chemicals consisting of carbon, hydrogen and chlorine. PCBs have no known taste or smell, and range in consistency from an oil to a waxy solid.
Due to their non-flammability, chemical stability, high boiling point and electrical insulating properties, PCBs were used in hundreds of industrial and commercial applications including:
1. Electrical, heat transfer and hydraulic equipment
2. Plasticizers in paints, plastics and rubber products
3. Pigments, dyes and carbonless copy paper
4. Other industrial applications

Radon
A toxic gas found in the soil beneath a house that can contribute to cancer and other illnesses.
Radon is a gas that has no color, odor, or taste and comes from the natural radioactive breakdown of uranium in the ground.
Most of the radon in indoor air comes from soil underneath the home.

Setback
In land use, a setback is a minimum distance which a building or other structure must be set back from a street or road, a river or other stream, a shore or flood plain, or any other place which is deemed to need protection.

Special land types
Government has the right to regulate special land types for the public good including coastal properties in wetlands. Standards have been set to keep construction a set distance from protected wetlands.

Special Use Permit
Permission granted by a local zoning agency that authorizes a use as a special exception to the applicable zoning. A special use permit in a residentially zoned area might allow for construction of a church or hospital. Such uses are considered conditional uses, only permitted upon the approval of the zoning authority. Sometimes referred to as a conditional use permit.

Spot Zoning
Spot zoning is the application of zoning to a specific parcel or parcels of land within a larger zoned area when the rezoning is usually at odds with a city's master plan and current zoning restrictions. Spot zoning may be ruled invalid as an "arbitrary, capricious and unreasonable treatment" of a limited parcel of land by a local zoning ordinance.

Subdivider
One who partitions a large parcel of land for resale as individual lots.

Superfund
In the late 1970s, toxic waste dumps such as Love Canal and Valley of the Drums received national attention when the public learned about the risks to human health and the environment posed by contaminated sites. In response, Congress established the Comprehensive Environmental Response, Compensation and Liability Act (CERCLA) in 1980. CERCLA is informally called Superfund. It allows EPA to clean up contaminated sites. It also forces the ☐ parties responsible for the cleanups or reimburse the government for EPA-led cleanup work. (☐ without excuse).

Superfund Amendments and Reauthorization Act
Added ☐ money to the Superfund. Included ☐ innocent landowner immunity. SARA reauthorized CERCLA to continue cleanup activities around the country. Several site-specific amendments, definitions clarifications, and technical requirements were added to the legislation, including additional enforcement authorities.

Underground Storage Tanks (USTs)
Approximately 544,000 underground storage tanks (USTs) nationwide store petroleum or hazardous substances. The greatest potential threat from a leaking UST ☐ (LUST) is contamination of groundwater, the source of drinking water for nearly half of all Americans.

Wetlands
☐ Set aside for conservation. Wetlands are areas where water covers the soil, or is present either at or near the surface of the soil all year or for a varying good period of time during the year, including during the growing season. They are often adjacent to, or tributaries to navigable waters. The soil is often saturated. The EPA regulates many wetlands.

Zoning
A public regulation of the use of private land through application of ☐ police power; accomplished by establishing districts or areas with uniform requirements relating to lot coverage, setbacks, type of improvement, permitted activities, signage, structure height, minimum lot area, density, landscaping, and other aspects of land use and development. Zoning regulations are established by enactment of a local (city, town, or country) zoning ordinance.

Zoning variance
A legally authorized modification in the use of property at a particular location that does not conform to the regulated use set forth in the zoning ordinance for the surrounding area; not an exception or change in the legally applicable zoning.

MODULE THREE: VALUATION AND MARKET ANALYSIS

Appraisals

Information sources include:

- The Appraisal Foundation
- 2020-2021 USPAP (Uniform Standards of Professional Appraisal Practice)
- CFPB (Consumer Finance Protection Bureau)

FIRREA

- The Financial Institutions Reform, Recovery, and Enforcement Act (FIRREA) passed in 1989 in response to the savings and loan crisis of the late 1980s. It is a set of regulatory changes to the U.S. savings and loan banking system and the real estate appraisal industry.
- FIRREA gives both Freddie Mac and Fannie Mae additional responsibility to support mortgages for low- and moderate-income families.

Appraisal Standards Board

The Appraisal Standards Board (ASB) develops, interprets, and amends the Uniform Standards of Professional Appraisal Practice (USPAP).

USPAP

- Standards for the appraisal profession are set forth in the Uniform Standards of Professional Appraisal Practice (USPAP) developed by the Appraisal Standards Board of The Appraisal Foundation. *
- USPAP specifies the procedures to be followed in developing and communicating an appraisal and the ethical rules for appraisal practice.

Uniform Residential Appraisal Report

- URAR is the form the appraiser uses to appraise a residential property.

The Valuation Process

- All appraisal problems can be solved through the systematic application of the valuation process.
- In the valuation process, the problem is identified, the work necessary to solve the problem is planned and relevant data is collected, verified, and analyzed to form an opinion of value.
- The valuation process is accomplished by following specific steps, the number of which depends on the nature of the appraisal assignment and the data available to complete it.

Steps in the Appraisal Process

1. State the Problem (Identify the problem.)
2. Scope of Work Determination
3. Data Collection and Property Description
4. Data Analysis
5. Site Value Opinion
6. Application of the Approaches to Value
7. Reconciliation of Value Indications
8. Final Opinion of Value
9. Report of Defined Value

Understanding the Appraisal

- An appraisal answers one or more specific questions about a real estate parcel's value, marketability, usefulness, or suitability.
- It is an opinion of value based on supportable evidence and approved methods.
- An appraisal assists buyers and sellers in arriving at a fair and equitable sales price

Appraiser

- One who is trained and educated in the methods of determining the value of property. (Appraised value). You will pay a fee for an appraisal report containing an opinion as to the value of your property and the reasoning leading to this opinion.

Appraisal fee
- An appraisal fee is the cost of a home appraisal of a house you plan to buy or already own. In most cases, the selection of the appraiser and any associated costs is up to your lender.

Purposes and Uses of Appraisals

The basic purpose of an appraisal is to estimate a particular value, i.e., market value, check for support of sales price, loan value, investment value, etc. Some uses for requiring the estimate of value are:

Appraisal for Taxation Purposes

- Appraisals are needed by governmental bodies to establish the proper relationship between land and improvements for real estate taxes (ad valorem taxation).
- Properties subject to estate taxes must be evaluated for the purpose of levying federal and state taxes.
- Appraisals of income-producing properties are necessary to property owners for the basis of depreciation.
- Normally, only improvements can be depreciated, not the land. An allocation of the market value between land and improvements is a requisite for accounting and taxation purposes.

Condemnation Actions

- With the right of eminent domain being vested in governmental agencies, it is important that properties under condemnation be evaluated at market value to properly estimate purchase price, benefits, and damages to the property being affected.

Insurance Purposes

- Appraisals are based principally upon the cost of replacement. This is important for the purpose of insuring properties for fire insurance.
- Appraisals are useful in setting claims arising from insurance contracts after a property has been destroyed.

Miscellaneous reasons for appraisals

- Catastrophic damage. Establishing market value of property before and immediately after the damage.
- Estimating market rents for negotiation of leases.
- Appraisals for inheritance and gift tax purposes.
- Fraud cases.
- Damage cases.
- Division-of-estate cases. A distribution of property under the terms of a will, in divorce proceedings, or between rival claimants, frequently requires that the value of the property involved be determined by appraisal.

☐ Situations requiring an appraisal by a certified appraiser

Transactions over 400,000 (was $250,000) require a certified appraisal.

<ul><li>If you use an FHA loan to buy a house, the property will have to be appraised and inspected by a HUD-approved home appraiser.</li><li>This individual will determine the current market value of the property and will also inspect it to ensure it meets HUD's minimum property standards. Here is an overview of FHA appraisal requirements and guidelines in 2018, based on current policy handbooks.</li><li>The same applies to VA Guarantee Loans.</li></ul>Read more: http://www.fhahandbook.com/appraisal-guidelines.php#ixzz5Zt7pMaHA

Appraisal License Levels

1. Appraiser Trainee Someone qualified to appraise those properties, which the supervising certified appraiser is qualified to appraise.
2. Licensed Real Property Appraiser Someone qualified to appraise non-complex one to four units with a transaction value of less than $1,000,000 and a complex one to four residential units having a transaction value less than $400,000. This classification does not include the appraisal of subdivisions.

3. Certified Residential Real Property Appraiser

Someone qualified to appraise one to four residential units without regard to value or complexity. This classification does not include the appraisal of subdivisions. To be a state-certified residential appraiser qualified to do appraisals for federally related transactions, a state must have requirements that meet or exceed this minimum standard.

4. Certified General Real Property Appraiser

Someone qualified to appraise all types of real property. To be a state-certified general appraiser qualified to do appraisals for federally related transactions, a state must have requirements that meet or exceed this minimum standard.

Types of Value

Market Value/Open Market Value

- The most probable selling price.
- The future worth.

Definition of Market Value

- buyer and seller are typically motivated.
- both parties are well informed or well advised, and each acting in his or her own best interest.
- a reasonable time is allowed for exposure in the open market.
- payment is made in terms of cash in U. S. dollars or in terms of financial arrangements comparable thereto.
- a competitive and open market.
- the property being marketed for a reasonable amount of time.
- buyer and seller acting with full knowledge and without any undue pressures (divorce, foreclosure, etc.)

Source: Appraisal Foundation Group

Market Price

The actual selling price.

Value-in-use	Insurable Value
Value-in-use is the value to one user and may be above or below the market value of a property.	The value of real property covered by an insurance policy. Generally, it does not include the site value.
Assessed Value	**Salvage Value**
The value from a local municipality for Ad Valorem Taxes	Property value at the end of its economic life.

The four principles necessary for a property to have value: DUST

1. Demand/desirability: supported by purchasing power
2. Utility: satisfies wants and needs
3. Scarcity: limited supply
4. Transferability: ease of transfer

Principles of Value

Principle of Supply and Demand

Interaction between the supply of goods and the demand for goods establishes both the price and quantity of goods demanded.

Supply	Demand
• The real estate market takes a long time to create; therefore, if the demand for real estate increases, the price of the real estate will also increase, because the supply of real estate will be slow to adjust.	• Buyers and sellers tend to set the price or value of real estate based on the supply and the demand. If the supply of a real estate is stable, and demand for real estate increases, sellers of real estate tend to increase the price

Principle of Anticipation

- Property is valuable because of the future benefits it is expected (anticipated) to provide.
- Investors buy income-producing properties for the future benefits, or income, that is anticipated they will produce in the future.
- Changes in anticipated demand caused by off-site improvements in the form of highways, freeways, bridges, schools, and parkways have an important impact on value even though such improvements may be in the planning stage and not visible at the time of the appraisal. Because the present value of real estate depends on expected future benefits, the principle of anticipation requires the appraiser to be fully informed of community affairs and economic changes anticipated in the market area in which the subject property is located.
- ☐ It is the future, and not the past, with which an appraiser must be concerned.

Concept of Highest and Best Use

- Highest and best use is a critical step in the development of a market value opinion.
- In the highest and best use analysis, the appraiser considers the use of the land as though it were vacant and the use of the property as it is improved.
- To qualify as the highest and best use, a use must satisfy four criteria: it must be legally permissible, physically possible, financially feasible, and maximally productive.

Principle of Substitution

- This principle is the basis of the appraisal process. Simply stated, value will tend to be set by the cost of acquiring an equally desirable substitute.
- In a free market, the buyer can be expected to pay no more, and a seller can expect to receive no less, than the price of an equivalent substitute.

Principle of Conformity

- The principle of conformity states that maximum value is realized when a reasonable degree of

architectural homogeneity exists, and land uses are compatible.
- This principle implies reasonable similarity, not monotonous uniformity, tends to create and maintain value.
- The principal purpose of zoning regulations and private deed restrictions is to maintain conformity.

Principle of Change

- Nothing is static; change is constantly occurring.
- In real estate, the change affects not only individual properties, but also neighborhoods, communities, and regions.
- Change is the law of cause and effect.
- Individual properties, districts, neighborhoods, and entire communities often follow a four-phase life span:

1. Growth

A period during which the area gains in public favor or acceptance.

2. Stability

A period of equilibrium without significant gains or losses.

3. Decline

A period of diminishing demand and acceptance.

4. Renewal/Revitalization

A period of rejuvenation and rebirth of market demand.
The principle of change is closely related to the principle of anticipation.

Gentrification

Gentrification happens when a neighborhood is revitalized, and rents increase to the point where the original residents can no longer afford to live in their neighborhood.

Principle of Competition

- Competition is created where substantial profits are being made. If there is a profitable demand for residential construction, competition among builders will become very apparent.
- This could lead to an increase in supply in relation to the demand, resulting in lower selling prices and unprofitable competition, leading to renewed decline in supply.

Principle of Increasing and Decreasing Returns

- Recognizes that increments of production produce greater net income (increasing returns) up to a point (surplus productivity).
- Any further increase in the amount of production will decrease the margin between the cost .and the gross income they will produce, resulting in a decrease in the proportionate net income returns.

- Increasing and decreasing returns applies to the maximum size that should be placed on a parcel of land.
- Adding stories to a building may result in *property value exceeding costs.*

Principle of Contribution

- This principle holds that the value of a property component is measured in terms of its contribution to the value of the total property rather than as a separate component. Note that the cost of an item does not necessarily equal its contributory value.
- For instance, it may cost $30,000 to build a pool in a 20-unit apartment complex; however, it may only add $20,000 to the overall value of the complex.

Principle of Balance

- The principle of balance is closely related to the principle of **increasing and decreasing returns**; it holds that maximum value is achieved and maintained when all elements of production are in economic balance.
- The value of a property depends on the balance of:
  - o Land
  - o Labor
  - o Capital
  - o Entrepreneurship

Regression	Progression
Largest house in the neighborhood.	Smallest house in the neighborhood.

Cycles and Factors Affecting Real Estate

- Cycle: Condition of the economy
- Economic: Employment and Salary, company investment in commercial real estate
- Physical and Environmental: Is the property in a Hurricane Zone, Tornado Alley, Earthquake Fault?
- Social: Age of community. Older communities inspire homes for aging. Younger communities inspire younger amenities such as pools, walk paths…
- Government and Legal: What is the zoning? Is it being rezoned?

Obtaining Your Appraisal

- **ECOA** requires your lender or mortgage broker to tell you that you have a right to get a copy of the appraisal report. The notice will also tell you how and when you can ask for a copy

The Three Approaches to Value

Sales Comparison (or Market Data) Approach	Cost Approach	Income Approach

Sales Comparison Approach

Market Data

- Most appropriate for residential property and sets the upper limit of value as it is concerned with most recent sales. Formerly known as the market data approach.
- Very Important: Sold price and date sold.
- The principle of substitution states that the upper limit of value tends to be set by the cost of acquiring an equally desirable substitute.
- Using this approach, an appraiser develops a value indication by comparing the subject property with similar properties, called comparable sales.
- The appraiser estimates the degree of similarity or difference between the subject property and the comparable sales by considering various elements of comparison:
- The property must have sold in an **ARMS LENGTH TRANSACTION**
- An arm's length transaction indicates a transaction between two independent parties in which both parties are acting in their own self-interest. Both buyer and seller are independent, possess equal bargaining power, are not under pressure or duress.

Three Comparable Property Minimum

Comparable Properties

- Similar properties in the vicinity of the subject (property being appraised) in the direct sales comparison approach to value.
- An appraiser will compare the comps to the subject and make adjustments to the comparable properties accordingly.

| There are comparable properties currently offered for sale in the subject neighborhood ranging in price from $ to $ |
| There are comparable sales in the subject neighborhood within the past twelve months ranging in sale price from $ to $ |

FEATURE	SUBJECT	COMPARABLE SALE # 1		COMPARABLE SALE # 2		COMPARABLE SALE # 3	
Address							
Proximity to Subject							
Sale Price	$	$		$		$	
Sale Price/Gross Liv. Area	$ sq. ft.	$ sq. ft.		$ sq. ft.		$ sq. ft.	
Data Source(s)							
Verification Source(s)							
VALUE ADJUSTMENTS	DESCRIPTION	DESCRIPTION	+(-) $ Adjustment	DESCRIPTION	+(-) $ Adjustment	DESCRIPTION	+(-) $ Adjustment
Sale or Financing Concessions							
Date of Sale/Time							
Location							
Leasehold/Fee Simple							
Site							
View							
Design (Style)							
Quality of Construction							
Actual Age							
Condition							
Above Grade Room Count	Total Bdrms. Baths	Total Bdrms. Baths		Total Bdrms. Baths		Total Bdrms. Baths	
Gross Living Area	sq. ft.	sq. ft.		sq. ft.		sq. ft.	

Always adjust the comparable property.

| If the comparable property is superior in a feature, you subtract value from the comparable. |

Comp #l has a patio and sold for $70,000.
The subject property does not have a patio.
The value of a patio is $2,000.

What would be the adjustment?
Solution: Subject Comparable $70,000
No Patio -$2,000
Value: $68,000

Cost Approach

Examples

Hospitals.	City Hall.	Library.	Historic Homes.
Schools.		The first home built in an area with no other properties.	

- Mostly used for Insurable value.
- Relates value to cost.
- In the cost approach, the property's value is equal to the cost of land, plus total costs of construction, less depreciation.

Replacement Cost
- Cost to replace a structure to a similar utility using current materials and modern construction methods.
- Estimating replacement cost methods include square-foot, unit-in-place, quantity-survey, or index.

Reproduction Cost
Used for historic properties.

☐ This approach is particularly useful in valuing new or nearly new improvements and properties that are not frequently exchanged in the market.

Unit-in-Place Method

- A method of determining replacement cost based primarily on the value of materials per square foot or yard (or another unit of measurement) *plus labor, profit*, etc.
- Less technical and involved than the quantity survey method.

Quantity Survey Method

- The most complex, technical, time-consuming, and accurate method of determining replacement/reproduction cost is considering materials and labor, *regulatory fees, survey, taxes, profit*, etc.
- QSM is applied primarily to historic structures.

Square-Foot Method

The most common and easiest method of determining replacement cost based on cost-per-square-foot of a comparable, recently constructed building multiplied by the square footage of the subject property.

Depreciation (appraisal)
• Loss of property value due to any physical, functional, or external condition.   • The loss of value in an improvement over time.   • The cost of the structure divided by its economic life equals the annual amount of depreciation. (taxes)   • Land Does Not Depreciate   • Only the **wasting assets** depreciate.

Depreciation is of three different types (physical deterioration, functional obsolescence, and external obsolescence) and is measured through market research and specific procedures.

Physical Deterioration	Physical/Functional Obsolescence	External/Economic obsolescence
• Ordinary wear and tear, age, and breakage. • Physical Deterioration– a leaky roof, a cracked foundation wall, worn-out window tracks. **Fixable.** • Normal wear and tear on a building is neither external nor functional (internal) obsolescence. It's deterioration. **Deferred Maintenance** • Deferred maintenance is the practice of postponing maintenance activities such as repairs real property to save costs, meet budget funding levels, or realign available budget monies.	**Curable Depreciation** • Depreciation that is not cost-prohibitive to repair. • A home with three bedrooms on the second floor and one bathroom on the first floor. • Loss in value due to something on the property. • Usually, **Fixable**. • A poor floor plan can cause functional obsolescence. • A single car garage could cause functional obsolescence.	**Incurable Depreciation** • Loss of property value that **cannot be fixed** due to external factors. • Loss in value due to an airport expanding its runway, and now planes fly over a neighborhood at a low altitude. • A deteriorating neighborhood with buildings not being maintained. • External is something outside the property.

Effective Age

Age of an improvement, taking into consideration all forms of depreciation. A building may be ten years old, but poor maintenance may have an effect of 20 years.

Income Approach to Value
Capitalization   • The CAP Rate is an investor's rate of return.   • A capitalization rate incorporates return on land and building and recapture of the building.   • With the income approach, the "highest and best use property" is the one that delivers the highest

net return.

Capitalization Approach

- Income-producing real estate is typically purchased as an investment, and earning power is the critical element affecting property value from an investor's perspective.
- Value is measured as the present value of the future benefits of property ownership.
- The yield of an investment is expressed as a percentage that the investor expects to make over ownership

Yield

- Annualized amount of return to an investor; expressed as a percentage of the original investment. (profit)

Operating Expenses

- Fixed expenses, variable expenses, and replacement reserves of operating and maintaining a property.
- Expenses do NOT include debt service (value is the same whether mortgaged or purchased with cash), capital improvements, or depreciation. Loans are considered incidental.

Net Operating Income (NOI)

- Projected income from a property.

Effective Gross Income
- Estimated income from a property after vacancy and collection loss is subtracted from gross income.

Residual Method

- An appraisal process is used in the income approach to estimate the value of the building by deducting the land's value.
- The appraiser must remember to add in the value of the land.

Gross Rent Multiplier	Gross Income Multiplier
Residential homes	Big Stuff
Steps • Sales price divided by gross monthly income = the GRM • Monthly rental income x GRM = value	**Steps** • Estimate gross annual income. • Deduct vacancy and rent loss. • Deduct annual operating expenses. • Sales price divided by annual rental income = GIM
MONTHLY INCOME	ANNUAL INCOME
	DEDUCT EXPENSES AN VACANCIES

	(RATE)

Automated Valuation Method (AVM)

Zillow and Trulia
- An AVM is a residential valuation report that can be obtained in a matter of seconds. It is a technology-driven report.
- The product of an automated valuation technology comes from analysis of public record data and computer decision logic combined to provide a calculated estimate of a probable selling price of a residential property.
- The Zestimate® home valuation model is Zillow's estimate of a home's market value.
- The Zestimate incorporates public and user-submitted data, considering home facts, location, and market conditions.

Competitive/Comparable Market Analysis

- CMA – Comparative Market Analysis is based on the Sales Comparison Approach
- A broker or salesperson uses them in attempting to find a listing price range.
- It's a scaled-down version of the appraiser's sales comparison approach.
- A CMA estimates a home's value done by a real estate broker to establish a listing or offer price.
- This service is usually offered free of charge and without obligation.
- A CMA should only be used as a reference for deciding at what price you should list or buy a home.
- A tool for real estate professionals.
- It is NOT an appraisal.
- It does NOT indicate the value`

□ When an agent wants to do a CMA in a mostly foreclosed neighborhood, he/she will take the actual arm's length (or more) sales comparisons from the bank instead of the foreclosed price.

Broker Price Opinion (BPO)

- Lenders often use them in conjunction with loan portfolio valuation, loss mitigation, short sales, or collections.
- A lender will contact a real estate professional in the property's area and ask for specific information.
- A sales professional can be paid for conducting BPOs.
- BPOs cannot be used to generate a mortgage.
- The National Association of Broker Price Opinion Professionals set the standards for BPOs.

Assemblage creates Plottage

Assemblage is combining adjacent properties to create one large property. Plottage is the increased value.

Quiz: Valuation and Market Analysis

1. The first step in the appraisal process is to…? a. estimate the value of the land b. state the problem c. analyze the neighborhood d. gather data	b. state the problem The appraiser first determines why he/she has been hired to make an appraisal on the property.
2. Which of the following situations would NOT normally require an appraisal? a. condemnation b. home purchase c. life insurance d. foreclosure	c. life insurance Life Insurance has no reason for a property appraisal.
3. An appraiser must be licensed or certified to handle Federally related work on residential, residential income, commercial, and all other real estate properties valued at a. $1,000,000. b. $550,000. c. $400,000 d. $525,000.	c. $400,000 The Licensed Residential Appraiser may appraise non-complex 1-4 residential units having a transaction value less than $1,000,000 and complex 1-4 residential units having a transaction value less than $400,000.
4. A real estate licensee may perform which of the following services? a. Prepare a CMA for a buyer. b. Conduct a fee appraisal of a residential property for an attorney interested in establishing market value for estate purposes. c. Conduct an appraisal and give an opinion of value for a fee for any valuation assignment. d. Conduct an appraisal on real property associated with a federally related transaction, provided he does not represent himself as a licensed or certified appraiser.	a. Prepare a CMA for a buyer. Only appraisers can do appraisals. A competitive/comparable market analysis is MOST often used for estate tax purposes. setting a listing price. Figuring an offer price for a buyer. divorce proceedings. property tax assessment. Sellers benefit from a CMA. It helps them to find a listing price.
5. Which characteristic would NOT be associated with a good appraiser? a. competent b. objective c. biased d. logical	c. biased Appraisers remain impartial and objective. They are not biased.
6. MATCH: The process of estimating the market value of real property a. Appraisal b. Brokerage c. Property management d. Subdivision and development	a. Appraisal An appraisal is the professional opinion of an appraiser.
7. Who retains final authority over revisions to USPAP? a. the Appraisal Practices Board b. the Appraisal Subcommittee c. the Appraisal Standards Board d. the Appraiser Qualifications Board	c. the Appraisal Standards Board The Appraisal Standards Board (ASB) sets the minimum standards, known as the Uniform Standards of Professional

	Appraisal Practice (USPAP).
8. A real estate broker or salesperson in the ordinary course of his business may give an opinion as to the price of real estate for the purpose of a prospective listing or sale, however this opinion as to the listing price or sale price? a. must not refer to this as an appraisal. b. neither c. must not take compensation.	a. must not refer to this as an appraisal. CMAs and BPOs should have a similar statement as below: A disclaimer stating that, "This opinion is not an appraisal of the market value of the property and may not be used in lieu of an appraisal. If an appraisal is desired, the services of a licensed or certified appraiser must be obtained."
9. A professional opinion of a property's market value, based on established methods and using trained judgment, is performed by a. A real estate attorney b. A real estate appraiser c. A real estate counselor d. A home inspector	b. A real estate appraiser Value is determined by an appraiser. They must be unbiased and independent of the buying and selling parties.
10. When an appraiser estimates the value of a property under each of the three approaches to appraising, the appraiser must consider the following: a. Estimates averaged out b. Calculates the average by assigning weights to each estimate c. Appraiser chooses and uses the approach he or she feels is best d. Justifies not using the other approaches, then choses the one the appraiser believes is the most appropriate	d. Justifies not using the other approaches, then choses the one or several the appraiser believes is the most appropriate. In arriving at the final estimate of value, an appraiser may use one or a combination of all three of the major approaches to appraising.
11. The general term "value" means? a. the function of an object b. the average use of an object to all people c. the worth, usefulness, or utility of an object to someone for some purpose d. a good buy	c. the worth, usefulness, or utility of an object to someone for some purpose The definition of appraisal (value) is the worth, usefulness, or utility of an object to someone for some purpose.
12. The "price that a willing, informed, and unpressured seller and buyer agree upon for a property, assuming a cash price and reasonable exposure of the property to the market" describes which of the following concepts of value? a. Highest and best value b. Substitution value c. Desirability d. Market value	d. Market value Market value is an opinion of what a property would sell for in a competitive market based on the features and benefits of that property (the value), the overall real estate market, supply, and demand, and what other similar properties have sold for in the same condition.
13. Assuming all factors are the same, which location would probably bring the highest price for a parking lot for sale? a. Business district zoned for one story small businesses.	d. Business zoned for 20 story high rises. Supply and demand. More people, More cars, More demand.

b. Recreational area. c. A residential area zoned for single-family homes. d. Business zoned for 20 story high rises.	
14. Rental rates have increased by 4% in the last twelve months. Which appraisal concept could explain the rent increase? a. Principle of substitution b. Principle of supply and demand c. Principle of contribution d. Principle of highest and best use	b. Principle of supply and demand The fewer properties that become available for rent or sale, the owner can increase the rents.
15. All the following would affect demand EXCEPT a. Population b. Demographics c. Wage levels d. Monetary policy	d. Monetary policy Money supply is determined by monetary policy.
16. A population's detailed characteristics, including its age, education, and other characteristics, is called? a. Population analysis b. Demographics c. Family averages d. Automobile data	b. Demographics Demographic data is socioeconomic information expressed statistically, and includes employment, education, income, birth, and death rates, among other factors.
17. Three identical homes in a neighborhood were listed at the same time in a market where demand was constant. According to the law of supply and demand, which would have sold for the lowest price? a. The first one sold. b. The property on the lot with the largest street frontage. c. The last one sold. d. The corner lot property.	a. The first one sold. The law of supply and demand dictates the equilibrium price of a property. A low supply or housing inventory may drive prices up, which is what tends to result in bidding wars.
18. The price of single-family residences may be affected by a. An increase in the number of homes built. b. An increase in employment in the community. c. A decrease in mortgage interest rates. d. All of these.	d. All of these. Demand for real estate may be affected by increasing population and employment, mortgage financing, and increases in purchasing power. Building new homes increases supply. Price is determined by market supply and demand in free-market economies.
19. The overproduction of new homes? a. Causes lower prices. b. Increases the demand. c. Increases higher prices. d. Causes a state of fair trade.	a. causes lower prices. Excess supply causes prices to decrease when market supply exceeds market demand. When market demand is greater than market supply there is excess demand, causing price to increase. Real estate prices rise quickly when demand is high.
20. The principle of increasing and decreasing returns	a. True

says that too much of a good thing is bad. a. True b. False	Increased production of property improvements will eventually have diminishing returns when the other properties in the neighborhood remain constant.
21. A buyer invests in a strip mall because he believes the property will net $100,000 per year. This is an example of? a. Contribution b. Supply c. Asset Demand d. Anticipation	d. Anticipation Anticipation is one reason for investing in real estate income producing properties. The principle holds that a person invests in property, real or personal, in anticipation of future benefits.
22. The principle of anticipation can be applied to? a. A single-family residence. b. A condominium c. An apartment building. d. A commercial structure. e. All the above.	e. All the above A person invests in property, real or personal, for future benefit.
23. A major manufacturer of automobiles announces that it will relocate one of its factories, along with 2,000 employees, to a small town. What effect will this announcement MOST likely have on the small town's housing market? a. Houses will likely become less expensive b. Houses will likely become more expensive c. Because the announcement involves an issue of demographics, not of supply and demand, housing prices will stay the same d. The announcement involves an industrial property, residential housing will not be affected	b. Houses will likely become more expensive Anticipation and supply and demand will affect the value of the real estate.
24. In an analysis of highest and best use, the appraiser must consider which of the following? a. The legally permissible b. The physically possibilities c. The financially feasibility d. All of these	d. All of these To qualify, as a property's highest and best use, the use must meet four criteria. The use must be: (1) legally permissible, (2) physically possible, (3) financially feasible, and (4) maximally productive
25. To be considered the highest and best use of a site, the use must? a. Conform to zoning b. Have development expansion future uses c. Conform to current zoning d. Have no external obsolescence	c. Conform to current zoning Properties are appraised based on a use consistent with the zoning.
26. According to the principle of contribution, some components may add value equal with their costs, while others may fall short.	a. True

a. True b. False	Contribution theory holds that a component's value depends on how much it contributes to the overall value. A component's value does not necessarily equal its cost.
27. A doctor built a five-bedroom house with five bathrooms on a lot in a neighborhood where all the homes are three bedrooms and one bath. The doctor's home will most likely suffer from a. subrogation. b. novation. c. progression. d. regression.	d. regression. The doctor will suffer in value due to the smaller properties in his neighborhood.
28. An office building has physical deterioration that can be corrected for $35,000. If the correction is made, the owner will receive more offers for renting. The yearly value added to the property could reach $50,000. This would be an example of? a. Increasing and decreasing returns b. Progression and Regression c. Economic Considerations d. Amenities and additional features	a. Increasing and decreasing returns In this case, the real estate investment would be economically justified if benefits equal or exceed costs.
29. A neighborhood's life cycle consists of which of the following stages? a. Growth, stability, decline and gentrification b. Acceptability, stability, decline and rezoning c. Growth, stability, decline; and rehabilitation d. Social aging, decline in revenue, gentrification, and revitalization	c. Growth, stability, decline; and rehabilitation Properties usually go through four phases: growth, stability, decline, and rehabilitation. Property values are affected by local, regional, and national trends.
30. An appraiser is using the sales comparison approach to estimate the value of a residential home. The appraiser will make positive and negative adjustments to the sold comparable properties for all the following factors EXCEPT? a. square footage of the sold properties. b. lot size and location of each sold comparable in relation to the subject. c. actual replacement and reproduction cost. d. date of sale of each sold comparable.	c. actual replacement and reproduction cost. Appraisers using the sales comparison approach will adjust for square footage, lot size and location, and date of sale in a rapidly changing market.
31. If the comparable properties have a feature that is not present in the subject property, the value of that feature will be? a. Identified in the report but given no consequences b. Ignored since no two properties are alike c. Subtracted from the sales price of the comparable properties d. Added to the sales price of the subject	c. Subtracted from the sales price of the comparable properties When using the market data approach to appraising, an appraiser finds comparable properties that are comparable to the subject property being appraised. If the comparable properties have a feature which the subject property does not have, then the value of that feature will be

	subtracted from the sales prices of the comparable properties to arrive at the value of the subject property.
32. What is the most difficult part about estimating the value of a property? a. Determining the condition of the market b. Understanding the seller's motivation c. Determining the condition of the home d. Determining the sales price of the home.	C. Determining the condition of the home Determining the condition of a home requires a professional inspector.
33. Which of the following single-family residences would get the MOST accurate appraisal by applying the reproduction cost approach to value? a. A rental property. b. A vacant property. c. A new property. d. An historic property.	d. An historic property The Reproduction Cost Approach is used for historic properties.
34. An example of functional obsolescence is? a. a building that, because of wear and tear, is no longer suitable for its intended purpose. b. a large commercial structure with inadequate onsite parking. c. an encroaching use. d. a political change that has reduced value.	b. a large commercial structure with inadequate onsite parking. Commercial structures typically need large parking areas for customers. An example would be a mall.
35. Depreciation is based on? a. land and the building. b. land only. c. building only. d. economic obsolescence.	c. building only Land does not depreciate.
36. The methods to calculate the reproduction and replacement cost of a building include all the following except? a. quantity survey method. b. straight-line method. c. unit in place method. d. square foot method.	b. straight-line method. straight-line method refers to depreciation.
37. Flight patterns were changed and now airplanes fly directly over a subdivision. What term best describes the loss in value to this subdivision? a. Deterioration b. Condemnation c. Physical obsolescence d. External/economic obsolescence	d. External/economic obsolescence Economic Obsolescence is the loss of value from causes outside the property itself.
38. Which of the following would be considered an example of economic obsolescence? a. A broken window. b. Carpet that is outdated. c. No parking at the site d. Deteriorating neighborhood.	d. Deteriorating neighborhood. The economic obsolescence of a property is caused by something outside of its bounds that decreases its value.
39. The BEST approach for an appraiser trying to	b. income approach to value.

determine market value of a shopping center, apartment building, or office building would be the? a.　replacement approach to value. b.　income approach to value. c.　sales comparison approach to value. d.　Additional approach to value.	The income approach is used when a property, such as a mall, creates revenue.
40. When a buyer of a four-plex refers to the property renting for 1000 dollars a month, therefore, the property is worth $100,000, the buyer is using the a.　IRS. b.　HUD. c.　GRM. d.　BRB.	c. GRM. Gross Rent Multiplier is used for income residential properties to help determine value.
41. When a broker is compiling information for a CMA. The broker will look for similar properties with similar features that? a.　were sold for all cash. b.　had been extensively advertised. c.　were offered by the owner with no broker. d.　were located near the property being listed.	d. was located near the property being listed. A broker should look for properties close to the subject property. Also looks for the closest in time.
42. Gross Rent Multiplier is used for income residential properties to help determine value. A competitive market analysis (CMA) considers? a.　demographics b.　unknown friable asbestos. c.　square footage of the subject property. d.　original price of the property.	c. square footage of the subject property. Don't let the question throw you off because the first line that has nothing to do with the question. The question is about a CMA. A comparative market analysis (CMA) is an estimate of a home's value based on recently sold, similar properties in the immediate area The square footage of the subject property is important.
43. Gross rent multiplier (GRM) is the ratio of the price of a real estate investment to its annual rental income before accounting for expenses such as property taxes, insurance, and utilities. A competitive market analysis is MOST often used for? a.　setting a value. b.　setting a sales value. c.　setting a listing price.	c. setting a listing price. The question is trying to confuse you by giving a statement about a GRM before asking the question. A CMA is most used in setting a list price.
44. A broker who is attempting to determine the current market value for a residential listing would get the BEST estimate of value by using? a.　a GRM b.　the reproduction estimates. c.　Comparable properties that are no more than six months old. d.　a GIM	c. Comparable properties that are no more than six months old. Comparable properties that are less than six months old. Recent comparable properties are more likely to reflect price changes up or down in a changing market.

45. The principle of substitution can be applied to? a. The cost approach. b. All the approaches. c. The income approach. d. The comparative sales approach.	b. All the approaches. The principle of substitution is fundamental to the cost, comparative sales, and income approaches to value.
46. The document given to the client upon completion of an appraisal assignment is the? a. appraisal report b. evaluation c. invoice d. CMA	a. appraisal report The "real estate appraisal report." This is a written report that estimates the current fair market value of the property that you are buying or selling.
47. MATCH: The process of estimating the market value or real property. a. property management b. appraisal c. subdivision d. CMA	b. appraisal An appraisal is the professional opinion of an appraiser.
48. When preparing a market data estimate of value, which of the following categories of adjustment is NOT important? a. the square footage of the subject house. b. Recent sales in the neighborhood. c. The original price of the property. d. The location of the subject property.	c. The original price of the property. The original price of the property does not matter in an appraisal. The property value may have appreciated over time. There may have been additions or other alterations.
49. Carol and Tom are interested in a house. It is their favorite floor plan, but the house is on a very busy street. Carol and Tom have decided not to make an offer on the house because of? a. Immobility. b. Permanence of investment. c. Area preference. d. Physical deterioration.	c. Area preference Area preference, or location, is situs and is the single most important economic characteristic of land.
50. According to the principle of contribution, some components may add value equal with their costs, while others may fall short. a. False b. True	b. True The principle of contribution holds that the value of a component of property depends upon its contribution to the value of the total property. The cost of an improvement does not necessarily equal the value the component adds to the property.
51. Alan, who is a doctor was tired of the commute from his home to the hospital where he works. He decided to buy two vacant lots near the hospital. The homes in the neighbor are all three bedrooms with one bath. Alan built a five-bedroom house with five bathrooms Alan's home will most likely suffer from? a. subrogation. b. novation. c. progression.	d. regression. Alan will suffer in value due to the smaller properties in his neighborhood.

d. regression.	
52. Outdated lighting fixtures are an example of? a. Curable external obsolescence b. Regression c. Curable functional obsolescence d. Incurable external obsolescence	c. Curable functional obsolescence Curable functional obsolescence is measured as the cost to cure the condition.
53. Tiny Town, a suburb near Big City has a growing need for single-family housing. The land available for new construction is restricted because of the National Forest boundary. There is a demand for the new community because it is an easy drive to Big City. In this case, it is likely that the price of existing homes a. will stabilize b. will increase. c. will not show any predictable movement. d. will decline.	b. will increase. supply and demand
54. Tawana purchased a new home in a planned gated community. She loves that all the homes in the neighborhood have uniformity. She is moving from a home where all the homes are different and zoned for multiuse construction. The term nonhomogeneity refers to? a. Immobility b. Indestructible c. Uniqueness d. Scarcity	c. Uniqueness No two properties are the same.
55. Daniel bought his home from a developer when the neighborhood was new. His three children and his wife have lived there. His children are now grown and have children of their own. His son Charlie visited him yesterday and attempted to talk Daniel into moving closer to the grandchildren. Charlie said the neighborhood his dad lives in has deteriorated. Daniel, because he has taken a real estate course after he retired from his thirty-year job told his son about the four neighborhood life cycles. The cycles are? a. Growth, stability, decline; and rehabilitation. b. Acceptability, stability, decline and rehabilitation. c. Stability, decline, gentrification, and revitalization. d. Growth, stability, decline and disintegration.	a. Growth, stability, decline; and rehabilitation. Properties often follow a four-phase life cycle: growth, stability, decline, and rehabilitation. Local, regional, national, and even international trends have strong effects on property values.
56. Andrew, the appraiser, was given an assignment to find the value of an income property. Which of the following is most important to Andrew in approaching the income property? a. capitalization rate. b. accrued depreciation. c. original cost to build. d. market changes since comparable sales.	a. capitalization rate. Capitalization rate for the income approach, the net income is divided by the capitalization rate.

57. Maryann and Tina are next door neighbors. They both decided to sell their homes at the same time. Both houses are identical. Tina is asking $20,000 more for her house because she just remolded her kitchen and she does not like it. If two homes in the same neighborhood are the same except for the price, which of the following statements is most true? a. The lower-priced home will sell for more than the higher-price home. b. The higher-priced home will attract more demand. c. The lower-priced home will attract more demand. d. The higher-priced home will sell faster than the lower-priced home.	a. The lower-priced home will sell for more than the higher-price home It is reasonable to assume the. Lower priced home will sell quicker.
58. An example of functional obsolescence is a. a political change that has reduced value. b. a building that, because of wear and tear, is no longer suitable for its intended purpose. c. a large commercial strip center with no vacancies has limited parking. d. an encroaching use.	c. a large commercial strip center with no vacancies has limited parking. Commercial structures typically need large parking areas for customers.

Definitions Module Three

Anticipation
The perception that value is created by the expectation of benefits to be derived in the future

Appraisal
The act or process of developing an opinion of value; an opinion of value.

Appraisal Practice
Valuation services performed by an individual acting as an appraiser, including but not limited to appraisal, appraisal review, or appraisal consulting.

Appraisal Report
The written or oral communication of an appraisal.

Appraiser
One who is expected to perform valuation services competently and in a manner that is independent, impartial, and objective.

Appreciation
An increase in the market value of a home due to changing market conditions and/or home improvements.

Approaches to Value
The traditional methods or techniques by which market data may be processed into an indication of value. The three approaches to value include the Direct Sales Comparison Approach, commonly referred to as
1.   the **Market Data Approach** or **Market Approach**.
2.   the **Cost Approach,** sometimes referred to as the **Summation Approach**.
3.   the **Income Approach,** sometimes referred to as the **Income Capitalization Approach.**

As Is Value
An estimate or opinion of property in its current state, which may be in disrepair or scheduled for improvement.

Assemblage
The combining of two or more parcels, usually but not necessarily contiguous, into one ownership or use; the process that may create plottage; the combining of separate properties into units, sets or groups, i.e., integration or combination under unified ownership.

Assessed Value
The value placed on property for the purpose of taxation.

Balance, Principle of
It holds that value is created and maintained in proportion to the equilibrium attained in the amount and location of essential uses of real estate. The degree of value of a property is governed by the balance or apportionment of the four factors in production; land, labor, capital and management.

Capitalization Rate (Cap Rate)
A measure of the ratio between the cash flow produced by an asset (usually real estate) and its capital cost (the original price paid to buy the asset) or alternatively its current market value.

Change, Principle of

It holds that economic and social forces are constantly at work and changes brought about by these forces affect real property.

The appraiser views real property and its environment as in transition and observes evidence of trends which may affect the property in the future.
The law of change is fundamentally the law of cause and effect.

Competition, Principle of

It holds that profit tends to breed competition and excess profit tends to breed ruinous competition.

Conformity, Principle of

It holds that the maximum value of a property is realized when a reasonable degree of sociological and economic homogeneity is present.

Contributory Value

The change in the value of a property as a whole, whether positive or negative, resulting from the addition or deletion of a property component.

Cost Approach

A set of procedures through which a value indication is derived for the fee simple interest in a property by estimating the current cost to construct a reproduction of (or replacement for) the existing structure including an entrepreneurial incentive, deducting depreciation from the total cost, and adding the estimated land value. Adjustments may then be made to the indicated fee simple value of the subject property to reflect the value of the property interest being appraised.

Cost to Cure

The cost to restore an item of deferred maintenance to new or reasonably new condition.

Curable Functional Obsolescence

An element of depreciation; a curable defect caused by a flaw in the structure, materials, or design, which can be practically and economically corrected.

Depreciation

A decline in the value of a house due to changing market conditions or lack of upkeep on a home.

Economic age-life method

A method of estimating depreciation in which the ratio between the effective age of a building and its total economic life is applied to the current cost of the improvements to obtain a lump-sum deduction; also known as the age-life method.

Economic Obsolescence

Caused by impairment of desirability or usefulness arising from factors external to the property. Also referred to as locational obsolescence.

Economic Rent

The rent which a property can be expected to bring in the open market as opposed to contract rent which is the rent the property is actually realizing at a given time. It is the market rent that a property should most probably command on the open market as of the effective date of the appraisal. Used synonymously with market rent.

Effective Age
The age of the property that is based on the amount of deterioration and obsolescence it has sustained, which may be different from its chronological age.

Effective Date
The date on which the analyses, opinions, and advice in an appraisal, review, or consulting service apply. In the case of a lease, it's the date upon which the lease goes into effect.

Effective Gross Income (EGI)
The anticipated income from all operations of the real property after an allowance is made for vacancy and collection losses and an addition is made for any other income.

External Obsolescence
An element of depreciation; a diminution in value caused by negative externalities and generally incurable on the part of the owner, landlord, or tenant.

Market Value
The price at which property would be transferred between a willing buyer and willing seller, each of whom has a reasonable knowledge of all pertinent facts and is not under any compulsion to buy or sell.

Functional Obsolescence
The impairment of functional capacity of a property according to the market tastes and standards.

Gross Income Multiplier
A multiplier that represents the relationship between the gross income of a property and its estimated value. It is calculated by dividing the sales price of a property by its gross income at the time of sale. The multiplier to be used in an appraisal is developed through an analysis of a sufficient number of comparable properties which were rented at the time of sale. When the gross income multiplier, also called the gross rent multiplier, is applied to a property's potential gross income, an estimate of value is indicated.

Highest and Best Use
The reasonably probable and legal use of vacant land or an improved property that is physically possible, appropriately supported, financially feasible, and that results in the highest value. The four criteria the highest and best use must be meet are legal permissibility, physical and possibility, financial feasibility, and maximum productivity. alternatively, the probable use of land or improved property – specific with respect to the user and timing of the use – that is adequately supported and results in the highest present value.

Income Approach
One of the three traditional approaches to value which measures the present worth of the future benefits of a property by the capitalization of the projected net income stream over its remaining economic life. The approach involves estimating the gross **possible income**; subtracting a reasonable vacancy and credit loss from the gross possible income to determine effective gross income; subtracting allowable operating expenses from effective gross income to determine net operating income; determining the proper capitalization method; computing the correct capitalization rate; and then capitalizing that projected net income into an indication of value.

Income Property

Real estate developed or purchased to produce income, such as a rental unit.

Increasing and Decreasing Returns, Principle of
A theory that additions to a property will produce an increase in value that exceeds the additional cost of production up to a certain point; at which point, the maximum true value in money is achieved and any additional investment of an agent of production will not produce an increase in "True Value in Money" equal to the cost of the additional improvements.

Market Data Approach
An appraisal valuation approach, also called the Sales Comparison Approach, which is used to develop an indication of value for a property by compiling data on properties which are comparable to the subject property and which recently sold.
An adjustment is made to the selling price to account for differences in time, location and property characteristics between the comparables and the subject property. The adjusted sale prices should provide an indication of value for the subject property.

Market Value
A type of value, stated as an opinion that presumes the transfer of a property as of a certain date, under specific conditions, set forth in the definition of the term identified by the appraiser as applicable in an appraisal.

Mass Appraisal
The process of valuing a area of properties as of a given date using standard methodology, employing common data, and allowing for statistical testing. Zestimate is a Mass Appraisal product.

Neighborhood Life Cycle
As reflected by the *Principle of Change*, a neighborhood typically evolves through three discernible life patterns.
The three stages in the lifecycle of a neighborhood include:
(1) Growth – the period during which the neighborhood is characterized by development and growth;
(2) Stability – the period characterized by an equilibrium or leveling off of values; and
(3) Decline – the life stage characterized by diminishing demand and decay.
Neighborhood renewal and rehabilitation may cause the life cycle of a neighborhood to be repeated.

Net Worth
The value of a company or individual's assets, including cash, less total liabilities.

Obsolescence
One cause of depreciations; an impairment of desirability and usefulness caused by new inventions, changes in design, improved processes for production, or external factors that make a property less desirable and valuable for a continued use; may either functional or external.

Operating Expenses
The necessary charges or expenses incurred by ownership of or investment in income-producing property. Net operating expenses are those fixed expenses, variable operating costs and reserves for replacements which are required for the production of income from the operation of a property.

Over Improvement
An improvement that does not represent the most profitable use for the site on which it is placed because it is too large or costly and cannot develop the highest possible land value; may be temporary or permanent.

Oversupply
An excess of supply over demand; indicated by high vacancy rates, sluggish absorption rates, and declining rents.

Physical Deterioration
The loss in value due to the physical wear and tear experienced by the structure as reflected by its age and the actions of the elements on the improvements. Physical deterioration may be classified as either curable, sometimes referred to as deferred maintenance, and incurable.

Quantity Survey Method
The most detailed and comprehensive method of projecting an estimate of a reproduction cost. It involves the itemization and summation of all materials and their respective costs, labor hours and costs, and all indirect costs (permits, insurance, office expense, and other overhead plus a margin for profit) into a total cost estimate.

Recapture Rate
A component of the capitalization rate which provides for a return of the original capital investment in a wasting asset. The rate is equal to the annual amount of dollars to be returned to the investor over the life of the property divided by the amount of the original investment.

Remaining Economic Life
As of the date of the appraisal, it is the number of years that represents the economic usability left in the improvements, or components thereof. At the end of the remaining economic life, the improvements will not contribute to the value of the property.

Replacement Cost
The cost to replace damaged personal property without a deduction for depreciation.

Sales Comparison Approach
The process of deriving a value indication for the subject property by comparing market information for similar properties with the property being appraised, identifying appropriate units of comparison, and making qualitative comparisons with or quantitative adjustments to the sale prices of the comparable properties based on relevant, market-derived elements of comparison.

Substitution, Principle of
It affirms that value tends to be set by the cost of acquiring a substitute property that is equally desirable and provides similar utility.

The principle assumes that there will be no costly delay in acquiring the substitute property, the property is available on the open market, and the actions would be those of a knowledgeable and prudent purchaser. This principle serves as a basis for all three approaches to value.

Sweat Equity
A borrower's contribution to the down payment for the purchase of a property in the form of labor or services rather than cash.

Unit-in-Place Method
A method of cost estimating in which the costs of individual structural components (foundations, walls, roof, etc.) are specified in appropriate unit measurements (area, volume, length), multiplied by the

estimated quantity of structural components contained within a particular structure, and summed to obtain an estimate of the cost of the entire structure.

Valuation Process
A systematic procedure used in the valuation of real property.

Value in Use
The value of a property assuming a specific use, which may or may not be the property's highest and best use on the effective date of the appraisal. Value in use may or may not be equal to market value but is different conceptual.

Wasting Asset
A property or resource whose value diminishes with the passage of time. Such assets include buildings, mineral deposits, and manmade structures.

MODULE FOUR: FINANCING

Financing: Basic Concepts and Terminology

Financing is the business of providing funds that make real estate transactions possible.

Mortgagor	Mortgagee
• The borrower • Mortgagor – borrower • The Mortgagor is the GIVOR. of the payment.	• The lender, bank or person who lends the money • If the Mortgagee doesn't give the payment, the Mortgagee says: gimee, gimee, gimee the propertee

Down payment
A down payment is the amount you pay toward the home upfront. You put a percentage of the home's value down and borrow the rest through your mortgage loan.

Down payment programs or grants
• A down payment grant or program typically refers to assistance provided by an organization such as a government or non-profit agency, to a homebuyer to assist them with the down payment for a home purchase. • The funds may be provided as an outright grant or may require repayment, such as when the home is sold.

Points
• Increases the lender's yield. (profit) • A Discount Point = 1% of the loan amount. • They are often used for buy-downs, where they may be called Discount Points. • A financing technique used to reduce the monthly payments of a loan • AKA: Discount Points • An upfront lender charges to increase the yield or lower the interest rate on the loan.

LTV (Loan to Value)

• The relationship between the amount of the mortgage loan and the real estate value is pledged as collateral.
• The amount of money borrowed compared to the value (or price) of the property.
• The amount of a first mortgage divided by the lesser of.
    (1) the appraised value of the property or
    (2) the purchase price of the property.

Loan Balance

The amount a person owes on a loan.

Mortgage Insurance

- Mortgage insurance lowers the risk to the lender of making a loan to you, so you can qualify for a loan that you might not otherwise be able to get.
- Mortgage insurance protects the lender if you fall behind on your payments.
- Mortgage insurance is required if your down payment is less than 20 percent of the property value. Mortgage insurance also is typically required on FHA and USDA loans.
- If you have a conventional loan and your down payment is less than 20 percent, you will most likely have private mortgage insurance (PMI).

Mortgage insurance protects the lender, not you.

M.I.P. (FHA)

Mortgage Insurance Premium
- To qualify for an FHA-approved loan, you will be required to pay a mortgage insurance premium.
- This insurance protects lenders from incurring a loss in case you are unable to make monthly payments.
- Charged up-front and annually (in each monthly loan payment) to insure the lender against default on that portion of a loan above the borrower's equity.

Homeowners Protection Act (HPA)

The federal Homeowners Protection Act (HPA) provides rights to remove Private Mortgage Insurance (PMI) under certain circumstances. The law generally provides two ways to remove PMI from your home loan:
(1) requesting PMI cancellation or
(2) automatic or final PMI termination.

Interest Rate and Other Fees

- The interest rate is the rate of interest you'll pay for the loan; the fees are what the lender can charge you to obtain the loan.
- Your annual percentage rate (APR) reflects the total cost of repaying the loan annualized over the course of a year.
- In terms of fees, there are several important ones to look out for in your loan terms and conditions, including:
  - Origination fees
  - Closing costs (in the case of a mortgage or home refinance loan)
  - Prepayment penalties
  - Late payment penalties
  - Application fees

- o   Annual fees
- Lenders can decide which fees to charge and when to apply them.
- Annual Percentage Rate (A.P.R.)
- How much a loan costs over the loan term expressed as a rate.

The A.P.R. Includes the interest rate, points, broker fees, and certain other credit charges a borrower must pay.
This is not the interest rate that is used in setting your monthly payment.
Side-by-side APR's allow true comparison loan shopping.

Interest

The charge for borrowing money.

Homeowner's (hazard) insurance

- Homeowner's (hazard) insurance protects your property in the event of a loss such as fire.
- Many lenders require that you get a homeowner's policy before settlement.

Flood insurance

- Flood insurance will be required if the house is in a flood hazard area.
- After your loan is settled, if a change in flood insurance maps brings your home within a flood hazard area, your lender or servicer may require you to buy flood insurance at that time

PITI

- principal, interest, taxes, and insurance
- The four elements of a monthly mortgage payment; payments of principal and interest go directly towards repaying the loan while the portion that covers taxes and insurance (homeowner's and mortgage, if applicable) goes into an escrow account to cover the fees when they are due.

Mortgage Loan Instruments

Mortgage	Promissory Note
- A two-party security instrument for a promissory note that pledges the property in the event of loan default and creates personal liability for the borrower. - Automatically released when paid off. - Mortgage foreclosure must be pursued through the courts.	- The promise to pay. A promissory note pledges the property in loan default and creates personal liability for the borrower. - Terms of the note usually include Names of note holder and borrower, the total amount to be repaid, interest rate, payment intervals, and amounts. - A note alone is unsecured (without collateral) unless accompanied by a security instrument, which is a deed of trust or mortgage in real estate. ☐ A promissory note is NOT evidence of ownership. (title)

Mortgage documents are recorded in the county where the property is located.

Hypothecated Loans
Occurs when an asset is pledged as collateral to secure a loan, without giving up title, possession, or ownership rights.

Mortgage Clauses

Defeasance Clause	Satisfaction (of Mortgage)
You defeated the mortgage. It is paid in full.	Payment of a debt or obligation such as a judgment or mortgage.

Alienation (Due-on-Sale) Clause	Acceleration Clause
A loan provision makes the balance due and payable immediately upon a sale or transfer of ownership.	A provision in a note, mortgage, or deed of trust that makes the entire loan amount due immediately (accelerates all future payments to now) in the event of default.

Mortgage term
The term of your mortgage loan is how long you must repay the loan. For most types of homes, mortgage terms are typically 15, 20 or 30 years.

Automatic payment
Automatic payments allow you to set up recurring mortgage payments through your bank. Automatic payments can be a convenient way to make sure that you make your payments on time.

Co-signer or co-borrower
<ul><li>A co-signer or co-borrower is someone who agrees to take full responsibility to pay back a mortgage loan with you.</li><li>This person is obligated to pay any missed payments and even the full amount of the loan if you don't pay.</li><li>Some mortgage programs distinguish a co-signer as someone who is not on the title and does not have any ownership interest in the mortgaged home.</li><li>Having a co-signer or co-borrower on your mortgage loan gives your lender additional assurance that the loan will be repaid. But your co-signer or co-borrower's credit record and finances are at risk if you don't repay the loan.</li></ul>

Forbearance
<ul><li>Forbearance is when your servicer allows you temporarily to pay your mortgage at a lower rate or</li></ul>

temporarily to stop paying your mortgage.
- Your servicer may grant you forbearance if, for example, you recently lost your job, suffered from a disaster, or from an illness or injury that increased your health care costs.
- Forbearance is a type of loss mitigation.

Assumption of Mortgage

- An assumable mortgage is a loan that can be transferred from one party to another with the initial terms remaining in place.
- For buyers and sellers in a rising interest rate environment, taking advantage of an assumable mortgage is a great option that makes financial sense—if done properly.

Subject to the Mortgage

- Buying "Subject to."
- The term "taking subject to" is when the buyer incurs no liability to repay the loan. The loan stays in the seller's name, but the buyer gets the deed and therefore controls the property.
- The buyer gets his/her own loan.

Maturity Date

The due date of the loan. (30 years for most residential loans).

"Or More" Clause

A contract provision that allows prepayment without penalty.

Prepayment

By making prepayments on a home loan, you pay off your principal loan earlier than the amortization schedule and reduce the total amount you pay in interest towards the mortgage

Prepayment Penalty

The amount set by the creditor as a penalty to the debtor for paying off the debt before it matures

Subordination Agreement

An agreement between lenders where one changes position with another lender. The lender in first position gets paid first.

Types of Loans

Straight Loan

- An interest-only mortgage is a loan with scheduled payments that require you to pay only the interest for a specified amount of time.
- Paying off the loan balance all at once.
- Creates a Balloon Payment

Partially Amortized

- A partially amortized loan doesn't settle the loan in full.
- It repays it partially. The part of the loan that hasn't been repaid is called a balloon payment.
- You and the lender decide when the balloon payment is scheduled. Balloon Payment

Balloon Payment Loan

- For mortgages, a balloon loan means that the loan has a larger-than-usual, one-time payment, typically at the end of the loan term.
- This one-time payment is called a "balloon payment, and it is higher than your other payments, sometimes much higher.
- If you cannot pay the balloon amount, you might have to refinance, sell your home, or face foreclosure.

Amortized Loans

- Amortization focuses on spreading out loan payments over time.
- When applied to an asset, amortization is like depreciation.
- REVERSES OVER TIME
- Amortization means paying off a loan with regular payments over time, so that the amount you owe decreases with each payment.
- Most home loans amortize, but some mortgage loans do not fully amortize, meaning that you would still owe money after making all your payments.

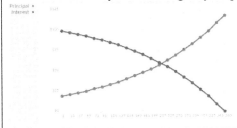

Negative Amortization

- Negative amortization means that even when you pay, the amount you owe will still go up because you are not paying enough to cover the interest.

- The quickest way to go underwater.

Adjustable-Rate Mortgage (ARM)

- An adjustable-rate mortgage (ARM) is a type of loan for which the interest rate can change, usually in relation to an index interest rate.
- Your monthly payment will go up or down depending on the loan's introductory period, rate caps, and the index interest rate.
- With an ARM, the interest rate and monthly payment may start out lower than for a fixed-rate mortgage, but both the interest rate and monthly payment can increase substantially.
- ARMs come with the risk of higher payments in the future that you might not be able to predict. But in some situations, an ARM might make sense for you. If you are considering an ARM, be sure to understand the tradeoffs.

Initial adjustment cap

- This cap determines how much the interest rate can increase the first time it adjusts after the fixed-rate period expires.

Interest rate cap

- An interest rate cap, sometimes referred to as an annual cap, is the maximum interest rate increase that can occur annually for an adjustable-rate mortgage (ARM) even if the rate would have increased more under market interest rates.

Lifetime adjustment cap

- This cap determines how much the interest rate can increase in total, over the life of the loan.

Margin

- The margin is the number of percentage points added to the index by the mortgage lender to set your interest rate on an adjustable-rate mortgage (ARM) after the initial rate period ends.
- The margin is set in your loan agreement and won't change after closing.

Fixed Rate vs. Adjustable-Rate Mortgages

This choice affects:
1. Whether your interest rate can change.
2. Whether your monthly principal and interest payment can change and its amount.
3. How much interest you will pay over the life of the loan.

Two of the most common types of mortgage loans are fixed-rate mortgages and adjustable-rate mortgages. The interest rate on a fixed-rate mortgage will remain the same for the entire life of your loan, while the interest rate on an adjustable-rate mortgage (ARM) may adjust at regular intervals and may be tied to an economic index, including a rate for Treasury securities. When the interest rate on an ARM adjusts, it may cause your payment to increase.

Fixed rate	Adjustable rate
• Lower risk, no surprises. • Higher interest rate. • Rate does not change. • Monthly principal and interest payments stay the same. • Historically: Chosen by 70-75% of buyers. • With a fixed-rate loan, your interest rate and monthly principal and interest payment will stay the same. • Your total monthly payment can still change—for example, if your property taxes, homeowner's insurance, or mortgage insurance might go up or down.	• Higher risk, uncertainty. • Lower interest rate to start. • After initial fixed period, rate can increase or decrease based on the market. • Monthly principal and interest payments can increase or decrease over time. • Historically: Chosen by 25-30% of buyers. • Adjustable-rate mortgages (ARMs) offer less predictability but may be cheaper in the short term. • You may want to consider this option if, for example, you plan to move again within the initial fixed period of an ARM. • ARMs are. marketed to people with lower credit scores tend to be riskier for the borrower.

Conventional Mortgage Loan

- A conventional loan is any mortgage loan that is not insured or guaranteed by the government (such as under Federal Housing Administration, Department of Veterans Affairs, or Department of Agriculture loan programs).
- There are two main categories of conventional loans:

Conforming loans
- Conforming loans have maximum loan amounts that are set by the government. Other rules for conforming loans are set by Fannie Mae or Freddie Mac, companies that provide backing for conforming loans.

Non-conforming loans
- Non-conforming loans are less standardized. Eligibility, pricing, and features can vary widely by lender, so it's particularly important to shop around and compare several offers.

Many of the loans that got people in trouble during the loan and foreclosure crisis of 2005-2008 fell in the "non-conforming (other)" category.

Jumbo Loan is a non-conforming loan
- A jumbo mortgage is a mortgage loan that may have high credit quality but is in an amount above conventional conforming loan limits.

Reverse Mortgage

- A reverse mortgage allows homeowners aged 62 or older to borrow against their home equity. It is called a "reverse" mortgage because, instead of making payments to the lender, you receive money from the lender.

- Most reverse mortgage loans are Home Equity Conversion Mortgages (HECMs). A HECM must be paid off when the last surviving borrower or Eligible Non-Borrowing Spouse*:
  - Dies
  - Sells their home, or
  - No longer lives in the home as their principal residence, including wanting to move closer to family, downsizing, or moving into an assistive living or a nursing facility.

An "Eligible Non-Borrowing Spouse" is a term used for your spouse when he/she is not a co-borrower but qualifies under the U.S. Department of Housing and Urban Development's (HUD) rules to stay in your home after you have died.

Home Equity Line of Credit (HELOC)

- A home equity line of credit (HELOC) is a line of credit that allows you to borrow against your home equity.
- Equity is the amount your property is currently worth, minus the amount of any mortgage on your property.
- For most HELOCs, you will receive special checks or a credit card, and you can borrow money for a specified time from when you open your account.
- This period is known as the "draw period."
- During the "draw period," you can borrow money, and you must make minimum payments.
- When the "draw period" ends, you will no longer be able to borrow money from your line of credit.
- After the "draw period" ends you may be required to pay off your balance all at once or you may be allowed to repay over a certain period. If you cannot pay back the HELOC, the lender could foreclose on your home.

Subprime Loan

- Historically, subprime borrowers were defined as having FICO scores below 600.
- Interest rates are higher because of the greater risk of default.

Seller Financing

- Seller (Owner) financing (installment and land contract/contract for deed)
- The seller loans the buyer the money to purchase the property.
- The seller gets a note instead of cash.
- Seller financing might be offered when a buyer cannot qualify for a bank loan.
- Under a land contract, the seller retains the legal title to the property, while permitting the buyer to take possession of it for most purposes other than legal ownership.
- When the full purchase price has been paid including any interest, the seller is obligated to convey (to the buyer) legal title to the property.
- An initial down payment from the buyer to the seller is usually also required.
- The most common use is used as a form of short-term seller financing.

Package Mortgage

- A package mortgage is a loan that covers real estate and personal property being sold with the real estate.

- The buyer of a house in which furniture is being included in the sale may want to apply for a package loan.

Blanket Mortgage

- A blanket mortgage is a developer loan.
- It is used when a subdivider would like to finance the entire project but be allowed to release certain lots.

Partial Release Clause

- The partial release clause is often used with a blanket mortgage.
- The partial release is a mortgage provision allowing some of the pledged collateral to be released from the mortgage contract if certain conditions are met.
- In other words, the partial release allows some of your collateral can be taken off the mortgage once a certain amount of the loan has been paid.
- The application process could require submitting a survey map to show which part of the property will be released and what will remain with the lenders as the mortgage continues to be paid.

Bridge Loans

- A bridge loan is a type of short-term loan, typically taken out for a period of 2 weeks to 3 years pending the arrangement of larger or longer-term financing.

Bi-weekly Payment

- In a bi-weekly payment plan, the mortgage servicer is collecting half of your monthly payment every two weeks, resulting in 26 payments over the course of the year (totaling one extra monthly payment per year).
- By making additional payments and applying your payments to the principal, you may be able to pay off your loan early.

Deed of Trust

- A three-party security instrument for a promissory note conveys "naked title." It gives the trustee a right and process to foreclose without resort to courts in the event of default.
- The three parties are the borrower (trustor), the trustee, and the lender (beneficiary of the trust).

Trustor	Trustee	Beneficiary
The borrower	The third party	The Lender

Second Mortgage

- A second mortgage or junior lien is a loan you take out using your house as collateral while you still

have another loan secured by your house.
- Home equity loans and home equity lines of credit (HELOCs) are examples of second mortgages.

Mortgage Refinance

Mortgage refinance is when you take out a new loan to pay off and replace your old loan. Common reasons to refinance are to lower the monthly interest rate, lower the mortgage payment, or to borrow additional money.

Wrap Around Loan

A loan wrapped around another loan. It is used in Seller Financing when the seller has a remaining balance secured by his/her property.

Lien Theory States	Title Theory States
• In lien theory states, the borrower holds the title to the property.	• The lender is viewed as the owner of mortgage property. • Title theory state's function where banks or mortgage lenders hold the title of a property until it is paid in full.

Government Loans

- Owner Occupied Mortgages
- These programs usually require a smaller down payment. They most likely will be owner-occupied loans.

FHA

- FHA is most like an insurance company.
- FHA insures lenders against loss. FHA ensures the bank that the bank will get its money.
- To get an FHA loan, you will go to a qualified lender.
- Down-payments are as low as 3.5%.
- FHA Loans require an FHA approved appraiser.
- FHA has no pre-payment penalties.
- Loan is assumable for qualified individuals.

Mortgage Insurance (MIP) for FHA Insured Loan - FHA funding fee

- Mortgage insurance is a policy that protects lenders against losses that result from defaults on home mortgages.
- FHA requires both upfront and annual mortgage insurance for all borrowers, regardless of the amount of down payment.

Closing Costs and Allowable Charges

- While FHA requirements define which closing costs are allowable as charges to the borrower, the specific costs and amounts that are deemed reasonable, and customary are determined by each local FHA office.
- All other costs are generally not allowed and are usually paid by the seller when buying a new home or paid by the lender when refinancing your existing FHA loan.

Sources of acceptable down payments

- Savings
- Financial gift from a family member
- Grant or down-payment assistance

FHA Limits

- The FHA has a maximum loan amount that it will insure, which is known as the FHA lending limit.
- Loan limits are based on geographic location.

Example of Loan Limits

Single	Duplex	Triplex	Four-plex
$356,362	$456,275	$551,500	$685,400

VA Mortgage

- VA acts a guarantee company.
- The VA guarantees a portion of the loan to reduce the risk of loss to the lender.
- A VA loan is a loan program offered by the Department of Veterans Affairs (VA) to help servicemembers, veterans, and eligible surviving spouses buy homes.
- The VA does not make the loans but sets the rules for who may qualify and the mortgage terms.
- The loans generally are only available for a primary residence.
- The Department of Veterans' Affairs (VA) has a loan program for eligible veterans, current servicemembers, and surviving spouses.
- The loans are made by private lenders and guaranteed by the VA.
- No pre-payment penalty.
- The VA guarantee takes effect when the loan closes.
- VA will loan up to the Certificate of Reasonable Value.
- Qualified individuals can purchase with no down payment if the Certificate of Reasonable Value equals the purchase price.

Entitlement

- The VA guarantees a portion of these loans to help lenders offset the risk of loans.
- To get your basic entitlement, take $36,000 and multiple by four. That's the initial amount you could borrow using a VA loan. To get your bonus entitlement, take the conforming loan limits for your county (let's say $548,250 in this case) and divide by four: $548,250 / 4 = $137,062.
- Certificate of Eligibility
- Your Certificate of Eligibility (COE) verifies you meet service requirements for a VA loan.
- Every veteran must meet one of the following service requirements before they can obtain a VA loan:

- 181 days of service during peacetime
- 90 days of service during war time
- 6 years of service in the Reserves or National Guard
- Some surviving spouses of service members who have died in the line of duty are also eligible
- Assumptions
- VA Loans may be assumed by qualified non-veterans. The veteran must have the assumption approved by the lender.

USDA Loans

- The Rural Housing Service, part of the U.S. Department of Agriculture (USDA) offers mortgage programs with no down payment and generally favorable interest rates to rural homebuyers who meet the USDA's income eligibility requirements.
- The US Department of Agriculture_ offers a similar program to the FHA and VA, designed for low- and moderate-income borrowers in rural areas.
- USDA loans can be a good option for borrowers who have little available savings. They offer zero down payments and are usually cheaper than FHA loans.
- Borrowers will pay an upfront fee as well as ongoing mortgage insurance premiums to the USDA.
- USDA loans are direct loans to the borrower.
- Homes must be modest housing.

Farm Service Agency

Through USDA, the Farm Service Agency lends mortgage money to farmers in rural areas.

Warehousing (Mortgage Money Markets)

Federal Reserve System

THE FED
- The United States Money Market is regulated by the FED.
- The FED regulates the flow of money through banks.
- The FED controls reserve requirements and discount rates.
- The FED is the bank's bank.

Lender of last resort
- The Federal Reserve serves as the lender of last resort to those institutions that cannot obtain credit elsewhere and the collapse of which would have serious implications for the economy.

The Discount Rate

- The discount rate is the interest rate charged to commercial banks and other depository institutions on loans they receive from their regional Federal Reserve Bank's lending facility—the discount window.
- Simply put. Discount rates are the interest charged to banks.

The U.S Treasury

The U.S. Treasury is the United States money fiscal manager.

FDIC

Federal Deposit Insurance Corporation insures bank deposits up to $250,000.

Sources of Real Estate Money

- Commercial Banks
- Savings and Loans
- Northeastern United States Mutual Savings Banks
- Mortgage Banking Companies
- Life Insurance Companies

Mortgage Brokers	Mortgage Bankers - Lenders
Some companies, known as "mortgage brokers," offer to find you a mortgage lender willing to make you a loan. A mortgage broker may operate as an independent business and may not be operating as your "agent" or representative.	A lender typically makes loans to borrowers directly. They receive payment through fees charged to you at settlement, payment from interest when you make your monthly mortgage payments and payments if they sell your loan or the servicing of your loan after settlement.

The Primary Mortgage Market	The Secondary Mortgage Market
• The first point of contact. • The bank. • The Mortgage broker	• The secondary mortgage market is a marketplace where lenders sell mortgages and investors buy financial products backed by those mortgages.

Warehousing

Fannie Mae	Freddie Mac	Ginnie Mae
Federal National Mortgage Association	Federal Home Loan Mortgage Corporation	Government National Mortgage Association
Government Sponsored Publicly Traded.	Government Sponsored Government Chartered.	Federal Agency.
Sells government guaranteed bonds.	Created for the Conventional Mortgage Market (NON-government).	
Purchases FHA, VA, and Conventional Mortgage.	Purchases FHA, VA, and Conventional Mortgages.	Purchases FHA, VA, and Rural Development Mortgages.
Works with larger banks.	Works with smaller thrift banks.	

Fannie Mae and Freddie Mac directly affect conventional lending for home buying.
☐ Conventional Mortgages are all mortgages that have no direct relationship to the government. (Non-VA, Non-FHA, Nonfarm Loans)

Government Sponsored Entities

• A government-sponsored enterprise (GSE) is a quasi-governmental entity established to enhance the flow of credit to specific sectors of the American economy.
• Government-sponsored enterprises (GSEs) do not lend money to the public directly; instead, they guarantee third-party loans and purchase loans in the secondary market, ensuring liquidity.
• Government-sponsored enterprises (GSEs) also issue short- and long-term bonds (agency bonds) that carry the implicit backing of the U.S. government.
• Mortgage issuers Fannie Mae and Freddie Mac are examples of government-sponsored enterprises (GSEs).

Mortgage-Backed Securities

• Fannie Mae, Freddie Mac, and private firms buy loans and package them into mortgage-backed securities. Then, investors from all over the world buy those products and keep the cycle going.
• Fannie and Freddie guarantee the loans that are bundled into the mortgage-backed securities they sell to investors.

The Community Reinvestment Act (CRA)

- The Community Reinvestment Act (CRA), enacted in 1977, requires the Federal Reserve and other federal banking regulators to encourage financial institutions to help meet the credit needs of the communities in which they do business, including low- and moderate-income (LMI) neighborhoods.
- Requires Fannie Mae and Freddie Mac, to attempt to make housing more affordable.
- Affordable housing goals are set, with both are required to have at least 30% of their mortgage purchases come from mortgages taken out by low- to moderate-income families and individuals.
- For Fannie and Freddie to be able to provide a guarantee, they require originating banks (the banks that originally lend the money directly to the borrower) to make sure they check the creditworthiness of the borrower.
- Originating banks must follow certain rules and guidelines (e.g., at least 20% down payment or the requirement to pay mortgage insurance premiums); documented proof of income and ability to repay; documented appraisal of the home by a professional and neutral third party; and so on. These rules and guidelines are meant to reduce the likelihood of a default on the loan.
- When all parts of the whole are functioning as they should, more people are able to afford to buy a home, debts are repaid, and investors make money

Credit Laws and Regulations

Truth in Lending Act (TILA)

Regulation Z

- Protects consumers against inaccurate and unfair credit billing and credit card practices.
- Provides consumers with rescission rights.
- Provides for rate caps on certain dwelling-secured loans.
- Imposes limitations on home equity lines of credit and certain closed-end home mortgages.
- Provides minimum standards for most dwelling-secured loans; and
- Prohibits unfair or deceptive mortgage lending practices.

Regulation Z is the implementing regulation of the Truth in Lending Act.

☐ TILA and Regulation Z do not tell financial institutions how much interest they may charge or whether they must grant a consumer a loan.

- The Truth in Lending Act (TILA) was enacted on May 29, 1968, as title I of the Consumer Credit Protection Act.
- Disclosure of the cost of credit transactions.
- Disclosure of the APR.
- Finance charges must include.
  - o Interest
  - o Loan fees
  - o Points
  - o Service charges
  - o Property insurance

- o Credit insurance
- o Finder's fees

Regulation Z Three day right of rescission (cooling off period)

The right to rescind a financing contract for credit if the person's primary residence is used as collateral.

Regulation Z Advertising

- Trigger terms may not be used in advertising unless the ad includes full disclosure.

Trigger Terms
- o Amount of down payment
- o Amount of loan or cash price
- o Finance charges
- o Annual percentage rate
- o Number of payments
- o Amount of payments
- o Due dates of payments
- o Total of all payments unless it is a mortgage for a first mortgage.

Advertising Defined

Regulation Z broadly defines advertisements as commercial messages provided in any medium that promote — directly or indirectly a credit transaction.
This definition encompasses messages in

newspapers	magazines	leaflets,	radio
internet	signage	fliers	television

However, advertisements do not include direct, personal contacts such as follow-up letters to customers about specific transactions (including oral or written negotiations).

Regulation Z Coverage

- Loans for real estate purposes
- Loans on non-real estate purposes for up to $25,000

RESPA (Also Known as Regulation X)

Real Estate Settlement Procedures Act
PURPOSE:
The main objective was to protect homeowners by assisting them in becoming better educated while shopping for real estate services, and
☐eliminating kickbacks and referral fees when no services were rendered.

RESPA Requirements

- Deliver informational book, Settlement Costs and You delivered to each loan applicant(s).

- Provide a Good Faith Estimate no later than 3 business days of the loan application.
- Loan closing expenses prepared on a HUD 1.
- RESPA applies to first mortgages only of homes of one to four dwelling units.

Mortgage Application and Processing Fees

In addition to the charges to originate your loan, there are other charges for services that will be required to get your mortgage. Examples include

Appraisal	Credit report	Flood Certificate	Tax Services
Inspection's	Recording charges	HOA fees	Transfer Tax

Survey
- Lenders or title insurance companies may require a survey to disclose the location of the property.
- The survey is a drawing of the property showing the location of the house and other improvements on the property.
- Even if not required by your lender, information provided by a current property survey, such as the true property

Homeowner's Insurance

As a condition to settle, many lenders will require that you procure homeowner's insurance, flood insurance or other hazard insurance to protect the property from loss.

Loan Application

To get the mortgage process underway, you must fill out and submit a loan application to your lender. The application form and its supporting documents are used to determine your eligibility for the home mortgage.

Loan Approval

Your loan is approved when the lenders officially grant you a mortgage, based on the information you proved in your loan application.

Equal Credit Opportunity Act

Prohibits Discrimination

Protected Classes

The Federal Trade Commission (FTC), the nation's consumer protection agency, enforces the Equal Credit Opportunity Act (ECOA), which prohibits credit discrimination based on:
1. race
2. color
3. religion

4. national origin
5. sex
6. marital status
7. age
8. or because you get public assistance

Creditors may ask you for most of this information in certain situations, but they may not use it when deciding whether to give you credit or when setting the terms of your credit.

Not everyone who applies for credit gets it or gets the same terms.

Redlining

- Redlining is a discriminatory practice that puts services (financial and otherwise) out of reach for residents of certain areas based on race or ethnicity. It can be seen in the systematic denial of mortgages, insurance, loans, and other financial services based on location (and that area's default history) rather than on an individual's qualifications and creditworthiness. Notably, the policy of redlining is felt the most by residents of minority neighborhoods.
- ☐ Redlining cases are often very difficult to prove because the courts recognize that lenders must be free to consider legitimate business interests by making investments that are economically sound.

CFPB

 Consumer Financial Protection Bureau

- As a result of the Great Recession in 2008, a new government agency that protects consumers was formed, the Consumer Financial Protection Bureau.

The Dodd-Frank Wall Street Reform and Consumer Protection Act of 2010 ended the "TOO BIG TO FAIL" policy.

- The CFPB was charged with protecting consumers against abuses related to credit cards, mortgages, and other financial products.

The stated aim of the legislation is

- To promote the financial stability of the United States by improving accountability and transparency in the financial system, to end "too big to fail," to protect the American taxpayer by ending bailouts, to protect consumers from abusive financial services practices, and for other purposes.

TILA RESPA Integrated Disclosure Law

- The CFPB Combined the four forms from Regulation Z (2 forms) and Regulation X (2 forms) and developed two new forms that makes financing real estate easier to understand. `
- The Good Faith Estimate
- The Closing Disclosure

This law is also known as Know Before you Owe.

The Good Faith Estimate Provides for Comparing Loans

Good Faith Estimate

- Provide a Good Faith Estimate no later than 3 business days of the loan application.
- The GFE is a three-page form designed to encourage you to shop for a mortgage loan and settlement services so you can determine which mortgage is best for you.
- It shows the loan terms, and the settlement charges you will pay if you decide to go forward with the loan process and are approved for the loan.
- It explains which charges can change before your settlement and which charges must remain the same.
- It contains a shopping chart allowing you to easily compare multiple mortgage loans and settlement costs, making it easier for you to shop for the best loan.
- The Loan Estimate tells you important details about the loan you have requested.
- Your loan officer cannot require you to provide documents verifying this information before providing you with a Loan Estimate.

Closing Disclosure

A Closing Disclosure is a required five-page form that provides final details about the mortgage loan you have selected. It includes the loan terms, your projected monthly payments, and how much you will pay in fees and other costs to get your mortgage.

Timing

- A Loan Estimate is required to be delivered to the homebuyer within three business days of the lender's receipt of the mortgage application.
- The final Closing Disclosure needs to be delivered to the homebuyer at least three business days before closing is scheduled.
- Upon receiving the Closing Disclosure, homebuyers are instructed to compare their Loan Estimate with the Closing Disclosure to ensure no significant changes have occurred.
- A change by more than 10%; will require a revised loan Estimate

Business day means a day on which your offices are open to the public for carrying on substantially all its business functions.

After Settlement

- RESPA requires that lenders give you disclosures concerning the servicing of your loan and any escrow account. RESPA also gives you certain protections regarding the timely payment of your taxes and insurance.

Loan Servicer

The company that collects your mortgage payments is your loan servicer.

Denial of Credit

- The lender has 30 days to notify the potential borrower that they have been denied a loan.

Obtaining Your Credit Report

- The Fair Credit Reporting Act ("FCRA") requires a lender or mortgage broker that denies your loan application to tell you whether it based its decision on information contained in your credit report. If that information was a reason for the denial, the notice will tell you where you can get a free copy of the credit report.
- You have the right to dispute the accuracy or completeness of any information in your credit report. If you dispute any information, the credit reporting agency that prepared the report must investigate free of charge and notify you of the results of the investigation.

Credit Agencies

The Fair Credit Reporting Act (FCRA) requires each of the three nationwide credit reporting companies — Equifax, Experian, and Trans Union — to give you a free copy of your credit report, at your request, once every 12 months.

CFPB Rules on Financing and Risky Loan Features

- A high-risk mortgage is a mortgage loan that falls outside of the normal scope of risk that lenders are used to. When you are dealing with a high-risk mortgage, everything else that has to do with the loan changes. Your lender will have different programs for you and different options within those programs.

Sub-Prime Mortgage – Risky

- Subprime borrowers typically have weakened credit histories and reduced repayment capacity. Subprime loans have a higher risk of default than loans to prime borrowers.

Jumbo Loans – Risky

- Each year Fannie Mae, Freddie Mac, and their regulator, the Federal Housing Finance Agency (FHFA), set a maximum amount for loans that they will buy from lenders.
- Jumbo loans are allowed to exceed these loan limits.
-

Risky

Balloons	Longer than 30 years	Interest Onlys
Negatives	Adjustable-Rate Mortgages	Non-conforming

Fraud in Lending

Mortgage Fraud

- The FBI investigates mortgage fraud.
- Mortgage loan fraud can be divided into two broad categories:
1. Fraud for housing, in which someone submits inaccurate information to be able to buy a home under more favorable terms.
2. Fraud for profit, in which a real estate professional falsifies information so that they can get more money out of a transaction.

PENALTIES
- Prison sentence of 30 years can be imposed, as well as a $1,000,000 fine.

Predatory Lending

- Lending in hopes that the borrower defaults and the lender can take the borrower's equity.
- **USURY**: Charging higher interest rates for people with not-perfect credit. The rates may violate interest rates maximums.
- Bait and Switch is moving a borrower to a different loan they can't afford at the last moment.
- The Homeownership and Protection Act of 1994 was created at identifying predatory practices.

Underwriting

- The process of evaluating a mortgage loan application to determine the risk involved for the lender. Underwriting involves an analysis of the borrower's creditworthiness and the quality of the property.
- Person in a lending institution who determines if a borrower qualifies for a loan.
- Computerized Loan Origination System is a specialized computer software that ties directly into the underwriter.

Ability-to-repay rule

- The ability-to-repay rule is the reasonable and good faith determination most mortgage lenders are required to make that you can pay back the loan.

Debt to Income Ratio

The debt-to-income ratio is all your debt payments divided by your gross monthly income.
In most cases □ 43% is the highest debt to income ratio to get a qualified mortgage.

Credit Scoring

- A credit score predicts how likely you are to repay a loan on time.
- A credit score is a numerical expression based on a level analysis of a person's credit files, to represent the creditworthiness of an individual. A credit score is primarily based on a credit report, information typically sourced from credit bureaus.

Module Four: Financing Quiz

□ QUESTION	ANSWER
1. The owner of the loan on a property. a. Mortgage Holder b. Grandparent c. Mortgage Giver d. Investor	a. Mortgage Holder A mortgage holder is a person or company that has a right to enforce a mortgage loan agreement. Mortgagee
2. Mortgage companies specialize in a. purchasing mortgages originated by other financial institutions. b. borrowing money through the creation of mortgages that is used to invest in real estate. c. investing and maintaining mortgages that they create. d. originating mortgages and selling those mortgages.	d. originating mortgages and selling those mortgages. Mortgage companies are in the primary mortgage market. They originate mortgages and sell those mortgages.
3. A mortgage loan in which one party pays an initial lump sum to reduce the homeowner's monthly payments. a. Balloon Mortgage b. Reverse Mortgage c. Buy-down Mortgage (pay points) d. Interest Only Mortgage	c. Buy-down Mortgage (pay points) A mortgage rate buydown is when a borrower pays an additional charge in exchange for a lower interest rate on their mortgage. (points)
4. As a cost of obtaining a real estate loan, one point equals 1 percent of the…? a. Loan amount. b. Purchase price c. Down payment. d. Appraised value	a. loan amount. Points paid to the lender increases the lender's yield. Your lender may offer you the option of paying points when you take out a mortgage on a house purchase or refinance an existing home loan.
5. A point is a. 10% of the sale price b. The Sale Price c. 1% of the loan amount d. 1% of the sale price	c. 1% of the loan amount A point is 1% of the loan amount and may be called a discount point. This is interest paid at the closing to "buy down" the rate to a lower rate.
6. MATCH: a fee paid in exchange for a reduction in the interest rate. a. Discount points b. Earnest money c. Equity d. DTI Ratio	a. Discount points One point costs 1 percent of your mortgage amount (or $1,000 for every $100,000.
7. MATCH: the difference between the fair market value of a property and the current balances of any mortgages and other liens against the property. a. Escrow account	d. Equity Equity is the difference between what you owe on your mortgage and what your home is

b. Escrow c. Discount point d. Equity	currently worth.
8. It is calculated by dividing the mortgage balance by the home's current market value. a. Loan-to-Value b. Loan-to-Appraisal c. Negative Equity d. Loan-to-Sales Price	a. Loan-to-Value The loan-to-value (LTV) ratio is a financial term used by lenders to express the ratio of a loan to the value of an asset purchased.
9. MATCH: describes the relationship between the value of a home and the mortgage loan for which it is serving as security a. Promissory b. Premium c. Mortgage d. LTV ratio	d. LTV ratio Loan-to-value is an often-used ratio in mortgage lending to determine the amount necessary to put in a down-payment and whether a lender will extend credit to a borrower.
10. A buyer is getting a new mortgage with a 95% loan-to-value ratio. The final loan amount the lender will lend the buyer is determined by? a. The appraised value only. b. sales price only. c. higher of the sales price or appraised value. d. lower of the sales price or appraised value.	d. lower of the sales price or appraised value. Loan-to-value (LTV) ratios are based on the lower of the sale price or the appraised value.
11. It is calculated by dividing the mortgage balance by the home's current market value? a. Loan-to-Value b. Loan-to-Appraisal c. Negative Equity d. Loan-to-Sales Price	a. Loan-to-Value The loan-to-value (LTV) ratio is the ratio of a loan to the value of an asset purchased. It's calculated on the appraised value, not the purchase price.
12. Usually, borrowers making a down payment of less than _____ percent of the purchase price of the home will need to pay for mortgage insurance. a. 30 b. 20 c. 5 d. 10	b. 20 Private mortgage insurance, or PMI, is required on most home loans with a down payment of less than 20%.
13. MATCH: It is required if the buyer's down payment is less than 20% of the purchase price. a. Forced Place Homeowners/Tenants Insurance b. Underwriting Insurance c. Trust Fund Insurance d. Mortgage Insurance	d. Mortgage Insurance Mortgage Insurance is required for buyers that hold less than 20% equity in a property.
14. MATCH: Insurance policy that protects lenders in case Mortgage borrowers can't pay? a. disability insurance for housing b. life of loan insurance policy c. public mortgage insurance d. private mortgage insurance (PMI)	d. private mortgage insurance PMI, or private mortgage insurance, protects a lender in case you default on your primary mortgage and the house goes into foreclosure.
15. MATCH: What is the cost of borrowing money and	b. interest

is the money you pay a lender for a loan? a. rated interest b. interest c. gross income d. net interest	Interest is what is paid to borrow money. Interest is calculated as a percentage of a loan (or deposit) balance, paid to the lender periodically for the privilege of using their money.
16. MATCH: The cost of borrowing money. a. interesting charges b. charge back c. charge d. Interest	d. Interest Interest- The price that people pay to borrow money.
17. The interest rate that banks charge to preferred customers is known as the? a. Prime Rate b. Table Rate c. Capitalization Rate d. Index Rate	a. Prime Rate Prime rate by definition.
18. Why do mortgagees (the bank) require mortgagors (the person taking the loan.) to pay taxes and insurance with an escrow account? a. So those monthly payments are maximized. b. So that they can create a surplus of funds eligible to be transferred when the property is sold. c. So, they can make sure that the ownership bills get paid. d. So that an overage can be calculated and refunded for an emergency expense.	c. So they can make sure that the ownership bills get paid. An escrow account is usually an account that helps to manage a mortgage borrower's annual tax and insurance costs.
19. Property taxes and insurance premiums _____. a. stay the same when you purchase another home. b. stay consistent. c. change over time. d. fluctuate with the money supply.	c. change over time. Your monthly payment can go up over time: If property taxes or homeowners' insurance premiums rise. These costs are included in most mortgage payments.
20. When are borrowers required to have a Mortgage escrow account? a. escrow accounts are required if your down payment was less than 30%. b. escrow accounts are required if your down payment was less than 20%. c. escrow accounts are required if your down payment was less than 5%. d. escrow accounts are required if your down payment was less than 10%.	b. escrow accounts are required if your down payment was less than 20%. You may have the option to cancel your escrow payments to your lender once you have built up at least 20% equity in your home and are current on your payments.
21. Typically, it is required if the homeowner's down payment is less than 20% of the purchase price. a. Mortgage Insurance b. Forced Place Homeowners/Tenants Insurance c. Underwriting Insurance d. Trust Fund Insurance	a. Mortgage Insurance Mortgage Insurance is required for buyers that hold less than 20% equity in a property.

22. MATCH: a two-party instrument that assigns the borrower's ownership interest to the lender who may sell the property for non-payment of the debt. a. Mortgage b. Premium c. amortization d. Interest	a. Mortgage Mortgages are also known as "liens against property" or "claims on property." The mortgage is the security document.
23. While every loan program has specific forms you need to fill out and documents you need to submit, you will likely need to submit much of the same information for different loan packages. a. True b. False	a. True An agreement to lend money is documented with a set of mutual promises between the parties. Documents vary.
24. Which of the following defines a "mortgage loan"? a. An instrument that is used only in the exchange of real property b. A financial obligation that is unsecured but is used to buy a building c. A promissory note that is unpaid d. A loan collateralized with real estate.	d. A loan collateralized with real estate. A mortgage loan is a loan that is obtained by a borrower using real estate as the collateral or the security.
25. If there has not been an agreement to the contrary, all the following would qualify as a negotiable instrument, except a. A mortgage securing a promissory note b. A bank draft. c. A personal check d. An installment note	a. A mortgage securing a promissory note Mortgages are not negotiable. A promissory note is a negotiable instrument.
26. Hypothecation means? a. Retaining possession of the property while making payments b. A mortgage amount higher than the property is worth c. Homeowners' association fees d. A partial release clause	a. Retaining possession of the property while making payments Examples would be a car loan or a home loan.
27. Jim stopped making payments on his mortgage six months ago. What clause in the mortgage allows the bank to call the entire amount due to prepare for foreclosure? a. Acceleration b. Due-on-sale c. Exculpatory d. Penalty	a. Acceleration An acceleration clause is a contract provision that allows a lender to require a borrower to repay all an outstanding loan if certain requirements are not met.
28. When a borrower defaults on a loan that has an acceleration clause it permits the lender? a. seize the personal assets of the borrower. b. seize the real assets of the borrower. c. demand the entire note be paid immediately. d. All the above.	c. demand the entire note be paid immediately. An acceleration clause is a contract provision that allows a lender to require a borrower to repay all an outstanding loan if certain requirements are not met.

29. When a mortgage requires loan repayment, which clause can the lender use? a. Defeasance b. Alienation c. Prepayment d. Acceleration	b. Alienation Alienation is used upon the transfer of the property. Acceleration is used for a foreclosure.
30. The mortgage or deed of trust will contain a/an _____ that permits the lender to demand that the entire balance of the loan be repaid if the borrower defaults. a. Due on sale clause b. Acceleration clause c. Balloon clause d. Alienation clause	b. Acceleration clause If the borrower defaults, the lender can request repayment in full through an acceleration clause. Borrowers who don't pay back the loan may face foreclosure.
31. A person who is equally responsible for paying back debt under certain terms. a. co-op b. co-seller c. co-buyer d. collection agency e. co-signer	e. co-signer A co-signer is someone who joins you in applying for a loan. When they co-sign with you, they also take on the legal responsibility of paying back the loan if you don't. The loan will appear on their credit reports as well as yours.
32. MATCH: A clause in a trust deed stating that the rights of the beneficiary shall be secondary to a subsequent trust deed is called? a. a subordination clause. b. a subdivision clause. c. an alienation clause. d. an acceleration clause.	a. a subordination clause. The subordination clause stipulates that the current claim on any debts will have priority over any other future claims
33. MATCH: A mortgage where the homeowner pays only the interest on the loan for a specified amount of time. a. Reverse Mortgage b. Interest-Only Mortgage c. Fully Amortized Mortgage d. Partially Amortized Mortgage	b. Interest-Only Mortgage Interest-only mortgages are loans secured by real estate and often contain an option to make an interest payment.
34. Which payment plan requires periodic payments of interest only, with the principal due as a lump sum payment at maturity? a. straight b. amortized c. partially amortized d. amortized	a. straight With a straight (term) mortgage, interest is paid. The last payment is a balloon payment.
35. You are paying interest on a $75,000 mortgage for three years after which the entire loan is due. This is called a(n)? a. term mortgage b. amortized mortgage c. fully amortized mortgage	a. term mortgage (straight) Term (straight) mortgages are typically five years or less in length. During the loan's term, only the interest is paid off. Once the

d. reverse mortgage	mortgage matures, the entire principal becomes due.
36. A partially amortized mortgage requires a? a. Junior Lien b. Due on sale clause c. Partial Release d. Balloon Payment	d. Balloon Payment A partially amortized loan has periodic payments that do not fully amortize the loan by the end of the loan term. The larger final payment is known as a balloon payment.
37. MATCH: Loan – occurs when the mortgage payment includes the interest due and a small payment towards the principal that is not adequate to reduce the principal balance to zero by the end of the loan term? a. Partial amortization b. Interest-only loan c. amortization d. Negative amortization	a. Partial amortization The partial amortization method means that some principal is paid back each month. The loan balance is still outstanding at the end of the term. It has not yet been fully repaid.
38. Which of the following best describes a mortgage loan with initially low interest payments, but that requires one large payment due upon maturity (for example, at the end of five or seven years)? a. Balloon Mortgage b. Variable Rate Mortgage c. Partial release Mortgage d. Fixed thirty years	a. Balloon Mortgage A balloon mortgage is a loan that has an initial period of low or no monthly payments, at the end of which the borrower is required to pay off the full balance in a lump sum.
39. The final payment of a mortgage loan that is considerably larger than the required periodic payments because the loan amount was not fully amortized? a. balloon payment b. reversed payment c. amortized payment d. half payment	a. balloon payment The balloon payment is a large lump sum paid at the end of the loan term. Borrowers can reduce the fixed payment amount by making balloon payments at the end of their loan terms.
40. During the early years of an amortizing mortgage loan, the lender applies a. all the monthly payments to the outstanding principal balance. b. All of these are true. c. most of the monthly payment to the outstanding principal balance. d. most of the monthly payment to interest on the loan.	d. most of the monthly payment to interest on the loan. The interest is paid first.
41. MATCH: A loan in which the principal as well as the interest is payable in monthly or other periodic installments over the term of the loan. a. reverse mortgage b. amortized loan c. partially amortized loan d. term loan	b. amortized loan Each month, a portion of the payment goes toward the loan's principal and part of it goes toward interest. Also known as an installment loan, fully amortized loans have equal monthly payments.

42. A mortgage loan in which the interest rate remains the same for the life of the loan? a. Fixed-Rate Mortgage b. 6 months-no interest c. Variable Mortgage d. Interest Free Mortgage	a. Fixed-Rate Mortgage A fixed-rate mortgage (FRM) is a fully amortizing mortgage loan where the interest rate on the note remains the same through the term of the loan.
43. An interest rate that is set and does not change over a specific period. a. Indexed Rate b. Fixed interest rate c. Variable Rate d. Reverse Rate	b. Fixed interest rate In a fixed interest rate loan, the interest rate doesn't fluctuate during the fixed rate period. The borrower can then accurately predict their future payments.
44. What type of (ARM) Adjustable-Rate Mortgage loan that can be converted into a fixed-rate mortgage during a certain period. a. Convertible Fixed b. Convertible Reverse c. Convertible Annuity d. Convertible ARM	d. Convertible ARM Convertible ARMs are adjustable-rate mortgages (ARMs) that can be converted to fixed rate mortgages. Convertible ARMs are marketed to take advantage of falling interest rates. In general, the financial institution charges a switch fee.
45. Which best describes a mortgage loan with an interest rate that can change at any time, usually in response to the market or Treasury Bill rates. These types of loans usually start off with a lower interest rate comparable to a fixed-rate mortgage. a. Adjustable-Rate Mortgage b. Equitable mortgage c. Straight line mortgage d. Vacation home mortgage	a. Adjustable-Rate Mortgage There are various types of interest rate caps on adjustable-rate mortgages (ARMs).
46. A characteristic of an ARM is? a. There is no such thing as an ARM loan. b. The mortgage will vary over the life of the loan depending on fluctuations in the interest rate to which the loan is referenced. c. An arm loan is a direct reduction loan. d. The loan will remain the same over the life of the loan.	b. The mortgage will vary over the life of the loan depending on fluctuations in the interest rate to which the loan is referenced. A variable rate mortgage (ARM) allows the interest rate to vary throughout the loan's maturity period.
47. Once the initial rate has been set for an adjustable-rate mortgage (ARM), future interest rate adjustments are based on the upward and downward movements of? a. The price of houses. b. The stock market. c. Income tax returns. d. A standard index.	c. A standard index. Interest rate adjustments are based on the upward and downward movements of the selected index.
48. What term would be used for the maximum increase in the interest rate on an ARM? a. Cap b. Amortization	a. Cap Over the life of the loan, the cap says how much the interest rate can increase

c. Convertible	
49. Which of the following statements correctly identifies a defining characteristic of conventional mortgages? a. Their interest rates are set by the money supply. b. Their interest rates are set by the FED. c. Their interest rates are set by the lender. d. Their interest rates are set by Fannie Mae.	c. Their interest rates are set by the lender. This applies not only to conventional mortgage. All mortgage rates are set by the lender.
50. Which of the following loans fail to meet the bank or secondary market criteria for funding? a. FHA Loans b. Non-Conforming Loans c. VA Loans d. Conforming Loans e. outside normal underwriting guidelines.	b. Non-Conforming Loans Non-Conforming Loan: Loans not eligible for sale to Fannie Mae or Freddie Mac due to various reasons including loan amount, credit outside normal underwriting guidelines.
51. With a conventional loan, all the following are correct except? a. It requires anywhere from 5-20% down. b. The LTV typically does not exceed 80% without PMI. c. It is never insured by a private agency. d. It is used if a property loan is outside the FHA limits.	c. It is never insured by a private agency. A conventional loan is a mortgage that is not guaranteed or insured by any government agency,
52. Which is TRUE about nonconforming loans? a. They generally cost a homeowner more in fees. b. They can be sold on the secondary market. c. All states prohibit them from being predatory. d. They meet Fannie Mae/Freddie Max standards.	a. They generally cost a homeowner more in fees. Non-conforming loan are not compliant with Fannie Mae/Freddie Mac standards and can't be sold on the secondary market. Generally, nonconforming loans charge higher fees, but they are not always predatory.
53. A loan program that allows older homeowners to use part of the equity in their property as tax free income without having to sell is known as? a. Subprime loan b. Money mortgage c. Reverse mortgage d. Purchase and lease back	c. Reverse mortgage With a reverse mortgage, the borrower can access the value of the property he or she owns. The loans are offered to older homeowners (62+) and don't require monthly mortgage payments.
54. An arrangement in which an elderly homeowner borrows against the equity in his home and in return receives a regular monthly tax-free payment from the lender is a? a. Back Load Mortgage. b. Front Load Mortgage. c. Inverse Annuity. d. Reverse Mortgage.	d. Reverse Mortgage. If you're 62 or older – and want money to pay off your mortgage, supplement your income, or pay for healthcare expenses – you may consider a reverse mortgage. It allows you to convert part of the equity in your home into cash without having to sell your home or pay additional monthly bills.
55. MATCH: A way of borrowing money against the equity or assets that the homeowner has in the home to	d. Home Equity Line of Credit

pay for things such as home repairs, college education, or other personal uses. a. HAARP Loan b. Hard Money Loan c. A Shark Loan d. Home Equity Line of Credit	A HELOC Uses a Percentage of Your Home Equity to Provide a Revolving Line of Credit.
56. MATCH: Below the qualifications set for prime borrowers. Loans for borrowers who have poor credit, an unstable income history, or high debt ratios. a. Prepaids b. Table funding c. Subprime d. Payment shock	c. Subprime A subprime mortgage is a type of home loan issued to borrowers with low credit scores (often below 640 or 600, depending on the lender). Because the borrower is a higher credit risk, a subprime mortgage comes with a higher interest rate and closing costs than conventional loans.
57. When the sellers are lending part of the purchase price, they may secure the debt either with a deed of trust or a mortgage. For the seller, one benefit of the deed of trust is that? a. It is easier to pay. b. It guarantees a payment. c. It is easier to foreclose. d. It is easier to set up.	c. It is easier to foreclose. Nonjudicial foreclosures tend to be much quicker than judicial foreclosures.
58. When a blanket mortgage is placed upon a property and a "release schedule" is put into the mortgage showing the amount of the loan that must be paid off for each of the lots, those individual amounts would likely be proportionately larger for the first lots that are sold. The reason for this practice is? a. To increase the security value of the remaining lots b. To compensate for the loss of security as the lots under the blanket encumbrance are removed c. To compensate for the loss of security due to the best lots being sold first d. All the above.	d. All the above. All three of these are good reasons for requiring larger repayment when the first lots are sold under a blanket mortgage
59. When a principal has one mortgage covering two or more specific parcels of realty it would be considered a(n)? a. Assumption of Mortgage b. Conventional Mortgage c. Blanket Mortgage d. Balloon Mortgage	c. Blanket Mortgage Builders and developers use blanket loans to buy large tracts of land, then subdivide them into individual parcels and sell them one at a time.
60. A mortgage that covers more than one parcel of real estate is a? a. Plottage Mortgage b. Reverse Mortgage c. Blanket Mortgage d. Quick Equity Mortgage	c. Blanket Mortgage A blanket mortgage covers more than one parcel of land or lot and is usually used to finance subdivision developments.

61. A mortgage that occurs between the termination of one mortgage and the beginning of the next is known as a? a. Wraparound Mortgage b. Bridge Mortgage c. Package Mortgage d. Blanket Mortgage	b. Bridge Mortgage A bridge mortgage is used to cover the termination of one mortgage and the beginning of the next.
62. MATCH: a lien on the property that is junior, or subsequent, to another lien, or liens based on the order of recordation or by agreement among the lenders. a. Subprime lien b. Revolving lien c. Senior lien d. Subordinate lien	d. Subordinate lien Subordinate financing is not funded until prior liens are paid. Subordinate liens are also known as junior liens and junior financing.
63. Which is NOT a type of mortgage? a. Bi-Weekly b. Bi-monthly c. Reverse d. Construction	d. Construction There is not a bi-monthly mortgage product
64. Which of the following statements is most correct concerning the activities of mortgage companies? a. They are organized under federal laws and thus are not subject to state regulations b. They are not active in the field of government-insured loans c. They never service the loans they create d. They prefer negotiating loans that are salable in the secondary market	d. They prefer negotiating loans that are salable in the secondary market Mortgage companies often negotiate loans that are sold on the secondary market.
65. Which of the following is not true of the FHA (Federal Housing Administration)? a. The FHA provides the money for the mortgage b. The lender is insured against loss c. The loan is given through a qualified lender. d. In most cases mortgage insurance is charged	a. The FHA provides the money for the mortgage An FHA loan is a mortgage issued by an FHA-approved lender and insured by the Federal Housing Administration (FHA). Designed for low-to-moderate-income borrowers, FHA loans require a lower minimum down payments and credit scores than many conventional loans.
66. The mortgage insurance on an FHA loan? Is paid for by the lender. a. Protects the lender in the event of default b. Protects the lender in the event of the trustor's death c. Protects the borrower from a fire loss	b. Protects the lender in the event of default The mortgage insurance on an FHA loan protects the lender in the event of a default on the loan. It is paid for by the borrower.
67. Which of the following may not be a requirement of an FHA loan? a. The buyer must meet credit criteria b. Make a 15% down payment c. Work with an FHA approved lender	b. Make a 15% down payment As of 2019, you can borrow up to 96.5% of the value of a home with an FHA loan (meaning you'll need to make a down

	payment of only 3.5%). You'll need a credit score of at least 580 to qualify. With FHA loans, your down payment can come from savings, a financial gift from a family member or a grant for down-payment assistance.
68. The FHA is most like a? a. insurance company. b. guarantee company. c. a thrift. d. a savings and loan.	a. insurance company. An FHA loan is a mortgage issued by an FHA-approved lender and insured by the Federal Housing Administration (FHA).
69. A retired Air Force officer purchased a home using his VA loan. Several years later he sold the property and with the lender's approval the buyer assumed the loan. The buyer defaulted on the loan 6 months later. What is the responsibility of the retired Air Force officer is? a. Required to pay the interest not paid. b. Responsible for the PMI payments c. Required to pay the origination fees d. No longer responsible for anything regarding the property or the loan	d. No longer responsible for anything regarding the property or the loan The "lender's approval" is the key here. The lender will check the credit and finances of the person assuming your loan. Unlike a home sale, an assumption does not automatically remove your liability. Lender approval is required. Homeowners must ask for and obtain a release of liability from the lender or servicer.
70. What is not true of a VA loan? a. Little or no money down is required. b. The loan is insured. c. The veteran may have to supply the difference between the appraisal and the price he is paying. d. It is a government guaranteed loan.	a. The loan is insured. VA guarantees a portion of the loan, enabling the lender to provide you with more favorable terms.
71. Funds for a VA loan are provided by which of the following? a. Approved lenders b. Freddie Mac c. The VA department d. FHA	a. Approved lenders VA Home Loans are provided by banks and mortgage companies.
72. In helping a buyer to select a lender, if the buyer believes he has good credit and his income is documentable as a salary and by tax returns, the licensee might recommend a mortgage banker, instead of a mortgage broker, for all the following reasons EXCEPT a. confidence with the bank. b. previous relationships with the bank. c. more variety of loan programs available. d. keeping the business local.	c. more variety of loan programs available. A mortgage banker works for a bank or similar lending institution which provides you the money for the loan. A mortgage broker doesn't represent one institution but works with many to shop for a loan for a specific individual.
73. What is the term used for the person or organization who acts as an intermediary for the purpose of obtaining financing? a. mortgage broker b. mortgage banker c. credit repair specialist	a. mortgage broker A mortgage banker works for a bank or similar lending institution which provides you the money for the loan. A mortgage broker doesn't represent one institution but

d. 1031 specialist	works with many to shop for a loan for a specific individual.
74. Which entity is best suited to meet all borrowers' needs and goals while considering their financial situations? a. Savings & Loan b. Savings banks c. Mortgage Brokers d. Commercial Banks	c. Mortgage Brokers Brokers can select from a variety of lending options the best one for each client.
75. MATCH: a person that lends its own funds to borrowers for the purpose of purchasing a home. a. Fannie Mae b. Mortgage broker c. FHA d. Mortgage lender	d. Mortgage lender A mortgage lender is a bank or financial company that lends money to borrowers to purchase real estate.
76. A secured type of loan used for buying property? a. mortgage b. escrow mortgage c. bill of sale d. chattel bill	a. mortgage A mortgage is a loan secured by real estate. Borrowers have an agreement with lenders (usually banks) where they receive funds upfront and make payments over a set time until they pay the lender in full.
77. The secondary mortgage market evolved to develop? a. a market that Bankers can trade mortgages. b. a need for money to be deposited into Wall Street for any bail outs. c. a market that mortgage originators can sell mortgages to and replenish funds to make new loans. d. a need for collateralized loan packages.	c. a market that mortgage originators can sell mortgages to and replenish funds to make new loans. The secondary mortgage market is extremely large and liquid and helps to make credit equally available to all borrowers.
78. Which of the following is NOT a guarantor or insurer of federally insured mortgages? a. Federal Housing Administration (FHA) b. Veterans Administration (VA) c. Federal Deposit Insurance Corporation (FDIC)	c. Federal Deposit Insurance Corporation (FDIC) The Federal Deposit Insurance Corporation (FDIC) is an independent agency created by Congress to maintain stability and public confidence in the nation's financial system. Federal Deposit Insurance Corporation (FDIC) insures bank deposits up to $250,000.
79. Created in 1968 as a corporation that is wholly owned by the federal government. It guarantees payment on mortgages that meet specific criteria. a. Freddie Mac b. Ginnie Mae c. None of these are correct. d. Fannie Mae	b. Ginnie Mae Ginnie Mae is owned by the US Government
80. Fannie Mae and Freddie Mac experienced financial problems during the credit crisis because they?	c. invested heavily in subprime mortgages.

a. were unwilling to finance new mortgages. b. invested heavily in balloon mortgages. c. invested heavily in subprime mortgages. d. invested only in prime mortgages that offered very low returns.	A subprime mortgage is a type of loan granted to individuals with poor credit scores—640 or less, and often below 600—who, because of their deficient credit histories, would not be able to qualify for conventional mortgages.
81. Which of the warehousers are controlled by HUD (owned by the government), and offered by Congress to buy FHA loans or VA loans? a. Government National Secured Funds (GNSF) b. Federal Association of New Mortgage Activity (Fannie) c. Government National Mortgage Association (GNMA) d. Federal Home Loan Mortgage Association (FHLMA)	c. Government National Mortgage Association (GNMA) This federal government agency guarantees the timely repayment of principal and interest on mortgage-backed securities (MBSs) issued by approved lenders. Ginnie Mae is commonly known as GNMA.
82. What is the purpose of the secondary mortgage market? a. To underwrite mortgages. b. To create mortgage back securities to sell to countries for country diversification. c. To buy existing loans from banks and freeing up cash for primary mortgage entities to re-lend. d. To create more real estate buyers.	c. To buy existing loans from banks and freeing up cash for primary mortgage entities to re-lend. Prior to the secondary market, only large banks had the funds needed to provide the funds for the life of the loan, usually for 15 to 30 years.
83. The activities of Fannie Mae in the secondary mortgage market serve to? a. make construction standards uniform. b. insure or guarantee home loans. c. encourage lenders to make commercial loans. d. helps reduce mortgage rates by creating liquidity for mortgage lenders.	d. helps reduce mortgage rates by creating liquidity for mortgage lenders. By buying FHA, VA, and conventional loans made by direct lenders money is freed to re-lend.
84. Rate of interest charged on a loan, calculated to consider up-front loan fees and points. Usually higher than the contract interest rate. a. annual percentage rate b. Interest rate c. finance rate d. quarterly interest rate	a. annual percentage rate An annual percentage rate (APR) is the annual rate charged for borrowing or earned through an investment. APR is expressed as a percentage that represents the actual yearly cost of funds over the term of a loan
85. Who does the three-day right of rescission apply to? a. Refinances and junior loans b. Individual seller financing loans c. Quick loans d. Hypothecated loans	a. Refinances and junior loans The right of rescission is a right under the Truth in Lending Act (TILA) that allows a borrower to cancel a home equity loan or line of credit within three days of closing.
86. What Act was established to regulate loans that are publicly advertised? a. The Truth in Lending b. Equal Credit Opportunity c. Commercial Lending Practices d. Blind Advertising and Negotiations	a. The Truth in Lending TILA protects consumers in credit transactions by requiring clear disclosures of key terms in the lending arrangement. In most states, interest rates are capped.

87. Mortgage lenders are required to disclose financing costs and annual percentage rate to the borrower under which law or regulation? a. Equal Credit Opportunity Act b. Real Estate Settlement and Procedures Act c. Fair Housing laws d. Truth in Lending Act	d. Truth in Lending Act Truth in Lending Act deals with financing and disclosure.
88. MATCH: A word or phrase that, when used in advertising literature, requires the presentation of the terms of a credit agreement. a. Ginnie Mae b. Trigger terms c. Fannie Mae d. FDIC	b. Trigger terms Triggering terms are intended to help consumers compare credit offers on a fair and equal basis.
89. When a "trigger term" is used in an ad, The Truth in Lending Act requires the following disclosures except? a. amount of loan or cash price. b. pre-payment penalties. c. number, amount, and frequency of payments. d. amount of the down payment required.	b. pre-payment penalties. Pre-payment penalties are not a cost of the loan.
90. MATCH: fees involved in arranging for a mortgage or in transferring ownership of property? a. Amortization b. Discount point c. DTI Ratio d. Closing Costs	d. Closing Costs Closing costs are the expenses, beyond the property cost, that buyers and sellers incur to finalize a real estate transaction.
91. The Equal Credit Opportunity Act does not address? a. factors for borrower's analysis. b. interest rates. c. discrimination in lending. d. written credit denial letters.	b. interest rates. Interest rates do not fall under the ECOA.
92. Denial of a mortgage would be allowed if the denial was based on? a. Lack of income b. Sex c. Age d. Race	a. Lack of income The applicant must have a source of income to qualify for a loan.
93. Which of the following does the federal RESPA law require the lender to provide to all loan applicants within three days of application? a. Good faith estimate of all closing costs b. Truth-in-lending statement c. Notice of the three-day rescission right d. HUD-1 settlement form	a. good faith estimate of all closing costs RESPA requires the lender to provide the borrower with a good faith estimate within three days of loan application.
94. The intended purpose of the Dodd-Frank Wall Street Reform and Consumer Protection Act (Dodd-	a. promotes the financial stability of the United States by improving accountability and

Frank Act) is to? a. promote the financial stability of the United States by improving accountability and transparency in the marketplace. b. promote the standards in real estate by improving accountability. c. promote housing availability in the sub-prime mortgage market. d. promote integrity with real estate professionals.	transparency in the marketplace. The Dodd–Frank Wall Street Reform and Consumer Protection Act (commonly referred to as Dodd–Frank) is a United States federal law that was enacted on July 21, 2010. The law overhauled financial regulation in the aftermath of the Great Recession, and it made changes affecting all federal financial regulatory agencies and almost every part of the nation's financial services industry.
95. Which disclosure is required by TRID and summarizes potential closing costs for the borrower? a. 1099S b. Loan Estimate (LE) c. HUD 502 d. HUD 1099	b. Loan Estimate (LE) In a Loan Estimate, a borrower's principal, interest rates, closing costs, and mortgage features are estimated.
96. MATCH: Number between 350-850 you are given based on your credit history, The higher the number, the better your history and the more likely you are to get a loan. a. Credit history b. Credit rating c. Credit report d. Credit limit	b. Credit rating A credit rating is a quantified assessment of the creditworthiness of a borrower in general terms or with respect to a particular debt or financial obligation.
97. The three credit reporting agencies include the following, except? a. Experian b. TransUnion c. Equifax d. Equinox	d. Equinox There are three credit agencies: TransUnion, Equifax, and Experian.
98. MATCH: The relationship, expressed as a percentage, between a borrower's monthly obligations on long-term debts and his or her gross monthly income. a. DTI Ratio (Debt to Income) b. Closing Costs c. Discount point d. Amortization	a. DTI Ratio (Debt to Income) DTI is calculated by dividing all your monthly debt payments by your gross monthly income. A lender uses this number to measure your ability to repay the money you plan to borrow.
99. A state statute has set the maximum interest rate allowed on loans originated within the state. This type of law is known as? a. usury law. b. statute of limitations. c. nominal interest rate. d. discount points.	a. usury law. Interest rates on credit cards and loans are capped by law. Usury laws are present in more than half of U.S. states, and each imposes its own legal limit.
100. Usury laws prohibit which of the following? a. Life insurance companies providing mortgages b. Hypothecation	d. Charging interest rates higher than allowed by law

c. Insurance on real estate d. Charging interest rates higher than allowed by law	Usury laws specifically target the practice of charging excessively high rates on loans by setting caps on the maximum amount of interest that can be levied. These laws are designed to protect consumers.
101. A loan that doesn't require any collateral. a. Down Payment b. Secured Loan c. Installment Loans d. Unsecured Loan	d. Unsecured Loan An unsecured loan is made solely based on the borrowers' creditworthiness, without collateral.
102. Usury Laws regulate? a. the maximum amount of interest which can be charged on a security instrument b. the right to use the surface of real property c. the return of his earnest money deposit back before the offer is accepted. d. applicable to the prescriptive easement of ingress and egress	a. the maximum amount of interest which can be charged on a security instrument The purpose of Usury laws is to prevent excessively high interest rates on loans by limiting the maximum that can be charged. The laws protect consumers.
103. The use of borrowed money to finance investment is called? a. Capital gain b. Leverage c. Depreciation d. Appreciation	b. Leverage To undertake an investment or project, leverage is used (borrowed capital). The term "highly leveraged" means that an item has more debt than equity. Investors and companies both use leverage.
104. MATCH: Actions taken by a lender to entice, induce and/or assist borrowers to take a mortgage that carries high fees, a high interest rate, or strips the borrower of equity to benefit the lender. a. Predatory lending b. Subprime Mortgage c. Fraud d. Participation Agreement	A. Predatory lending Predatory lending is any lending practice that imposes unfair or abusive loan terms on borrowers.

Definitions Module Four

Adjustable-Rate Mortgage (ARM)
Adjustable-rate mortgages change their interest rates at predetermined time intervals (6 month or 1 year is typical). This change in rate may or may not change the monthly payment, depending on what was agreed to prior to accepting signing up for the Mortgage. The interest rate is usually tied to the banks source of funds, often called the one-year treasury index. The better mortgages have caps on how much the interest rate can go up in any one year and/or over its lifetime. These caps also apply to the payment. Typically interest rates and monthly payments are lower than 30-year fixed rate mortgages for the first couple of years.

Annual Percentage Rate (APR)
Includes the interest charge, points, broker fees and other credit charges.

Assignment of Mortgage
A document evidencing the transfer of ownership of a mortgage from one person to another.

Assumable Mortgage
A mortgage loan that can be taken over (assumed) by the buyer when a home is sold. An assumption of a mortgage is a transaction in which the buyer of real property takes over the seller's existing mortgage; the seller remains liable unless released by the lender from the obligation. If the mortgage contains a due-on-sale clause, the loan may not be assumed without the lender's consent.

Automated Underwriting
An auto-mated process performed by a technology application that streamlines the processing of loan applications and provides a recommendation to the lender to approve the loan or refer it for manual underwriting.

Balloon Mortgage
☐ A predetermined largest and final payment. A mortgage with monthly payments often based on a 30-year amortization schedule, with the unpaid balance due in a lump sum payment at the end of a specific period of time (usually 5 or 7 years).

Before-tax Income
Income before taxes are deducted. Also known as "gross income."

Biweekly Payment Mortgage
A mortgage with payments due every two weeks (instead of monthly).

Bridge Loan
A short-term loan secured by the borrower's current home (which is usually for sale) that allows the proceeds to be used for building or closing on a new house before the current home is sold. Also known as a "swing loan."

Certificate of Eligibility
A document issued by the U.S. Department of Veterans Affairs (VA) certifying a veteran's eligibility for a VA-guaranteed mortgage lo

Co-borrower

Any borrower other than the first borrower whose name appears on the application and mortgage note, even when that person owns the property jointly with the first borrower and shares liability for the note.

Collateral
An asset that is pledged as security for a loan. The borrower risks losing the asset if the loan is not repaid according to the terms of the loan agreement. In the case of a mortgage, the collateral would be the house and real property.

Construction Loan
A loan for financing the cost of construction or improvements to a property; the lender disburses payments to the builder at periodic intervals during construction.

Credit Bureau
A company that gathers information on consumers who use credit. These companies sell that information to lenders and other businesses in the form of a credit report.

Credit Report
Information provided by a credit bureau that allows a lender or other business to examine your use of credit. It provides information on money that you've borrowed from credit institutions and your payment history.

Credit Score
A numerical value that ranks a borrower's credit risk at a given point in time based on a statistical evaluation of information in the individual's credit history that has been proven to be predictive of loan performance.

Creditworthy
Your ability to qualify for credit and repay debts.

Debt-to-Income Ratio
The percentage of gross monthly income that goes toward paying for your monthly housing expense, alimony, child support, car payments and other installment debts, and payments on revolving or open-ended accounts, such as credit cards.

Deed of Trust
A legal document in which the borrower transfers the title to a third party (trustee) to hold as security for the lender. When the loan is paid in full, the trustee transfers title back to the borrower. If the borrower defaults on the loan the trustee will sell the property and pay the lender the mortgage debt.

Default
Failure to fulfill a legal obligation. A default includes failure to pay on a financial obligation, but also may be a failure to perform some action or service that is non-monetary. For example, when leasing a car, the lessee is usually required to properly maintain the car.

Delinquency
Failure to make a payment when it is due. The condition of a loan when a scheduled payment has not been received by the due date, but generally used to refer to a loan for which payment is 30 or more days past due.

Discount Point

A fee paid by the borrower at closing to reduce the interest rate. A point equals one percent of the loan amount.

Down Payment

A portion of the price of a home, usually between 3-20%, not borrowed and paid up-front in cash. Some loans are offered with zero down-payment.

Due-on-Sale Clause

A provision in a mortgage that allows the lender to demand repayment in full of the outstanding balance if the property securing the mortgage is sold.

Equal Credit Opportunity Act (ECOA)

A federal law that requires lenders to make credit equally available without regard to the applicant's race, color, religion, national origin, age, sex, or marital status; the fact that all or part of the applicant's income is derived from a public assistance program; or the fact that the applicant has in good faith exercised any right under the Consumer Credit Protection Act. It also requires various notices to consumers.

Equity

The value in your home above the total amount of the liens against your home. If you owe $100,000 on your house but it is worth $130,000, you have $30,000 of equity.

Fair Credit Reporting Act (FCRA)

A consumer protection law that imposes obligations on (1) credit bureaus (and similar agencies) that maintain consumer credit histories, (2) lenders and other businesses that buy reports from credit bureaus, and (3) parties who furnish consumer information to credit bureaus. Among other provisions, the FCRA limits the sale of credit reports by credit bureaus by requiring the purchaser to have a legitimate business need for the data, allows consumers to learn the information on them in credit bureau files (including one annual free credit report), and specifies procedure for challenging errors in that data.

Federal housing administration (FHA) Mortgage

Federal housing administration mortgage made in conformity with the requirements of the national housing act and insured by the federal housing administration.

FHA-Insured Loan

A loan that is insured by the Federal Housing Administration (FHA) of the U.S. Department of Housing and Urban Development (HUD).

Good-Faith Estimate

A form required by the Real Estate Settlement Procedures Act (RESPA) that discloses an estimate of the amount or range of charges, for specific settlement services the borrower is likely to incur in connection with the mortgage transaction.

Government Mortgage

A mortgage loan that is insured or guaranteed by a federal government entity such as the Federal Housing Administration (FHA), the U.S. Department of Veterans Affairs (VA), or the Rural Housing Service (RHS).

Gross Annual Income

The total income, before taxes and other deductions, received by all members of the tenant's household. There shall be included in this total income all wages, social security payments, retirement benefits, military and veteran's disability payments, unemployment benefits, welfare benefits, interest and dividend payments and such other income items as the Secretary considers appropriate.

Gross Monthly Income
The income you earn in a month before taxes and other deductions. It also may include rental income, self-employed income, income from alimony, child support, public assistance payments, and retirement benefits.

Growing-Equity Mortgage (GEM)
A fixed-rate mortgage in which the monthly payments increase according to an agreed-upon schedule, with the extra funds applied to reduce the loan balance and loan term.

Home Equity Line of Credit (HELOC)
A type of revolving loan, that enables a homeowner to obtain multiple advances of the loan proceeds at his or her own discretion, up to an amount that represents a specified percentage of the borrower's equity in the property.

Hybrid Loan
An adjustable-rate mortgage (ARM) that offers a fixed rate for an initial period, typically three to ten years, and then adjusts every six months, annually, or at another specified period, for the remainder of the term.

Index
A number used to compute the interest rate for an adjustable-rate mortgage (ARM). The index is generally a published number or percentage, such as the average interest rate or yield on U.S. Treasury bills. A margin is added to the index to determine the interest rate that will be charged on the ARM. This interest rate is subject to any caps on the maximum or minimum interest rate that may be charged on the mortgage, stated in the note.

Initial Interest Rate
The original interest rate for an adjustable-rate mortgage (ARM). Sometimes known as the "start rate."

Interest
The cost you pay to borrow money. It is the payment you make to a lender for the money it has loaned to you. Interest is usually expressed as a percentage of the amount borrowed.

Jumbo Loan
A loan that exceeds the mortgage amount eligible for purchase by Fannie Mae or Freddie Mac. Also called "non-conforming loan."

Junior Mortgage
A loan that is subordinate to the primary loan or first-lien mortgage loan, such as a second or third mortgage.

Lease-Purchase Option
An option sometimes used by sellers to rent a property to a consumer, who has the option to buy the home within a specified period of time. Typically, part of each rental payment is put aside for the purpose of accumulating funds to pay the down payment and closing costs.

Lifetime Cap

For an adjustable-rate mortgage (ARM), a limit on the amount that the interest rate or monthly payment can increase or decrease over the life of the loan.

Liquid Asset
A cash asset or an asset that is easily converted into cash.

Loan Origination
The process by which a loan is made, which may include taking a loan application, processing and underwriting the application, and closing the loan.

Loan-To-Value (LTV) Ratio
The relationship between the loan amount and the value of the property (the lower of appraised value or sales price), ex-pressed as a percentage of the property's value. For example, a $100,000 home with an $80,000 mortgage has an LTV of 80 percent.

Maturity Date
The date on which a mortgage loan is scheduled to be paid in full, as stated in the note.

Mortgage
A loan using your home as collateral. In some states the term mortgage is also used to describe the document you sign (to grant the lender a lien on your home).

Mortgage Broker
An individual or firm that brings borrowers and lenders together for the purpose of loan origination. A mortgage broker typically takes loan applications and may process loans.

Mortgage Insurance (MI)
Insurance that protects lenders against losses caused by a borrower's default on a mortgage loan. MI typically is required if the borrower's down payment is less than 20 percent of the purchase price.

Mortgagor
The owner of real estate who pledges property as security for the repayment of a debt, the borrower.

Negative Amortization
An increase in the balance of a loan caused by adding unpaid interest to the loan balance; this occurs when the payment does not cover the interest due.

Net Monthly Income
Your take-home pay after taxes. It is the amount of money that you actually receive in your paycheck.

Origination Fee
A fee paid to a lender or broker to cover the administrative costs of processing a loan application. The origination fee typically is stated in the form of points. One point is one percent of the mortgage amount.

Owner Financing
A transaction in which the property seller provides all or part of the financing for the buyer's purchase of the property.

Partial Payment
A payment that is less than the scheduled monthly payment on a mortgage loan.

PITI
An acronym for the four primary components of a monthly mortgage payment: principle, interest, taxes, and insurance (PITI).

Point
One percent of the amount of the mortgage loan. For example, if a loan is made for $50,000, one-point equals $500.

Pre-Approval
A process by which a lender provides a prospective borrower with an indication of how much money he or she will be eligible to borrow when applying for a mortgage loan. This pro-cess typically includes a review of the applicant's credit history and may involve the review and verification of income and assets to close.

Pre-Qualification
A preliminary assessment by a lender of the amount it will lend to a potential home buyer. The process of determining how much money a prospective home buyer may be eligible to borrow before he or she applies for a loan.

Predatory Lending
Abusive lending practices that include making mortgage loans to people who do not have the income to repay them or repeatedly refinancing loans, charging high points and fees each time and "packing" credit insurance onto a loan.

Prepayment
Any amount paid to re-duce the principal balance of a loan before the scheduled due date.

Prepayment Penalty
A fee that a borrower may be required to pay to the lender, in the early years of a mortgage loan, for repaying the loan in full or pre-paying a substantial amount to reduce the unpaid principal balance.

Principal
The amount of money borrowed or the amount of the loan that has not yet been repaid to the lender. This does not include the interest you will pay to borrow that money. The principal balance (sometimes called the outstanding or unpaid principal balance) is the amount owed on the loan minus the amount you've repaid.

Promissory Note
A written promise to repay a specified amount over a specified period.

Purchase Money Mortgage
A mortgage loan that enables a borrower to acquire a property.

Qualified Mortgage
An entity approved by the HUD Secretary that is capable of servicing, as well as originating, FHA-insured mortgages, and is not suspended or debarred by the Secretary, is not suspended or on probation imposed by HUD's Mortgagee Review Board and is not in default under any Government National Mortgage Association obligation.

Qualifying Guidelines

Criteria used to determine eligibility for a loan.

Qualifying Ratios
Calculations that are used in determining the loan amount that a borrower qualifies for, typically a comparison of the borrower's total monthly income to monthly debt payments and other recurring monthly obligations

Real Estate Settlement Procedures Act (RESPA)
A federal law that requires lenders to provide home mortgage borrowers with information about transaction-related costs prior to settlement, as well as information during the life of the loan regarding servicing and escrow accounts. **RESPA also prohibits kickbacks and unearned fees in the mortgage loan business.**

Redlining
Discrimination based on location is often referred to as redlining, because historically, some lending institutions were found to have maps with red lines delineating neighborhoods within which they would not do business.

Refinance
Getting a new mortgage with all or some portion of the proceeds used to pay off the prior mortgage.

Sale-Leaseback
A transaction in which the buyer leases the property back to the seller for a specified period of time.

Second Mortgage
A mortgage that has a lien position subordinate to the first mortgage.

Service Members Civil Relief Act
A federal law that restricts the enforcement of civilian debts against certain military personnel who may not be able to pay because of active military service. It also provides other protections to certain military personnel.

Servicer
A firm that performs servicing functions, including collecting mortgage payments, paying the borrower's taxes and insurance and generally managing borrower escrow accounts.

Subordinate Financing
Any mortgage or other lien with lower priority than the first mortgage.

Subprime Loan
A mortgage that carries] a higher rate of interest than prime loans to compensate for increased credit risk.

Truth-In-Lending Act (TILA)
A federal law that requires disclosure of a truth-in-lending statement for consumer credit. The statement includes a summary of the total cost of credit, such as the annual percentage rate (APR) and other specifics of the credit.

Underwriting
The process used to determine loan approval. It involves evaluating the property and the borrower's credit and ability to pay the mortgage.

Uniform Residential Loan Application
A standard mortgage application you will have to complete. The form requests your income, assets, liabilities, and a description of the property you plan to buy, among other things.

VA Guaranteed Loan
A mortgage loan that is guaranteed by the U.S. Department of Veterans Affairs (VA).

Veterans Affairs (U.S. Department of Veterans Affairs)
A federal government agency that provides benefits to veterans and their dependents, including health care, educational assistance, financial assistance, and guaranteed home loans.

Yield
A return measure for an investment over a set period of time, expressed as a percentage.

MODULE FIVE: GENERAL PRINCIPLES OF AGENCY

Creation of Agency, Agency, and Non-Agency Relationships

Agency

- To create agency, there must be delegated authority and consent to act.
- Agency is the foundation upon which real estate brokerage is practiced.
- Agency describes a legal and ethical relationship between a real estate licensee and a party to a transaction that may include a buyer, a seller, a rental property owner, or a tenant.
- The agency relationship governs the day-to day actions of every real estate licensee.

How Agencies are Created

Expressed Agency
(Actual Agency)
- Established by agreement.
- Oral or written.
- Clearly stated.
- Agreement can be oral unless written agreement is required by law.
- Real estate agency agreements required to be in writing.

Implied Agency

- No written or clearly stated agreement.
- Agency is created by the conduct of the "principal".
  Implied agencies arises where one person behaves as an agent would and the "principal," knowing that the "agent" is behaving so, acquiesces, allowing the person to hold himself out as an agent.

Agency by Ratification

- No expressed agency.
- Agency created retroactively when "principal" approves or accepts the benefits of a transaction negotiated by the "agent".
- "Principal" later finds out about and, with full knowledge, approves or accepts the benefits of the transaction.

Types of Agents

There are five types of agents.

1. Special Agent (Buyer's Agent or Seller's Agent)

- One authorized by the principal to perform a narrow or specific task.
- A listing broker employed to sell one home is a special agent.

- Appointed to carry out a single act or transaction.
- Example: Real estate agent in sale transaction.

2. General Agent

- A Property Manager.
- A property manager's primary responsibility is to get the highest net return for the owner.
- The general agent possesses the authority to carry out a broad range of transactions in the name and on behalf of the principal.
- The general agent may be the manager of a multi-unit complex or may have a more limited but nevertheless ongoing role—for example, as a rental agent.
- In either case, the general agent has authority to alter the principal's legal relationships with third parties.
- One who is designated a general agent has the authority to act in any way required by the principal's business.
- A Property Manager is given a broad scope of authority to handle a variety of things. A property manager is a general agent because of the wide range of activities necessary to rent and maintain it.

3. Universal Agent

- Holds Power of Attorney

Powers of attorney and other delegation of authority
  a. **Power of Attorney**
     A written document appointing an "attorney-in-fact" to act independently and with signature authority on behalf of another person in matters specified. It May be either specific (e.g., attend a closing and sign on behalf of a seller) or general (e.g., manage extensive business and personal matters).
  b. **General Power of Attorney**
     Appointment of an attorney-in-fact with signature authority and with wide-ranging discretion in handling the delegated matters in the appointment.
  c. **Attorney in Fact**
     A person named in a written power of attorney document acts on behalf of the person who signs the document. The attorney-in-fact's authority and responsibilities depend on the specific powers granted in the power of attorney document. An attorney-in-fact is an agent of the principal.

4. Designated Agent

- Practice under the law in some states, which the employing broker 'designates' a licensee as the exclusive company representative (agent or facilitator/transaction broker) to a seller(s), buyer(s), landlord(s), or tenant(s).
- This enables another licensee in the firm to be designated to the other side of the transaction without creating dual agency.

Other Brokerage Relationships (non-agents)

Transactional Agent

- A non-agent. The closing attorney.
- The Purchase Agreement is delivered to the Transactional Agent. (Closing Attorney)
- The job of the Transactional Agent to make sure the legal rights of the seller and buyer have been completed before the property transfers ownership.

Facilitator

A facilitator may assist the Buyer and Seller in the same transaction without creating a dual agency.

Gratuitous Agency

An agency relationship with no charges.

Agency Coupled with an Interest

An agency relationship in which the agent is given an estate or interest in the property that is the subject of the agency relationship.

Client vs. Customer

Principal/Client	Customer
- The person the agent has a written agreement with. - The person appointing an agent in an agency relationship. - A Client is someone you work for. - A client is due Fiduciary Duties.	- A Customer is someone you work with. A customer is not represented. - The customer is not represented. - A customer is due, "fair and honest dealings". - This duty to disclose known material facts is based upon a real estate broker's duty to treat all persons honestly and fairly. **Customer-Level Services** - Reasonable care and skill. - Honest and fair dealing. - Disclosure of material facts.

Agency Duties to Third Person

(Someone who is not a principal)
- Agent does not owe fiduciary duties to a third party.
- Agent does owe duties of honesty and fair dealing to third person.
- No fraud or misrepresentations.
- Agent representing the seller only also owes to the buyer the duty to disclose material facts about the property.
- Defined as facts that affect the value or desirability of the property.

Fiduciary Duties

Whether through implied or expressed agency, a real estate broker acting as an agent to a seller or buyer is considered a fiduciary. Fiduciary duties are among the highest obligations. In addition to any duties or obligations set forth in a listing agreement or other contract of employment, a real estate broker is held under the law to owe certain specific duties to his principal. Among the specific fiduciary duties are:
COLDAC

Confidentiality

- Agents have a duty to protect their principal's confidential information.
- As a result, real estate brokers must protect any information that might weaken the bargaining power of their principals.
- Under this duty of confidentiality, a broker representing a seller cannot disclose to a buyer that the seller can, or must, sell his property below its listed price. For the buyer, the broker representing the buyer cannot disclose the highest price the buyer will pay.

Obedience

The agent must comply with all lawful instructions issued by his principal promptly and efficiently.

Loyalty

- Fiduciary duties owed by an agent to his principal include the duty of loyalty.
- Real estate brokers must always act exclusively in the best interests of their principals, including their own self-interest.
- Brokerage firms are legally bound to avoid any conflicts of interest that may compromise or dilute their undivided loyalty to their principals.

Disclosure

- Any relevant information that an agent knows and is related to his principal's business is required to be disclosed to him.
- A real estate broker representing a seller has a duty to disclose to the seller:
    - Offers to purchase the seller's property.
    - Identification of all potential purchasers.
    - Factors that affect a property's value.
    - Information about the buyer's ability or willingness to complete the sale or to offer a higher price.
- The real estate broker representing a buyer must disclose to the buyer:
    - The seller's willingness to accept a lower price.
    - Facts relating to the urgency of the seller's need to sell the property.
    - Relationship with, or interest in, the seller of the property for sale.
    - Aspects that affect the property's value.

- o The length of time that the property has been listed and any other offers or counteroffers made for it.
- o Other information that could affect a buyer's ability to get the property at the lowest price and on the most favorable terms.

Accounting

- Agents are obligated to account for all money and property belonging to their principal that they are entrusted with.
- The duty of a real estate broker is to safeguard any money, deeds, or other documents entrusted to him relating to a client's business.

(Reasonable) care and diligence

- The agent must exercise reasonable care and diligence in pursuing the principal's affairs.
- A real estate broker is expected to provide the same level of service as a competent real estate professional when representing buyers or sellers.
- Due to his license, a real estate broker is considered to have superior skill and expertise in real estate matters.
- An estate broker is obligated to discover facts regarding the principal's affairs which a reasonable and prudent broker would probably investigate. Basically, this is the same responsibility every professional owes to his or her patient or client.
- Estimating a seller's net profit from an income property before listing the property for sale is an example of Care.
- When a salesperson doesn't know something but should have, he did not practice care.

Single vs. Dual Agency

Single Agency	Dual Agency
• Working on behalf of one person. • Representing either the seller(s) or buyer(s).	• Representing both sides of the same transaction with written permission explaining what is due to each party is Dual Agency. • Undisclosed dual agency is an illegal form of real estate representation.

☐ It is unethical for a broker representing the seller to tell the buyer the lowest price a seller will accept.

Caveat Emptor	Caveat Venditor
When the customer is the Buyer.	When the customer is the Seller.

Parties in Agency

1. Real Estate Broker

Any licensed person, firm, partnership, association, or corporation who, in consideration of valuable compensation or intending to receive such compensation, acts as a special agent for parties in the sale or lease of real estate.

2. Real Estate Salesperson

One who is employed by a real estate broker, usually as an independent contractor.

3. Associate Broker – Affiliate Broker

A salesperson with a broker's license who is not the responsible broker for the company.

4. Cooperating Broker

One working with or representing the buyer or tenant; Cooperates with the listing broker by providing a prospective buyer/tenant for the listed property.

Agency Disclosure

- Real estate professionals are required to disclose to the parties they represent that they represent then and to the parties they don't represent that they don't represent them.
- Agency Disclosure is informing clients/fiduciaries and customers of your relationships which each person.

☐ If a broker wants to buy his seller's property, he should make his true intentions known.

Imputed Knowledge

- The Principal/Client is responsible for the acts of the agent.
- The Principal/Client is deemed to have knowledge of anything known by the agent.

Conflict of Interest

A real estate professional must disclose any conflict of interest in the transaction. Examples include, but are not limited to:

Agent seller
Agent buyer
Buyer or seller is a family member of agent

Agency, Listing Agreements and Buyers

Requirements for Validity

1.   Real Estate Contracts must be/have
Competent parties
18 years or older
Sobor, sane adult
2. Legal Purpose (Legality of Object)
An essential element of a valid contract. A contract for an illegal purpose is void.
3. Consideration
Anything of value that induces one to enter a contract.
4. An accurate legal description
5. Written and Signed

Everything in real estate must be in writing, according to the Statute of Frauds.

Upon selecting a listing broker, the seller enters a contract known as a "listing agreement" in which the broker agrees to market and sell their home for a fixed fee, typically in a percentage commission.

Listing Agreements

☐ Listing agreements are service contracts.
- The Listing Agreement ☐ (Employment Contract)
- In real estate, a listing agreement is a contract between a property owner and a real estate broker that authorizes the broker to represent the seller and find a buyer for the property.

Commissions

- Commission "fees" are the total dollar amount paid by consumers for real estate brokerage services. This contract often specifies the commission the homeowner will pay the listing broker if the home is sold within a specified period, how the home is to be listed in the MLS, and, as discussed below, the share of the commission to be offered by the listing broker to a so-called "cooperating broker," who works with the buyer.
- The listing broker typically markets the home, both within his or her brokerage firm and to other brokers in the community, by uploading the listing data, including the offer of compensation to cooperating brokers, into the MLS database so that the information can be disseminated to cooperating brokers, who in turn can inform potential buyers of the listing.
☐ The commission is negotiable.

Multiple Listing Service

The multiple listing service is an organization with a suite of services that real estate brokers use to establish contractual offers of cooperation and compensation and accumulate and disseminate information to enable appraisals.

☐ Listing Agreements must be in writing to be enforceable in court according to the Statutes of Frauds.

Types of Listing Agreements

1. Exclusive right-to-sell listing

- An exclusive right-to-sell listing is the most used contract. With this type of listing agreement, one broker is appointed as the sole seller's agent and has exclusive authorization to represent the property.
- The broker receives a commission no matter who sells the property while the listing agreement is in effect.

2. Exclusive Listing

- Exclusive agency listing.
- With an exclusive agency listing, one broker is authorized to act as the exclusive agent for the seller. The seller retains the right to sell the property, without obligation to the broker.
- However, the seller is obligated to pay a commission to the broker if the broker is the procuring cause of the sale.

3. Open Listing

- With an open listing, a seller retains the right to employ any number of brokers as agents.
- It's a non-exclusive type of listing, and the seller is obligated to pay a commission only to the broker who successfully finds a ready, willing, and able buyer.
- The seller retains the right to sell the property independently without any obligation to pay a commission.
- An Open Listing is a unilateral contract.
- ☐ the phrase "procuring cause" is most important to the broker and seller in an open listing contract. "Procure the Buyer".

Listings Must:
- Be in writing
- Name the broker
- Include the listing price
- Include commission amount
- Include terms of the sale
- Include a termination date

Net Listing

- A net listing can be any of the listing agreements above.
- Net listings are considered unethical.
- Net Listings are prohibited in most states because of the uncertainty of the selling price. An example would be your client says to you that he needs $500,000 from the sale, and you can keep anything you above that.

- The type of listing in which the listing agent is least likely to know what his commission will be is a net listing.

Ready Willing and Able Buyer to Meet the Terms of the Listing Agreement

- When a listing broker brings a ready, willing, and able buyer who can meet the terms of the listing agreement, the listing broker has earned the commission.

Procuring Cause

- The "procuring cause" of a real estate transaction is the agent whose actions and efforts result in the sale of a property.
- It's the agent who ultimately caused the buyer to purchase the home.
- As such, that agent is entitled to compensation in the form of a commission.

Protection Clause

- The Protection Clause in the listing extends the period that a seller agrees to pay a commission.
- The broker is not entitled to a commission if the seller sells the property one day after the expiration of the listing unless there is a protection clause in the listing and the agent was the procuring cause of the transaction.
- In every listing there is a "protection clause".
- It states that if a buyer purchases your property within_? Months, days, years, the seller will owe the agent a commission because they were the procuring cause.
- Salespeople should keep a list of the people who they showed the property to or introduced the property to. When the listing expires, give the seller a copy of the list.

◻ A listing agreement terminates immediately upon the death of the seller or listing agent.
◻ Bob secured a six-month Exclusive Right Listing Agreement with Sam. Two months into the contract, Sam gave Bob a written notice he no longer wanted to sell.
The contract will be cancelled, but Sam will be liable for any expenses incurred by agent Bob.
◻ A salesperson listed Bob's property. Bob died in a car accident before the salesperson could procure a buyer. What happens to the listing?
The listing terminates immediately.

The Buyer's Relationship with the Cooperating Broker

- The broker who works with the buyer is often referred to as the "cooperating broker" "or "buyer's broker."
- Cooperating brokers typically attempt to find housing from the available stock that match buyers' preferences, show prospective buyers' homes for sale, provide them information about comparable home sales that have occurred in the area, assist prospective buyers in becoming pre-qualified for a certain level of financing, advise them on making offers, and assist in closing the transaction. Buyers typically do not pay their brokers directly.
- Listing brokers compensate cooperating brokers according to the terms stated in the MLS listing, which usually specifies an unconditional offer of compensation to any broker that is the "procuring cause" of the sale.

Buyer Agency Agreements

- The Buyer is the person who makes an offer to purchase real estate.
- Buyer Agency Agreements
    - Exclusive
    - Non-exclusive
    - Non-exclusive/Not for Compensation

Termination of Agency

Mutual Agreement (Rescission)

- If a principal and an agent mutually agree to form an agency contract, they can mutually agree to terminate the contract. This is called rescission.

Expiration Date

- All listing agreements must have an expiration date. When that date is reached, the principal and agent have mutually agreed in advance that the listing agreement is over.

Completion

- Fulfillment of the Purpose
- If the goal of the agreement is reached, the agent has Tendered Performance. The agent has completed his/her requirement under the agreement.

Revocation by the Principal

- The principal can unilaterally (one-sided) revoke the agent's authority to represent the principal.
- This can be done if no injury is caused to parties.

Termination by Force of Law

Tax sale, eminent domain.

Destruction of the Property

Fire, windstorm, hurricane, tornado

Death of a Principal

Client or Broker died.

Broker Bankruptcy

Legal event

Broker Insanity

Legal event

Negligent Misrepresentation

- When a salesperson should have known something but didn't.
- Examples
- You know your client wants to use the garage as a hair salon. You sell her the property without researching the fact that the neighborhood is not zoned for home-based business'.
- You tell a buyer how wonderful the fire in the fireplace will be. The fireplace is a fake fireplace front.

Intentional Misrepresentation

Illegality

- The person selling the property didn't have the Covenant of SEISIN. They didn't seize the property.
- Meaning, they did not own the property at all. FRAUD

Mistake of Fact / Non-Facts

- A statement like, "this farm has the best tasting water well I have ever tasted". Upon inspection, the water well is tainted and can never be utilized.
- Not telling a buyer that a freeway will be built 100 yards from the backyard and it never is.

Agent's Lack of Authority

- The agent didn't have a legal listing or a buyer's agreement.

Fundamental Breaches / Discharge by Breach

- An actual breach occurs when one person refuses to fulfill their side of the bargain on the due date or performs incompletely.
- An anticipatory breach occurs when one party announces that he intends not to meet his side of the deal in advance of the due date for performance.

Pre-contractual Misrepresentations

- The property was not what was held out/advertised by the agent.

Renunciation / Refusal to Perform

- One of the parties to the contract backed out of the deal.

Inside the Brokerage

- There is only one responsible broker in the office.
- The salesperson and broker agree in writing to the amount the salesperson will be paid.
- When a commission arrives at the broker's office, before a salesperson receives their money, the broker will take their split.

☐ Brokers own everything the salespeople do.
☐ Brokers own all listings.

Employment Agreement

- Each salesperson has an Employment Agreement with their broker.
- To be legally compliant, every broker must have an employment agreement with every salesperson. (In writing)
- The employment agreement spells out the conditions of your association with the broker.
- Payment, commission splits, desk fees, expectations, and other conditions.

Salespeople

There can be salespeople with salesperson's licenses or broker's licenses.

☐ A broker cannot pay another broker's salesperson.

Subagency

Salespersons are Agents to the Broker and Sub Agents to the Broker's Clients.

Module Five: Agency Quiz

1. Law of agency a. Laws designed to preserve the free enterprise of the open marketplace by making illegal certain private conspiracies and combinations formed to minimize competition. b. Laws that govern RESPA. c. The action that starts a chain of events that results in the sale of real estate. d. The body of law that governs the rights and duties of principals, agents and third parties.	d. the body of law that governs the rights and duties of principals, agents and third parties.
2. MATCH: Ratification a. A method of creating an agency relationship in which the principal confirms the conduct of someone who initially acted without authority. b. A contract that is inferred by the actions and conduct of the parties. c. A main party to a transaction; the person for whom the agent works. d. A contract between a property owner and a real estate broker by which the broker is employed as agent to sell the owner's real estate on the owner's terms within a set period.	a. A method of creating an agency relationship in which the principal confirms the conduct of someone who initially acted without authority. A method of creating an agency relationship in which the principal confirms the conduct of someone who initially acted without authority.
3. The type of agency a real estate broker and seller enter when they execute a listing agreement is generally considered to be? a. universal agency. b. a special agency. c. a general agency. d. conditional agency.	b. a special agency. a special agency in a specific transaction
4. Match: Special agent a. A contract that is inferred by the actions and conduct of the parties. b. An agent who is authorized to represent the principal in one specific transaction or business activity only. c. A main party to a transaction; the person for whom the agent works. d. An agent who is authorized to represent the principal in a specified range of matters.	b. An agent who is authorized to represent the principal in one specific transaction or business activity only. Special Agents are responsible to a client in a specific transaction.
5. A broker has supplied the money for a developer to build a new neighborhood with the stipulation that the broker becomes the sole agent for the builder when the properties are ready for sale. This is a? a. Open Agency. b. Agency coupled with an interest. c. Riparian Rights d. Specific Agency.	b. Agency coupled with an interest. The agent receives an estate or interest in the property that is the subject of the agency.
6. Which of the following is not essential to the creation of an agency relationship? a. Agreement to pay a consideration b. Agreement of the parties to the agency	a. Agreement to pay a consideration Compensation is not a requirement

c. Competency on the part of the principal d. A fiduciary relationship	
7. The position of trust assumed by the broker as an agent for a principal is described more accurately as? a. an employment relationship b. a gratuitous relationship c. a trustor relationship d. a fiduciary relationship	d. a fiduciary relationship A fiduciary relationship exists with the Principle/Client.
8. An agent is authorized by a principal to perform an act or transaction. This is an example of a? a. general agency. b. transactional agency. c. special agency. d. universal agency.	c. special agency. A Special Agent is hired to do one specific act.
9. Which best describes a "Principal"? a. A person that is a party to a transaction, and the person for whom the licensee acts b. A person that acts on behalf of someone else c. A person in a position of trust and loyalty d. A person that has agency representation with a licensee	a. A person that is a party to a transaction, and the person for whom the licensee acts "A party to the transaction". The principal is the Client.
10. Which term describes a "Customer"? a. Someone you work with but not for and is not represented by an agent or broker b. A person that acts on behalf of someone else c. A person in a position of trust and loyalty d. A person that has agency representation with a licensee	a. Someone you work with but not for and is not represented by an agent or broker A customer is not represented. An agent works WITH a customer. Not FOR the customer.
11. "Customer" maybe the buyer, seller, landlord, or tenant. A Customer is? a. Represented in an agency agreement. b. Not represented in a transaction. c. Represented in a specific transaction. d. Represented as the universal agent' client.	b. Not represented in a transaction. A customer is not represented. The Client/Principle is represented. When disclosing Agency to the Customer you must disclose that they are not represented.
12. Which best describes a "Principal"? a. A person that is a party to a transaction, and the person for whom the licensee acts b. A person that acts on behalf of someone else c. A person in a position of trust and loyalty d. A person that has agency representation with a licensee	a. A person that is a party to a transaction, and the person for whom the licensee acts "A party to the transaction". The principal is the Client.
13. A real estate agent lists a woman's home for sale for $250,000. On the same day, a man enters the broker's office and requests general information about homes for sale in the $200,000 to $225,000 price range but declines representation by the broker's company. Who are the women and men's relationships with the broker? a. Both the man and the woman are customers. b. Both the man and the woman are clients	d. The woman is the broker's client, and the man is a customer

c. The man is the broker's client; the woman is a customer	
d. The woman is the broker's client, and the man is a customer	
14. A realty firm has just entered into an agreement to represent a home builder in the sale of a new subdivision. The firm has located several potential buyers and four homes have been sold with earnest money deposited by the buyers. The realty firm has an agency relationship with? a. the builder. b. the buyers. c. neither because it is a dual agency. d. both builder and buyers.	a. the builder. There is a contract agreement with the builder.
15. Buyers who are not represented ask the licensee who listed the home whether a property inspection is necessary as part of the due diligence process for purchasing the home. Is it appropriate that the listing agent respond in one of the following ways? a. If you feel it is in your best interest, please do. b. Don't bother, the seller will only come down so far on their price. c. I have all the information here. d. Maybe you should just do it yourself.	a. If you feel it is in your best interest, please do. Third parties and customers are owed fair and honest dealings.
16. The listing agent meets an unrepresented buyer at an open house. The buyer asks the agent to prepare an offer to purchase. When the agent meets with the buyer to prepare the offer, she says, "I'm sure I can get the seller on board and get you the financing you need." What has the listing agent just done? a. The agent is being a fiduciary to the client. b. The agent has created an implied agency. c. The agent made the seller very happy. d. The agent has done nothing inappropriate.	b. The agent has created an implied agency and as a result, an undisclosed dual agency. Agency can be created by implied actions.
17. MATCH "Fiduciary Responsibility". a. Loyalty, Obedience, Disclosure, Confidentiality, Reasonable Skill, Care and Diligence and Full Accounting. b. Due Diligence. c. Care, Honesty. d. Honest and Fair Dealing.	a. Loyalty, Obedience, Disclosure, Confidentiality, Reasonable Skill, Care and Diligence and Full Accounting. Correct answer by definition.
18. There was a listing agreement with an agent for a $150,000 home. Due to the seller being under duress, the agent knew the seller would take $140,000. A buyer viewed the property during an open house. However, he couldn't afford more than $135,000. An offer was encouraged by the agent. Buyers were told to offer $135k as she suspected the seller would take $140,000. What did the agent do wrong? a. Nothing, the buyer was ready, willing, and able to meet the terms of the contract. b. Yikes, regardless of intent, an agent can never reveal the lowest amount a seller will take for a property. c. Getting it sold is all that matters.	b. Yikes, regardless of intent, an agent can never reveal the lowest amount a seller will take for a property. This is a violation of fiduciary duties to the seller.
19.MATCH: Relationship built on trust.	a. Fiduciary

a. Fiduciary b. Specific Agency c. Customary d. General Agency	A fiduciary is any person or institution that has the power to act on behalf of another in situations that require the utmost trust, honesty, and loyalty. But it's more than just the power to act.
20.MATCH: Fiduciary a. One who is placed in a position of trust and confidence, as an agent is to his or her principal. b. A contract that is inferred by the actions and conduct of the parties. c. The intentional misrepresentation of a material fact to harm or take advantage of another person. d. A broker who cooperates in the sale of property listed by another broker; subagent of the principal.	a. One who is placed in a position of trust and confidence, as an agent is to his or her principal. One who is placed in a position of trust and confidence, as an agent is to his or her principal.
21. An agent's fiduciary duty to his/her client includes all these below, EXCEPT? a. obedience. b. fair and honest dealing with the customer. c. care. d. loyalty.	b. fair and honest dealing with the customer. Fair and honest dealing with the buyer. — Fiduciary duties are to the principal.
22. What is a client level duty relating to accounting of earnest money, communication, and actions a. Accounting b. Attorney-in-fact c. Care d. Confidentiality	c. Care Special care should always be paid.
23. When is a broker relieved of the obligation to present an offer to purchase real property to the principle? a. When the offer is for the purchase of nonresidential property b. When the offer contains more than 3 contingency clauses c. When the offer is patently frivolous, or the broker is acting on written instructions of the principal d. When the broker notifies the seller in writing of his decision not to present the offer	c. When the offer is patently frivolous, or the broker is acting on written instructions of the principal Brokers don't have to present an offer if they are obvious frivolous or if they are told in writing not to make frivolous types of offers.
24. A broker was hired by an owner to sell his property. The broker must reveal all significant and material information to the principal. Which of the following would be considered material information and must be revealed? a. None of these are correct b. The agent's knowledge that a better offer to purchase is imminent c. The new lender will require the buyer to maintain an impound account d. The prospective buyer is of oriental descent	b. The agent's knowledge that a better offer to purchase is imminent It may very well be a material fact to the seller if a better offer is imminent. This would probably influence his decision on the present offer
25. If a buyer asks for early occupancy, which of the following statements describe(s) the best way to protect the seller? a. The early occupancy should be made a separate clause in the	d. The best protection is to avoid the early occupancy, if possible.

purchase agreement so that if the sale falls through, it is easy to require the buyer to pay. b. Give the keys to the seller immediately. c. A separate lease between the parties should cover the early occupancy. d. The best protection is to avoid the early occupancy, if possible.	Avoid early occupancy at all costs.
26. Under the law of agency, a real estate broker owes all the following duties to the principal except? a. obedience b. disclosure c. care d. advertising	d. advertising Fiduciary duties are confidentiality, obedience, accountability, care, loyalty, disclosure.
27. To what party or parties does the broker owe the fiduciary duty of care? a. The party employing the broker. b. The customer. c. Everyone. d. His agent.	a. The party employing the broker. The party employing the broker is the client.
28. A seller of a property going into foreclosure has told the broker that he or she is very motivated to sell the property and will consider all offers. The broker should? a. say nothing unless the seller gives the broker written notice to disclose motivation. b. put "motivated seller" on the MLS listing and all other advertising. c. lower the listing price in the MLS to generate more offers. d. tell any buyers or buyers' agents to make offers lower than the listing price.	a. say nothing unless the seller gives the broker written notice to disclose motivation. Brokers must remain silent unless they have written permission to reveal motivation under the fiduciary obligation of confidentiality. Without the seller's written permission, a broker cannot tell others to bring lower offers, advertise "motivated seller," or lower the listing price.
29. A dual agency is in effect when? a. the seller sells her own home. b. both the buyer and seller accept dual agency and acknowledge the dual agency agreement in writing. c. the document is notarized. d. the listing agent finds a buyer.	b. both the buyer and seller accept dual agency and acknowledge the dual agency agreement in writing. Both the buyer and seller must accept dual agency and acknowledge the dual agency agreement in writing.
30. "Disclosed Dual Agent" is when? a. an agent representing both parties to a real estate transaction with the informed consent of both parties, with written understanding of specific duties and representation to be afforded each party. b. an agent representing both parties to a real estate transaction with the verbal commitment to do one's best c. an agent is selling two houses at the same time. d. an agent representing the seller and two parties making	a. an agent representing both parties to a real estate transaction with the informed consent of both parties, with written understanding of specific duties and representation to be afforded each party. Disclosed dual agency is when an agent representing both parties to a

offers on the same property on the same day.	real estate transaction has informed consent of both parties, with written understanding of specific duties and representation to be afforded each party.
31. MATCH: Dual agency. a. One who is placed in a position of trust and confidence, as an agent is to his or her principal. b. A contract that is inferred by the actions and conduct of the parties. c. Situation in which a person is legally prevented from denying that an agency relationship existed, usually due to acts or words on which a third party relied. d. Representing both parties to a transaction; while this practice is illegal in many states, in other states it is legal if disclosed and agreed to by the parties.	d. Representing both parties to a transaction; while this practice is illegal in many states, in other states it is legal if disclosed and agreed to by the parties. Representing both parties to a transaction; while this practice is illegal in many states, in other states it is legal if disclosed and agreed to by the parties.
32. A dual agency is legal and in violation of the fiduciary duty of loyalty unless both parties give their prior consent based on full knowledge of all the facts. a. false b. true	b. true A dual agency is illegal and in violation of the fiduciary duty of loyalty unless both parties give their prior.
33. What activity would be illegal and violate the requirement of common-law duties? a. An agent represents only one party to the transaction. b. An agent has dual agency with the consent of both parties on separate, unrelated property transactions. c. An agent has an express agreement with the seller and an implied agreement with the buyer, and neither party is aware of the agreements. d. A newly licensed broker without appointees negotiates a transaction with the informed, written consent of all parties to a transaction.	c. An agent has an express agreement with the seller and an implied agreement with the buyer, and neither party is aware of the agreements. Dual agency requires expressed written consent of both parties to the transaction.
34. A dual agent works? a. Primarily for the sellers b. For both the buyer and the seller c. As a subagent of the listing agent d. Primarily for the buyers	b. For both the buyer and the seller Dual agents work equally (according to state law.) for the buyer and the seller. It is imperative that the agent disclose dual agency to both parties and explain its implications.
35. Brokers have been asked to act as agents for friends selling their homes. One of the friends asks a broker to be her agent for finding a home before listing her friend's home. The broker is also serving as an agent for relatives of the two friends. Which statement is true? a. The broker may have one client at a time. b. The broker may serve as agent for any of the buyers and sellers.	b. The broker may serve as agent for any of the buyers and sellers. A salesperson is not limited on the number of clients and customers.

c. The broker may have one seller at a time. d. The broker may serve as agent for buyers during this transaction.	
36. Why is a designated agency a good alternative to a traditional dual agency? a. Only the broker is involved in the transaction and the parties do not have an exclusive agent. b. Designated agency is legal in all 50 states while dual agency is banned in every state. c. Even though the same broker represents each party, both the buyer and seller have a licensee who exclusively acts as their agent in the transaction. d. Fair housing laws do not apply to transactions involving designated agency.	c. Even though the same broker represents each party, both the buyer and seller have a licensee who exclusively acts as their agent in the transaction Even though the same broker represents each party, both the buyer and the seller has a licensee who exclusively acts as their agent in the transaction.
37. What would one call a selling agent who is NOT the listing agent? a. Sellers's agent b. General agent c. Cooperating agent d. Universal agent	c. Cooperating agent A cooperating broker is a non-listing third-party broker that finds a buyer
38. Which of the following is a broker who attempts to find a buyer for a property listed by another broker? a. cooperating broker b. dual agency broker c. transactional agent. d. agency broker	a. cooperating broker The agent that finds the buyer is cooperating with the listing agent.
39. When must you disclose your agency relationship to the seller if the property is a residential property of one-to-four units? a. After escrow is complete b. Prior to taking a listing agreement c. After holding an open house d. After the buyers move into the new property	b. Prior to taking a listing agreement Make your agency disclosure as soon as practicable.
40. The broker is selling an investment property she has owned for many years. She listed the property and put it in the MLS. If an interested buyer calls to inquire about the property? a. the broker has no obligation to disclose her ownership until closing. b. should first get the buyer's name and contact information so she can set a showing. c. will be required to disclose her ownership to the buyer if the buyer decides to make an offer. d. should disclose she is the owner and agent for the property before further discussion.	d. should disclose she is the owner and agent for the property before further discussion. Brokers are required to disclose ownership whenever they are agents for properties.
41. A broker has decided to buy his client's house, which the broker has listed. The broker should? a. buy the property through a straw man. b. not accept any offers on the property to protect his interest. c. wait six weeks.	d. makes his true intention known to his client. Provide full disclosure to your client.

d. make his true intention known to his client.	
42. A real estate broker learns that her neighbor wishes to sell his house. The broker knows the property well and can persuade a buyer to make an offer for the property. The broker then asks the neighbor if the broker can present an offer from the prospective buyer, and the neighbor agrees. At this point, which of the following statements is true? a. The neighbor is obligated to pay the broker a commission. b. The buyer is obligated to pay the broker for locating the property. c. The neighbor is not obligated to pay the broker a commission. d. The broker may not be considered the procuring cause without a written contract.	c. The neighbor is not obligated to pay the broker a commission. There is no contract in writing
43. All exclusive Listing Agreements shall? a. properly identify the property to be sold b. contain all the conditions under which the transaction is to be consummated. c. all the answers are correct d. contain a definite date of expiration, sales price, consideration, and signatures.	c. all the answers are correct All must be included.
44. If an owner refuses to pay the broker an earned commission, the broker may properly seek relief by? a. bringing a formal complaint with the division of real estate b. filing a mechanics lien c. bringing a quiet title action against the seller d. bringing court action	d. bringing court action Look to the seller for compensation.
45. To reduce the chance of misunderstandings and lawsuits, licensees should explain the listing agreement carefully to the seller. a. False b. True	b. True Salespeople should explain contracts and disclosures to their clients and customers.
46. Brokers receive listings of houses for sale, and the sellers specify that they won't sell to any Russian families. Which of the following should the broker do? a. Require that the owner sign a separate legal document. b. Advertise the property exclusively in Asian-language newspapers. c. Explain to the owner that the instruction violates federal law and that the broker cannot comply with it. d. Abide by the principal's directions even though they conflict with the fair housing laws.	c. Explain to the owner that the instruction violates federal law and that the broker cannot comply with it. Never violate fair housing laws.
47. Listing agreements between seller and brokers have been, and continue to be, the most common employment agreements in real estate. a. True b. False	a. True Buyer Agreements are a relatively new contract. Listing Agreements are most common.
48. A listing agreement is an employment contract between an owner and a real estate broker.	b. True

a. False b. True	Listing Agreements are between the seller and the real estate broker.
49. The listing agent for a residential property can legally complete the entire Real Property Transfer Disclosure Statement? a. When the buyer gives the agent a written waiver b. When authorized in writing by the seller c. Under no circumstances d. When the seller lives in another state and has not seen the property;	c. Under no circumstances Agency prohibits an agent from completing forms for the seller.
50. During the listing presentation, the seller questions the amount of commission to be paid and is told? a. the amount is set by law. b. everyone charges the same amount. c. the agent that charges a lower commission will not do as good a job selling the property d. the amount of commission is negotiable.	d. the amount of commission is negotiable. The commission is not set. It is always negotiable.
51. A broker wants to pay his neighbor a referral fee for sending the broker the neighbor's sister who purchased a home through that broker. a. The broker can pay anyone he wants to pay. b. The broker can pay his neighbor by automatic deposit. c. The broker can pay his neighbor a referral fee because no one will find out. d. The broker cannot pay his neighbor a fee unless the neighbor is a licensed real estate agent and then the broker would need to pay his broker.	d. The broker cannot pay his neighbor a fee unless the neighbor is a licensed real estate agent and then the broker would need to pay his broker. No Finder's Fees to unlicensed people. An agent cannot accept payment from anyone except his/her broker.
52. What is the duty of a listing agent upon receiving several offers on a property they have listed? a. Suggest that the seller counter each offer at the same time. b. Deliver each offer to the seller immediately upon receipt. c. All are correct. d. Accept the highest and best offer on behalf of the seller	b. Deliver each offer to the seller immediately upon receipt. Deliver immediately.
53. An exclusive right to sell listing obtained by a broker associate belongs to? a. the broker associates b. all the agents c. the seller d. the responsible broker	d. the responsible broker The listing belongs to that broker.
54. In an exclusive right to sell listing, an owner lists the property for sale with how many brokers? a. five b. six c. one d. two	c. one An "exclusive right to sell listing" is a listing agreement between a real estate broker granting the exclusive right to sell a property. The seller agrees to pay a commission if the property sells during the term of the listing.
55. Of the following, what constitutes an open listing?	b. The seller can employ any

a. The first listing broker is guaranteed a commission. b. The seller can employ any number of brokers. c. The seller only employs one exclusive agent. d. No counteroffers will be considered	number of brokers. The seller can employ any number of brokers.
56. You would like to hire more than one broker to sell your house and be able to sell the house yourself without paying a commission to a broker. Which of the following listing agreements should you choose? a. Net b. Exclusive Right c. Exclusive d. Open	d. Open In an open listing, the seller is free to hire as many agents as he/she wishes
57. Of the following listings, which one is a broker guaranteed a commission regardless of who sells the property? a. Exclusive listing b. Open listing c. A net listing d. Exclusive right	d. Exclusive right In an Exclusive RIGHT Listing, the agent will collect a commission if the agent brings a ready, willing, and able buyer who can meet the terms of the listing.
58. What type of listing could create the most competition between the owner and listing agent selling the home? a. A lease option. b. An open listing c. An exclusive right to sell agreement d. An exclusive agency agreement	b. An open listing In an open listing, the seller may hire as many agents as he/she wishes.
59. An exclusive agency listing allows the seller to sell without owing the broker a commission a. True b. False	a. True Only an Exclusive Right Listing Agreement pays the broker if the seller sells the property.
60. An exclusive agency listing allows the seller to sell without owing the broker a commission a. False b. True	b. True Only an Exclusive Right Listing Agreement pays the broker if the seller sells the property.
61. An agent brought a ready, willing, and able buyer that met the terms of the contract. The broker has earned her commission. a. when the buyer gives a counteroffer. b. when the seller gives a counteroffer. c. when the seller accepts the offer. d. when the buyer accepts the counteroffer.	c. when the seller accepts the offer. A Listing agent has earned their money when they bring a ready, willing, and able buyer that can meet the terms of the listing. If a buyer's offer is presented that does not meet the terms of the listing and the seller accepts it anyways, the listing agent has earned their money upon the seller's acceptance.
62. MATCH: Ready, willing, and able buyer a. A contract that is inferred by the actions and conduct of the parties.	d. One who is prepared to buy property on the seller's terms, is ready to take positive steps to

b. The agent of an agent; associated salesperson or cooperating broker in relation to the principal. c. A main party to a transaction; the person for whom the agent works. d. One who is prepared to buy property on the seller's terms, is ready to take positive steps to consummate the transaction and has the financial ability to do so.	consummate the transaction and has the financial ability to do so. A prepared buyer who can afford the property.
63. Which of the following statements best explains the meaning of this sentence: "To recover a commission for brokerage services, a broker must be employed as the agent of the seller"? a. The broker must have asked the seller the price of the property and then found a ready, willing, and able buyer. b. The broker must have a salesperson employed in the office. c. The seller must have made an express or implied agreement to pay a commission to the broker for selling the property. d. The broker must work in a real estate office	a. The broker must have asked the seller the price of the property and then found a ready, willing, and able buyer. Agents or brokers may earn commissions only if the purchaser is 'willing, able, and ready' to execute an unconditional contract as specified by the seller. In such a case, if the agent fulfills that condition, even if the seller refuses to conclude the sale or withdraws the property, he has earned his commission.
64. The phrase, "procuring cause" is most important to real estate agents in a? a. Exclusive Right Net Listing. b. Net listing c. Exclusive Right to Sell Listing Agreement. d. Open Listing.	d. Open Listing. Open listing can refer to a property for sale whose owner is using multiple real estate agents.
65. A broker lists a property and begins marketing it. The seller sold the property to a neighbor and upon closing pays the broker a full commission. What type of listing agreement did the brokerage firm have with the seller? a. Exclusive agency with a "seller may not sell" contingency b. Open c. Exclusive agency d. Exclusive right to sell	d. Exclusive right to sell Exclusive right to sell. Only an exclusive right-to-sell listing allows anyone to sell the property and the broker will still get paid.
66. A buyer hired an agent under an exclusive buyer's agency agreement. The buyer client wanted to submit an offer on a house that had been stigmatized by a recent murder-suicide. What is the agent's ethical responsibility to her client? a. Not say anything, it doesn't affect the structure of the property. b. Remain silent to protect the seller. c. Disclose it prior to signing any offer to purchase. d. Keep quiet.	c. Disclose it prior to signing any offer to purchase. Murder or suicide are not material facts. When representing the Buyer, ethically, you should disclose it.
67. A real estate salesperson is representing only the buyer in a transaction. Which of the following actions would be a violation of the salesperson's agency duties to the client? a. disclosing no price, the buyer is willing to pay.	b. disclosing the highest price the buyer is willing to pay. The Fiduciary Duty of

b. disclosing the highest price, the buyer is willing to pay. c. all of these are violations of agency. d. disclosing the lowest price, the buyer is willing to pay.	Confidentiality: The agent must keep confidential any information given to her by her client, especially information that may be damaging to the client in a negotiation.
68. MATCH: A real estate broker appointed by a buyer to find property for the buyer. a. buyer's agent. b. transactional agent. c. dual agent. d. seller's agent.	a. buyer's agent. Buyer's agents are bound to help buyers. Listing agents have a fiduciary duty to the home seller.
69. In a traditional brokerage, commissions are paid, and commissions can be? a. reduced if the salesperson is a female. b. reduced for expenses. c. reduced depending on religious group. d. reduced for attitude adjustments.	b. reduced for expenses. Agreements may be made for reductions due to expenses.
70. Without checking the facts, a broker who is the seller's agent tells a buyer that the property taxes in a particular neighborhood are among the lowest in the area. The buyer relies on the broker's statement and makes an offer on a house in the neighborhood. Before closing, it is determined that the taxes are among the highest in the area. The buyer could seek to rescind the contract based on. a. nothing; property taxes are a matter of public record, and it was the buyer's responsibility to check them. b. lack of care and diligence. c. misrepresentation. d. puffing.	c. misrepresentation. Don't state facts when you are unaware of the truth.
71. Which of the following would most buyers and sellers consider important in selecting a real estate professional? a. Licensed b. Accredited c. Success d. Trust	d. Trust Trust is the primary concern of the consumer.
72. A real estate professional who has several years of experience in the industry decided to retire from actively marketing properties. Now this person helps clients choose among the various alternatives involved in purchasing, using, or investing in property. What is this person's profession? a. Building inspector b. Real estate educator c. Real estate appraiser d. Real estate counselor	d. Real estate counselor Real Estate Counseling is a growing area of real estate.
73. Under no circumstances may a broker? a. receive a commission from both buyer and seller b. appoint a subagent c. misrepresents material facts d. sell the principal's property to a relative	c. misrepresents material facts A material misrepresentation is a violation of law.

74. When you know you are competing with another Agent for a listing? a. Always get permission from your broker. b. Never discuss that you are competing among colleagues. c. Use your competitive market analysis (CMA) skills. d. Never make a disparaging comment about your competition.	d. Never make a disparaging comment about your competition. Never talk bad about other professionals.
75. Which of the following would not be legally proper for a licensee to do? a. Tell a prospective buyer that the listed farm is the nicest in the county. b. Refuse to give his principal a serious verbal offer to purchase. c. Show a property only on sunny days. d. Keep the client's secret that the roof leaks.	d. Keep the client's secret that the roof leaks A licensee must reveal all material facts to a prospective buyer.
76. Brokers may give legal advice? a. Never. b. When a client asks how to take title. c. and accounting advice. d. When the client is under 18.	a. Never.
77. Which describes an "Agent"? a. A person that has agency representation with a licensee b. A person in a position of trust and loyalty c. A person that acts on behalf of someone else d. A person that is a party to a transaction, and the person for whom the licensee acts	c. A person that acts on behalf of someone else. Definition of Agency
78. Which of the following skillsets is most important for the buyer's representative? a. A strong grasp of financing options b. Counseling and negotiating c. None of the above d. Time management and computer literacy	b. Counseling and negotiating Real estate agency relationships demand the salesperson understand the needs of the client and communicate with them effectively.
79. A salesperson has a listing with his responsible broker, Broker A. The salesperson decided to transfer to a new broker before the listing expires. When the agent moves to the new broker, who owns the listing? a. Broker A b. The agent. c. The listing automatically gets cancelled. d. Broker	a. Broker A Broker A. Listings belong to the Responsible Broker under whose salesperson's contract the listing was obtained.
80. A salesperson, working for a broker, was able to complete a complex transaction that benefited both the buyer and the seller. The parties wanted to show their appreciation by giving the salesperson additional compensation. The salesperson can receive this compensation from? a. the seller. b. the seller. c. the broker. d. the buyer and seller equally.	c. the broker. The only party that can compensate a salesperson is the salesperson's own broker.
81. A salesperson has earned a commission on the sale of a	a. the selling brokerage

listing by another broker. The listing broker may pay part of her commission to? a. the selling brokerage b. the buyer's attorney c. the selling salesperson d. the out of state salesperson who referred the seller to her	All commissions get paid to the broker, who then splits the money with any involved agents. Being a fiduciary requires an agent to always act in good faith to the benefit of the principal.
82. States require real estate brokers and agents to be at least? a. a high school graduate. b. 21 years of age. c. licensed. d. 19 years of age.	c. licensed. Real estate practitioners must be licensed.
83. A salesperson lists a property with a contract that allows for subagency and dual agency. The salesperson is? a. An agent to the broker and a subagent to the principal. b. An employee of the sub-contractor. c. A subagent to the broker and no relationship to the client. d. An independent contractor to the broker and an agent to the client.	a. An agent to the broker and a subagent to the principal. The agent of the broker. All agents in that broker's office are sub agents of the client.

Offers, Counteroffers, Acceptance and Rejections

Offers

Present all offers.

A buyer makes an offer on a property
Offers must.
1. Identify the address (legal description and parties involved
2. Price and terms
3. Closing dates
4. Costs
5. Items included and excluded
6. Required disclosures
7. Delivery, acceptance date and offer expiration
8. Signatures

Offer and Acceptance

- Communication to an offeror that the recipient (offeree) finds the terms and conditions of an offer acceptable. Turns an offer into a binding contract.
- Any language or action that indicates an agreement forming a contract has been reached.

An offer is just an offer until acceptance.
- Mutual Assent or Agreement
- An essential element of a contract.
- Mutual assent is an agreement between two parties that intend to form a contract. Also known as a "meeting of the minds," mutual assent signifies that the parties agree to the terms they are setting, if the necessary requirements are in place.

Earnest money

- A buyer deposits an earnest money deposit to show his/her true intentions to move forward with the transaction.
- A good faith deposit is typically given to the seller by the buyer, which is often treated as liquidated damages in the event of the buyer's default
- Simply put, an earnest payment is a form of security deposit made in real estate offers to demonstrate that the buyer is serious and willing to demonstrate an earnest of good faith about wanting to complete the transaction.
- Although an earnest money deposit is not a mandatory condition of the sale, buyers will supply one to show their true intentions.
- The absence of a security deposit does not void the contract.
- A good faith deposit is typically given to the seller by the buyer, which is often treated as liquidated damages in the event of the buyer's default
- Simply put, an earnest payment is a form of security deposit made in real estate offers to demonstrate that the buyer is serious and willing to demonstrate an earnest of good faith about

---

- wanting to complete the transaction.
- The responsible broker is always responsible for earnest money deposits.
- The responsible broker is required to promptly account for and remit the full amount of the deposit or earnest money at the consummation or termination of transaction.
- A licensee is required to pay over to the responsible broker all deposits and earnest money immediately upon receipt thereof.
- Earnest money must be returned promptly when the purchaser is rightfully entitled to same allowing reasonable time for clearance of the earnest money check.
- Failure to comply with this regulation shall constitute grounds for revocation or suspension of license.
- Buyers may be legally entitled to get their earnest money back if their contingencies can't be met, such as if the buyer can't get the financing described in the financing contingency.
- A seller may be able to keep the earnest money if the buyer doesn't make a serious, good faith effort to close the deal after the offer has been accepted.
- The earnest money deposit received by the Broker goes into a federally insured escrow account and stays there until the transaction is completed, or it's been canceled.
- In the event of a failure to close, Broker/Trustee can give the earnest money to the rightful recipient depending on the terms of the contract.

☐ In the event of uncertainty as to the proper disposition of earnest money, the broker may turn earnest money over to a court of law for disposition. (The form is an interpleader.)

Liquidated damages

- Liquidated Damages are money set aside to be paid to the party that has been injured. Some agents will include liquidated damages into the offer to purchase. The liquidated damages would be paid to the seller if the buyer backs out after a meeting of the minds.
- Those damages are specified by contract in advance (usually loss of earnest money) if the buyer defaults.
- If specified, liquidated damages are the seller's only remedy against the buyer.

Counteroffer

- Counteroffers void the original offer.
- Legally, a rejection of the original offer; a new offer. In form, a counter usually states that the first offer is accepted "except for the following changes…" thus incorporating (merging) the first contract.
- Not binding on the buyer (who is now the offeree) until accepted.

Recission of Offer or Counteroffer

- An offer or a counteroffer may be rescinded before it has been accepted.
- In the case of the buyer, the buyer is entitled to their earnest money back.
- In the case of the seller, the seller may rescind a counteroffer before it is accepted and accept a better offer.

Acceptance /Binding Acceptance

Meeting of the minds

- A Purchase Agreement is signed by both seller and buyer once there has been an agreement.
- After all the parties sign the offer, it's "accepted." When the seller returns the offer to the buyer it becomes a binding contract.
- If the seller wants to change any of the terms of the buyer's offer, he/she will usually give the buyer a counteroffer.

Legal Title	Equitable Title
The seller retains legal title until the property transfers.	The buyer holds equitable title until the property transfers. Equitable title is an insurable interest to be the next owner.

☐ Both legal title and equitable title can be inherited.

Purchase Agreement (Contract)

- The purchase agreement defines the legal rights of the buyer and seller.
- The purchase agreement must identify the parties, describe the property, sets forth the price and method of payment, and sets the date for closing the transaction
- Everyone with an ownership interest must sign the contract; it is best for both spouses to sign the contract
- In a real estate transaction, there are two parties: the seller and the buyer.
- The purchase agreement is a bilateral contract.

Handy Definitions

Purchase Contracts
Purchase contracts are between the seller and buyer.
Offers
A buyer will supply an earnest money deposit to show their true intentions to carry the transaction forward.
Counteroffers
A counteroffer voids the original offer.
Recission of offer
A buyer may rescind their offer before it is accepted by the seller.
Recission of Counteroffer
A seller can rescind a counteroffer before it is accepted by the buyer.

Contract Clauses

A purchase or sale subject to an event, approval, or other contingency.

Contingency Clauses

- A contingency clause makes the contract conditional on something else happening, like the buyer receiving financing, an inspection, lead based paint.
- The buyer must remove the contingencies in a timely manner.

Loan Approval	Inspection report
Termite report	Title inspection

Other Contingencies

- The Property must appraise at, or above Purchase Price or Buyer shall not be obligated to complete the purchase of the Property and all Earnest Money shall be refunded to Buyer, except when Buyer has failed to secure a timely appraisal in good faith. Failure of Buyer to make good faith efforts to secure a timely appraisal shall constitute a Breach of this Contract.
- The contract is contingent upon satisfactory inspections to be conducted by Buyer.
- The Buyer retains the right to perform a final walk-through Inspection of the Property prior to Closing to verify the terms of the Contract have been fulfilled.
- An acceptable FHA/VA Wood Destroying Insect Report ("WDIR") from a licensed, bonded termite company indicating that Property shows no evidence of termite or other wood-destroying insect infestation.

Escrow Agreement

The parties will enter a contract called an *escrow agreement* that provides instructions for the closing process.

Transactional Agent (Escrow Period)

- The Purchase Agreement is delivered to the Transactional Agent. (Closing Attorney)
- The job of the Transactional Agent to make sure the legal rights of the seller and buyer have been completed before the property transfers ownership.

Delivery of the Property

- This Contract is conditioned upon delivery of the Property and all improvements in their present condition, reasonable wear and tear excepted.
- Damage to the Property or improvements before Closing by virtue of causes beyond the parties' control, such as fire, flood, war, acts of God or other causes can void the contract and the buyer's earnest money will be returned.

Transferring a Property with Tenants

Optional Provisions
Even if tenants are living on the property at the time the offer is made, the purchase of the property doesn't affect their lease rights. The seller and buyer may want to have a special agreement that explains

what the seller should do if there are certain issues with the tenants before closing, for example, does the buyer want the seller to renew or not renew a tenant's lease before closing?

Time is of the Essence Clause in the Purchase Agreement

- The Purchase Agreement contains a time is of the essence clause, which makes any failure to meet a deadline a breach of contract.
- Time is of the essence means "punctual performance." In other words, if one party holds up the transaction, that party may be responsible to the other party for damages.
- Failure of the Buyer to make timely application for loan and exercise good faith efforts to facilitate its approval shall entitle the Seller at its option to
- excuse the failure and proceed with the transaction on such terms as the parties may agree to in writing in the form of an amendment to the Contract, OR
- declare the Contract void and refund to Buyer the earnest money deposit, OR
- treat the failure as a Breach by Buyer under paragraph 10
- Here's the deal. Buyer can get a loan with different terms and conditions or close the deal with a different type of loan, if all other terms and conditions in this agreement are met.

Changes to the Purchase Agreement

Amendment	Addendum
An amendment is a change before the contract is signed.	An addendum is an attachment to the contract made prior to signing

☐ If a buyer makes an offer and pays an earnest money deposit, the buyer can withdraw the offer and buy another property if the offer has not been accepted.

☐ If a buyer receives a counteroffer and has not accepted it, the seller can withdraw the counteroffer and accept a better offer.

☐ If a seller receives multiple offers, the agent should caution their seller to counteroffer each offer one at a time.

☐ If your seller receives multiple offers, you should deliver them as they come in.

☐ If your seller goes on vacation and asked you to hold all the offers until he gets back. When he does get back, you will deliver all the offers simultaneously.

☐ If a buyer makes an offer on a home and gives his agent an earnest money deposit, but on his way home he saw an open house sign and stopped by. He loved that house even better than the one he put the earnest money deposit on. He made an offer on the second home and put an earnest money deposit down. Both offers were accepted. What is the Buyer responsible for?

He is responsible for both offers.

(He bought two properties.)

☐ PRESENT ALL OFFERS

☐ Brokers/Salespersons should caution the seller against countering on more than one offer simultaneously.

☐ Deliver offers to your client as soon as practicable.

BUT…

☐ Your client went on vacation and asked you to hold all the offers until he returns. While he was on vacation, you received six offers. One week later, your client visited your office. How should you deliver the offers?

Answer: All simultaneously.

CONTRACT FOR THE SALE AND PURCHASE OF REAL ESTATE

THIS IS AN EXAMPLE OF AN OFFER

For EDUCATIONAL PURPOSES ONLY

This form is provided as a courtesy to the parties only. It is not required to be used in this transaction and may not fit the needs, goals, and purposes of the parties. The Mississippi Association of REALTORS® makes no statement or warranty as to this form, its contents or use, and the parties, by their use of this form, acknowledge said facts and agree that neither the Mississippi Association of REALTORS® nor any member thereof shall be liable to any party or person for its contents or use. If any party to this transaction does not fully understand it, or has any questions, the party should seek advice from a competent legal professional before signing.

PARTIES.

Buyer	Seller

Buyer agrees to buy, and Seller agrees to sell the herein described property on the terms and conditions set forth herein.

PROPERTY Description:

☐ LEGAL DESCRIPTION
in County, MS. (street address, if available) (city) (zip code) (county)
The Property is further described as tax parcel #

A list of standard real property (This is added by Instructor for educational purposes.) ☐
together with any of the following presently located therein: all built-in appliances, ceiling fans, all plumbing and heating and air conditioning equipment including any window units, stationary laundry tubs, water heaters, doors, windows, storm doors and windows, window treatments (e.g., shutters, blinds, shades) and associated hardware, awnings, carpet, bathroom fixtures and mirrors, lighting fixtures and their shades, gas logs, fireplace doors and screens, security system components, smoke detectors, garage door openers, antennae and satellite dishes (including rotor equipment but excluding proprietary components), central vacuum systems/attachments, landscaping, fences, permanently installed pet fences and equipment (including collars), gates, outdoor lighting, swimming pools and equipment, mailboxes, water pump(s) and pressure tanks, permanently installed playgroup equipment, and permanently installed cooking grills, and keys to all doors with keyed locks or deadbolts.

all built-in appliances	ceiling fans	stationary laundry tubs	water heaters	doors
windows	storm doors and windows	carpet	gas logs	fireplace doors and screen
security system components	smoke detectors	garage door openers	landscaping	fences
gates	outdoor lighting	swimming pools and equipment	mailboxes	water pump(s) and pressu tanks
permanently	permanently	keys to all doors	permanently	central vacuum

installed playgroup equipment	installed cooking grills	with keyed locks or deadbolts	installed pet fences and equipment (including collars)	systems/attachments	
all plumbing and heating and air conditioning equipment including any window units	antennae and satellite dishes (including rotor equipment but excluding proprietary components)	lighting fixtures and their shades	bathroom fixtures and mirrors	window treatments (e.g., shutters, shades) and associated hardware awning	

PURCHASE PRICE.

Buyer agrees to pay a purchase price of $ _____ ("Purchase Price") by Federal Reserve wire transfer, Cashier's Check issued by a financial institution as defined in 12 CFR § 229.2(i), or such form as is approved in writing by Seller.

☐ EARNEST MONEY.

cash check is to be deposited with [Broker/Trustee], who shall hold it in trust, presuming clearance of check.

Upon acceptance of the Contract, earnest money deposit and down payment received by above named

Broker/Trustee shall be deposited in a *federally insured escrow account* and shall remain in that account until the transaction has been consummated or terminated.

In any event of failure to close, Broker/Trustee has authority to provide the earnest money to the rightfully entitled party based upon the terms of the Contract.

In the event the Broker/Trustee cannot determine by the terms of the Contract which party is rightfully entitled to the earnest money, the Broker/Trustee shall ☐ **interplead the funds**.

In the event interpleader is required, Buyer and Seller consent to the filing of same; jurisdiction in the county where the property, or any part of it, lies; entry of an order discharging Broker/Trustee or the interpleading party upon deposit of the funds into court; and deduction against the money interplead of all costs necessitated by the filing of the interpleader action, including filing and attorney's fees.

CONTINGENCIES.

(A) Loan. (Check One):

Applicable				Not Applicable		
☐						
FHA ☐	VA ☐	CONV ☐	Other:	To Be Determined	USDA ☐	Direct USDA Guaranteed ☐

If applicable, Contract is contingent upon Buyer being approved for a new loan sufficient to close, provided that Buyer makes timely application and good faith efforts to secure loan prior to Closing.

Within five (5) business days after the Effective Date of the Contract, Buyer will make application in proper form for the loan(s), shall cooperate with parties to obtain approval(s), diligently and timely pursue the same in good faith, execute all documents and furnish all information and documents required, and make timely payment of any costs of obtaining such loan approval.

Failure of the Buyer to make timely application for loan and exercise *good faith* efforts to facilitate its approval

A) excuse the failure and proceed with the transaction on such terms as the parties may agree to in writing in the form of an amendment to the Contract, OR

(B) declare the Contract void and refund to Buyer the earnest money deposit, OR

(C) treat the failure as a Breach by Buyer under paragraph 10 hereof.

Buyer may apply for a loan with different terms and conditions and also close the transaction with a different type of loan provided all other terms and conditions of this Agreement are fulfilled and Seller's costs are not increased.

(B) No Waste.

This Contract is conditioned upon delivery of the Property and any and all improvements in their present condition, reasonable wear and tear excepted.

Seller shall preserve the Property in its present general condition, normal wear and tear excepted, and shall not permit the Property to suffer waste avoidable by the reasonable exercise of due care.

 Any material change to the Property shall be disclosed in accordance with the Real Estate Brokers License Law of 1954, as amended, allowing for termination of the offer as prescribed by law.

Appraisal. (Check One):

Applicable	Not Applicable

If applicable, Property must appraise at or above Purchase Price or Buyer shall not be obligated to complete the purchase of the Property and all Earnest Money shall be refunded to Buyer, except when Buyer has failed to secure a timely appraisal in good faith.

Failure of Buyer to make **good faith efforts** to secure a timely appraisal shall constitute a Breach of this Contract.

Warranty And Inspections.

Sale Without Warranty;

No Home Inspection.

Buyer has inspected the Property and finds same to be in satisfactory condition and DOES NOT wish to secure a home inspection.

Buyer accepts the Property in its condition as of the Effective Date of this Contract and acknowledges that neither Seller nor Listing Broker nor Selling Broker or salespersons associated with this transaction have made any warranty, express, implied, or otherwise, as to the Property, except such express warranties as the parties agree to in writing attached hereto, which shall survive Closing.

☐ **Inspections.** Contract is contingent upon satisfactory inspections to be conducted by Buyer, at Buyer's expense.

Buyer shall have ☐ *ten (10) business days* from the Effective Date to conduct inspections using Mississippi licensed and bonded inspectors.

Buyer's inspector(s) shall have the right to enter the Property at reasonable hours with twenty-four (24) hour prior notice. On designated inspection date(s), Seller shall provide unlimited access to the Property, and shall see that all utilities are on.

UTILITIES ON
Should Seller fail to have utilities on, Seller shall be responsible to Buyer for foreseeable loss or expense resulting from failed inspections.

Within said ☐ ten (10) business day inspection period, Buyer shall submit a list of repairs to Seller accompanied by relevant portions of any inspection report(s) from a ☐ Mississippi licensed and bonded inspector or waive this inspection contingency and proceed to Closing.

If Buyer timely submits a list of repairs accompanied by relevant portions of any inspection report(s), Buyer and Seller shall have _____ business days to resolve how listed items shall be handled or this Contract shall terminate and Buyer's earnest money shall be returned.

Final Walk-Through Inspection.
Irrespective of the election made above, Buyer retains the right to perform a final walkthrough Inspection of the Property prior to Closing to verify the terms of the Contract have been fulfilled.

Wood Destroying Insect Report; Release. (Check One):

Buyer	Seller

shall, at their expense, furnish within thirty (30) calendar days before Closing approved ☐ FHA/VA Wood Destroying Insect Report ("WDIR") from a licensed, bonded termite company indicating that Property shows no evidence of termite or other wood-destroying insect infestation.

If infestation or damage is discovered, Seller shall amend the Property Condition Disclosure Statement as appropriate and, per 89-1-503 of the Mississippi Code of 1972

Buyer shall have ☐ *three (3) days after delivery in person or five (5) days after delivery by deposit in the mail*, of any amendment to PCDS to terminate his or her offer by delivery of a written notice of termination to the transferor (seller) or the transferor's agent (listing broker or salesperson), and have their earnest money refunded.

Irrespective of whether a WDIR (Wood Destroying Insect Report) is received or not, Buyer and Seller acknowledge that Listing and Selling Broker make no representations concerning wood destroying insects or the condition of the Property, and any damage found, either before or after Closing or after termination of this Contract shall not be the responsibility of said Broker(s).

By signing this Contract, Buyer and Seller acknowledge receipt of this notice and agree to hold the brokerages, their agents and the designated title company or closing attorney harmless from all claims arising out of or relating to wood destroying insects or the WDIR.

Pre-Closing Loss. ☐
In the event of damage to the Property or improvements before Closing by virtue of causes beyond the parties' control, such as
1. fire,
2. flood,
3. war,
4. acts of God or
5. other causes,

Seller(s) shall, within three (3) calendar days of a loss or as soon thereafter as reasonably possible, notify Buyer(s) in writing of said damage, at which time Buyer(s) may, at Buyer's option:
(1) cancel this contract and be entitled to the return of earnest money deposits; OR
(2) waive any objection and proceed to Closing on the terms set forth in this Contract; OR
(3) seek to reach suitable agreement with Seller(s) as to repair(s), extension of the Closing date and/or other adjustments to the Contract as may be agreed upon by the parties. Failure of the parties to reach a suitable agreement within five (5) calendar days after election by Buyer(s) to proceed under this option (3) shall automatically and without further notice cancel this Contract and entitle Buyer(s) to the return of earnest money deposits.

CLOSING.
(A) Deadline to Close. Closing (evidenced by delivery of deed and payment of Purchase Price) shall take place no later than 11:59 p.m. (CST) on the _____ (the closing date, or on such earlier date as agreed on by the parties in writing
(B) Title And Conveyance.
At Closing, Seller shall deliver to Buyer a(n):

☐ General Warranty Deed	☐ Special Warranty Deed	☐ Assignment of Lease	☐Quitclaim Deed

vesting title to the Property in (write names clearly):_____;

Seller shall, prior to or at Closing, satisfy and pay
all outstanding mortgages,
deeds of trust,
special liens,
taxes or special assessments,
escrow amount of Property Owner's Association or Condominium fees affecting the subject property which are not specifically assumed by Buyer herein.

Title shall be good, marketable, and insurable, subject only to the following items recorded in the

Chancery Clerk's Office of said county:			
easements without encroachments ☐	applicable zoning ordinances ☐	protective covenants ☐	prior mineral reservations ☐

otherwise, Buyer, at its option, may either

(A) if defects cannot be cured by designated Closing Date, cancel this Contract, in which case any earnest money deposit shall be refunded to Buyer;

(B) accept title as is and proceed to day of, (the "Closing Date") or on such earlier date as agreed to by the Closing; or

(C) if the defects are of such character that they can be remedied by legal action within a reasonable time, permit Seller such reasonable time to perform this curative work at Seller's expense.

In the event curative formed by Seller, the time specified herein for Closing shall be extended for a reasonable period necessary for such cure, said period not to exceed thirty (30) calendar days unless agreed to in writing by the parties.

(C) Proration ☐

All taxes, rents, utility and other assessments and appropriate condominium or Property Owner's Association fees are to be prorated as of the Closing Date for the year of the sale.

(D) Costs of Sale.

At Closing, Seller agrees to pay up to $ _____ toward total costs of sale not including home warranty, wood destroying insect report (WDIR), inspection cost, compensation to Brokers, Seller's repair costs (if any), cure of title defects under paragraph 6(B), or prorated items under paragraph 6(C) (subject to applicable law).

E. Possession.
Possession shall be delivered to Buyer (Check One):

Upon completion of Closing and full funding	By separate Possession Addendum attached and made a part of this Contract

DISCLOSURES. ☐
A. Multiple Listing Service ("MLS").
The Selling Broker is a participant of the Multiple Listing Service and the sales information will be provided to the MLS to be published and disseminated to its Participants.

B. Property Condition Disclosure. ☐
Buyer acknowledges receipt of the Informational Statement for Mississippi Property Condition Disclosure Statement AND

(Select One):

A fully completed Property Condition Disclosure Statement is not required in accordance with Sections 89-1-501 et seq. of the Mississippi Code of 1972 and a Seller's Statement of Exclusion From Completing the Property Condition Disclosure Statement (PCDS) has been completed and delivered to Buyer, and Buyer acknowledges receipt thereof.

Buyer acknowledges receipt of a **Property Condition Disclosure Statement.**
OR
The Property Condition Disclosure Statement is to be delivered after the Buyer has made an offer.

☐* STATE EXAM Buyer shall have three (3) days after delivery in person or five (5) days after delivery by deposit in the mail, to terminate his or her offer by delivery of a written notice of termination to the transferor (seller) or the transferor's agent (listing broker or salesperson), and have their earnest money refunded.

☐ **Equal Housing Opportunity.**
In accordance with the federal Fair Housing Act, it is illegal to block bust or to discriminate against any person because of race, color, religion, sex, handicap, familial status or national origin in the sale or rental of housing or residential lots, in advertising the sale or rental of housing, in the financing of housing or in the providing of real estate brokerage services.

☐ **Lead-Based Paint Disclosure.**
Every Buyer of any interest in residential property on which a residential dwelling was built prior to 1978 is notified that such subject property may present exposure to lead from lead-based paint that may place young children at risk of developing lead poisoning.

☐ Lead poisoning in young children may produce permanent neurological damage, including learning disabilities, reduced intelligence quotient, behavioral problems, and impaired memory.
☐Lead poisoning also poses a particular risk to pregnant women.
☐The Seller of any interest in residential real property is required to provide the Buyer with any information on lead-based paint hazards from risk assessments or inspections in the Seller's possession and notify the Buyer of any unknown lead-based paint hazards.

A risk assessment or inspection for possible lead-based paint hazards is recommended prior to purchase.
Wire Fraud Warning; Release.

Buyers and Sellers of real property are targets in scams regarding electronic transfers of money (i.e., wire transfers, direct deposits, electronic checks, etc.).

NEVER transfer funds associated with this transaction based upon electronic communications (such as email) that have not been verbally confirmed by you to be valid (from a person you know and trust) and accurate.
Email scammers can disguise emails, text messages and social media messages to appear to be from your real estate agent, title companies, your bank, or other parties.

Do not trust any communication you receive concerning transfer of funds without taking steps to verify that these funds are, in fact, going to the proper recipient.

Do not use telephone numbers or email addresses in electronic communications you receive; they may be fraudulent and part of a scam.

VERIFY telephone numbers, contact people and wiring instructions BEFORE you respond.

Fraudulent communications or acts should be reported immediately to the FBI and law enforcement authorities and should be done so immediately if funds are lost.

By signing this Contract, you acknowledge receipt of this notice and agree to hold the brokerages, their agents and the designated title company or closing attorney harmless from all claims arising out of inaccurate transfer instructions, fraudulent taking of such funds, and any and all other damages relating to conduct of third parties influencing implementation of wire transfers.

BROKERS AND SALESPERSONS

A. The Brokers and Salespersons
involved in the transaction associated with this Contract are as follows:

B. Agency Relationship. (Check One):

▷ The Listing Firm, the Selling Firm, and their salespersons represent the Seller as their Client. The Buyer is the customer.

▷ The Listing Firm and its salespersons represent the Seller. The Selling Firm and its salespersons represent the Buyer(s).

▷ The Listing Firm and its salespersons represent both Seller and the Buyer as dual agents by mutual agreement and all parties have signed and understand the Dual Agency Confirmation form provided to them by the Listing Firm.

▷ The Selling Firm and its salespersons represent the Buyer. The Seller is not represented and is a customer.

(C) Compensation. ☐
The parties under this Contract or through any other ☐ negotiated agreement agree to pay as per listing agreement or prior offer of cooperation and compensation.

If Broker collects this compensation or any part thereof through legal action, the defaulting party agrees to pay court costs, including reasonable attorney fees.

☐ Compensation due hereunder is deemed earned, due and payable upon presentation of a ☐ *buyer ready, willing, and able to purchase on terms acceptable to Seller*, though Broker agrees to accept payment at Closing as an accommodation to the parties.

(D) No Reliance; Release.

Seller and Buyer acknowledge that neither them, nor their agents, have relied upon any statement, representation or omission made or documentation provided by the Broker, salesperson(s), or their representatives, relating to any aspect of this transaction, the Property or otherwise including, but not limited to, terms or conditions of sale, tax or legal considerations, liability, size, square footage or condition of the Property, presence or lack thereof of urea formaldehyde foam insulation (UFFI), presence or lack thereof of exterior insulation finish systems (EIFS), previous or present flooding, flood zones, flood insurance, history of title or use, effect of or location within Mississippi State Tidelands or Federal wetlands, presence or absence of mold or other toxic substances, presence or lack of expansive soils, presence or absence or enforceability of acceleration clauses or tax or balloon notes, names or recommendations concerning vendors of any sort whatsoever or validity or accuracy of any reports rendered thereby.

By signing this Contract, Buyer and Seller acknowledge receipt of this disclosure and agree to hold the brokerages, their agents and the designated title company or closing attorney harmless from all claims arising out of or pertaining in any way to any representations in this section.

(E) Liability
Broker's liability to Buyer and Seller in this transaction shall not exceed the amount it has received as compensation.

GENERAL.
A) Agreement Complete.
This Contract incorporates all prior agreements between the parties, contains the entire and final agreement of the parties and cannot be changed except by their written mutual consent.
Neither party shall be bound by any terms, conditions, oral statements, warranties, or representations not herein contained.

B. Read and Understood.
Each party acknowledges and hereby affirms that it has read and understands this Contract.

☐ C. Assignment.
This Contract shall not be assignable by either party without consent of the other party.

D. Effective Date.
For purposes of this Contract the Effective Date is the date the last necessary party signs.

E. Notices.
Any notices required or permitted to be given under this Contract shall be delivered by hand or mailed by certified or registered mail, return receipt requested, in a postage prepaid envelope or by nationally recognized overnight carrier service; by facsimile with receipt acknowledgment (if the fax number is listed below); or by email (if the email address is listed below), at Sender's option, and addressed as follows:

F. Survival of Contract.
All *express representations*, ☐ warranties and covenants shall survive termination of the Contract or Closing unless specified to the contrary. All other contractual obligations shall terminate at Closing.

☐ G. Time Is of The Essence.
Time is of the essence as to all time periods and deadlines stated in this Contract, and delay in performance is not excused unless expressly excused in writing signed by all parties. The foregoing or any other provision in this Contract notwithstanding, any unavoidable delay necessitated by applicable law or regulations shall extend any affected deadline by no more than the actual number of days of delay necessitated by such law or regulation.

BREACH. ☐

In the event of a default by either party under this Contract, the non-breaching party shall have the right to receive from Broker/Trustee the Earnest Money paid under Section 4 of this Contract, to be a credit against any other damages, in addition to such other remedies as it may have under applicable law including, but not limited to, specific performance.

SPECIAL PROVISIONS.
(If None, Write "NONE" Below):
EXPIRATION OF OFFER.

This offer expires at _____ o'clock AM, PM Central Time on_____ if not accepted, countered, or rejected by Seller by that time.

ATTACHMENTS. (Check All That Apply)

Dual Agency Confirmation ☐	Pre-Closing Repair/Improvement Addendum ☐	First Right of Refusal Addendum ☐	Pre-Closing Possession Addendum ☐
Lead-Based Paint Disclosure ☐	Option Agreement ☐		Back-Up Agreement Contingency
VA/FHA Disclosures (as required) ☐	Other		

Quiz: AGENCY Listings

1. You listed a home for sale under an exclusive-right-to-sell agreement and showed the property to a person who wrote an offer with an earnest money check that was subsequently rejected by the owner. What should happen to the earnest money check? a. It should be given to the seller for the trouble. b. It should be put into the Listing Agent's business account. c. It should be put into the Listing Agent's trust account. d. It should just be returned to the buyer.	d. It should just be returned to the buyer. Earnest money deposits are returned to the person making the offer when the offer is rejected.
2. Salesperson Tina presented to Broker Wrightford Buyer King's offer to purchase Seller Bright's real estate, accompanied by an earnest money deposit in the form of a personal note in the amount of $1,000. Broker Wright should inform Salesperson Tina that: a. Seller Bright should be informed prior to acceptance that the deposit is a personal note b. Buyer King should be told that this offer cannot be presented to Seller Bright c. Buyer King must be told that the note will have to be redeemed within five days by cash d. Without Seller Bright's express permission, Salesperson Tina should not have accepted the note	a. Seller Bright should be informed prior to acceptance that the deposit is a personal note A promissory note is legal consideration as an earnest money deposit, but the principal should be informed of this information.
3. Which of the following statements is (are) true of a buyer's earnest money deposit? a. While a postdated check is illegal, the broker must note clearly on the deposit receipt that the check is postdated, and he must get the seller's approval before the contract is signed. b. While a postdated check is not illegal, the broker must note clearly on the deposit receipt that the check is postdated, and he must get the seller's approval before the contract is signed. c. the broker will lose his license. d. if the broker deposits the check by the close of the next banking day, the broker is not responsible if the check is dishonored.	b. While a postdated check is not illegal, the broker must note clearly on the deposit receipt that the check is postdated, and he must get the seller's approval before the contract is signed. While a postdated check is not illegal, the broker must note clearly on the deposit receipt that the check is postdated, and he must get the seller's approval before the contract is signed.
4. A buyer made an offer and the seller responded with a counteroffer. When the buyer was reviewing the counter offer the seller received a better offer from another buyer. The seller can accept the second offer? a. if the second offer is coupled with a higher down payment. b. if the seller withdraws the counteroffer before the buyer accepts it. c. if the first buyer has been informed in writing that the seller is going to accept the second offer. d. the seller is forced to wait for the response of the first	b. if the seller withdraws the counteroffer before the buyer accepts it. Offers and counteroffers can be withdrawn before they are accepted.

buyer.	
5. A written agreement between a buyer and seller when the buyer wants to buy, and the seller wants to sell is called? a. a disclosure agreement. b. an appraisal. c. contract. d. an estoppel	c. contract. Definition of contract a binding agreement between two or more persons or parties especially: one legally enforceable
6. When a buyer withdraws his offer to purchase real property prior to acceptance by the seller, the? a. Broker may sue buyer for specific performance b. Seller may sue the buyer for specific performance and will probably win the suit c. Buyer is entitled to the refund of the earnest money deposit d. Seller is entitled to one-half of the earnest money deposit	c. Buyer is entitled to the refund of the earnest money deposit A "meeting of the minds" is a three-step process. The offeror makes an offer the offer is received by the offeree and accepted the offeree's acceptance must be communicated back to the offeror Until this takes place, there is no contract, and the offeror may withdraw or cancel the offer without a reason.
7. Bender made an offer on the purchase of a vacant residence and gave a cash deposit with the offer. The offer was presented through Broker Harris. The offer was accepted by the seller. Prior to the close of the transaction, Bender requested permission from Harris to enter the house for the purpose of painting and making minor repairs. Which of the following is true? a. If Bender signs a rental agreement, Harris may give permission. b. Bender is an equity owner and doesn't need to obtain permission from anyone. c. Harris should obtain written approval of Bender's request from the owner. d. For Bender to do this, there must be a written agreement signed by the buyer and seller setting forth the limits of the repairs to be made.	c. Harris should obtain written approval of Bender's request from the owner The seller remains the owner of the property until the close of escrow and, therefore, the seller's written approval must be obtained before anything is done to the property.
8. A buyer's agency contract should include a. A dual agency disclosure b. Information about potential environmental hazards in the area c. Exclusivity d. An extremely detailed description of what the buyers want	c. Exclusivity Exclusivity and fee structure are vital parts of a buyer's agency contract. Dual agency disclosure would be necessary only if it applies.

MODULE SIX: PROPERTY DISCLOSURE

Property Defects

Patent Defects	Latent Defects
Defects readily seen.	A defect that is not visible or apparent; a hidden defect that would not be discovered in a reasonably thorough inspection of the property. The least apparent lead product to be found on a property is a lead pipe. It's a latent defect. (Latent Defect is an unseen defect.) .

Material fact	Nonmaterial fact
The fact that a reasonable person would recognize as significant. In other words, it is a fact, the suppression of which would reasonably result in a different decision.	Homicide, suicide felony on the property, HIV AND AIDS – Things that do not affect the property's physical condition or the surrounding area. Varies state to state.

Seller's Property Disclosure Act

Legislation requiring the seller to reveal the property's honest condition, whether a defect is observed or a latent defect.

SELLER of residential real property consisting of not less than one (1) nor more than four (4) dwelling units shall provide a Property Condition Disclosure

Property Owner's Role Regarding Property Condition

- The Seller will provide the buyer with a written property condition disclosure.
- The Seller must identify all material facts relating to the property and its surrounding area.
- The seller must identify latent defects if aware of the defect.
- Full seller disclosure
- Sellers must disclose material facts even if not asked.

Licensee's Role Regarding Property Condition

- A duty of an agent to the principal to discover and reveal information that might adversely affect the principal's position.
- The agent's obligation to the seller regarding disclosure is to have him disclose all material defects.
- Both the Listing Agent and the Selling Agent must conduct a reasonably competent visual inspection and disclose facts that an inspection would reveal
- A licensee is not responsible for identifying latent defects.
- If the agent is aware of a latent defect, he must disclose it.
- The agent must disclose what is readily seen.
- When in doubt, licensees should make full disclosure.

- Agents have no duty to inspect:
- reasonably inaccessible areas.
- areas off-site.
- public records and permits.

Property Condition Disclosure Statement (PCDS)

FOR EDUCATIONAL PURPOSES ONLY
Visit the MREC website for a true copy.

A document required by law that reveals specific information. Must be filled out by the Seller.

The following is a Property Condition Disclosure Statement (PCDS) of the Mississippi Real Estate Brokers Act of **1954,** as Amended, and made by the SELLER(S) concerning the condition of the RESIDENTIAL PROPERTY ☐ (1 TO 4 UNITS) located at_____ SELLER(S): _____
Approximate Age of the Residence_____

This document is a disclosure of the condition of real property known by the SELLER on the date that this statement is signed, and it is based on their *actual knowledge* of the property.

☐ It is *NOT a warranty* of any kind by the Seller or any Real Estate Licensee representing a principal in this transaction and this PCDS ☐ is not a substitute for any home inspection(s) or warranties the purchaser(s) may wish to obtain. However, the purchaser(s) may rely on the information contained herein when deciding to negotiate the terms for the purchase of the residential real property. This statement may be made available to other parties and is to be attached to the Listing Agreement and signed by the SELLER(S). This statement is NOT intended to be part of any contract between the seller and the purchaser.

☐ IF THE RESIDENCE IS NEW (NEVER OCCUPIED) OR PROPOSED RESIDENTIAL CONSTRUCTION and a real estate licensee is involved in the transaction, the BUILDER/OWNER/SELLER must complete the PCDS in its entirety and should reference specific plans/specifications, building material lists and/or change orders.

DO NOT LEAVE ANY QUESTIONS UNANSWERED AND DO NOT LEAVE BLANK SPACES.

THE SELLER(S) MAY ATTACH ADDITIONAL PAGES IF NECESSARY TO FULLY EXPLAIN A PROPERTY'S CONDITION. THE ACRONYM "N/A" MAY BE USED FOR "NOT APPLICABLE" AND "UNK" MAY BE USED FOR "UNKNOWN".

A. GENERAL INFORMATION:
1. Does the Transferor/Seller currently have a deeded title to the residence?
2. Does the Transferor/Seller currently occupy the residence?
3. Is the site improved with a Factory Built (Manufactured Housing Unit) or a Modular Home constructed on a permanent foundation?
4. Was the residence built in conformity with an ☐ approved building code?

B. STRUCTURAL ITEMS & SOILS:
Are you aware of any ☐ settlement/heaving of soils, any collapsible or expansive soils or poorly compacted fill on the Property?

Are you aware of any past or present ☐ movement, shifting, deterioration or other problems with the walls (interior or exterior) or the foundation of the Property?

Are you aware of any ☐ foundation repairs made in the past?

To your knowledge, are any ☐ foundation repairs currently needed?

Except for "Cosmetic Upgrades" (carpet, paint, wallpaper, etc.) have you ☐ remodeled, made any room additions, made structural modifications or other alterations or improvements to the Property?

To your knowledge, were all necessary work PERMITS and approvals secured ☐ in compliance with local/city/county building codes?

C. ROOF:

Are you aware of any current ☐ leaks or defects with the roof such as structural issues, dry rot, water backups, moisture issues, wind damage or hail damage?

D. HISTORY OF INFESTATION: TERMITES, CARPENTER ANTS, ETC:

1. Are you aware of any ongoing, recurring or ☐ habitual problems with termites, dry rot, mildew, vermin, rodents, or other pests which affect the Property?

2. Are you aware of any DAMAGE to the Property, which was caused by ☐ termites, dry rot, mildew, vermin, rodents, or other pests?

E. STRUCTURE/FLOOR/WALLS/CEILINGS/WINDOWS/FEATURES:

1. During your ownership, has there been DAMAGE to any portion of the physical structure resulting from fire, windstorm, hail, tornados, hurricane, or any other natural disaster?

2. Are you aware of any past or present problems, ☐ malfunctions or defects with the windows (including storm windows and screens), the flooring (hardwood, marble, stone, tile, or carpeting), fireplace/chimneys, ceilings, walls (interior), jetted bathtub, hot tub, sauna, skylights, shower, or wet bar; including any modifications to them?

3. Are you aware of any past or present problems, ☐ malfunctions or defects with the lawn sprinkler system, swimming pool, hot tub, rain gutters, tile drains (French drains), driveway, patio, storage building, gazebo, outdoor fireplace, or outdoor kitchen appliances (which are remaining with the property)?

4. During your ownership, have there been any notices concerning ☐ safety issues with a swimming pool or other improvements to the property?

5. Except for regular maintenance of the exterior surfaces of the Property (painting, staining, etc.) are you aware of any ☐ past or present problems, malfunctions, or defects with any portion of the exterior walls, facias, soffits, stucco, windows, doors, or trim?

F. LAND AND SITE DATA:

2. Are you aware of the existence of any of the following, to wit:

Encroachments:	Boundary Dispute:	Easements:	Soil/Erosion:
Soil Problems:	Standing Water:	Land Fill:	Drainage Problems

3. Are you aware of any ☐ current pending litigation, foreclosure, zoning regulations, restrictive covenants. building code violations, mechanics liens, judgments, special assessments, or any other type of restriction which could negatively affect your property?

4. Other than the utility easements, are you aware of any easement which impacts the residence?

5. Are there any ☐ rights-of-way, easements, eminent domain proceedings or similar matters which may negatively impact your ownership interest in the Property?

6. Are you aware if any portion of the Property (including a part of the site) is currently located in or

near a ☐ FEMA Designated Flood Hazard Zone?

8. Are you aware if any portion of the Property (Site) is currently designated as being located within a ☐ WETLANDS area and is subject to specific restrictive uses?

9. Are you aware if the Property has ever had ☐ standing water in the front, rear, or side yards for more than forty-eight (48) hours following a heavy rain?

10. Are you aware, FOR ANY REASON, in the past or present of water penetration problems in the walls, windows, doors, crawl space, basement or attic?

11. FOR ANY REASON, past or present, has any portion of the ☐ interior of the Property ever suffered water damage or moisture related damage, which was caused by flooding, lot drainage, moisture seepage, condensation, sewer overflow, sewer backup, leaking or broken water pipes (during or after construction) pipe fittings, plumbing fixtures, leaking appliances, fixtures, or equipment?

12. Are you aware, FOR ANY REASON, of ☐ any leaks, back-ups, or other problems relating to any of the plumbing, water, sewage, or related items during your ownership?

G. APPLIANCES/MECHANICAL EQUIPMENT:

Following is a list of appliances and mechanical systems which may or may not be present in the residence. Please complete the information to the best of your knowledge.

APPLIANCES/ITEMS/SYSTEMS REMAINING WITH THE PROPERTY:	GAS/ ELECTRIC REPAIRS COMPLETED IN LAST TWO YEARS	AGE BUILT-IN COOKTOP	BUILT-IN OVEN(S)	BUILT-IN DISHWASHER
GARBAGE DISPOSAL	ICE-MAKER (STAND ALONE)	MICROWAVE OVEN	TRASH COMPACTOR	KITCHEN VENT FAN(S)
CENTRAL AIR SYSTEM(S)	CENTRAL HEATING SYSTEM(S)	HUMIDIFIERS OR EVAPORATORS	AIR PURIFIERS	WATER HEATER(S)
TANKLESS WATER HEATER(S)	CEILING FAN(S)	ATTIC FANS	BATHROOM VENT FAN(S)	GARAGE DOOR OPENER(S)
SMOKE/MONOXIDE DETECTORS	SECURITY SYSTEM	INTERCOM/SOUND SYSTEM	REFRIGERATO FREE STANDING	STANDING STOVE

H. OTHER:

1. Are you aware of any past or present hazardous conditions, substances, or materials on the Property such as ☐ asbestos or asbestos components, lead-based paint, urea-formaldehyde insulation, the presence of Chinese dry-wall, methane gas, radon gas, underground storage tanks and lines or any past industrial uses occurring on the premises?

2. Are you aware of any past or present contaminations which have resulted from the storing or the manufacturing of ☐ methamphetamines?

3. Are you aware if there are currently, or have previously been, any inspections by qualified experts or orders issued on the property by any governmental authority requiring the remediation of ☐ MOLD or any other public health nuisance on the Property?

4. Are you aware of any problems or conditions that affect the desirability or functionality of the ☐ Heating, Cooling, Electrical, Plumbing, or Mechanical Systems?

5. The water supply is: Public _ Private _ On-site Well _ Neighbor's Well _ Community___

6. If your drinking water is from a well, when was the water quality last checked for safety, what were the results of the test and who was the qualified entity who conducted the test?

7. Is the water supply equipped with a water softener?

8. The Sewage System is: Public __ Private __ Septic __ Cesspool __ Treatment Plant __ Other ___
9. If the sewer service is by an individual system, has it been ☐ inspected by the proper state/county Health Department officials?
10. How many bedrooms are allowed by the Individual Wastewater Permit?
11. Is there a ☐ sewage pump installed?

I. MISCELLANEOUS:
1. Is the residence situated on ☐ Leasehold or Sixteenth Section land?
2. Are you aware of any ☐ hidden defects or needed repairs about which the purchaser should be informed PRIOR to their purchase?
3. What is the APPROXIMATE SQUARE FOOTAGE of the Heated and Cooled Living Area?
4. How was the approximation of the Gross Living Area (square footage) determined?
5. Are there any finished hardwood floors beneath the floor coverings?
6. Are there ☐ Homeowner's Association Fees associated with ownership?
7. Does the HOA levy dues or assessments for maintenance of common areas and/or other common expenses?
8. Are you aware of any☐ HOA, Public (municipal) special improvement district (PID) or other assessments that are presently owing or that have been approved but not yet levied against the Property?
9. Please indicate the contact information for the HOA
10. What is the YEARLY Real Estate Tax Bill?
County Taxes _____ City Taxes _____ Special District Taxes _____.
11. Has Homestead Exemption been filed for the current year?
12. Are you aware of any ☐ additional tax exemptions which accrue to the Property?
13. What is the average YEARLY Electric Bill?
What is the average YEARLY Gas Bill?
14. Is the residence serviced by Propane (LP) Gas?
15. The Propane Tank is: Owned _____ Leased _____
If leased, how much is the lease payment?
16. Is Cable Television Service available at the site?
Service Provider
17. Is Fiber Optic Cable (Internet) available at the site?
Service Provider
18. List any item remaining with the Property which is financed separately from the mortgages

MECHANICAL EQUIPMENT WHICH IS CONSIDERED PERSONAL PROPERTY AND IS NOT CONVEYED BY DEED AS PART OF THE REAL PROPERTY SHOULD BE NEGOTIATED IN THE CONTRACT OF SALE OR OTHER SUCH INSTRUMENT IF THE ITEMS ARE TO REMAIN WITH THE RESIDENCE.

To the extent of the Seller's knowledge as a property owner, the Seller(s) acknowledges that the information contained above is true and accurate for those areas of the property listed.
The owner(s) agree to save and hold the Broker harmless from all claims, disputes, litigation and/or judgments arising from any incorrect information supplied by the owner(s) or from any material fact known by the owner(s) which owner(s) fail to disclose except the Broker is not held harmless to the owner(s) in claims, disputes, litigation, or judgments arising from conditions of which the Broker had actual knowledge.

Percolation tests are used to determine if a septic tank can be installed. Soil that absorbs and drains water can be the basis for the installation of a septic system

Home Inspectors

- A person hired to examine systems and components of a building.
- An inspection is not a warranty.
- Home Inspection
- Home inspection means the process by which a home inspector examines the observable systems and components of improvements to residential real property that are readily accessible.
- Home inspection means a written evaluation prepared and issued by a home inspector concerning the condition of the improvements to residential real property.

Other Disclosures

Zoning and Planning Information

There are zoning maps available. It is the duty of the agent to investigate the zoning of a property

Boundaries of School/Utility/Taxation Districts, Flight paths Disclose everything.	**Encroachments** Encroachments must be disclosed. Hire a professional to survey the property or look toward public records for the measurement.
Local Taxes and Special Assessments, Other Liens Neighborhoods in the same city may have different tax amounts due or special assessments.	**Special Assessments** An added tax to the property owner. An example of a special assessment would be if a school district needed a new school; the city would build it and then tax the district's homes with a special assessment. Only the people who benefit from an improvement will pay special assessments.

Megan's Law

A federal law requiring residence registration of convicted sexual predators, in effect creating a stigmatized property. Real Estate licensees should direct buyers/tenants to the source of such registration lists instead of providing the information personally

Stigmatized Property

What do you do?
Properties that have been the scenes of murders, suicides, or are alleged to be haunted, are stigmatized.

Red Flag Issues

- A red flag issue is an indication that a property may have a problem that may require a closer inspection. You would like to inspect further."

- Examples would be a brown spot on the ceiling, musty mold smells, or several cracks in a driveway going up or down a hill.
- A professional should inspect all red flags.

Property Conditions that may warrant extra inspections

• slipping hill • wood rot • noisy pipes • easements • encroachments • lawsuits	• destruction, damage, or material alteration of property • not fit for occupancy • fire • soil	• meth house • sinking foundation' • bad electrical • sewer well • plumbing problems

- Disclose Government Controls
- Freeway addition
- Zoning Changes
- Airport Expansion
- Special assessments
- New highway in backyard
- Railroads

Comprehensive Loss Underwriter Exchange

CLUE
CLUE is a claims-information report generated by LexisNexis®, a consumer-reporting agency. The report generally contains up to seven years of personal-auto and personal-property claims history.

Lead Based Paint Disclosure

Lead Based Paint (ten days to inspect) (from EPA)

- Many homes and condominiums built before ☐ **1978** have lead-based paint.
- Paint that has chipped or is deteriorating, or on surfaces that rub together such as windows and doors, creates lead dust which can pose *serious health hazards* to occupants and visitors.
- Homebuyers and renters have important rights to know about whether lead is present — before signing contracts or leases.
- Lead poisoning has been called *"the silent disease"* because its effects may occur gradually and imperceptibly, often showing no obvious symptoms.
- Blood-lead levels as low as ☐ *10 mg/d*L have been associated with **learning disabilities, growth impairment, permanent hearing and visual impairment, and other damage to the brain and nervous system.**
- In large doses, lead exposure can cause ☐ **brain damage, convulsions, and even death.**
- Lead exposure before or during pregnancy can also alter fetal development and cause miscarriages.
- EPA and HUD estimate that **83 percent** of the privately owned housing units built in the United States before 1980 contain some lead-based paint.
- Lead from exterior house paint can flake off or leach into the ☐ **soil around the outside of a home**, contaminating children's playing areas.
- Dust caused during normal lead-based paint wear (especially around windows and doors) can create a hard-to-see film over surfaces in a house.
- In some cases, cleaning and renovation activities can increase the threat of lead-based paint exposure by dispersing fine lead dust particles in the air and over accessible household surfaces.
- If managed improperly, both adults and children can receive hazardous exposures by inhaling the fine dust or by ingesting paint dust during hand-to-mouth activities.
- Children under age 6 are especially susceptible to lead poisoning.

Violation of Disclosure

- Violation may result in civil and criminal penalties and potential triple damages in a private civil suit.

☐ Exclusions to Lead Paint Disclosure

- Housing built after 1977, housing for the elderly, housing for the disabled, 0- bedroom dwellings, and commercial lodging.
- Foreclosure properties are excluded.
- Rental housing found to be free of lead-based paint are excluded.
- Excluding housing transactions involving leasing agreements of **100 days or less**, where no lease renewal or extension can occur.
- **Lease renewals.** The final rule does not require repeated disclosure during the renewal of existing leases in which the lessor has previously disclosed.
- The purchase, sale, or servicing of mortgages.
- The sale or lease of 0-bedroom dwellings.
- Informal rental agreements.

Seller's Disclosure for Lead Based Paint

For educational purposes only

(a) Presence of lead-based paint and/or lead-based paint hazards
(Check (I) or (ii) below):
(i) _____ Known lead-based paint and/or lead-based paint hazards are present in the housing (explain).
_____
(ii) _____ Seller has no knowledge of lead-based paint and/or lead-based paint hazards in the housing.
(b) Records and reports available to the seller (check (i) or (ii) below):
(i) _____ Seller has provided the purchaser with all available records and reports pertaining to lead based paint and/or lead-based paint hazards in the housing (list documents below).
_____
(ii) _____ Seller has no reports or records pertaining to lead-based paint and/or lead-based paint hazards in the housing. Purchaser's Acknowledgment (initial)
(c) _____ Purchaser has received copies of all information listed above.
(d) _____ Purchaser has received the pamphlet Protect Your Family from Lead in Your Home.
(e) Purchaser has (check (i) or (ii) below):
(i) _____ received a ☐ 10-day opportunity (or mutually agreed upon period) to conduct a risk assessment or inspection for the presence of lead-based paint and/or lead-based paint hazards; or
(ii) _____ waived the opportunity to conduct a risk assessment or inspection for the presence of lead-based paint and/or lead-based paint hazards.
Agent's Acknowledgment (initial)
(f) _____ Agent has informed the seller of the seller's obligations under 42 U.S.C. 4852d and is aware of his/her responsibility to ensure compliance.

Real Estate Agents and Home Sellers
As real estate agents and home sellers, you play an important role in protecting the health of families purchasing and moving into your home. ☐ Buildings built before 1978 are much more likely to have lead-based paint. Federal law requires you to provide certain important information about lead-based paint and/or lead-based paint hazards before a prospective buyer is obligated under a contract to purchase your home.
Real estate agents must: ☐
. Homebuyers may choose to waive this inspection opportunity.
IMPORTANT!
Lead From Paint, Dust, and ☐ Soil in and Around Your Home Can Be Dangerous if Not Managed Properly
Children under 6 years old are most at risk for lead poisoning in your home.
Lead exposure can harm young children and babies even before they are born.
Homes, schools, and childcare facilities built before 1978 are likely to contain lead-based paint.
Even children who seem healthy may have dangerous levels of lead in their bodies.
Disturbing surfaces with lead-based paint or removing lead-based paint improperly can increase the danger to your family.
People can get lead into their bodies by breathing or swallowing lead dust, or by eating soil or paint chips containing lead.
• People have many options for reducing lead hazards. Generally, lead-based paint that is in good condition is not a hazard.

Percolation tests are used to determine if a septic tank can be installed. Soil that absorbs and drains water can be the basis for the installation of a septic system

Property Disclosure Quiz

1. Lead would likely be found in all the following EXCEPT a. paint. b. dry board. c. soil. d. pipes.	b. dry board. Lead was an additive in paint and gasoline, which can end up in ☐ soil. For many years, plumbing pipes were made of lead.
2. On discovering a latent defect in a property, a salesperson should discuss the problem with the seller and then? a. arrange for the repairs. b. tell the seller that the defect must be repaired. c. inform any prospective buyers of the defect. d. contact the city building inspector about the defect.	c. inform any prospective buyers of the defect. A salesperson / broker must disclose information about material defects in the property to prospective buyers.
3. An owner's grease fire spread to the ceiling. The paint was used to seal charred ceiling joints in the kitchen. When the seller sells the property, the hidden charred ceiling joists should be disclosed as? a. nothing, because they were repaired. b. discoverable defects. c. caveat emptor. d. latent defects.	d. latent defects An inspection before the sale may not uncover a latent defect in the property.
4. The listing broker visually inspected the property and found no issues. The seller's property disclosure states that there are no problems. After closing, the buyers find long-standing issues with water entering the basement. Who is MOST likely to be held liable for nondisclosure of this latent material defect? a. The listing broker and the seller, because they must disclose all defects, even latent b. The listing broker because the listing broker should have had the property inspected. c. The seller because brokers are not responsible for latent defects the seller does not disclose. d. The buyers, because they should have had an inspection before they closed; after closing, they own the property and have no recourse.	c. The seller because brokers are not responsible for latent defects the seller does not disclose The broker is expected to complete a visual inspection and obtaining a seller's disclosure. The seller who covered up the defect would be liable.
5. Salesperson Jim has listed Mary's house. Mary has been advised not to disclose that the foundation is cracked since the latent defect will probably scare off potential buyers. Tom buys the house and soon sees the problem. Who might be liable? a. The buyer's agent. b. The buyer's broker. c. Jim's broker. d. Toms' inspector.	c. Jim's broker Fraud.
6. Hidden defects, which are not easily discovered during a property inspection, are called?	d. latent defects.

a. material facts. b. observable defects. c. fraudulent defects. d. latent defects.	Any fact influencing a decision to buy a property is a material fact. A visible defect is one that can be seen. Falsely concealed or hidden defects are fraudulent.
7. Which of the following transfers is exempted from the property condition disclosure requirement? a. Tom is selling his duplex to his mother-in-law. b. Tony is transferring his empty lot to his neighbor. c. Terry is selling his newly constructed house to a buyer he just met. d. Tim is offering a lease on his house with an option to purchase to his best friend.	b. Tony is transferring his empty lot to his neighbor. There is no building on the empty lot.
8. A nonmaterial fact which need not be disclosed is? a. A felony committed on the property. b. The foundation of the house has shifted, and it is built on a hill that's sliding. c. Illegal drug activity that affects the physical condition of the property. d. The property is in a flood plain.	a. A felony committed on the property. A felony committed on the property is not a material fact.
9. All the following are material facts except? a. Leak in the roof b. Crack in the basement wall c. Problem with plumbing d. Seller is anxious to sell	d. Seller is anxious to sell Property Condition Disclosure deals with the building, not the owner.
10. During his absence from the office, the listing broker found out there was a large hailstorm and heavy rain that caused some flooding about the property he is expected to close this week. Though many properties in the neighborhood were damaged, the seller has not reported any issues with the property. The listing broker. a. has no duty to inform the buyer since he represents the seller. b. has no responsibility because it will be the buyer's broker who should request an inspection. c. should verify no damage has occurred to the property. d. does not need to worry since only the seller will be liable if there is undisclosed damage.	c. should verify no damage has occurred to the property. It is important to make sure that the seller understands that material facts must be disclosed before title is transferred.
11. A broker discovers the previous owner of a home she has listed died of AIDS. a. The broker must disclose the fact to prospective buyers. b. should consult an attorney to determine if the fact creates a stigmatized property. c. may disclose the fact if asked by a prospective buyer. d. may not disclose that the previous owner died of AIDS.	d. may not disclose that the previous owner died of AIDS. A disclosure that a property owner or occupant died of AIDS is illegal discrimination against the handicapped under the federal Fair Housing Act.
12. How does the seller's property disclosure benefit the buyer? a. It informs the buyer as to which defects exist. b. It provides a basis for further investigation by the buyer	d. It allows the buyer to make an informed decision as to buying the property.

c. It allows the buyer to make an informed decision as to buying the property. d. It gives the buyer full knowledge of all issues with the property.	The seller's property disclosure gives the buyer full knowledge of the seller's representation of the issues asked on the form.
13. A salesperson working with a customer knows the neighborhood he is showing is very near an airport with low-flying planes that create a lot of noise. The salesperson should disclose the level of airplane noise in the neighborhood because it is? a. a material defect. b. material information. c. a material breach. d. a material fact.	d. a material fact. Airplane noise is a material fact and should be disclosed to the buyer.
14. Information that is important to buyers that could change their decision to purchase a property is known as a. a latent defect. b. a physical defect. c. a material fact. d. an observable defect.	c. a material fact. A material fact is any fact relevant to a person deciding to buy a property.
15. What is the intent of seller disclosures regarding property conditions? a. Shifts the burden onto the buyer to discover what is wrong with the property. b. Helps the buyer determine what price to offer. c. Encourages the broker to share in liability issues. d. Assists the seller in determining a fair asking price.	b. Helps the buyer determine what price to offer. After consulting the property disclosure, the buyer is in a better position to make an offer based on the condition of the property
16. The seller has completed a property disclosure for an "as is" sale, which states all items are in working order. After closing, the buyer finds out the sewer system has had long-term problems. The person or persons MOST likely to be held responsible for the misrepresentation is? a. the buyer's broker. b. no one since it is an "as is" sale. c. the seller. d. the listing broker and seller.	c. the seller. "As is" simply means the seller is not repairing issues—not that the seller has no obligation to disclose them. Full disclosure must still be made.
17. Who should fill in the blanks of the seller property disclosure form? a. Seller b. Home inspector hired by the real estate licensee c. Home inspector hired by the seller d. Real estate licensee who is listing the property	a. Seller Do not fill-in anything.
18. Requiring the seller to make certain disclosures about the property is an attempt to? a. increase the liability of the licensee who lists the property. b. guarantee that the buyers will not be surprised. c. avoids surprises for the buyer. d. provide a warranty to the buyers.	c. avoids surprises for the buyer. The seller can only disclose that of which the seller is aware.
19. Most states have a requirement that the broker and the	a. the broker completes the form, and the

seller give a written disclosure of material facts to buyers. All the following are true about the seller's property disclosure EXCEPT? a. the broker completes the form, and the seller signs it. b. the seller completes the form and signs it. c. it represents the seller's current knowledge of the property. d. the buyer signs the form to acknowledge receipt of the disclosure.	seller signs it. The seller's property disclosure is completed by the seller, never the broker, to the best of the seller's knowledge.
20. Who is responsible for completing the Property Condition Disclosure Statement? a. The listing agent b. The seller c. The listing agent	b. The seller The seller must disclose all known defects.
21. When a property is misrepresented because defects are not disclosed to a buyer, the buyer may be able to rescind a sales contract or receive? a. compensatory damages for repair of the defect. b. incidental damages that occur in every real estate transaction. c. a return of any earnest money paid to the seller. d. special damages due to the inconvenience to the buyer.	a. compensatory damages for repair of the defect. Compensatory damages (actual damages) are a monetary payment for the repair of the defect.
22. The property disclosure form is usually given to a buyer? a. after an offer is made. b. before an offer is made. c. at the initial contact with the buyer. d. at the closing of the transaction.	b. before an offer is made. The property disclosure form is given to the buyer before an offer is made. It is uploaded to the Multiple Listing Service. The buyer's agent downloads it and reviews it with the buyer before the offer is made.
23. Ground water contamination could come from the following except? a. Underground gas storage tanks b. Waste disposal sites c. Cement d. Sodium hydrogen carbonate	c. Cement Cement is not liquid.
24. When asked about the condition of the building foundation, a wise agent will respond? a. "I have a friend in engineering school who can give you an opinion." b. You probably should discuss this with a qualified engineer." c. "The seller has lived here for more than 20 years, and she hasn't had a problem." D) "It looked fine to me."	b. You probably should discuss this with a qualified engineer." Stay within your area of competence.
25. Brokers are aware of properties near their new listings that may be environmental hazards. Environmental issues in this case? a. do not need to be disclosed because issues outside the neighborhood have no impact on value.	b. needs to be disclosed because they can impact the value of the listing. Environmental issues may impact value and must be disclosed.

b. needs to be disclosed because they can impact the value of the listing and neighborhood. c. need to be disclosed only if they are not obvious.	
26. While the buyer and his agent are doing a walk-through inspection, the agent discovers that the recent hurricane caused damage. What should be the agent's next step? a. Have the buyer call his insurance agent. b. Tell the buyer not to worry. c. Terminate the contract d. Disclose the issue to the buyer.	d. Disclose the issue to the buyer. The damage is a material fact.
27. Some of the boxes indicating structural damage on the seller's property disclosure form provided by the listing broker are unchecked. How should a buyer's agent act? a. Contact the sellers. b. Tell the buyers that a property inspector will handle it. c. Contact the listing broker and ask for a completed form. d. File a complaint with the state real estate commission.	c. Contact the listing broker and ask for a completed form. The buyer's agent should contact the listing broker.
28. Before a buyer makes an offer on a property, the buyer should have received and read? a. the independent contractor agreement. b. the seller's property condition disclosure form. c. the general warranty deed. d. the broker policy manual.	b. the seller's property condition disclosure form. The property Condition Disclosure Form (PCFDS) will reveal any known defects.
29. The seller indicates that his home is serviced by a city water system. The broker relies on the seller's statement. After moving in the home, the buyer's wife realizes that it does not have city water. The broker? a. maybe liable for misrepresentation since she should have checked if the property was on city systems. b. is not liable for misrepresentation. c. may file a complaint against the seller with the state real estate commission. d. May sue the seller.	a. maybe liable for misrepresentation since she should have checked if the property was on city systems. A real estate agent may be guilty of negligent misrepresentation by failing the duty of care.
30. What critical aspect of the property inspection process MUST licensees convey to prospective buyers? a. That the inspection is done by a contractor. b. That the inspection can be done by themselves. c. That the inspection is done within the inspection period. d. That the inspection could help them re-negotiate.	c. That the inspection is done within the inspection period. Time is of the essence in contracts.
31. A licensee is listing a property in a known flood plain. The seller flatly denies that the structure and the property have ever been flooded. What is the licensee required to do in this situation? a. Tell the seller to not disclose the flood plain. b. Disclose the flood plain on a separate amendment signed by the broker. c. Disclose the flood plain on a separate addendum notarized by the broker. d. Remind the seller of the obligation to disclose material	d. Remind the seller of the obligation to disclose material facts The seller is required to disclose all material facts.

facts	
32. A seller tells the listing broker that a recent plumbing leak has been fixed. The broker suspects this might not be true. To protect himself and his broker, the listing broker should inform buyers that? a. the broker relied on the seller' disclosure. b. the house is sold "as is." c. they should have a plumber inspect the leak. d. the leak has been fixed.	c. they should have a plumber inspect the leak. Recommend experts inspect issues that may be a material fact.
33. The listing agent for a residential property can legally complete the entire Real Property Transfer Disclosure Statement? a. Under no circumstances b. When authorized in writing by the seller c. When the seller lives in another state and has not seen the property. d. When the buyer gives the agent a written waiver	a. Under no circumstances Don't do it.
34. A person who performs a visual survey of a property structure and write a report for a buyer is? a. An educator b. A home inspector c. An appraiser d. A property manager	b. A home inspector A home inspector inspects and reports on the condition of a property.
35. Regarding home inspections, all the following are correct except? a. The home inspection could be a contingency. b. It's a good idea that the buyer attends the inspection. c. The home inspection needs to be completed within 10 days of the accepted offer. d. Home inspections should be conducted by a licensed home inspector.	b. The buyer needs to be present during the inspection process. The buyer doesn't need to be there during the buyer's inspection.
36. All the following statements correctly describe a home warranty program EXCEPT? a. the program is generally offered to the seller by a home warranty company. b. the program is often purchased by the seller as a marketing tool. c. the program protects buyers for up to two years after the move d. Incorrect	c. the program protects buyers for up to two years after the move The stipulations in a home warranty will vary.
37. A broker listing an older home performs a visual property inspection to discover any patent defects. He discovers the foundation is slipping on the northeast side of the home. What should the broker advise the seller to do? a. Disclose the problem. b. Leave the problem up to the buyers to find. c. Hide the problem. d. Tell buyers that the foundation is not slipping.	a. Disclose the problem. A broker must disclose any known material fact to a buyer or a buyer's agent.
38. While looking at a property, the potential buyers ask	c. have a survey conducted.

their salesperson if a fence is the boundary line of the property. The salesperson should recommend that the buyers? a. ask the owners of the property. b. ask the neighbors. c. have a survey conducted. d. read the legal description.	Hire a professional.
39. A property owner granted an easement to his neighbor 30 years ago. The owner has the property under contract. At closing, the easement a. will not pass with the deed. b. is listed on the bill of sale. c. passes the title of the property with easement. d. is automatically released.	c. passes the title of the property with easement Unless an easement is released, it will automatically transfer.
40. A listing broker knows a sex offender lives near the house she is listing. Prospective buyers are families with small children. The broker? a. lie to the buyers and tell the buyers that the home is under contract. b. inform the buyers of the offender's presence in the neighborhood. c. has no responsibility under any law since states release information about convicted sex offenders to the public. d. should inform the seller not to accept an offer from any families with small children.	b. may have a responsibility under state law to inform the buyers of the offender's presence in the neighborhood. Some state laws require active notification to a buyer about a sex offender living in the area.
41. Megan's Law requires which of the following? a. The disclosure of convicted sex offenders in a community. b. The home inspector be licensed. c. Lawful disclosure of a stigmatized property d. The transactional agent cannot have a dual agency.	a. The disclosure of convicted sex offenders in a community. Megan's Law is the name for a federal law, and informal name for subsequent state laws, it requires law enforcement authorities to make information available to the public regarding registered sex offenders.
42. If a buyer's agent knows the house her buyer desires to purchase has been stigmatized by a recent murder-suicide ethically what should the buyer's agent do? a. Remain silent to protect the seller b. Remain silent because the incident didn't harm the structure c. Disclose it to the buyer after the purchase agreement is signed d. Disclose it to the buyer before the buyer writes an offer	d. Disclose it to the buyer before the buyer writes an offer As the buyer's agent. In Mississippi, death on the property is not a material fact.
43. Which of the following would be a nonmaterial fact that does not require a property condition disclosure? a. A house has a leaking roof. b. A basement floods. c. A previous occupant died in the house. d. A previous occupant contaminated the house by	c. A previous occupant died in the house. Death does not affect the condition of the property. If asked about a death, salespersons must tell the truth.

manufacturing methamphetamine in the basement.	
44. When a property experiences a bad reputation because of something that happened on the property or nearby, it is an example of? a. a dangerous property. b. a stigmatized property. c. a polluted property. d. considered a physical hazard.	b. a stigmatized property Stigmatized properties are properties that gain a reputation that is not pleasant. These properties may not present a danger.
45. Mineral deposits may indicate basement flooding, as can cracks in a foundation wall. These visual facts may be? a. evidence of more serious latent defects. b. red flags that warrant further investigation. c. easily repairable defects. d. patent defects that do not need to be pointed out because they should be observed by a prospective buyer.	a. red flags that warrant further investigation. Hire a professional and investigate further.
46. The seller has just learned that a nearby industrial property may have environmental issues. As part of the disclosure, the seller? a. can ignore the environmental issue because it might not be true. b. may wait until more information is disclosed by the EPA. c. May investigate other properties with similar problems and disclose that information to buyers. d. should disclose because the issue might be important to a reasonable person's decision to purchase the property.	d. should disclose because the issue might be important to a reasonable person's decision to purchase the property. Disclose material facts may be known or suspected.
47. Abandoned factories, former dry-cleaning properties, and vacant gas stations that may contain environmental hazards are classified as? a. priority list sites. b. Greenfields. c. brownfields. d. wetlands.	c. brownfields. The presence of brownfields can prevent redevelopment and decrease a neighborhood's property values.
48. Prospective purchasers interested in building on vacant lots ask their salesperson if an onsite septic system can be installed. A salesperson may advise the buyer to conduct or have a? a. get a hydroponic test. b. have a percolation test. c. have a clay test. d. have a rock test.	b. have a percolation test. Soil that absorbs and drains water can be the basis for the installation of a septic system.
49. Which of the following would NOT require abatement, mitigation, or cleanup? a. A sealed well b. Radon c. Mold d. Asbestos	a. A sealed well A sealed well does not require any of these, and it should be disclosed.
50. MATCH: A naturally occurring mineral composite that once was used extensively as insulation in residential and	a. asbestos

commercial buildings, in brake pads, and in fire-retardant products, such as furniture. a. asbestos b. UFFI c. lead d. radon	Asbestos is a group of six naturally occurring fibrous minerals composed of thin, needle-like fibers.
51. Hidden leaks can cause condensation or wet spots on walls and can also lead to mold growth in many places, such as behind walls. a. True b. False	a. True Mold is created by wetness.
52. All the following are true about asbestos EXCEPT? a. it was commonly used as insulation. b. it is most dangerous when airborne. c. removal can cause further contamination of a building. d. HUD requires all residential buildings be tested for asbestos-containing materials.	d. HUD requires all residential buildings be tested for asbestos-containing materials. Friable asbestos can get into lings and cause cancer.
53. An asbestos wrapping was found on the furnace ducts during a property inspection. Instead of removing the asbestos, you should? a. encapsulate the ducts. b. clean it up using an oil-based cleaner. c. leave it alone until it starts to shed and then remove it. d. spray it with bleach.	a. encapsulate the ducts. Asbestosis tapes and *wraps were* often placed directly inside of the *heating vents in* older homes.
54. Mold is MOST likely to develop a. when there is adequate air circulation. b. with humidity. c. in a basement. d. in attics with high heat levels.	b. with humidity. Mold needs wet conditions.
55. Which of the following is TRUE regarding asbestos? a. The level of asbestos in a building is affected by weather conditions. b. The removal of asbestos can cause further contamination of a building. c. HUD requires that all asbestos-containing materials be removed from all residential buildings. d. Asbestos causes health problems only when it is eaten.	b. The removal of asbestos can cause further contamination of a building. Once disturbed, asbestos can remain suspended in the air for long periods of times. (friable). The friable particles can stick in the lungs.
56. This seller discovered radon and has sealed the foundation cracks and feels certain that his issue is resolved. What should a listing broker do? a. Disclose the radon if the buyer if asked about it. b. Say nothing, the buyer's inspector will find any problems. c. Not disclose, because the broker represents the seller, and it might cause the seller harm. d. Disclose the radon issue to all potential buyers.	d. Disclose the radon issue to all potential buyers. The discovery of radon is a material fact.
57. A radioactive, odorless gas which may build up inside buildings is? a. urea-formaldehyde.	c. radon. Radon is an odorless, colorless gas that

b. polychlorinated biphenyls (PCBs). c. radon. d. asbestos.	you can't see. It can cause lung cancer. Inspectors will inspect up to the third floor.
58. The greatest health risk from radon is when it is exposed to humans and? a. emitted by malfunctioning appliances. b. contained in insulation material used in residential properties during the 1970s. c. found in high concentrations in unimproved land. d. trapped and concentrated in inadequately ventilated areas.	d. trapped and concentrated in inadequately ventilated areas. Poor ventilation in a structure can increase radon's harmful effects.
59. In regulations regarding lead-based paints for houses built before 1978, HUD requires that? a. the seller is required to give all buyers a lead-based paint disclosure. b. the buyer completes a lead inspection and testing before closing. c. the broker must make sure the buyer receives the required lead-based paint disclosure. d. lead-based paint must be removed from surfaces before selling.	a. the seller is required to give all buyers a lead-based paint disclosure. Sellers, as well as any listing agents hired by the sellers to market the property, must comply with the federal lead-based paint disclosure requirements.
60. The federal lead-based paint disclosure regulations require that sellers (or their agents) provide lead-based paint disclosures to purchasers and lessees in what time frame? a. At any time before closing or move-in, in the case of rental property b. At least 10 days before closing or move-in, in the case of rental property. c. Before the purchaser or lessee is obligated under a contract for sale or lease. d. At the earliest possible time after the purchaser or lessee expresses serious interest in purchase or lease of the property.	c. Before the purchaser or lessee is obligated under a contract for sale or lease. The purchaser or lessee has ten days to inspect for lead-based paint. The owner/seller does not have to remove it.
61. An agent shows a prospective buyer a house built in 1912. The buyer is concerned about possible health hazards for her two toddlers. Which of the following statements is TRUE? a. Because of the age of the house, there is a good chance of the presence of lead-based paint. b. Removal of lead-based paint and asbestos hazards is covered by standard title insurance policies. c. Because the salesman is a licensed real estate salesperson, he can offer to personally inspect for lead and remove any lead risks. d. Lead-based paint is more of a threat to adults than children.	a. Because of the age of the house, there is a good chance of the presence of lead-based paint. Because of the age of the house, there is a good chance of the presence of lead-based paint.
62. Lead would likely be found in all the following EXCEPT? a. paint.	b. dry board. Lead was an additive in paint and

b. dry board. c. soil. d. pipes.	gasoline, which can end up in ☐ soil. For many years, plumbing pipes were made of lead.
63. An agent listed a property that was built in 1922. By federal law, the agent must have the sellers fill out a? a. loan application. b. CLUE report. c. good faith estimate for cleanup. d. lead-based paint disclosure form.	d. lead-based paint disclosure form Lead-Based Paint Hazard Reduction Act of 1992 protects families from exposure to lead from paint, dust, and soil.
64. What statement about the Lead-Based Paint Hazard Reduction Act is TRUE? a. Residential property constructed prior to 1978 must be tested for the presence of lead-based paint. b. A lead hazard pamphlet must be distributed to all prospective buyers but not to tenants. c. A disclosure statement must be included with all sales contracts and leases involving residential properties built prior to 1978. d. Purchasers of housing built before 1978 must be given five days to test the property for the presence of lead-based paint.	c. A disclosure statement must be included with all sales contracts and leases involving residential properties built prior to 1978. A lead-based paint warning disclosure statement must be completed and signed by the parties and a copy included with any sales contract or lease for a residential property built before 1978.
65. Lung cancer kills thousands of Americans every year a. True b. False	a. True Lung cancer is by far the leading cause of cancer death among both men and women, making up almost 25% of all cancer deaths
66. Naturally occurring radioactive gas decay is caused by? a. mold. b. radon. c. formaldehyde. d. carbon monoxide (CO)	b. radon. Radon is an odorless, colorless gas that you can't see. It can cause lung cancer. Inspectors will inspect up to the third floor.
67. Water leaking into a homeowner's basement caused damage estimated in the range of $25,000 to $30,000. Due to financial limitations, the owner constructed a false floor over the entire basement and covered the damaged areas with carpet. On the property disclosure form, he did not disclose the leak or the damage to the basement. A basement that has been damaged can be used as an example of? a. a patent defect. b. a latent defect, and the listing brokerage firm may be liable for not discovering the false floor over the damage. c. a patent defect, and the brokerage firm is not liable for not discovering the false floor and the damage. d. a latent defect, and the listing brokerage firm is not liable for not discovering the false floor over the damage.	d. a latent defect, and the listing brokerage firm is not liable for not discovering the false floor over the damage. The listing brokerage firm is not liable for not discovering the false floor over the damage. Basement damage is a hidden structural defect that a seller knows about, but no brokerage firm, brokers, or purchasers will be aware of. Realtors are not responsible for discovering and disclosing latent defects

	due to the lack of disclosure by the seller.

Definitions Module Six

Home Inspection
A professional inspection of a home to determine the condition of the property. The inspection should include an evaluation of the plumbing, heating and cooling systems, roof, wiring, foundation and pest infestation.

Inspection
As an agent it is always a good idea to recommend an inspection. It is a licensee's responsibility to explain the property inspection process and the use of inspections to buyers.

Inspection Report
A document for the results of a thorough visual survey of the property.

Latent Defects
A defect that is not visible or apparent; a hidden defect that would not be discovered in a reasonably thorough inspection of the property.
The least apparent lead product to be found on a property is a lead pipe. It's a latent defect. (Latent Defect is an unseen defect.) .

Lead-Based Paint
Many homes and condominiums built before 1978 have lead-based paint. Paint that has chipped or is deteriorating, or on surfaces that rub together such as windows and doors, creates lead dust which can pose serious health hazards to occupants and visitors. Homebuyers and renters have important rights to know about whether lead is present, before signing contracts or leases.

Provide a 10-day period to conduct a paint inspection or risk assessment for lead-based paint or lead-based paint hazards. Parties may mutually agree, in writing, to lengthen or shorten the time period for inspection. Homebuyers may choose to waive this inspection opportunity.

Material Fact
Include Land/soil conditions, pest infestation, toxic mold and other interior environmental hazards, structural issues-roof, doors, foundation, windows, condition of electrical and plumbing system and fixtures location within natural hazard or especially regulated areas-nuclear power plants, landfill, floodplains, wetlands, endangered species.

Megan's Law
A federal law requiring residence registration of convicted sexual predators, in effect creating a stigmatized property. Real Estate licensees should direct buyers/tenants to the source of such registration lists instead of providing the information personally

Nonmaterial Fact
Homicide, suicide felony on the property, HIV AND AIDS – Things that do not affect the property's physical condition or the surrounding area. Varies state to state

Patent Defects
Defects readily seen.

Percolation Tests
Used to determine if a septic tank can be installed. Soil that absorbs and drains water can be the basis for the installation of a septic system

Red Flags
A licensee must also inquire about any red flag issue. A red flag is defined as something that would warrant a reasonably observant agent that there may be an underlying problem.

Seller's Property Disclosure Act
Legislation requiring the seller to reveal the property's honest condition, whether a defect is observed or a latent defect.

Seller's Disclosure of Information on Lead-Based Paint and/or Lead-Based Paint Hazards
Form for realtors to use in sales transactions when sellers of residential real property are required to disclose to the buyer any known information on the property's lead-based paint hazards.

Stachybotrys Chartarum
Black Mold produces mycotoxins. Has been linked with so-called sick building syndrome. Is detected in cellulose-rich building materials from damp or water-damaged buildings.

Stigmatized Property
Properties that have been the scenes of murders, suicides, or are alleged to be haunted, are stigmatized.

Walk-Through
A common clause in a sales contract that allows the buyer to examine the property being purchased at a specified time immediately before the closing, for example, within the 24 hours before closing.

Zoning and Planning Information
There are zoning maps available. It is the duty of the agent to investigate the zoning of a property

MODULE SEVEN: Contracts

Contracts

What is a contract?

A VOLUNTARY Contract is a voluntary, legally enforceable promise between two competent parties to perform some legal act in exchange for consideration.

Requirements for Validity

Real Estate Contracts must be/have
1. Competent parties
18 years or older
Sobor, sane adult
2. Legal Purpose (Legality of Object)
An essential element of a valid contract. A contract for an illegal purpose is void.
3. Consideration
Anything of value that induces one to enter a contract.
4. An accurate legal description
5. Written and Signed
Everything in real estate must be in writing, according to the Statute of Frauds.

Statute of Frauds

Everything in real estate must be in writing, according to the Statute of Frauds.

Parole Evidence Rule

Anything in writing (like the contract) takes precedence over verbal agreements.

Types of Contracts

Expressed	Implied
Clearly stated or written.	Shown by the actions of the parties.

Bilateral	Unilateral
Two people make a promise. A promise for a promise.	One party makes a promise.

A unilateral agreement is an open-end agreement offered by one party that requires acceptance to start, where a bilateral contract is a contract where both sides have made promises

An Option

- A unilateral contract in which the optionor (property owner) promises to sell when the optionee (prospective buyer) chooses to buy – at a price and before a date set in the option contract
- An option agreement is a contract to keep an offer open, giving a person a right to buy at a specific price during a specific period.
- the holder the first opportunity to purchase.
- An option can be recorded to give notice; an unrecorded option can create a cloud on title.
- A right of first refusal gives the holder the first opportunity to purchase.

Optionor	Optionee
The optionor (the seller, grants the option right).	The optionee is not bound to exercise the option, but the optionor must keep the offer open during the specified time and must go through with the sale if the optionee exercises the option.

Executory	Executed
- Something still needs to be done. - A contract that has not yet been entirely performed. (Example: when you are "under contract," you have an executory contract.)	- Completed - A contract that has been entirely performed. The closing executes the real estate purchase contract.

Valid	Voidable	Void	Unenforceable
- Has all the legal elements required for a contract. - Legally binding and has enforceability in a court of law.	- Lacks one or more elements and has no legal force or effect by one party. - Valid but it contains a flaw.	- Lacks one or more elements and has no legal force or effect. - Not an actual contract.	- Appears to have all legal elements but cannot be enforced in court. - Looks valid but can't be enforced.
Married Minor	**Unmarried Minor** - At any time, the minor can change their mind. - An adult cannot force a minor to complete a transaction	An agreement to commit a crime is not a legal contract.	Performance of the contract cannot be forced.

Performed or Discharge Contracts

Performance	Substantial Performance	Mutual Agreement	Operation of Law
A contract completed as stated.	• Contract is completed but the contract was not completed as agreed. • The violating party is still responsible (liable) for actions.	• Both parties agree to rescind the contract. • Both parties agree to cancel. • Termination of contract.	• Statute of limitations are enforced. (Ran out of time to complete.) • An unmarried minor has changed their mind.

Impossibility of Performance

Impossibility of performance is when the duties and contractual obligations of one or more parties cannot be fulfilled under normal circumstances.

Breach of Contract

A Breach of contract is failure to perform without a legal cause.

There are remedies for Breach of Contract

Recover money
Sue for damages
Sue for Specific Performance.

Specific Performance

- Specific performance is an equitable remedy in the law of contract. A court issues an order requiring a party to perform a specific act, such as to complete performance of the contract.
- The seller refused to sell their property after an agreement was validated.
- The seller took fixtures not entitled to take before they moved out.
- A contract remedy permitting either party to force the other to perform the contract and sue for damages. Buy-Sell contracts are often "specific performance" against the seller— it is the opposite of liquidated damages.

Payment Remedies for Damages

Liquidated Damages

- Those damages are specified by contract in advance (usually loss of earnest money) if the buyer defaults. If specified, liquidated damages are the seller's only remedy against the buyer.
- Actual damages refer to the financial amount that is paid to a victim that suffered loss that can be calculated.
- Actual damages are often known as real damages or, legally, as compensatory damages. These are damages that arose from the neglect or mistake of another party.

Exemplary Damages

- Damages above and beyond the actual cost of the loss, assessed to punish or set an example for others.

An affirmation

An affirmation is a formal statement, not under oath, that a statement is true or that the proponent will tell the truth.

Rescission

- The rescission of a contract is a return to the status quo.
- If a buyer withdraws his offer before the seller accepts it, the buyer is entitled to his earnest money deposit

Factors affecting enforceability of contracts

1. Incapacity

Valid Contracts must include sober sane adults.

2. Mistake (Negligent Misrepresentation)

An error of fact by both parties may cause a contract to be voidable.
Example: A contract's legal description depicts a different lot than the buyer was shown.

3. Misrepresentation

An untrue statement of material fact that induces a party to act. It may be intentional (fraud) or unintentional. A contract so signed is voidable by the injured party.

4. Fraud

Intentional deception or misrepresentation – a material misstatement of fact.

5. Discharge

Terminating a contract or agreement; when it has been completely performed for by another party's breach or default.

Undue influence	Duress

Undue influence is taking advantage of another person through a position of trust in the formation of a contract.	Duress is wrongful pressure exerted upon a person to coerce that person into a contract that he or she ordinarily wouldn't enter.

Vicarious Liability

- A principal's liability for an agent's acts performed within the scope of the agency.
- The employing broker is responsible for licensees' actions.

Land Contracts

Rights and responsibilities of parties

- The parties to a land contract (which is most often used in seller-financed transactions) are the vendor (seller) and vendee (buyer).
- The buyer takes possession immediately and pays the seller in installments but does not receive title until the purchase price has been paid off.
- The seller retains **legal title** to the property, while the buyer has **equitable title** to the property during the contract period.
- The seller and buyer both may encumber their interests during the contract period, but lenders are unlikely to accept that as security.

Notice, delivery, and acceptance of contracts

1. Actual Notice
That truly seen, heard, or read or observed and not presumed. Contrasts with constructive (legal) notice.
2. Acceptance
Any language or action that indicates an agreement forming a contract has been reached. An offer is just an offer until acceptance.
3. Acknowledgment
Written declaration by a person who signs a document that he or she is who they claim to be. Acknowledgments are witnessed by a notary public or other authorized official.

Electronic signature and paperless transactions

- The **Uniform Electronic Transactions Act (UETA)** was adopted in 1999, and it provides a framework for determining the legality of electronic signatures. It guarantees that electronic signatures are given the same legal weight as handwritten signatures.
- The UETA is applicable in both business and e-commerce transactions, and it provides some legal recourse if things go wrong in an electronic transaction.
- It doesn't apply to wills or testamentary trusts.

Novation	Assignment
- Novation is a mechanism where one party transfers all its obligations and rights under a contract to a third party, with	- A transfer of interest in a mortgage, lease, or other

the consent of his original counterparty. • It may be substituting a party to the transaction with another.	contract.

Contracts QUIZ

1. MATCH: Satisfies all legal requirements for a contract. a. Voidable Contract b. Valid Contract c. Void Agreement d. Unenforceable Contract	b. Valid Contract A valid contract satisfies all legal requirements.
2. All the following are essentials of every contract, except? a. A proper writing b. Capable parties c. Mutual consent d. Lawful object	a. A proper writing A lease for a year or less does not have to be in writing. (Leases are not covered by the Statute of Frauds unless they're of a year or more in length.)
3. The law that requires contracts in real estate to be in writing is? a. Statute of Governing Transactions b. Statute of Limitations c. Statute of Frauds d. Statute of Contracts	c. Statute of Frauds The statute of frauds refers to the requirement that certain kinds of contracts be memorialized in writing, signed by the party to be charged, with sufficient content to evidence the contract.
4. A contract shown by the actions of the parties would be a/an? a. Unilateral b. Implied c. Expressed d. Bilateral	b. Implied When two parties lack a written contract, the law creates an implied contract based on the parties' conduct or circumstances.
5. MATCH: IMPLIED CONTRACT a. Contingencies b. Can't legally accomplish c. Demonstrated by ACTS and CONDUCT	c. Demonstrated by ACTS and CONDUCT A legal obligation is created based on the conduct of the parties.
6. You order dinner at a fine dining restaurant. What type of 'contract' do you have in reference to your actions? a. Implied b. Void c. expressed d. imagined	a. Implied When two parties lack a written contract, the law creates an implied contract based on the parties' conduct or circumstances.
7. MATCH: Express agreement. a. An agent who is authorized to represent the principal in a specified range of matters. b. An oral or written contract in which the parties state the contract's terms and express their intentions in words. c. A contract that is inferred by the actions and conduct of the parties. d. Payment to a broker for services rendered, such as in the sale or purchase of real property, usually a flat fee or a percentage of the selling price.	b. An oral or written contract in which the parties state the contract's terms and express their intentions in words. Something is spoken or in writing.

8. A _____ contract is an exchange of promises, which binds both parties. a. Implied b. Executory c. Bilateral d. Unilateral	b. Bilateral Two parties exchange performance promises in a bilateral contract. The promise of one party is consider for the promise of the other. Consequently, each party is both an obligee and an obligor.
9. The seller tells the broker, "If you bring me a buyer, I will pay you a commission." The broker MOST likely has what type of agreement with the seller? a. Exclusive buyer representation agreement b. Unilateral open listing c. Unilateral exclusive agency listing d. Unilateral open listing	d. Unilateral open listing An open listing is when the seller pays the broker who brings the buyer. The contract is unilateral because the seller is the only party obligated to act.
10. Ann has a contract with Ben in which she must perform if Ben decides to go forward. This is what type of contract? a. Nonbinding b. Unilateral for Ben c. Bilateral for both d. Unilateral for Ann	d. Unilateral for Ann Ann must perform if Ben acts by going forward. This makes the contract unilateral for Ann.
11. An option does NOT become a binding contract on both parties until? a. the option is signed by both parties. b. the option is signed by both parties. c. the consideration is paid. d. the option is exercised.	d. the option is exercised. The option is exercised. When exercised, the optionee agrees to be bound.
12. A contract has been drawn which obliges the sellers to convey title to their land to the buyers if the buyers come up with $22,000 on or before December 31st. This is called? a. an option contract. b. an open-ended contract c. a bilateral contract. d. an executed contract.	a. an option contract. For a fixed price during a given period, the buyer can buy a property from the seller. By the end of the holding period, the buyer has the option to buy or not buy the property.
13.Buying a home for $300,000 with 10% down, the buyer asks the seller to provide him six months to close the deal. The buyer agreed to give the seller $3,000 to keep the offer open for the next six months, with the seller keeping the cash if the buyer does not buy. This contract is? a. an open listing agreement. b. a bilateral agreement with both the buyer and seller bound because there was a payment. c. an option agreement. d. an implied sales agreement with both parties bound.	c. an option agreement. In this case, the seller will keep the buyer's option money.
14. A buyer and a seller enter into a purchase	a. executory contract.

agreement. The agreement includes a contingency that the buyer can terminate the contract if she cannot sell her current home. This type of agreement is an? a. executory contract. b. executed contract. c. unilateral contract. d. option contract.	This contract has a contingency. Contingencies can void contracts.
15. Which of the following describes a contract that has not yet been fully performed? a. Executory b. Executed c. Unenforceable d. Voidable	a. Executory It has not been fully executed.
16. Under what type of contract is a seller obligated to sell, but the buyer is not obligated to buy? a. Bilateral b. Recovery c. Option d. Chance	c. Option Option agreements are between a seller (optionor) who must sell and a buyer (optionee) who may decide not to purchase.
17. The buyer and seller exchanged several counteroffers before reaching an agreement. During this stage of the process, the contract is not yet performed. The status of the contract is? a. executory. b. unilateral. c. executed. d. voidable.	a. executory. The contract is not fully performed.
18. How many parties make a promise in an option contract? a. three b. one c. one d. four	b. one An option is a unilateral contract.
19. Contracts with an unmarried minor are considered? a. Void b. Voidable c. Valid d. Unenforceable	b. Voidable A contract with a married minor is valid. An unmarried minor would be voidable.
20. A 15-year-old recently inherited a parcel of real estate and has decided to sell it. If the 15-year-old executes a deed conveying the property to a purchaser, such a conveyance would be? a. Void b. Voidable c. Valid d. Invalid	b. Voidable Unmarried minors can sign contracts, but the contracts are voidable at any time by the minor. The adult in the deal cannot force the minor to complete the transaction.
21. A minor has inherited a large old house from her father. The minor sells it to her aunt. Is the purchase	c. No, it is voidable by the minor.

contract valid? a. Yes, it is valid and enforceable. b. No, it is void. c. No, it is voidable by the minor. d. No, it is voidable by the minor.	The answer is no, it is voidable by the minor. Contracts with minors entered by adults are always voidable by the minor.
22. A mentally disabled person that was declared incompetent can't enter a contract unless? a. A person appointed by the court may enter the contract on the disabled person's behalf. b. A disabled person can under no circumstances enter a contract without the written certification acquired while in school. c. A disabled person can correctly spell his/her name. d. A person appointed by a parent can sign legal contracts for the disabled person.	a. A person appointed by the court may enter the contract on the disabled person's behalf. Contracts (except those that cover necessities) can be voided by those lacking mental capacity, or by a guardian.
23. An offer was made on a property. The seller counteroffered but did not accept. Counteroffers are signed and delivered by the real estate agent to the seller. After finding a better house, the same buyers made an offer on a new home. Which of the following is TRUE? a. All the following are common law requirements for a valid listing agreement EXCEPT b. specific performance remedies should one of the parties' defaults. c. be an expressed written agreement to enforce the commission clause. d. a definite termination date.	b. specific performance remedies should one of the parties' defaults. Employment agreements do not have specific performance remedies. Employment agreements do not use specific performance clauses
24. Of the following, what is not necessary for a contract to be valid? a. An earnest money deposit b. Competent Parties c. Offer and acceptance (mutual assent) d. Consideration	a. An earnest money deposit An earnest money deposit is a representation of a buyer's good faith to buy a house. Money gives the buyer time to get financing and conduct the title search, appraisal, and inspections before closing. They are not required.
25. A contract that has no legal object is considered. a. Null b. Valid c. Voidable d. Void	d. Void Some contracts are automatically void because of some aspect of the law. Both parties are freed from contractual obligations with void contracts.
26. Death of the broker or principal, or incapacity, insanity, or bankruptcy of the principal are all ways agency can be terminated by? a. full performance. b. acts of the parties. c. operation of law.	c. operation of law. Insanity or death (including both) will terminate the agency. In the event of death or incapacity of a licensee that represents a

d. expiration of its term.	broker, the agency will not be terminated. It is an Operation of Law.
27. The real estate contract for a specific property for use as an unlicensed whiskey sales operation was forced to terminate. The termination was the result of? a. impossibility of performance. b. breach of contract. c. novation. d. operation of law.	a. impossibility of performance. It can't be done.
28. A woman bought a house subject to her getting approval to run her beauty shop from the city. The city refused her request. The contract was? a. Canceled because of inability to pay points. b. Cancelled because financing based on homes rather than businesses was not accepted. c. Impossibility of performance. d. Her mother	c. impossibility of performance. If something is impossible, that means there is no way for it to happen.
29. A _____ happens when one or more of the contracting parties either partially or completely fails to fulfill the contractual obligations? a. Novation b. Breach of Contract c. Breach of Agency Law d. Estoppel	b. Breach of Contract Contract Breach is a legal process and civil wrong where a party to a contract fails to perform or interferes with the other party's performance of the contract.
30. A seller decides NOT to sell a property despite having an executory contract with a buyer. The buyer's remedy is? a. file criminal charges to void the agreement. b. file criminal charges to void the agreement. c. sue the seller for specific performance to force compliance with the agreement. d. amend the contract and change the terms to get the buyer's earnest money returned.	c. sue the seller for specific performance to force compliance with the agreement. The specific performance clause in the contract allows the buyer to sue the seller for failure to comply with its terms.
31. If an owner refuses to pay the broker an earned commission, the broker may properly seek relief by? bringing a quiet title action against the seller bringing court action filing a mechanics lien bringing a formal complaint with the division of real estate	b. bringing court action Look to the seller for compensation.
32. Every day that the completion of a home is delayed beyond a stated due date, a contractor will reduce his amount by $100. This is an example of? a. compulsory damages. b. punitive damages. c. compensatory damages. d. liquidated damages.	d. liquidated damages. Agreeing to reasonably estimated damages before a breach
33. A property is under contract. The buyer finds major structural issues that the seller is unable to fix	a. mutual rescission of the contract.

before closing. They agree to end the contract, which is known as? a. mutual rescission of the contract. b. specific performance for both parties with no monetary remedy. c. a valid contract that has become voidable by both parties d. mutual rescission of the contract.	In mutual rescission, both parties return all things of value including earnest money to the original state.
34. MATCH: The ability to cancel a transaction for a refinance or for a home equity loan? a. Reliction b. Foreclosure c. transfer d. Rescission	d. Rescission Rescission is the act of voiding a contract that cannot be recognized as binding.
35. Mutual rescission, when the parties rescind a contract and return all things of value to each party, would likely occur in all the following situations EXCEPT? a. the buyer deciding to buy another home. b. the inspection finding major heating problems. c. financing not being available. d. the property being destroyed.	a. the buyer deciding to buy another home. Sellers do not have to return earnest money if the buyer finds another home.
36. Common Contingencies in real estate include all the following except? a. inspections b. financing c. lead based paint d. size of family	d. size of family The size of the family is not a contingency.
37. A condition in a contract, which has not yet been met, is a _____. a. contingency b. implied agreement c. escape clause d. voidable clause	a. contingency Contingencies may create a voidable contract.
38. After an accepted offer, the buyer was unable to obtain a mortgage. Both parties agreed to cancel the contract. Who does the earnest money deposit belong to? a. The purchaser is entitled to the entire amount of the earnest money. b. The seller for compensation of the failed transaction c. The courts d. The agents	a. The purchaser is entitled to the entire amount of the earnest money. The earnest money deposit belongs to the buyer.
39. Which of the following real estate contracts is a service contract? a. a purchase agreement. b. a purchase contract. c. a listing agreement.	c. a listing agreement. Listing contracts (or listing agreements) are contracts between a real estate broker and a

d. an executed listing	homeowner in which, in the event of finding a buyer, the agent receives a fee (commission).
40. Whether a legal agreement is valid, void, or voidable depends on whether it contains all the essential elements of a contract. All the following would render a contract voidable EXCEPT. a. the broker misrepresented the property. b. a minor has signed the document. c. it isn't in writing. d. the buyer is under duress.	c. it isn't in writing. An unwritten real estate contract is void, not voidable.
41. A broker lists and markets a property. The seller sells the property to a neighbor and pays the broker a full commission upon closing. The brokerage firm and the seller had what type of listing agreement? a. Open b. Exclusive agency with a "seller may not sell" contingency c. Exclusive agency d. Exclusive right to sell	d. Exclusive right to sell An exclusive right-to-sell listing allows anyone to sell the property and the broker still gets paid.
42. What is one way a listing agreement would not be canceled? a. The seller loses the property due to bankruptcy. b. The broker sells the property and the property transfers. c. The broker (salesperson) and the seller mutually agree that it is in the best interest of all parties to cancel the listing d. The seller is late on their mortgage payment.	d. The seller is late on their mortgage payment. A contract can be canceled in many ways and for many reasons, but being late on a listing agreement is not one of them
43. Listing Agreements include which of the following? a. An open listing and an exclusive right to sell listing. b. An exclusive right to sell listing only. c. An open listing only. d. A contract for deed.	a. An open listing and an exclusive right to sell listing. Watch out for the words" ONLY" or similar limiting words.
44. John listed his property with Tracy, a sales agent. He sold his own home to his cousin. There was no commission to be paid to Tracy by John. The type of listing most likely was a/an? a. exclusive listing. b. net listing. c. Exclusive Right to Sell. d. net listing.	a. exclusive listing. Exclusive listings allow the seller to sell the property themselves and not have to pay a commission.
45. Of the following listings, which one is a broker guaranteed a commission regardless of who sells the property? a. A net listing b. Open listing c. Exclusive listing	d. Exclusive right In an Exclusive RIGHT Listing, the agent is rewarded if a ready, willing, and able buyer meets the seller's terms. With an Exclusive Listing, the Seller reserves the right to sell the

d. Exclusive right	property directly, without paying a commission to the Realtor.
46. A buyer hired an agent under an exclusive buyer's agency agreement. The buyer client wanted to submit an offer on a house that had been stigmatized by a recent murder-suicide. What is the agent's ethical responsibility to her client? a. Not say anything, it doesn't affect the structure of the property. b. Remain silent to protect the seller. c. Disclose it prior to signing any offer to purchase. d. Keep quiet.	c. Disclose it prior to signing any offer to purchase. Murder or suicide are not material facts. BUT when representing the Buyer, ethically, you should disclose it.
47. Which of the following events may cancel a listing agreement? a. Property owner's marriage. b. Property seller's death. c. Salesperson's relocation to another agency. d. Salesperson's retirement.	b. Property seller's death. The seller's death terminates the agency relationship between the seller and real estate agent.
48. An exclusive right to sell listing obtained by a broker associate belongs to? a. all the agents b. the seller c. the responsible broker d. the broker associate	c. the responsible broker Listings belongs to that broker.
49. All exclusive Listing Agreements shall? a. contain a definite date of expiration, sales price, consideration, and signatures. b. properly identify the property to be sold c. contain all the conditions under which the transaction is to be consummated. d. all the answers are correct.	d. all the answers are correct. All must be included.
50. In which of the following does the listing agent earn a commission even if the owner sells the property to his cousin, who never met the listing agent and never saw any advertising by the agent? a. Exclusive right to sell agency b. None of these c. Exclusive right to list agency d. Protection clause	a. Exclusive right to sell agency In this type of agency arrangement, the agent receives a commission regardless of who sells the property
51. All the following actions would be acceptable in a sales transaction EXCEPT? a. the seller excludes transfer of the built-in microwave in the contract. b. the buyer receives the earnest money after terminating per the financing contingency. c. the seller removes the built-in microwave after closing and before giving possession of the property to the buyer. d. the buyer waives the lead-based paint inspection.	c. the seller removes the built-in microwave after closing and before giving possession of the property to the buyer. The seller may not remove any fixtures or other real property without first excluding it from the contract. The seller would be in breach.

52. A counteroffer usually accepts some of the terms of the original offer and changes others. The offer becomes a _____ when it is accepted, and acceptance is communicated. a. estoppel b. contract c. arrangement d. conditional estoppel	b. contract A counteroffer voids the original offer. When there is a "meeting of the minds", a contract can be established.
53. The document the buyer and seller sign to establish their legal rights is the? a. HUD statement b. buyer's agreement. c. listing agreement. d. purchase contract.	d. purchase contract. The purchase agreements describe the legal rights of the buyer and seller.
54. A written agreement between a buyer/customer and seller/client when the buyer wants to buy real property and the seller wants to sell real property to the buyer, it is called? a. A contract. b. An appraisal. c. A BPO. d. A disclosure agreement.	a. A contract A contract is a written agreement.
55. All the following make a purchase agreement voidable EXCEPT? a. the seller being under extreme duress. b. the buyer signing the contract without reading it. c. the seller misrepresenting the property. d. the buyer being a minor.	b. the buyer signing the contract without reading it. The contract is valid once the buyer signs it and acceptance is communicated, even if the buyer failed to read the document.
56. Which of the following is TRUE about the execution stage of a real estate contract? a. The buyer has legal title and possessory rights once all the contingencies have terminated. b. This stage is for the seller to determine if the buyer's offer is acceptable or if the seller should counteroffer. c. The seller has possession and equitable title. d. The seller has legal title, and the buyer is the equitable.	d. The seller has legal title, and the buyer is the equitable The seller has possession and legal title until the deed is delivered to the buyer conveying title.
57. Lisa owns an apartment building. She orally leases an apartment to Tina "for 5 years, with rents to be paid on the first of every month." Is this lease enforceable under these terms? a. Yes, because only permanent sales of land need to be in writing. b. Yes, because the periods of the lease are only one month. c. No, because all transfers of interest in real estate need to be in writing. d. No, because this is a transfer of interest in real	d. No because this is a transfer of interest in real estate for five years. Under the Statute of Frauds, a transfer of an interest in real estate for more than one year must be in writing to be enforceable.

estate for five years.	
58. To reduce the chance of misunderstandings and lawsuits, licensees should explain the listing agreement carefully to the seller. a. True b. False	a. True Salespeople should explain contracts and disclosures to their clients and customers.
59. A novation is? a. an assignment. b. a new contract. c. an addendum. d. a unilateral agreement.	b. a new contract. · A novation is a new contract that forms a new agreement and removes the liability of the old agreement from the previous parties. It may be unilateral or bilateral.
60. When an existing contract is replaced by an entirely new contract, it is an act of? a. Reversion b. Rescission c. Novation d. Reformation	c. Novation Novation comes from the Latin word "nova," indicating something new.
61. When one party is substituted for another party in a contract, the process is appropriately called a? a. regulation b. unilateral option c. counteroffer d. novation	d. novation
62. A word or phrase in a contract that requires the performance of a certain act within a stated period? a. Option b. Breach of Contract c. For Consideration d. Time is of the essence	d. Time is of the essence Real estate contracts have time-of-the-essence clauses, which require one party to perform within a set timeframe. It is considered a breach of contract if the party fails to complete the required task on time.

Definitions Module Seven

Acceptance
Any language or action that indicates an agreement forming a contract has been reached. An offer is just an offer until acceptance.

Acknowledgment
Written declaration by a person who signs a document that he or she is who they claim to be. Acknowledgments are witnessed by a notary public or other authorized official.

Actual Notice
That truly seen, heard, or read or observed and not presumed. Contrasts with constructive (legal) notice

Affirmation
An affirmation is a formal statement, not under oath, that a statement is true or that the proponent will tell the truth.

Assignment
Assignment transfers benefits only
A transfer of interest in a mortgage, lease, or other contract.

Bilateral Contract
Two people make a promise.
A promise for a promise

Breach of Contract
A Breach of contract is failure to perform without a legal cause.

Consideration
Anything of value that induces one to enter a contract.

Discharge of Contract
Terminating a contract or agreement, when it has been completely performed for by another party's breach or default.

Duress
Duress is wrongful pressure exerted upon a person to coerce that person into a contract that he or she ordinarily wouldn't enter.

Electronic Signature and Paperless Transactions
The Uniform Electronic Transactions Act (UETA) was adopted in 1999, and it provides a framework for determining the legality of electronic signatures. It guarantees that electronic signatures are given the same legal weight as handwritten signatures.

Expressed Contract
Clearly stated or written.
Takes precedence over verbal agreements.

Executed Contract

Completed

Executory Contract
Something still needs to be done.

Exemplary Damages
Damages above and beyond the actual cost of the loss, assessed to punish or set an example for others.

Fraud
Intentional deception or misrepresentation – a material misstatement of fact.

Implied Contract
Shown by the actions.

Impossibility of Performance
Impossibility of performance is when the duties and contractual obligations of one or more parties cannot be fulfilled under normal circumstances.

Incapacity
Valid Contracts must include sober sane adults.

Liquidated Damages
Those damages are specified by contract in advance (usually loss of earnest money) if the buyer defaults. If specified, liquidated damages are the seller's only remedy against the buyer.

Misrepresentation
An untrue statement of material fact that induces a party to act. It may be intentional (fraud) or unintentional. A contract so signed is voidable by the injured party.

Mistake (Negligent Misrepresentation)
An error of fact by both parties may cause a contract to be voidable.
Example: A contract's legal description depicts a different lot than the buyer was shown.

Mutual Agreement
Both parties agree to rescind the contract.
Both parties agree to cancel.
Termination of contract.

Novation
Novation is a mechanism where one party transfers all its obligations and rights under a contract to a third party, with the consent of his original counterparty.

Operation of Law
Statute of limitations are enforced. (Ran out of time to complete.)
An unmarried minor has changed their mind.

Option
A unilateral contract in which the optionor (property owner) promises to sell when the optionee (prospective buyer) chooses to buy – at a price and before a date set in the option contract

Optionee
The optionee is not bound to exercise the option, but the optionor must keep the offer open during the specified time and must go through with the sale if the optionee exercises the option.

Optionor
The optionor (the seller, grants the option right).

Specific Performance
Specific performance is an equitable remedy in the law of contract. A court issues an order requiring a party to perform a specific act, such as to complete performance of the contract.

Statute of Frauds
Everything in real estate must be in writing, according to the Statute of Frauds.

Undue Influence
Undue influence is taking advantage of another person through a position of trust in the formation of a contract

Unenforceable
Appears to have all legal elements but cannot be enforced in court.
Looks valid but can't be enforced.

Unilateral Contract
One party makes a promise.

Valid Contract
Has all the legal elements required for a contract.
Legally binding and has enforceability in a court of law.

Vicarious Liability
A principal's liability for an agent's acts performed within the scope of the agency.
The employing broker is responsible for licensees' actions.

Void Contract
Lacks one or more elements and has no legal force or effect.
Not an actual contract.

Voidable Contract
Lacks one or more elements and has no legal force or effect by one party.
Valid but it contains a flaw.

MODULE EIGHT: LEASING AND PROPERTY MANAGEMENT

Leasing

☐ The property manager is a General Manager
☐ (Leasehold) It's a piece of paper that gives a lessee the right to live in a landlord's real property.
☐ A lease is Personal Property.
☐ A leasehold is a non-freehold estate.
☐ the landlord holds a reversionary interest in his real property when his property is rented.

Property Owners	Tenants/Renters
Leased Fee Lessor	Leasehold Lessee

Tenement

Everything that may be occupied under a lease by a tenant.

Management Agreement

The property manager establishes an agency relationship with the property owner by Property Management Agreement.

Landlord Responsibilities

a. Owners pay property managers a fee or a percentage of the property's rent while under a management agreement.
b. An obligation to their tenants to keep a "warranty of habitability." This is accomplished by making sure the rental is livable, safe, and clean for your tenant.
c. The landlord is ultimately responsible for financials, taxes, utilities, and property maintenance.
d. The landlord/owner has a reversionary right when there is a lease. (Leased fee estate with reversionary rights.).
e. Advice from the property manager may be sought.

Property Manager's Fiduciary Duties to the Owner

The owner is due:
1. Confidentiality
2. Obedience
3. Loyalty
4. Disclosure
5. Accountability
6. Care

- As an agent, the property manager has a fiduciary responsibility to the property owner and must abide by all the requirements of license law, including depositing all funds collected on behalf of the oner or principal into a designated and registered trust account.
- A property manager's primary responsibility is to get the highest NET return for the owner.

Property Manager's Job Responsibilities

☐ the highest NET return for the owner is the primary responsibility of a property manager.

Maximize the Financial Return
- The property manager's primary responsibility is to maximize the owner's financial return over the life of the property so that the owner can achieve the rate of return he or she desires.
- To maximize the return on the property, the property manager oversees or undertakes various activities.

Supervisory Duties
- Property managers help owners create budgets, advertise rental properties, qualify tenants, collect rent, comply with local landlord-tenant laws, maintain properties, oversee preventative maintenance, cleaning, and construction.

Rental Responsibilities
- A manager is responsible for renting the space in a building.
- The manager is responsible for providing necessary services to the tenants as agreed to in the lease.
- Settle disputes between tenants.
- Engaging in eviction activities.
- Knowledge of Landlord-Tenant Law
- Landlord–tenant law is a part of the common law that details the rights and duties of landlords and tenants. It includes elements of both real property law and contract law.

Budgeting and Record Keeping

- Responsible for maintaining records and budgeting.
- Records are kept a minimum of three years.

Risk Management

- Building managers or insurance experts may analyze a building's insurance needs.
- Large complex buildings often require multiple insurance policies to protect specific items, as opposed to a single policy for a single-family house.
- A property manager needs to consider proper insurance coverage as part of an overall risk management strategy.
- Risk management, or some other aspect of resolving potential liabilities, can be handled by a CART-based system.
- CART
  - controlling
  - avoiding
  - retaining
  - transferring risk

Controlling Risk	Avoiding Risk	Retaining Risk	Transferring Risk
Controlling risk means anticipating it and preparing for it. ☐ an apartment owner raised his air conditioners two feet off the ground. He is Controlling his Risk.	Avoiding risk means removing the source of danger.	Retaining risk means accepting the liability.	Transferring risk means buying the appropriate type and amount of insurance to cover the payment whenever an insured incident occurs.

Landlord Property and Business Insurance

Casualty Insurance	Co-insurance	Errors and Omissions Insurance
This type of insurance covers losses caused by theft, vandalism, and burglary.	This coverage essentially is for situations in which the owner takes on the risk by self-insuring for a portion of the risk. Incorporating a large deductible before the insurance policy starts to pay off is one example.	This type of insurance can cover property managers against any errors they make in the performance of their duties. This insurance doesn't cover losses caused by fraud or other dishonest or malfeasant activities.
Fire and Hazard Insurance Depending on what it covers, this type of policy sometimes is called an all-risk, all-peril policy. It covers loss of property caused by fire, storms, and other types of dangerous conditions. This type of policy usually does not cover flooding and earthquake damage.	**Liability Insurance** This type of insurance covers losses caused by injuries resulting from negligence on the landlord's part. The classic case is the person who falls on an icy sidewalk that the landlord was supposed to have cleaned.	**Rent Loss Insurance** This insurance sometimes is called business interruption insurance or consequential loss insurance. It pays the building owner for the loss of rent from tenants if the building is destroyed by fire.

Types of Lease Agreements

Gross Lease	Net Lease
• A type of lease where the Tenant pays a flat rental amount and the landlord pays for all property charges regularly incurred by the ownership, including taxes, utilities, and water. Most apartment leases resemble gross leases. • Mostly higher rental charge	• A net lease requires the Tenant to pay, in addition to rent, some or all the property expenses that usually would be paid by the property owner. • These include property taxes, insurance, maintenance, repair, operations, utilities, and other items.
Residential Leases	Commercial Leases

Landlords Pay	Tenants Pay

More About Net Leases		
Triple Net	**Double Net**	**Single Net**
• NNN Lease / Triple Net Lease • property taxes • insurance • maintenance/utilities • NNN Lease, or triple-N for short and sometimes written NNN.	• NN Lease / Double Net Lease • property taxes • insurance	• N Lease / Single Net Lease • property taxes.
Percentage Lease • A percentage lease is a commercial lease in which the rental amount is computed as a certain percentage of the monthly or annual gross sales generated at leased property. In a percentage lease, the Tenant pays a base rent plus a percentage of any revenue earned while doing business on the rental premises. • This type of lease is more common in commercial real estate markets. • There is a charge for rent, operating expenses, maintenance of common areas, and even a share of the gross revenues generated	**Index Lease** • A lease that makes some or all the rent dependent upon calculations with reference to some type of index. Cost of living index could be used.	**Graduated Lease** • A long-term lease on a property where the rent is changed periodically to reflect the market value of the property. Rent goes up slowly.
Commercial Leases	Commercial Leases	Commercial or Residential Leases

Common Area Maintenance (CAMs)
Common Area Maintenance charges, or CAM for short, are one of the net charges billed to tenants in a commercial net lease and are paid by tenants to the landlord of a commercial property

Ground Lease	**Oil and Gas Lease**
• A ground lease is an agreement in which a tenant is permitted to develop a piece of property during the lease period, after which the land and all improvements are turned over to the property owner. • A ground lease indicates that the property owner will own the improvements. • A ground lease involves leasing land, typically for 99 years, to a tenant who constructs a property building. The ground lease defines who owns the land and who owns the building and improvements on the property.	• An oil and gas lease are essentially an agreement between parties to allow a Lessee (the oil and gas company and their production crew) to have access to the property and minerals (oil and gas) on the property of the Lessor. **Farm Lease** • Farmers to grow crops • The lease provides the basis for combining the landlord's and the tenant's

• Ground leases usually require the Tenant to pay all property expenses, such as taxes, utilities, and maintenance. In this respect, a ground or land lease is like a net lease. • ☐ You could find a (Ground Lease) Long Term Lease on a Section 16.	resources of land, labor, capital, and management to efficiently produce farm commodities. **Hunting Lease** A hunting lease is a legal arrangement or contract whereby a landowner grants access to his or her property for recreational hunting for a certain period.

A Lease Option to Purchase	Sales-Leaseback	Proprietary Lease
• A unilateral contract. • A lease option is an agreement that gives a renter a choice to purchase the rented property during or at the end of the rental period. • It also precludes the owner from offering the property for sale to anyone else. • When the term expires, the renter must either exercise the option or forfeit it. • Usually includes a First Right of Refusal.	• The sale of a property in which the seller immediately begins to rent the property from the buyer. • That is, the seller no longer has ownership of the property, but maintains residence and/or use for the duration of the rental agreement. • A sales-Leaseback frees up the seller's cash.	• In a cooperative apartment, residents buy shares of stock in a corporation that owns the apartment building. • They then rent a particular unit from the corporation, under a document called a proprietary lease.

☐ During a time of inflation, a property manager would not wish to have long-term leases.

☐ When Joe buys the commercial property with three existing leases, he must honor those three leases.

Timing of Leases

All the leases above can be for any of the below lengths of time.

Tenancy for Years	Periodic Tenancy
• A lease for a fixed period. • For a Tenancy for Years Lease, no notice is needed for termination, the lessee knows the termination date from the outset of the lease.	• The tenancy is originally created for a specific period, but the renter's tenancy can continue until there is some notification of the lease's termination. • Month to Month
Tenancy at Will / Estate at Will	**Holdover Tenancy**
• A tenancy-at-will is a property tenure that can be terminated at any time by either the tenant or the owner/landlord. It exists without a contract or lease and usually does not specify the duration of a tenant's rental or the exchange of payment.	• A tenant continues to occupy and use the premises after the term of the lease ends. • If the landowner continues to accept rent payments, the holdover tenant can continue to legally occupy the premises. … If the landowner does not accept continued payments, eviction proceedings can occur.

☐ How much notice do you need to give the landlord when you will be vacating your apartment when the one-year lease is up?

ANSWER: NONE

☐ When Joe rents the ski lodge from November 2nd to March 1st, it is an estate for years. It has a definite beginning and an actual definite end.

☐ If rent is not paid by the due date, the property manager <u>should first</u> determine the problem and then, if needed, pursue an eviction.

Tenancy at Sufferance

A tenancy at sufferance occurs when a tenant continues to live in a rental property after their lease has expired.

Actual Eviction	Constructive Eviction
<ul><li>An actual eviction is when a tenant is physically forced to leave the premises.</li><li>The landlord may sue for possession.</li></ul>	<ul><li>A landlord either does something or fails to do something that he or she has a legal duty to provide (e.g., the landlord refuses to provide heat or water to the apartment), rendering the property uninhabitable. A</li><li>A tenant who is constructively evicted may terminate the lease and seek damages.</li><li>To maintain an action for damages, the tenant must show that: the uninhabitable conditions (substantial interferences) were a result of the landlord's actions (not the actions of some third party) and that the tenant vacated the premises in a reasonable time.</li></ul>

Forcible entry and detainer

A summary proceeding for restoring to possession of land one who is wrongfully kept out or has been wrongfully deprived of the possession.

Security Deposit

- A renter's security deposit is to cover any repairs needed once the tenant vacates. It is not the last month's rent.
- Renter's Insurance
- The renter is responsible for insuring his personal property. Renter's Insurance is for the tenant's personal property.

Sublease

In a sublease, a tenant transfers the leasehold for just a portion of the remaining lease term; the subtenant pays rent to the tenant, who pays the landlord.

Requirements for a Valid Lease

- A lease is an agreement between a landlord and tenant that conveys a leasehold interest.
- Generally, in states with leases for longer than one year, the landlord must sign the lease in writing.
- There must be competent parties to the lease, agreement on its terms, and consideration (such as rent).
- Several leases allow tenants to renew the lease at the end of the term; a lease may also be renewed by implication if a landlord continues to accept payments.

Termination of a Lease

- The cancellation of a lease by the action of either party.
- Mutual Agreement.
- Actual Eviction.
- Constructive Eviction.
- Surrender.
- Breach.
- Violation of lease terms.
- Illegal Activities.
- Property Destroyed.
- Land leases do not terminate if a structure is destroyed.

Setting Rents and Lease Rates (BROKER ONLY)

1. Using the home's value
The amount of rent you charge your tenants should be a percentage of your home's market value.
Typically, the rents that landlords charge fall between 0.8% and 1.1% of the home's value.
For example, for a home valued at $250,000, a landlord could charge between $2,000 and $2,750 each month
2. Researching Comparable Units.
3. Calculate rental price per square foot.
4. Consider the location.
5. Consider available amenities.

Fair Housing in Property Management

Fair Housing Act

Protected Classes

1. race
2. color
3. religion
4. national origin
5. sex
6. disability
7. familial status

In the Sale and Rental of Housing:
It is illegal discrimination to take any of the following actions because of race, color, religion, sex, disability, familial status, or national origin:
- Refuse to rent or sell housing
- Refuse to negotiate for housing
- Otherwise make housing unavailable
- Set different terms, conditions or privileges for sale or rental of a dwelling
- Provide a person different housing services or facilities
- Falsely deny that housing is available for inspection, sale, or rental
- Make, print, or publish any notice, statement, or advertisement with respect to the sale or rental of a dwelling that indicates any preference, limitation, or discrimination
- Impose different sales prices or rental charges for the sale or rental of a dwelling
- Use different qualification criteria or applications, or sale or rental standards or procedures, such as income standards, application requirements, application fees, credit analyses, sale or rental approval procedures or other requirements
- Evict a tenant or a tenant's guest
- Harass a person
- Fail or delay performance of maintenance or repairs
- Limit privileges, services, or facilities of a dwelling
- Discourage the purchase or rental of a dwelling
- Assign a person to a particular building or neighborhood or section of a building or neighborhood
- Refuse to provide or discriminate in the terms or conditions of homeowner's insurance because of the race, color, religion, sex, disability, familial status, or national origin of the owner and/or occupants of a dwelling

Equal Housing Opportunity Poster

Every real estate office must predominately display the EHO poster, or they are guilty of prima facie discrimination.

Covid 19 * NEW

People who currently have COVID–19, those who have a history of having the virus, and those who are perceived as having the virus may be protected against housing discrimination under long-standing interpretations of the Fair Housing Act and other civil rights laws.

Convicted Drug User vs. Convicted Drug Dealer

Convicted Drug User	Convicted Drug Dealer
☐ Convicted drug users may be protected if they are currently or have sought treatment. Or, they haven't used for some time.	Convicted drug dealers are not protected.

☐ in general, the definition of "person with a disability" does not include current users of illegal controlled substances but does provide protections for individuals with drug or alcohol addiction. Individuals would also be protected under Section 504 and the ADA if a purpose of the specific program or activity is to provide health or rehabilitation services to such individuals.

Sexual Harassment

- Sexual harassment occurs when there is deliberate or repeated unsolicited verbal comments, gestures, or physical contact that makes for an offensive environment or when sexual favors are sought as a "quid pro quo" for housing.
- Actions taken by a landlord against a victim of domestic violence have a disproportionate effect on women and possibly other protected classes.

Sexual Orientation

- Discrimination because of sexual orientation or gender identity is not explicitly prohibited by the Fair Housing Act.
- Nonetheless, discrimination against lesbian, gay, bisexual, and transgender (LGBT) individuals in housing assisted by HUD or subject to a mortgage insured by the Federal Housing Administration is prohibited by HUD regulation.
- The regulation also prohibits inquiries about sexual orientation or gender identify.

Undocumented Immigrants

- A person's immigration status does not affect his or her federal fair housing rights or responsibilities.
- Currently, there is no federal law which prevents or penalizes landlords from renting to undocumented persons.
- Asking for immigration or citizenship documentation only from people who speak with an accent or seem to be "foreign" is a civil rights violation.

Public-law occupancy standards

- Local maximum occupancy standards aren't superseded in their application by the Fair Housing Act.
- For example, if a local law provides a maximum occupancy of two people per bedroom and you

rent out a studio apartment in a building you own, you can't be forced to rent the apartment to a couple with a child.

Retaliation for Complaints

- It is illegal to retaliate against any person for making a complaint, testifying, assisting, or participating in any manner in a proceeding under HUD's complaint process at any time, even after the investigation has been completed.
- The Fair Housing Act also makes it illegal to retaliate against any person because that person reported a discriminatory practice to a housing provider or other authority. If you believe you have experienced retaliation, you can file a complaint.

Who Is a Person with a Disability?

Federal nondiscrimination laws define a person with a disability to include any
(1) individual with a physical or mental impairment that substantially limits one or more major life activities.
(2) individual with a record of such impairment; or
(3) individual who is regarded as having such an impairment.

Physical or Mental Impairment
In general, a physical or mental impairment includes, but is not limited to, examples of conditions such as

orthopedic	hearing impairments	cerebral palsy	autism
visual	epilepsy	muscular dystrophy	multiple sclerosis
speech	drug addiction alcoholism	developmental disabilities	Human Immunodeficiency (HIV)
cancer	diabetes	heart disease	mental illness

Some impairments are readily observable, while others may be invisible.

Observable impairments may include, but are not limited to
- blindness or low vision
- deafness or being hard of hearing
- mobility limitations
- other types of impairments with observable symptoms or effects
- intellectual impairments (including some types of autism)
- neurological impairments (e.g., stroke, Parkinson's disease, cerebral palsy, epilepsy, or brain injury)
- mental illness
- other diseases or conditions that affect major life activities or bodily functions

A landlord can refuse to rent to a person with a violent criminal history.

A Landlord May Not Ask Discriminatory Questions

- If there is not an accommodation request, the Fair Housing Acts prohibit the landlord from asking whether the applicant has a disability or about the severity of the impairment.

- Landlords must treat disabled applicants and tenants in the same way as those without a disability:
    1. Landlords cannot request medical records, nor guide a tenant to a specific unit.
    2. A landlord may ask all prospective tenants, including disabled applicants, about whether:
    3. The applicant can meet tenancy requirements.
    4. The applicant abuses or is addicted to an illegal controlled substance.
    5. The applicant qualifies for a rental unit available only to people with a disability or a certain type of disability; or
    6. The applicant qualifies for a rental unit that is offered on a priority basis to people with a disability or with a certain type of disability.

☐ An apartment complex cannot segregate families in one section of the complex.

Reasonable Accommodations	Reasonable Modifications
A reasonable accommodation is a change, exception, or adjustment to a rule, policy, practice, or service that may be necessary for a person with disabilities to have an equal opportunity to use and enjoy a dwelling, including public and common use spaces, or to fulfill their program obligations.	A reasonable modification is a structural change made to existing premises, occupied or to be occupied by a person with a disability, to afford such person full enjoyment of the premises.
Reasonable accommodations eliminate barriers that prevent persons with disabilities from fully participating in housing opportunities, including both private housing and in federally assisted programs or activities.	Reasonable modifications can include structural changes to interiors and exteriors of dwellings and to common and public use areas.
Examples of Reasonable Accommodations 1. Assigning an accessible parking space 2. Permitting a tenant to transfer to a ground-floor unit 3. Adjusting a rent payment schedule to accommodate when an individual receives income assistance 4. Permitting an applicant to submit a housing application via a different means 5. Permitting an assistance animal in a "no pets" building 6. Permission to mail a rent payment	**Examples of Reasonable Modifications** 1. the installation of a ramp into a building 2. lowering the entry threshold of a unit 3. installation of grab bars in a bathroom 4. wheelchair ramps 5. lowered countertops 6. special door handles 7. There must be a relationship between the modification and the disability.
Housing providers may not require persons with disabilities to pay extra fees or deposits or place any other special conditions or requirements as a condition of receiving a reasonable accommodation.	A housing provider is required to provide and pay for the structural modification as a reasonable accommodation unless it amounts to an undue financial and administrative burden or a fundamental alteration of the program.
A Landlord may not refuse to make reasonable accommodations in rules, policies, practices, or services if necessary for the disabled person to use the housing. o An example would be an accessible Parking Spot.	A landlord may not refuse to let a disabled person make reasonable modifications to the dwelling or common use areas, ☐ at their expense, if necessary for the disabled person to use the housing.
Not all persons with disabilities will have a need to request a reasonable accommodation. However, all persons with disabilities have a right to request or be provided a reasonable accommodation at any time	If reasonable, disabled tenants may modify a rental unit to make it safe and comfortable to live in. (Where reasonable, the landlord may permit changes ☐ only if the disabled person

	agrees to restore the property to its original condition when they move)
If the landlord owns an older building and accommodating a tenant with a disability would require a major remodel, the landlord is usually not required to add the accommodations.	If the modification will create an inappropriate living condition for the next Tenant, the landlord may agree to the modification upon the condition that the Tenant restore the unit to its original condition prior to leaving. In this circumstance, the landlord may require the Tenant to put money in an interest-bearing escrow account.
	All modifications are subject to approval with the landlord. The landlord may ask for a description of the proposed modification and any necessary building permits.

Under federal law, disabled tenants and prospective tenants with a disability have the right to apply for and live in a rental unit regardless of their impairment.

☐ What's the least likely thing a handicapped person would bring back to the original condition before they move out?
Answer: handrails screwed into the shower tile.

Four or More Units

The Fair Housing Act requires all "covered multifamily dwellings" designed and constructed for first occupancy after March 13, 1991, to be readily accessible and usable by persons with disabilities.
- Public and common use areas must be accessible to persons with disabilities,
- All doors and hallways must be wide enough for wheelchairs.

All units must have:
- An accessible route into and through the unit.
- Accessible light switches, electrical outlets, thermostats, and other environmental controls.
- Reinforced bathroom walls to allow later installation of grab bars.
- Kitchens and bathrooms that can be used by people in wheelchairs.

Undue burden	Undue hardship	Undue financial and administrative burden
Significant difficulty or expense. A public accommodation is not required to provide any auxiliary aid or service that would result in an undue burden.	An action that requires "significant difficulty or expense" in relation to the size of the employer, the resources available, and the nature of the operation. The concept of undue hardship includes any action that is unduly costly, extensive, substantial, disruptive, or would fundamentally alter the nature or operation of the business. Accordingly, whether a	A public entity does not have to take any action that it can demonstrate would result in an undue financial and administrative burden. This applies in program accessibility, effective communication, and auxiliary aids and services. The determination of an undue financial and administrative burden must be:

	particular accommodation will impose an undue hardship must always be determined on a case-by- case basis.	• Made by the head of the public entity or his/her designee. • Accompanied by a written statement of the reasons. • Based on all resources available for use in the program.

What Is an Assistance Animal?

- An animal that works, aids, or performs tasks for the benefit of a person with a disability, or that provides emotional support that alleviates one or more identified effects of a person's disability. ☐ an assistance animal is not a pet.

Obligations of Housing Providers

- Individuals with a disability may request to keep an assistance animal as a reasonable accommodation to a housing provider's pet restrictions.

Examples
A reasonable accommodation request for an assistance animal may include, for example:
- A request to live with an assistance animal at a property where a housing provider has a no-pets policy.
- A request to waive a pet deposit, fee, or other rule as to an assistance animal.

Service Animals

- A service animal is any dog that is individually trained to do work or perform tasks for the benefit of an individual with a disability, including a physical, sensory, psychiatric, intellectual, or other mental disability. Other species of animals, whether wild or domestic, trained, or untrained, are not considered service animals.
- The work or tasks performed by a service animal must be directly related to the individual's disability. Examples of work or tasks include, but are not limited to:
  1. Assisting individuals who are blind or have low vision with navigation and other tasks.
  2. Alerting individuals who are deaf or hard of hearing to the presence of people or sounds.
  3. Providing non-violent protection or rescue work.
  4. Pulling a wheelchair.
  5. Assisting an individual during a seizure.
  6. Alerting individuals to the presence of allergens.
  7. Retrieving items such as medicine or the telephone.
  8. Providing physical support and assistance with balance and stability to individuals with mobility disabilities.
  9. Helping individuals with psychiatric and neurological disabilities by preventing or interrupting impulsive or destructive behaviors.

The crime deterrent effects of an animal's presence and the provision of emotional support, well-being, comfort, or companionship are not considered work or tasks under the definition of a service animal.

When and Where a Service Animal is Allowed Access

- Individuals with disabilities can bring their service animals into all areas of public facilities and private businesses where members of the public, program participants, clients, customers, patrons, or invitees are allowed.
- A service animal can be excluded from a facility if its presence interferes with legitimate safety requirements of the facility (e.g., from a surgery or burn unit in a hospital in which a sterile field is required).
- A public entity or a private business may ask an individual with a disability to remove a service animal if the animal is not housebroken or is out of control and the individual is not able to control it.
- A service animal must have a harness, leash, or other tether, unless the handler is unable to use a tether because of a disability or the use of a tether would interfere with the service animal's ability to safely perform its work or tasks. In these cases, the service animal must be under the handler's control through voice commands, hand signals, or other effective means.
- If a service animal is excluded, the individual with a disability must still be offered the opportunity to obtain goods, services, and accommodations without having the service animal on the premises.

Asking Questions

to determine if an animal is a service animal, a public entity or a private business may ask two questions:

1. Is this animal required because of a disability?	2. What work or task has this animal been trained to perform?

These questions may not be asked if the need for the service animal is obvious (e.g., the dog is guiding an individual who is blind or pulling a person's wheelchair). A public entity or private business may not ask about the nature or extent of an individual's disability, or require documentation, such as proof that the animal has been certified, trained, or licensed as a service animal, or require the animal to wear an identifying vest.

Allergies and fear of dogs are not valid reasons for denying access or refusing service to people using service animals.

Other Provisions

- A public entity or private business is not responsible for the care and supervision of a service animal.
- A public entity or private business cannot ask nor require an individual with a disability to pay a surcharge or deposit, even if people accompanied by pets are required to pay such fees.
- If a public entity or private business normally charges individuals for the damage they cause, an individual with a disability may be charged for damage caused by his or her service animal.

Miniature Horses

- A public entity or private business must allow a person with a disability to bring a miniature horse on the premises if it has been individually trained to do work or perform tasks for the benefit of the individual with a disability.

- However, an organization can consider whether the facility can accommodate the miniature based on the horse's type, size, and weight.
- The rules that apply to service dogs also apply to miniature horses.

Psychiatric Service Dog

PSD is a dog that has been trained to perform tasks that assist individuals with disabilities to detect the onset of psychiatric episodes and lessen their effects. Tasks performed by psychiatric service animals may include reminding the handler to take medicine, providing safety checks or room searches, or turning on lights for persons with Post Traumatic Stress Disorder, interrupting self-mutilation by persons with dissociative identity disorders, and keeping disoriented individuals from danger.

SSig DOG

(Sensory signal dogs or social signal dogs) is a dog trained to assist a person with autism. The dog alerts the handler to distracting repetitive movements common among those with autism, allowing the person to stop the movement (e.g., hand flapping).

Seizure Response Dog

A dog trained to assist a person with a seizure disorder. How the dog serves the person depends on the person's needs. The dog may stand guard over the person during a seizure, or the dog may go for help. A few dogs have learned to predict a seizure and warn the person in advance to sit down or move to a safe place.

Comfort / Emotional Support Animal

- An emotional support animal is an animal (typically a dog or cat though this can include other species) that provides a therapeutic benefit to its owner through companionship.
- The animal provides emotional support and comfort to individuals with psychiatric disabilities and other mental impairments.
- While Emotional Support Animals or Comfort Animals are often used as part of a medical treatment plan as therapy animals, they are not considered service animals under the ADA.
- These support animals provide companionship, relieve loneliness, and sometimes help with depression, anxiety, and certain phobias, but do not have special training to perform tasks that assist people with disabilities.
- Even though some states have laws defining therapy animals, these animals are not limited to working with people with disabilities and therefore are not covered by federal laws protecting the use of service animals.
- Therapy animals provide people with therapeutic contact, usually in a clinical setting, to improve their physical, social, emotional, and/or cognitive functioning.
- It does not matter if a person has a note from a doctor that states that the person has a disability and needs to have the animal for emotional support.
- A doctor's letter does not turn an animal into a service animal.

Families with Pregnant Women and Children

Familial status covers:

- families with children under the age of 18
- pregnant persons
- any person in the process of securing legal custody of a minor child (including adoptive or foster parents)
- persons with written permission of the parent or legal guardian

Familial Status Discrimination

Examples of familial status discrimination include:
- Refusing to rent to families with children.
- Evicting families once a child joins the family through, e.g., birth, adoption, custody.
- Requiring families with children to live on specific floors or in specific buildings or areas.
- Imposing overly restrictive rules about children's use of the common areas (e.g., pools, hallways, open spaces).
- Advertising that prohibits children.

The Familial Status Act also does not limit the applicability of reasonable local, state, or federal restrictions regarding the maximum number of occupants permitted to occupy a dwelling.

The Act also does not limit the applicability of reasonable local, state, or federal restrictions regarding the maximum number of occupants permitted to occupy a dwelling.
☐ an apartment complex cannot segregate all the families with children into a separate area.

Housing does not have to be made available to persons who would constitute a direct threat to the health and safety of other individuals or the substantial physical damage to the property.
Individual convicted of selling drugs can be denied housing.

Housing for Older Persons

The Fair Housing Act specifically exempts three types of housing for older persons from liability for familial status discrimination. Such exempt housing facilities or communities can lawfully refuse to sell or rent dwellings to families with minor children only if they qualify for the exemption. To qualify for the "housing for older persons" exemption, a facility or community must comply with all the requirements of the exemption.

The Housing for Older Persons exemptions apply to the following housing:

- Intended for, and solely occupied by persons 62 years of age or older; or
- Intended and operated for occupancy by persons 55 years of age or older.
- Provided under any state or federal program that the Secretary of HUD has determined to be specifically designed and operated to assist elderly persons (as defined in the state or federal program).

The 55 or older exemption is the most common of the three.

How to Qualify for the "55 or Older" Exemption - and 62 and Over

To qualify for the "55 or older" housing exemption, a facility or community must satisfy each of the following requirements:

- ☐ At least 80 percent of the units must have at least one occupant who is 55 years of age or older: and
- The facility or community must publish and adhere to policies and procedures that demonstrate the intent to operate as "55 or older" housing; and
- The facility or community must comply with HUD's regulatory requirements for age verification of residents.
- The "housing for older persons" exemption does not protect such housing facilities or communities from liability for housing discrimination because of race, color, religion, sex, disability, or national origin.

☐ You may legally turn away families with children, however, if your rental property qualifies as senior housing. (55+ Communities and 62+ Communities)

HUD enforces Fair Housing Complaints (except complaints of the Equal RIGHTS act of 1866.)

Exemptions to Fair Housing

The Fair Housing Act exempts

- owner-occupied buildings with no more than four units
- single-family houses sold or rented by the owner without the use of an agent
- housing operated by religious organizations
- private clubs that limit occupancy to members
- ☐ There must be no discriminatory advertising or using a professional real estate broker.

☐ A woman has been living in her small studio apartment for nine years. She loves the apartment because it overlooks a golf course and has a peek a boo view of the ocean. She knows the apartment is limited to one person or couples. Two months ago, the woman was in a car accident and was hurt. At the hospital, the doctor informed her that the health insurance company is going to supply a 24 hour "live in aide" to help her get around. The doctor believes "in time" the woman will fully recover and the nurse most likely will be temporary.
Can the landlord refuse to let the "live-in" aide move in based on square foot occupancy?
Approving a live-in aide, if needed by a disabled household, is an example of a reasonable accommodation.

Quiz – Leasing and Property Management

1. A property manager's duties typically include all the following except? a. Investing the property owner's funds. b. Handing out applications to potential renters. c. Screening tenants. d. Collecting rents.	a. investing the property owner's funds. Investing a client funds is not a duty for the agent.
2. An individual or company that maintains client properties and maximizes return on the client's investment is a? a. An investment counselor b. A rental agent c. A building maintenance specialist d. A property manager	a. A property manager Property managers fill vacancies, negotiate, and enforce leases, as well as maintain and secure rental properties.
3. MATCH: Property management. a. the activities involved in conducting a visual survey of a property's site conditions, structure, and systems and preparing an analytical report useful to both buyers and homeowners. b. the activities of splitting a large parcel of real estate into smaller ones and constructing improvements on the land. c. the business of arranging for or providing funds for real estate transactions. d. the business of managing real estate to protect the owner's investment and maximize the owner's return.	d. the business of managing real estate to protect the owner's investment and maximize the owner's return.
4. An owner of a car shop entered into a sale-and-leaseback agreement with a buyer. Which statement is TRUE of this arrangement? a. The owner is the lessor. b. The buyer is the lessor. c. The buyer receives possession of the property. d. The owner retains title to the ranch.	b. The buyer is the lessor. The buyer starts out as a grantee and ends up being a lessor.
5. Which of the following parties does a property manager always work for? a. the owner or principal. b. the appraiser. c. the lender or mortgagee. d. the tenant or lessee.	a. the owner or principal. It is the owner who hires the property manager. They have a fiduciary relationship.
6. A property manager produced a one-year lease for prospective tenants from Southern Europe who loved the apartment with three bedrooms. The price was a little high for the couple's budget, but the tenants agreed that the rent was fair. Unfortunately, the couple was unsure if they could fulfill the entire lease period of one year. What is the agent's responsibility to the property owner?	a. To get the highest net return for the owner. This is a superfluous question. Meaning, there is information in this question that is not needed to answer the question. Focus on the actual question. The answer is that a property manager's primary duty is to get the highest net return for the owner.

a. To get the highest net return for the owner. b. To get the highest gross return for the owner. c. To review the citizenship eligibility of the tenants before allowing them to sign the lease. d. Along with the financial eligibility, the agent should request immigration papers.	
7. An apartment manager expects residential rental demand to exceed residential rental supply soon, so he wants to renew leases for? a. a long-term commitment. b. be for relatively short terms. c. reflect the ARM. d. reflect the CPI.	b. be for relatively short terms. The property manager wants the new leases to reflect the economic condition when old leases expire.
8. When the property manager suspects an illegal activity is taking place in the building he or she manages, the manager should? a. tell the tenant they are being watched closely. b. notify the owner of their concerns. c. terminate the property management agreement with the owner. d. do nothing if the tenant pays the rent on time.	b. notify the owner of their concerns. Notify the Principal regarding the suspected behavior.
9. What is the foundation of a good landlord and tenant relationship? a. Great reputation for weekend parties. b. Good reputation for maintenance and management. c. No reputation of maintenance. d. Bad reputation for police visits to the property.	b. Good reputation for maintenance and management, Well-maintained properties and respectful leasing agents could increase the demand for the units.
10. What should be done when a tenant makes a service request? a. The tenant should be told when it will be taken care of, or why it will not be b. Tell the tenant the request must be in writing. c. Tell the tenant that there is a waiting list. d. Regardless of safety, check the balance sheet before responding.	a. The tenant should be told when it will be taken care of, or why it will not be The property manager should abide by lease agreements.
11. When should a property manager qualify a rental prospect? a. Before making an appointment to show the space. b. Before a deposit is made. c. Before a rental agreement is signed. d. After showing a sample of properties.	a. Before making an appointment to show the space Qualify potential renters ASAP.
12. What is one of the major objectives of professional property management? a. Maintain 100 percent occupancy. b. Maximize the return to the property management firm. c. Help control area rent schedules.	d. Minimize expenses while maximizing profits for the owner. Minimize expenses while maximizing profits for the owner. HIGHEST NET RETURN

d. Minimize expenses while maximizing profits for the owner.	
13. What factors realistically determine the level of rental amounts? a. Capitalization of income b. Cost of construction c. Market comparison d. Published surveys which report average housing costs	c. Market comparison Rent schedules can be established most realistically by comparing the local market.
14. A property manager has a subtracted the losses for vacancies and collection losses from the scheduled gross rental income. The resulting figure is? a. cash flow before tax b. operating expenses c. gross effective income d. net operating income	c. gross effective income BEFORE office and management expenses are deducted, the amount is "gross". After expenses, it is "net".
15. If a landlord collects two years rent in advance, how is that money recorded on his income tax? a. At income at the end of the lease period. b. As income each month as the rent can be applied c. It will be dependent on the structure of his business. d. In the year collected	d. In the year collected Prepaid rent is reported as income in the year received, not when it is earned.
16. Which of the following owners of an apartment building would emphasize maintenance of value over-income? a. HUD b. FCC c. FDIC d. An entrepreneur who owns several income properties.	a. HUD For HUD it is the safety of the building that is important. maintenance of value over-income
17. A property management plan may serve different purposes for different owners and generally must strike a balance between preservation of the property's value and generation of income. Which of the following owners would MOST likely prefer a property manager who emphasizes cash flow or income over the maintenance of value? a. FDIC b. FEMA c. The entrepreneur who owns several apartments. d. HUD	c. The entrepreneur who owns several apartments. An investor is more concerned with property income than HUD, FHA, or VA lenders. These organizations are more concerned with health and safety.
18. When renting residential property, the amount of a security deposit which a lessor may legally charge from a lessee is determined in part by which of the following? a. The number of children or pets. b. Whether the unit is furnished or not. c. The number of adults who will reside in the unit.	b. Whether the unit is furnished or not. If the unit is furnished, the lessor can charge a higher deposit than if it is not.

d. The number of square feet in the building.	
19. A property manager's duties typically include all the following except? a. Collecting rents. b. Handing out applications to potential renters. c. investing the property owner's funds. d. Screening tenants	c. investing the property owner's funds. Investing a client funds is not a duty for the agent.
20. A commercial tenant pays $16,000 per month in base rent plus a percentage of taxes, insurance, and maintenance. This type of lease is known as. a. a net lease b. a fixed lease c. a percentage lease d. an index lease	a. a net lease In a net lease, the tenant pays a portion of the owner's expenses in addition to the base rent.
21. Upon leasing a store, an agreement was signed that stipulated a fixed rent would be paid and all operating costs would be paid by the landlord. This is an example of a? a. gross lease b. income lease c. net lease d. graduated lease	a. gross lease Gross leases are types of easements in which the landlord pays all operating expenses, including taxes, electric, and water, for the owner
22. A tenant pays a base rent plus a percentage of all monthly sales over $20,000. This is an example of what type of lease? a. Residential percentage lease b. Double net lease c. Commercial percentage lease d. Gross or fixed lease with a sales rider	c. Commercial percentage lease Commercial percentage lease. A percentage lease has the tenant pay a portion of the sales as well as rent.
23. An apartment was leased to a couple for a period of one year. There is no automatic renewal clause in the lease. Rather than extending their lease, they plan to move out after the term ends. To comply with the lease term, how much notice must they give? a. 60 days. b. 45 days. c. No notice is required. d. 30 days.	c. No notice is required. No notice is needed. The lease contract states the specific date the lease ends.
24. A tenant signed a 23-month lease for an apartment. The tenant paid 1 month's rent after the lease expired. What kind of leasehold does the tenant have? a. Holdover Tenancy. b. Tenancy at will. c. Tenancy by the Entirety. d. Tenancy for Years.	b. Tenancy at will. You or your landlord/owner can end the tenancy at will at any time.
25. Which is NOT a Type of Leasehold? a. Estate at Opportunity b. Estate for period	a. Estate at Opportunity

c. Estate at will d. Estate for years	Leasehold estates can be classified into four main types based on features such as lease periods and relationships between landlords and tenants
26. A tenant in good standing under a valid five-year lease which makes no mention of assignment or sub-leasing, may legally do which of the following? a. May sublease or assign the leasehold to anyone, since the lease made no mention of any restrictions on such action. b. May sublease to another but can assign only with the consent of the lessor. c. May assign, but cannot sublease to another d. May sublease the property to another, but only with the consent of the lessor.	a. May sublease or assign the leasehold to anyone, since the lease made no mention of any restrictions on such action If the lease does not otherwise specify, it may be assigned or sublet without restriction.
27. MATCH: Tenancy for year-to-year, month-to-month, or week-to-week. From period to period. a. Periodic Tenancy b. Tenancy by the entirety c. Tenancy in Common d. Joint Tenancy	a. Periodic Tenancy From period to period.
28. A tenant signed a 21-month lease for an apartment. The tenant paid 1 month's rent after the lease expired. What kind of leasehold does the tenant have? a. Holdover Tenancy b. Tenancy at will c. Tenancy by the Entirety d. Tenancy for Years	b. Tenancy at will You or your landlord/owner can end the tenancy at will at any time.
29. MATCH: A leasehold estate without a specific amount of time when either the tenant or landlord can? a. end this lease b. stock cooperative c. freehold estate d. Tenancy at Will	c. Tenancy at Will Tenancy at Will is an informal lease. It can be terminated at will.
30. If leased premises become unusable for the purpose stated in the lease, the tenant may have the right to abandon the premises. This action is called. a. constructive eviction. b. primary eviction. c. actual eviction. d. Condemnation.	a. constructive eviction. An effective eviction occurs when a landlord takes steps that disturb or impair the enjoyment of the leased premises to the point that the tenant is effectively forced out of the premises without having to pay further rent.
31. MATCH: A tenant is unwilling to vacate. An eviction may be in effect. a. On Year Lease b. Tenancy from period to period c. Tenancy at Sufferance d. Tenancy for Years	c. Tenancy at Sufferance The tenant is making the landlord suffer

32. MATCH: A leasehold interest in property with a definite beginning and a definite end. a. Tenancy for Years b. Point to Point c. Period to Period d. Tenancy at Sufferance	a. Tenancy for Years Tenancy for years does not mean a term of a year; it means it has a definite beginning and a definite ending.
33. When qualifying a prospective buyer or renter, a licensee may question the prospect about? a. race. b. religion. c. marital status and the number of children in the household. d. rental history.	d. rental history. Familial status, race, and religion are protected classes.
34. For a brokerage firm to show it follows fair housing laws, the firm must? a. make sure all brokers and salespersons take an annual fair housing course. b. establish territories for all its licensees to prove equal treatment to all areas of the city. c. prominently display the equal opportunity poster in the office. d. survey all its licensees to make sure they are not steering.	c. prominently display the equal opportunity poster in the office. The office must display the poster, or it is prima facie discrimination.
35. The provisions of the 1968 Federal Fair Housing Act apply? a. only in states that have substantially equivalent laws. b. in all states. c. only states that do not have substantially equivalent laws. d. only in states that have ratified the act.	b. in all states. They are federal laws and statues they apply in all states.
36. The Fair Housing Act of 1968 was meant as a follow-up to the Civil Rights Act of 1964. It is called the? a. Fair Rental Housing Act. b. Fair Housing Act. c. Fair Housing Enactment. d. Fair Act.	b. Fair Housing Act. Also known as Title VIII of 1968.
37. When is a multiple-family dwelling with 4 or fewer units excluded by the Civil Rights Act of 1968? a. When the owner does NOT live in a unit. b. When the owner lives on the property. c. When the property is in a residential neighborhood. d. When the owner leases on to a certain nationality.	b. When the owner lives on the property. Exemptions include: 1. owner-occupied buildings with no more than four units 2. single-family housing sold or rented without the use of a broker if the private individual owner does not own more than three such single-family homes at one time

	3. housing operated by organizations and private clubs that limit occupancy to member.
38. Under federal fair housing law, which of the following is not a protected class? a. Children b. National origin c. Marital status d. Religion	c. Marital status Marital status is not protected under federal fair housing law.
39. The Civil Rights Act of 1866 prohibited discrimination based on? a. Pregnancy b. Race c. Familial Status d. National Origin	b. Race The Civil Rights Act of 1866, which declared that all people born in the United States were U.S. citizens and had certain inalienable rights, including the right to make contracts, to own property, to sue in court, and to enjoy the full protection of federal law.
40. What type of federal law prohibits discrimination in the provision of housing and housing-related services (including lending) based on an individual's race, color, national origin, religion, sex, familial status, or disability? a. Fair housing b. Lot size c. Licensing d. Homeownership	a. Fair housing The Fair Housing Act protects people from discrimination when they are renting or buying a home, getting a mortgage, seeking housing assistance, or engaging in other housing-related activities.
41. Ana, a property manager, may legally refuse to rent to? a. a person unable to live alone without help. b. pregnant single women. c. a person convicted of selling drugs. d. a person who wants to adjust the apartment and pay for it to fit her wheelchair.	c. a person convicted of selling drugs. A convicted drug dealer is not protected.
42. All the following are a violation of fair housing law EXCEPT? a. a landlord refusing to rent to a convicted drug dealer. b. homeowners refusing to rent a room in their house to Caucasians. c. a landlord refusing to rent to a recovering drug addict. d. helping a seller sell a home only to married couples without children.	a. a landlord refusing to rent to a convicted drug dealer. The answer is a landlord refusing to rent to a convicted drug dealer. Fair housing law does not cover those who have been convicted of dealing drugs.
43. Under federal fair housing laws, it is legal to prohibit which of the following in a housing unit? a. all of these b. live in care nurses c. modifications d. Drugs	d. Drugs Drug use is not protected.

44. The Americans with Disabilities Act (ADA) provides protection to those who? a. are receiving treatment for alcoholism. b. have suffered financial hardship because of health costs. c. are age 55 or older. d. have been convicted of selling drugs.	a. are receiving treatment for alcoholism. The answer is receiving treatment for alcoholism. Those who are receiving treatment for alcoholism are protected under ADA.
45. Federal Fair housing laws prohibit discrimination based on? a. Sex b. Political beliefs c. College affiliation d. Education	a. Sex When someone (an applicant or employee) is treated unfavorably because of their gender, sex discrimination. Discriminatory action against a person based on gender identity, including transgender status, or based on sexual orientation is prohibited under Title VII.
46. Of the following, which is considered a violation of fair housing laws regarding periodic tenancy? a. A landlord that requires all tenants pay first, second and last month's rent in advance. b. The requirement of a landlord that all tenants furnish references from their previous landlord. c. A landlord requiring that each tenant have a good credit rating and the assurance of a steady source of income. d. The requirement of a landlord of a co-signer exclusively for tenants who are single.	d. The requirement of a landlord of a co-signer exclusively for tenants who are single. The landlord singled out a certain group.
47. Federal fair housing laws protect all the following people against discrimination EXCEPT? a. homosexuals b. children c. Baptists d. Russians	a. homosexuals Although some city and state laws protect homosexuality (sexual orientation), the federal Fair Housing Act does not.
48. This federal act that prohibits discrimination against persons with disabilities, where disability is defined as a physical or mental impairment that substantially limits a major life activity? a. Redlining Act b. Americans with Disabilities Act c. Title VI d. Blockbusting	b. Americans with Disabilities Act A law enacted in 1990 by Congress prohibits unjustified discrimination against people with disabilities.
49. A mentally disabled person that was declared incompetent can't enter a contract unless? a. All the above under certain conditions. b. a person appointed by the court may enter the contract on the disabled person's behalf. c. a disabled person can under no circumstances enter a contract without the written certification acquired while in school. d. a person appointed by a parent can sign legal	c. a disabled person can under no circumstances enter a contract without the written certification acquired while in school. The court can appoint a guardian or agent on behalf of the disabled person.

contracts for the disabled person.	
50. The Smith family renewed their lease on their single-family home for another year. Smith recently became disabled and asked his landlord for permission to modify the property to suit his needs. Owners must? a. pay for a ramp and make any other needed changes. b. reduce the rent and make the house accessible. c. allow the tenant to make the changes if he gives the landlord an additional damage deposit to remove the changes if needed. d. allow the tenant to build a ramp and make other changes.	d. allow the tenant to build a ramp and make other changes. A landlord must allow tenants to make changes to accommodate tenants with disabilities. Landlords do not have to pay for tenants' changes, and tenants can be required to remove all changes upon leaving without incurring additional fees.
51. A handicapped tenant moved into a building and wishes to make changes to make the unit more accessible. The landlord may require the tenant to? a. move to the ground floor when an apartment becomes available there. b. get permission for all changes, even reversible ones. c. pay additional rent because of the changes. d. pay for the improvements.	d. pay for the improvements. is the landlord's responsibility to allow the tenant to make changes to the home. Landlords do not have to pay for the renovations, and tenants can take them away when vacating.
52. The applicant for rental housing has a child who uses a wheelchair. This dwelling unit has a narrow bathroom door that can't accommodate a wheelchair. The tenant asks the landlord for permission to widen the doorway at his or her expense. Can the landlord refuse to rent to this person for this demand? a. YES. The landlord can refuse for any reason. b. NO. But the state's local HUD program must subsidize the changes. c. YES. If extensive damage will be done to the property. d. NO. It is unlawful for the landlord to refuse to permit the applicant to make the modification.	d. NO. It is unlawful for the landlord to refuse to permit the applicant to make the modification. Housing providers are required by federal laws to provide reasonable accommodations and modifications for individuals with disabilities. In addition to tenants and home seekers who have disabilities, federal nondiscrimination laws cover buyers and renters who have no disabilities and live with individuals with disabilities.
53. A rental agent has allowed a person dependent on a wheelchair to make necessary, minor changes to a rental property. These changes are? a. Trade fixtures modification b. Reasonable modifications c. Replacement fixtures d. Disability accommodations	b. Reasonable modifications A reasonable accommodation is a modification, exception, or exception to a property policy, practice, or service. Changing the structure of a building is a reasonable modification.
54. When a handicapped person is allowed to make modifications to a rental property, the cost of such modifications is borne by? a. the city. b. the state under HUD statutes c. the tenant	c. the tenant The landlord may require that the renter restore the dwelling to the condition it was before the modification. Reasonable wear and tear can be excluded.

d. the landlord	
55. Which of the following would NOT be a requirement under ADA or fair housing laws? a. A landlord must allow disabled tenants to make changes to the property and may not charge the tenants or force them to move. b. The owner of a commercial building could refuse to make changes to the "first come first serve" parking to accommodate a disabled tenant. c. A building with a no-pets policy would have to allow service animals without an additional charge. d. A tenant who makes changes to an apartment to accommodate a disability can be required to return the unit to its original condition upon lease expiration.	b. The owner of a commercial building could refuse to make changes to the "first come first serve" parking to accommodate a disabled tenant. A commercial building owner could refuse to make changes to the "first come first serve" parking to accommodate a disabled tenant. Under reasonable accommodations, a commercial landlord would be expected to delegate a parking space for a disabled tenant.
56. Which of the following is allowed under federal fair housing laws? a. Segregating families in certain buildings. b. Charging higher rents to a person with a support animal. c. Requiring a higher security deposit for a pregnant woman. d. Charging higher rates for people with pets.	d. Charging higher rates for people with pets. Pets are not protected. Service and some medical support animals are protected.
57. The Fair Housing Amendment Act prohibits discrimination based upon familial status. Familial status includes? a. all of these. b. any pregnant person. c. those in the adoption process. d. persons under 18 living with a parent or guardian.	a. all of these. Established families with children • Persons planning on having a family • Pregnant women • Traditional and non-traditional families, such as single-parent families • Persons in the process of securing legal custody of children through foster care, adoption, or divorce • Unique or unexpected circumstances which may change the composition of a family, such as the death of the parents, temporary or permanent court-ordered custody or written permission from a parent or legal guardian.
58. There is an apartment complex that advertises its apartments as adult-only apartments. THIS ADVERTISING IS? a. A legal if the adults are married. b. legal if each unit has at least one person over 55 living in it. c. legal if each unit has at least one person over 55 living in it. legal per federal law but may be illegal per state laws.	b. legal if each unit has at least one person over 55 living in it. Federal law allows senior housing to discriminate if 80% of the units are rented to at least one person over 55 years old.

59. An unmarried mother with two preschool children applied for a condominium in a resort-style development designed for over 55s, which is 90% occupied by over 55s. Based on the children's age, the mother's application was denied. The Federal Fair Housing Act protects? a. the condo owner from being forced to rent to the family because of the age of over 80% of the occupants of the development. b. the condo owner only. the community must find housing for the family. c. the condo owner and the community because the condo, based on honest square footage, is too small.	a. the condo owner from being forced to rent to the family because of the age of over 80% of the occupants of the development. A senior living community might be lawfully exempt from the FHA's familial status protections if: • All occupants are at least 62 years of age • At least one person older than 55 lives in 80% of housing units • Assisted living communities are part of government-sponsored housing programs for the elderly
60. Which of the following is not allowed? a. Charging higher rents for families with children. b. A Catholic organization giving preference to other Catholics when renting a private lodge. c. An Italian landlord advertising his home available for 'Italian people only'. d. Allowing support animals.	a. Charging higher rents for families with children. When someone is treated differently based on their family status, for instance if one or more of the members are under 18 years old, that constitutes family status discrimination.
61. A buyer with six children was told by a broker that the neighborhood she wanted to view was not suitable for her family because it had very few children. The buyer decided to file a fair housing complaint against the broker and brokerage firm. In this type of case, the first step is for HUD to? a. require the buyer to prove that discrimination occurred. b. Request that the real estate commission start an investigation. c. take the broker's license until the hearing is completed. d. start an investigation to verify if the complaint is valid.	d. start an investigation to verify if the complaint is valid. The first step for HUD is to determine whether the law was broken.
62. A charge of violation of Federal Fair Housing laws can be heard by an administrative law judge within the Department of Housing and Urban Development (HUD) or by a federal district court judge in Federal court. The advantage of a federal court hearing to the complaining party is that? a. there is no dollar limit on damages paid. b. the federal district court is faster. c. there is no benefit. d. federal district court allows for the complaints to be heard locally.	a. there is no dollar limit on damages paid. If any party elects to have a federal civil trial, HUD must refer your case to the U.S. Department of Justice for enforcement.
63. Which of the following statements is true of complaints relating to the Civil Rights Act of 1866? a. They are handled by HUD.	d. They must be taken directly to federal courts.

b. They are handled by state enforcement agencies. c. They are no longer reviewed in the courts. d. They must be taken directly to federal courts.	Violations are the Fair Housing Act of 1866 are taken to the federal government.
64. The Americans with Disabilities Act applies to private employers when? a. they have state contracts. b. they have fifteen (15) or more employees. c. they have federal contracts. d. they have demonstrated past practices of discrimination.	b. they have fifteen (15) or more employees. The ADA applies to employers with 15 or more employees, including state and local governments. It also applies to employment agencies and to labor organizations. The ADA's nondiscrimination standards also apply to federal sector employees under section 501 of the Rehabilitation Act, as amended, and its implementing rules.
65. Ignorance of the law is? a. an acceptable legal defense for a charge of discrimination. b. not a legal defense for discrimination. c. a clause in the Fair Housing Act that excludes illegality. d. a cause of dismissal since there was no intent.	b. not a legal defense for discrimination. "Ignorance of the law excuses not" and "ignorance of law excuses no one" is a legal principle holding that a person who is unaware of a law may not escape liability for violating that law simply because they were unaware of it.
66. The Smith family leased their single-family home for another year. Smith recently became disabled and asked his landlord for permission to modify the property to suit his needs. Owners must? a. allow the tenant to build a ramp and make other changes. b. allow the tenant to make the changes if he gives the landlord an additional damage deposit to remove the changes if needed. c. Reduce the rent and make the house accessible. d. pay for a ramp and make any other needed changes	a. allow the tenant to build a ramp and make other changes. To accommodate tenants' disabilities, landlords must allow tenants to make changes. Changes do not have to be paid for by landlords, and tenants can be required to remove all changes upon leaving without incurring any additional fees.
67. A property manager's duties typically include all the following except? a. investing the property owner's funds. b. Handing out applications to potential renters. c. Screening tenants d. Collecting rents.	a. investing the property owner's funds. Investing a client funds is not a duty for the agent.
68. The single parent of two preschool children applies to rent a condominium in a resort-like development designed for those over 55, which is 90% occupied by adults over 55. The parent was denied based on the age of her children. The Federal Fair Housing Act protects? a. the condo owner from being forced to rent to the family because of the age of over 80% of the occupants of the development. b. the condo owner only. the community must find	a. the condo owner from being forced to rent to the family because of the age of over 80% of the occupants of the development. There are three exceptions that apply to senior living communities. These were created to allow elderly people to live peacefully and quietly in communities that attend to their unique needs. A senior living community might be lawfully exempt from the FHA's

housing for the family. c. The condo owner and the community because the condo, based on honest square footage, is too small. d. the single parent of two preschool children. d. THERE ARE NO EXCEPTIONS	familial status protections if: every occupant is 62 years of age or older80% of the housing units are occupied by at least one person over the age of 55, or the community is part of a state or federal housing program designed to assist elderly people.
69. Anthony, a property manager for ABC Realty, may legally refuse to rent to? a. pregnant single women. b. a person unable to live alone without help. c. a person convicted of selling drugs. d. a person who wants to adjust the apartment and pay for it in order to fit her wheelchair.	c. a person convicted of selling drugs. A convicted drug dealer is not protected.
70. Which of the following is allowed under federal fair housing laws? a. Segregating families in certain buildings. b. Charging higher rents to a person with a support animal. c. Requiring a higher security deposit for a pregnant woman. d. Charging higher rates for people with pets.	d. Charging higher rates for people with pets. Pets are not protected. Service and some medical support animals are protected.
71. What is the foundation of a good landlord and tenant relationship? a. Great reputation for weekend parties. b. Good reputation for maintenance and management. c. No reputation of maintenance. d. Bad reputation for police visits to the property.	b. Good reputation for maintenance and management. Well-maintained properties and respectful leasing agents could increase the demand for the units.
72. Under the terms of a valid five-year lease that does not mention assignment or subletting, a tenant in good standing may legally do the following? a. May sublease or assign the leasehold to anyone, since the lease made no mention of any restrictions on such action. b. With the consent of the lessor, may sublease. c. May assign, but cannot sublease to another d. Upon consent of the lessor, may sublet the premises to another.	a. May sublease or assign the leasehold to anyone, since the lease made no mention of any restrictions on such action. If the lease does not otherwise specify, it may be assigned or sublet without restriction.
73. An apartment building advertises its apartments as "adult only." This advertising is? a. legal if the adults are married. b. legal per federal law but may be illegal per state laws. c. illegal and discriminatory against children. d. legal if each unit has at least one person over 55 living in it.	d. legal if each unit has at least one person over 55 living in it.

Definitions Module Eight

Actual Eviction
An actual eviction is when a tenant is physically forced to leave the premises.
The landlord may sue for possession

Avoiding Risk
Avoiding risk means removing the source of danger.

Casualty insurance
This type of insurance covers losses caused by theft, vandalism, and burglary.

Comfort / Emotional Support Animal
An emotional support animal is an animal (typically a dog or cat though this can include other species) that provides a therapeutic benefit to its owner through companionship.

Constructive Eviction
A landlord either does something or fails to do something that he or she has a legal duty to provide (e.g., the landlord refuses to provide heat or water to the apartment), rendering the property uninhabitable. A
A tenant who is constructively evicted may terminate the lease and seek damages.
To maintain an action for damages, the tenant must show that: the uninhabitable conditions (substantial interferences) were a result of the landlord's actions (not the actions of some third party) and that the tenant vacated the premises in a reasonable time.

Controlling Risk
Controlling risk means anticipating it and preparing for it.

Errors and omissions insurance
This type of insurance can cover property managers against any errors they make in the performance of their duties. This insurance doesn't cover losses caused by fraud or other dishonest or malfeasant activities.

Familial status
families with children under the age of 18.
pregnant persons.
any person in the process of securing legal custody of a minor child (including adoptive or foster parents).
persons with written permission of the parent or legal guardian

Farm Lease
Farmers to grow crops
The lease provides the basis for combining the landlord's and the tenant's resources of land, labor, capital, and management to efficiently produce farm commodities.

Fire and hazard insurance
Depending on what it covers, this type of policy sometimes is called an all-risk, all-peril policy. It covers loss of property caused by fire, storms, and other types of dangerous conditions. This type of policy usually does not cover flooding and earthquake damage.

Forcible entry and detainer
A summary proceeding for restoring to possession of land one who is wrongfully kept out or has been

wrongfully deprived of the possession.

Graduated Lease
A long-term lease on a property where the rent is changed periodically to reflect the market value of the property. Rent goes up slowly.

Ground Lease
A ground lease is an agreement in which a tenant is permitted to develop a piece of property during the lease period, after which the land and all improvements are turned over to the property owner.

Gross Lease
A type of lease where the Tenant pays a flat rental amount and the landlord pays for all property charges regularly incurred by the ownership, including taxes, utilities, and water. Most apartment leases resemble gross leases.
Mostly higher rental charge

Holdover Tenancy
A tenant continues to occupy and use the premises after the term of the lease ends.
If the landowner continues to accept rent payments, the holdover tenant can continue to legally occupy the premises. … If the landowner does not accept continued payments, eviction proceedings can occur.

Housing for Older Persons
The Fair Housing Act specifically exempts three types of housing for older persons from liability for familial status discrimination. Such exempt housing facilities or communities can lawfully refuse to sell or rent dwellings to families with minor children only if they qualify for the exemption. To qualify for the "housing for older persons" exemption, a facility or community must comply with all the requirements of the exemption.

Hunting Lease
A hunting lease is a legal arrangement or contract whereby a landowner grants access to his or her property for recreational hunting for a certain period.

Index Lease
A lease that makes some or all the rent dependent upon calculations with reference to some type of index. Cost of living index could be used.

Lease Option to Purchase
A unilateral contract.
A lease option is an agreement that gives a renter a choice to purchase the rented property during or at the end of the rental period.

Liability insurance
This type of insurance covers losses caused by injuries resulting from negligence on the landlord's part. The classic case is the person who falls on an icy sidewalk that the landlord was supposed to have cleaned.

Management Agreement
The property manager establishes an agency relationship with the property owner by Property Management Agreement.

Net Lease

A net lease requires the Tenant to pay, in addition to rent, some or all the property expenses that usually would be paid by the property owner.
These include property taxes, insurance, maintenance, repair, operations, utilities, and other items

Oil and Gas Lease
An oil and gas lease are essentially an agreement between parties to allow a Lessee (the oil and gas company and their production crew) to have access to the property and minerals (oil and gas) on the property of the Lessor.

Percentage Lease
A percentage lease is a commercial lease in which the rental amount is computed as a certain percentage of the monthly or annual gross sales generated at leased property. In a percentage lease, the Tenant pays a base rent plus a percentage of any revenue earned while doing business on the rental premises.

Periodic Tenancy
The tenancy is originally created for a specific period, but the renter's tenancy can continue until there is some notification of the lease's termination.
Month to Month

Proprietary Lease
In a cooperative apartment, residents buy shares of stock in a corporation that owns the apartment building.

Psychiatric Service Dog
is a dog that has been trained to perform tasks that assist individuals with disabilities to detect the onset of psychiatric episodes and lessen their effects. Tasks performed by psychiatric service animals may include reminding the handler to take medicine, providing safety checks or room searches, or turning on lights for persons with Post Traumatic Stress Disorder, interrupting self-mutilation by persons with dissociative identity disorders, and keeping disoriented individuals from danger.

Public-law occupancy standards
Local maximum occupancy standards aren't superseded in their application by the Fair Housing Act.

Reasonable Accommodations
A reasonable accommodation is a change, exception, or adjustment to a rule, policy, practice, or service that may be necessary for a person with disabilities to have an equal opportunity to use and enjoy a dwelling, including public and common use spaces, or to fulfill their program obligations.

Reasonable Modifications
A reasonable modification is a structural change made to existing premises, occupied or to be occupied by a person with a disability, to afford such person full enjoyment of the premises.

Rent loss insurance
This insurance sometimes is called business interruption insurance or consequential loss insurance. It pays the building owner for the loss of rent from tenants if the building is destroyed by fire.

Retaining Risk
Retaining risk means accepting the liability.

Sales-Leaseback
The sale of a property in which the seller immediately begins to rent the property from the buyer.

Security Deposit
A renter's security deposit is to cover any repairs needed once the tenant vacates. It is not the last month's rent.

Renter's Insurance
The renter is responsible for insuring his personal property. Renter's Insurance is for the tenant's personal property.

Seizure Response Dog
A dog trained to assist a person with a seizure disorder. How the dog serves the person depends on the person's needs. The dog may stand guard over the person during a seizure, or the dog may go for help. A few dogs have learned to predict a seizure and warn the person in advance to sit down or move to a safe place.

Service Animals
A service animal is any dog that is individually trained to do work or perform tasks for the benefit of an individual with a disability, including a physical, sensory, psychiatric, intellectual, or other mental disability. Other species of animals, whether wild or domestic, trained, or untrained, are not considered service animals.

Sexual Harassment
Sexual harassment occurs when there is deliberate or repeated unsolicited verbal comments, gestures, or physical contact that makes for an offensive environment or when sexual favors are sought as a "quid pro quo" for housing

Sexual Orientation
Discrimination because of sexual orientation or gender identity is not explicitly prohibited by the Fair Housing Act.

SSig DOG
(Sensory signal dogs or social signal dogs) is a dog trained to assist a person with autism. The dog alerts the handler to distracting repetitive movements common among those with autism, allowing the person to stop the movement (e.g., hand flapping).

Sublease
In a sublease, a tenant transfers the leasehold for just a portion of the remaining lease term; the subtenant pays rent to the tenant, who pays the landlord

Tenancy for Years
A lease for a fixed period.
For a Tenancy for Years Lease, no notice is needed for termination, the lessee knows the termination date from the outset of the lease

Tenancy at Will / Estate at Will
A tenancy-at-will is a property tenure that can be terminated at any time by either the tenant or the owner/landlord. It exists without a contract or lease and usually does not specify the duration of a tenant's rental or the exchange of payment.

Tenancy at Sufferance

A tenancy at sufferance occurs when a tenant continues to live in a rental property after their lease has expired.

Transferring Risk
Transferring risk means buying the appropriate type and amount of insurance to cover the payment whenever an insured incident occurs.

Undue burden
Significant difficulty or expense. A public accommodation is not required to provide any auxiliary aid or service that would result in an undue burden.

Undue hardship
An action that requires "significant difficulty or expense" in relation to the size of the employer, the resources available, and the nature of the operation. The concept of undue hardship includes any action that is unduly costly, extensive, substantial, disruptive, or would fundamentally alter the nature or operation of the business. Accordingly, whether a particular accommodation will impose an undue hardship must always be determined on a case-by- case basis.

Undue financial and administrative burden
A public entity does not have to take any action that it can demonstrate would result in an undue financial and administrative burden. This applies in program accessibility, effective communication, and auxiliary aids and services. The determination of an undue financial and administrative burden must be:
Made by the head of the public entity or his/her designee.
Accompanied by a written statement of the reasons.
Based on all resources available for use in the program.

MODULE NINE: TRANSFER OF TITLE

Title Insurance

- Protection for the buyer against previous title defects that may become known in the future.
- The owner's policy purchased by seller insures up to contract price; Lender's policy purchased by the buyer insures lender up to the balance of the loan.
- Insures from the date it is issued.

TYPES OF POLICIES

Standard Coverage Policy	ALTA - Extended Policy
Coverage of Policy	
Insures against: - Defects found in public records. - Forged documents. - Incompetent grantors. - Incorrect marital statements. - Improperly delivered deeds. - The coverage typically only pertains to issues that can be uncovered by conducting a public records search, ensuring that: 1. the insured party owns the interest in the real property as set out in the policy. 2. there are no existing liens, defects, or encumbrances related to the title. 3. the owner has a right of access in and out of the property; and 4. The title is marketable. 5. Also offers protection if the grantor lacked capacity to complete the transaction. 6. The conveyance instrument was improperly recorded. 7. There was an instance of o forgery o fraud o duress o incompetency o impersonation	**ALTA stands for American Land Title Association** - Basically, the ALTA title insurance policy is issued to protect the lender and ensure that it has an enforceable lien that is also valid. - As with other title insurance policies, an ALTA title insurance policy will protect against problems in the title such as: 1. Undisclosed and unrecorded mechanic's liens. 2. Misrepresentation and identity theft – someone impersonating the owner. 3. Acts of forgery on the deed or will. 4. Easements. 5. Disputes regarding boundary lines. 6. Exercise of rights for water and mineral extraction. 7. Encroachments. 8. Life estates. 9. Contested deeds and wills. 10. The appearance of undisclosed heirs. 11. Misrepresentation of civil status (i.e., saying one is single when in fact he is married or divorced). The spouse may have an interest in the policy by virtue of their legal union.
	There is a property survey.

http://www.insuranceqna.com/home-insurance/what-is-alta-title-insurance.html

Title Insurance Premium

The title insurance premium is paid once, at the closing.

The insurer's liability cannot exceed the policy face amount unless an inflation rider is included.
☐ Title Insurance insures up to the date it is issued.

Certificate of Title

A statement of opinion prepared by a title company, licensed abstractor, or attorney on the status of title to a parcel of real property, based on an examination of public records.

TYPICAL EXCLUSIONS

- Defects and liens are listed in the policy—defects are known to the buyer.
- Changes in land use brought about by changes in zoning ordinances.

Title Search

- A title search is an examination of all the public records to determine whether any defects exist in the chain of title.
- Title searches also make a note of any other encumbrances on the property.

Public Records

- Public records are documents or pieces of information that are not considered confidential.
- Public records are subject to inspection, examination, and copying by any member of the public.
- Real property records that affect title, or ownership, of property, are filed with a recording office.
- An individual who files a real property record must file, that record in the county where the property is located.

Abstract of Title

- An abstract of title is a report of what was found in a title search, searching virtually all public records related to the property's title, such as previous deeds and liens.

Abstract and Opinion

An attorney providing a short summary of the title report.

Chain of Title

A historical "chain" linked from the first recorded title (ownership) of a property down through each subsequent conveyance.

Marketable Title vs. Insurable Title

Marketable Title	Insurable Title
• The chain of ownership (title) to a particular property is clear and free from defects. • It can be marketed for sale without additional effort by the seller or potential buyer.	• The property may have a known defect or defects in the chain of title. • A title insurance company has agreed in advance to provide insurance against the defects ever affecting the ownership or value of the property.

Unmarketable title can still be transferred, but its defects may limit or restrict its ownership.

Transferability

A characteristic of value indicating that a property has a good title and marketable title.

Potential Title Problems and Resolution

Cloud on Title	Suit to Quiet Title
• A cloud is something that casts doubts on the grantor's ownership of the property. • A defect that may adversely affect the marketability of a title, such as an unreleased lien. • Clouds may often be cleared up by a **quitclaim deed** or a quiet title suit.	• A court action to establish property ownership when the title is clouded. • A court action to remove a cloud on title and determine one's right to an ownership interest.

Defective Title

Title that is void due to an improper transfer such as error, fraud, signature flaw, or failure of delivery of consideration.

Deeds

Deed
A document that contains the agreement between the grantor and grantee to transfer property interests.

What is the purpose of a Deed?

Evidence of title ownership. Alienation of the seller. To show ownership from one person to another person.

Covenant of Seisin

The grantor's expression that he or she has possession and the right to convey the property.
☐ Deeds show the covenants by which a grantor is bound to the buyer in the transaction.

Parties to a Deed

Grantor(s)	Grantee(s)
The seller(s)	The buyer(s)

Only the Grantor(s) sign the deed.

Et Al	Et Con	Et Ux
And others (in deed)	And husband (in deed)	And wife (in deed)

Requirements for Valid Deed

1. In writing
2. Grantor (conveying interest) legally competent/sane.
3. Grantee (receiving prop) named in the deed.
4. Consideration required (something of value to convey interest).
5. Accurate legal description of property (measurements--specific).
6. Granting clause (Grants to/Conveys to).
7. Signed by Grantor.
8. Signed, delivered, and accepted.

Granting Clause (Habendum Clause)

To have and to hold.
"I grant (convey, bargain, or sell) the property to you."

Types of Deeds

General Warranty Deed

The deed that gives the most protection to the buyer.
It has five covenants.

Covenant of Seisen	Covenant of quiet enjoyment	Covenant against encumbrances	Covenant of further assurance	Covenant of warranty forever
The covenant of seisin (also seizin) is a promise that the grantor owns the property and has the right to convey title.	Quiet enjoyment means that the grantor guarantees that no one else can come along and claim ownership of the property. It also means that if a later party's title claim is found to be better than the owner's title, the grantor is liable for any losses.	The grantor guarantees that the title to the property has no encumbrances like an easement or lien. Easements are rights that enable someone else to use some of the property, and liens are financial claims against the property. The only exceptions to this warranty are encumbrances that are specifically stated in the deed.	In this covenant, the grantor promises to obtain and provide documents necessary to clear up any problem that comes up with the title.	The grantor guarantees to pay all costs to clear up any title problems at any time in the future. A particular feature of a general warranty deed is that warranties cover any title problems that may have occurred during all past owners' ownerships.

A particular feature of a general warranty deed is that warranties cover any title problems that may have occurred during all past owners' ownerships.

☐ When the seller can furnish title insurance, the buyer can be assured he is getting a fee simple title. (The highest form of ownership.

Special Warranty Deed

Likely to be encountered if the property is being acquired through a bank, a tax or foreclosure sale.to be encountered if the property is being acquired through a bank, a tax or foreclosure sale.
Because of the limited warranties, sometimes third parties will use special warranty deeds.
An executor of an estate uses a special warranty deed to transfer property owned by the estate or trust
Special Warranty Deeds have two covenants.

The grantor has title to the property.	The grantor guarantees that no damage was done to the title during their ownership, and that if problems did arise, they would fix them.

Quit Claim Deed

- Contains no warranties and gives no implication of how much or how good the grantor's title to the property is.
- Usually transferred between people who know each other.
- Used to clear up clouds/defects in the title or relinquish an inchoate interest.
- ☐ Least protection.
- Carries no covenants or warranties whatsoever.
- It may be used to transfer an easement.

- Quitclaim deeds sometimes are used for uncomplicated transfers.

Bargain and Sale Deed

- A buyer gets no protection from encumbrances whatsoever with a bargain and sale deed. This deed merely states that the grantor holds title to the property, but it doesn't assert that it's also free of liens.
- This type of deed has very specialized uses. It's most frequently found in tax sales and foreclosure actions when the history of a property might be a bit murky.
- The current owner is typically the lender or a taxing authority and doesn't know the property's history either the last owner or at any time prior to then.

Tax deed

An instrument, like a certificate of sale, given to a purchaser at a tax sale.

Gift Deed

A deed for which the only consideration is "love and affection".

Executor's Deeds, Administrator's Deeds, Sheriff's Deeds

a. A deed executed pursuant to a court order.
b. It is used to convey title to the property transferred by **court order or by will**.
c. An executor's deed in the case of a deceased person's estate.
d. A sheriff's deed in the case of a sale of property seized by a local unit of government, town or the bank are two examples such court-ordered deeds.

Contract for Deed

The seller passes possession but retains legal title until the total of the purchase price is paid. Seller Financing. The seller is called the vendor and buyer is the vendee.

Vendor(s)	Vendee(s)
Seller(s)	Buyer(s)
Legal Title	Equitable Title

Trust Deed

There are three parties in a deed of trust.

Lender (Beneficiary)	Borrower (Trustor) (GIVOR of the Payment)	Trustee (Third Party)

- Used with Seller Financing.

- Trust deeds are easy to foreclose.
- The trustee is a third party who plays the role of intermediary in the real estate transaction.
- The trust deed represents an agreement between the borrower and a lender to have the property held in trust by a neutral and independent third party until the loan is paid off.

Reconveyance Deed

- Executed by the Trustee to return (reconvey) title to property held in trust.
- A reconveyance deed is used to reconvey title to property from a Trustee back to a trustor after a debt for which the property is security has been paid off.

Sheriff's Deed

Deed used by county sheriff when they sell a property taken through failure to pay taxes or legal seizure proceedings.

Corporate Deeds

An authorized corporate officer must sign the deed.

Consideration

Good Consideration	Valuable Consideration
Love and affection; something of value given as consideration to secure property transfer; someone buys property for $1.	Money exchanged for purchase of a property or other item; price paid for unit (sometimes named in the deed/otherwise states "for consideration paid".

Importance of recording

Entering documents into the public record.
- Any written document that affects any estate, right, title, or interest in land will be recorded in the county where the land is located to serve as constructive notice.
- ☐ **Constructive Notice to the World**
- A term referring to the fact that the date and time of recording determine the priority of recorded documents, liens, etc. Comes from a "race" to the courthouse.
- ☐ the first person who records the deed owns the property.

☐ Bob executed a deed to Sally and then put it into a box.
When Bob died, the property went to his heirs because Sally's deed was not recorded.

Ways other than sale of property to have interest change hands.
• Will
• Adverse Possession

- Eminent Domain
- Involuntary Alienation

Transfer of Property from Deceased Persons

Intestate

- NO WILL.
- Administrator's Deed.
- Transfer of title by descent.
- The laws of the state determine to whom ownership passes when a person dies intestate.
- The laws of intestate succession vary from state to state.
- Generally, there are primary heirs (spouse, children).
- The closeness of one's relationship to the deceased determines the amount of the estate that will be received.
- The State law establishes deeds, and state law governs their form
- Descent and Distribution.
- Laws that govern distribution of property to heirs when someone dies intestate.

Escheat
- The reverting of property to the State when there are no heirs capable of inheriting.

Testate

- Executor's Deed
- Transfer by Will
- Passes by Devise

Devisor	Devisee
The person who died.	The living person receiving the gift.

Probate

- The property goes through Probate to verify the validity of the will and probate determines the precise assets of the deceased person.
- Probate is conducted in the county of the deceased person.
- Decedent's debts must be satisfied before any property can be disbursed to the devisees or heirs.
- Administrator/Administratrix are male/female.

- Legal procedures vary considerably from state to state.
- The State law establishes deeds, and state law governs their form.
- Taxes get paid first.

Terms

Intestate Succession

Statutory method of distribution of property that belonged to someone who died intestate.

Decedent

A person who has died.

Will

A testamentary instrument that becomes effective only after the death of its maker.

Codicil
A change in a will.

Heirs
Individuals who are scheduled to inherit property.

Legacy
A disposition of money or personal property by will.

Types of Wills

The Testamentary Will
<ul><li>A testamentary will is the most common type of will.</li><li>A testamentary will is the most frequently used will. The rules are clear, so it is less likely to be challenged or questioned.</li><li>This is a formal written will, often prepared by or with the assistance of an attorney, that meets all the formal requirements of state law.</li><li>It is written, and it is signed by the testator in the presence of witnesses. Most states require two witnesses, but some require more.</li><li>Among the advantages of a testamentary will is that it is less likely to be successfully contested by a disgruntled beneficiary or presumed beneficiary. In carefully meeting the law's requirements for a valid will, the testator makes it unlikely a challenge will succeed.</li><li>A standard testamentary will also has the advantage of illustrating the testator's wishes clearly.</li><li>Wills of other types may be incomplete or difficult to understand.</li></ul>

Holographic Will
<ul><li>A holographic will is one that has been written and signed by the testator.</li><li>A holographic will is written by the testator and not witnessed.</li><li>There are no witnesses to the document and no notarization of the signature.</li><li>Many states no longer recognize holographic wills as valid or accept them only in limited circumstances.</li><li>If the testator believes the document should be prepared quickly, such as when death may be imminent and witnesses are not available, a holographic will may be considered.</li><li>A holographic will may be challenged more often than a regular will, especially if the contents are not liked.</li><li>The chances of a challenge being successful are also higher than when a testamentary will is used.</li></ul>

Nuncupative Will

- The Oral Will.
- An oral will entail the testator telling one or more witnesses his or her last wishes.
- Many states only accept nuncupative wills on deathbeds.

☐ A husband and wife took ownership of their real estate as Joint Tenants to avoid probate.
Joint Tenants with **Rights of Survivorship**.

Transfer of Title: Escrow

The Escrow

Responsibilities of the transaction/escrow agent
In Mississippi, it is the closing attorney. **Transactional Agent** ● Holding documents and money in trust. ● Obtaining required documents. ● Ordering title searches. ● Preparing closing instructions. ● Coordinating with the buyer's lender ● Ensuring the legal rights of the buyer and seller are complete before closing. ● Recording documents. ● The escrow agent is responsible for overseeing and coordinating the closing activities, acting as a ☐neutral third party between the buyers and sellers. ● Your escrow officer must follow both parties' instructions (buyers and sellers) involved in the transaction.

Other Terms for the Transfer of Property

Escrow Instructions
Instructions, signed by a buyer and seller, that detail the procedures necessary to close a transaction and direct the escrow agent what needs to be done.

Closing Statement - Settlement Statement
● **Settlement:** the time at which the property is formally sold and transferred from the seller to the buyer. It is currently that the borrower takes on the loan obligation, pays all closing costs and receives title from the seller. ● **Settlement/Closing Agent:** a settlement agent, or closing agent, handles the real estate transaction when you buy or sell a home. It may also be an attorney or a title agent. ● A detailed breakdown of all cash received, all charges and credits made, and all costs incurred. ● The agreement identifies how much money will be "taken from" closing by the seller, as well as how much the buyer must bring to closing as of the closing day. ● **Settlement Costs/Closing Costs**: the customary costs above and beyond the sales price of the property that must be paid to cover the transfer of ownership at closing; these costs generally vary by geographic location and are typically detailed to the borrower at the time the GFE is given.

● **Tax certificate:** official proof of payment of taxes due provided at the time of transfer of

property title by the state or local government.
- **1099S.** The IRS document sent to the IRS by the Closing/Settlement Agent. The 1099S will include the Seller's Name, Social Security Number and Sold Price.

Vesting

The way title will be taken.
1. In Severalty
2. In Common
3. Joint Tenancy
4. Entirety

Proration

- A proration is an agreement between the buyer and seller that divides various property expenses so that each party only pays for the days they own the property. Several expenses are prorated at closing, including property taxes, homeowner's insurance, HOA dues, and mortgage interest.
- Proration is the fair-share buyer-seller splitting of expenses at closing.
- Two types of payments and costs that are allocated between the buyer and seller at closing are accrued items and prepaid items.

Accrued Expense	Prepaid Expenses
An accrued expense is an accounting expense recognized in the books **before** it is paid for.	A prepaid item is an accounting expense recognized in the books **after** it is paid for. A credit.

☐ the seller is responsible for the fees of the closing date.
☐ If the Seller Paid Taxes Already:
It is a credit for the seller.
Seller(s) get a refund.
Each party pays for the days they owned the property.

When Title Passes

Ownership passes when the buyer accepts the delivered and signed deed.

Special Transfers

Foreclosures

Judicial Foreclosure	Non-judicial Foreclosure
• The lender seeks to foreclose by filing a civil lawsuit against the borrower and serving the borrower with a formal summons and foreclosure complaint. • The foreclosure process is handled through the local court system. • The court appoints a referee to conduct the foreclosure auction on the courthouse steps. • The lender records a **Lis pendens** with the county clerk where the property is located. This **Lis pendens** becomes a lien on the property and gives notice of the pending foreclosure auction. • The court grants a **judgment** permitting the lender to conduct the foreclosure auction. • The Notice of Foreclosure Sale (NFS), which announces date, time, and place of the auction, is published, and sometimes posted (depending on the locale) for a certain period prior to auction.	• In the event of a power of sale clause in the mortgage or trust deed, the trustee may initiate foreclosure proceedings. • In deeds of trust and mortgages, power of sale clauses provides the trustee with the authority to begin foreclosure proceedings. Upon default, the trustee gives the county clerk notice **(NOD).** • In this document, the borrower is notified of an impending foreclosure and has a period to object to the lender's claim or pay what he owes. • After the expiration of this period, the borrower cannot stop the foreclosure. Upon the expiration of a predetermined period (which varies from state to state), the trustee files a Notice of Trustee's Sale **(NTS)** with the county clerk. • The notice specifies the date, time, and location of the foreclosure auction. • A foreclosure can take up to 12 months to complete, depending on the state. **Used in a Deed of Trust** A deed of trust conveys an interest in real property to a third party (the trustee) to hold as security for repayment of a debt.

Types of Property Redemptions

Equitable Right of Redemption	Statutory Right of Redemption
The borrower can stop the foreclosure by repaying what he owes up to the moment of sale.	The borrower is given time after the property sells to redeem the property.

Strict Foreclosure
• Only Connecticut and Vermont have laws that permit a strict foreclosure. • In the event of the mortgagor's default title will be vested in the mortgagee free of any right of the mortgagor to redeem.

Deed in Lieu of Foreclosure

- Friendly foreclosure - Voluntary surrender.
- A deed in lieu of foreclosure transfers ownership of your home to your lender to avoid foreclosure.

Short Sale

In a short sale, the property is sold for less than what is owed on the owner's mortgage, hence the term" short."

Deficiency Judgment

A deficiency judgment is an unsecured money judgment against a borrower whose mortgage foreclosure sale did not produce sufficient funds to pay the underlying promissory note, or loan, in full.

Real Estate Owned Property (REO) means Bank Owned Property

Priority of Payment of Debt Secured by Real Estate

- The priority of mortgages and other liens is determined by the order in which they were recorded.
- ☐ Mechanics liens begin on the first day of work or materials were supplied.

Subordination Agreements

Position of payments may be changed with subordination agreements between entities owed money.

Other Ways to Transfer Real Property

Accession
    Trade fixtures left behind by the commercial tenant become the real property of the owner.
Accretion/Alluvion
    Accession by Natural forces, such as alluvion.
Erosion
    Slow wearing a way of land.
Reliction
    The increase of a landowner's property by the receding of an adjacent body of water.
Avulsion
    The tearing or washing away of land along the bank of a body of water by natural forces.
Adverse Possession
    Occupying the property against the interests of the true owner.
Dedication
    Transfer of private land to public use or ownership.
Public Grant
    The transfer of title by the government to a private individual.
Eminent Domain
    Right of the government to acquire title to property for public use by condemnation, the property
    owner receives compensation, generally fair market value.
Forfeiture

Breach of a condition subsequent in a deed; entitles grantor or grantor's successor to reacquire title to the property

Partition Action

Court proceeding by which co-owners may force a division of the property or its sale.

Abandonment

Giving up possession or ownership of property by nonuse.

Land Trust

When buying property in the name of a land trust, the trust identity of the purchaser is hidden.

Transfer of Title Quiz

1. What protects real estate owners from challenges to their property titles? a. Property insurance b. Title insurance c. Land insurance d. Escrow insurance	b. Title insurance Before issuing title insurance, there is a title search of public records to determine and confirm a property's legal ownership and to find out whether there are any claims are on the property.
2. Title Insurance insures? a. up to the date the insurance is issued. b. into the future up to three title transfers c. ten years into the future. d. personal property financed.	a. up to the date the insurance is issued. Title insurance issuers up to the date it is issued.
3. The policyholder of a standard title insurance policy is protected against loss resulting from? a. Encumbrances and liens unrecorded. b. Rights of parties in possession. c. Recorded title forgery. d. A defect in the chain of title previously known to the insured.	d. A defect in the chain of title previously known to the insured. Standard policies cover fraud; extended policies cover unrecorded liens and rights in possession. No policy covers known defects.
4. A deed states that the grantors are conveying all their rights and interests to the grantees and to have and to hold? This statement is communicated in? a. The acknowledgment clause b. The restriction clause c. The covenant of seisin d. The habendum clause	d. The habendum clause Habendum clauses define or explain the ownership to be enjoyed by the grantee, and their provisions must match the grants. It begins with the words to have and to hold.
5. A clause in a mortgage that conveys title to a borrower once the loan is paid in full. a. Reconveyance b. Refinance c. re-neg d. reappraise	a. Reconveyance Reconveyance deeds are issued by mortgage holders when borrowers are free from mortgage obligations. (Paid in full)
6. Which one of the following deeds contains the most covenants? a. Bargain & Sale b. General Warranty c. Quit claim d. Special Warranty	b. General Warranty General Warranty Deed gives the most protection to the Grantee.
7. Which type of deed merely implies but does NOT specifically warrant that the grantor holds good title to the property? a. Special warranty b. Bargain and sale c. Quitclaim d. Trust deed	b. Bargain and sale Grantors are implying that they own and possess the property, but there are no express warranties against encumbrances.
8. Every deed must be signed by? a. The grantor(s)	a. The grantor(s)

b. The grantee(s) c. The grantor and grantee d. The devisee	Every deed must be executed (signed) by either the grantor(s), or someone acting under the grantor's authority.
9. A deed that makes no express or implied warranties that the grantor owns any interest in a property is? a. a warranty deed b. a trust deed c. a grant deed d. a quitclaim deed	d. a Quitclaim Deed A quitclaim deed gives the least protection to the buyer.
10. The owner of a property wishes to convey all interests in it to the next owner without encumbrances, liens, or other title defects. What type of deed would this party most likely use? a. A quitclaim deed b. A general warranty deed c. A deed in lieu of a warranty d. A guardian's deed	b. A General Warranty Deed A General Warranty provides the greatest potential to the buyer.
11. The grantee receives the greatest protection with what type of deed? a. Quitclaim b. General warranty c. Bargain and sale with the covenant d. Executor's Incorrect	b. General Warranty There are more covenants between the grantor and grantee in a general warranty deed than in any other deed.
12. If a buyer wants to be sure that he is buying a property with good title, he should rely on the following: a. an attorney's opinion of title. b. a title insurance policy.. c. a general warranty deed. d. a title commitment based on the abstract of title from the title company.	c. a General Warranty Deed. The buyer is most protected with this type of deed.
13. A deed states the title conveyed is good, as well as a promise to obtain and deliver any required documents. Which covenant does this deed illustrate? a. Further assurances b. Seisin c. Quiet enjoyment d. Warranty forever	a. Further assurances The covenant of further assurance is a promise to obtain documents to make the title good.
14. Who is usually in the weakest position when facing a claim of title by an outsider? a. Property owner who rents out their property. b. A certificate of title issued by a title company. c. Owner of an unrecorded deed who occupies the property. d. Owners of unrecorded quitclaim deeds who do not occupy the property.	d. Owners of unrecorded quitclaim deeds who do not occupy the property. Quitclaim deeds simply relinquish any claim the grantor may have to the property.
15. Who signs the deed? a. vendee b. grantee	c. grantor Only the grantor(s) sign the deed.

c. grantor d. vendor	
16. Homeowners are frantic because they want to sell their property and the deed is missing. Which of the following is TRUE? a. They may need to sue for quiet title. b. They must buy title insurance. c. They do not need the original deed if it has been recorded. d. They should execute a replacement deed to themselves.	d. They should execute a replacement deed to themselves. After the deed is recorded, copies of the deed can be found in the county where the property is located.
17. A deed has been properly recorded. Any subsequent purchasers, whether they have examined the record or not, have been given? a. bilateral notice b. written notice c. constructive notice d. executory notice	c. constructive notice A properly recorded deed provides constructive notice of its contents, which means that all parties concerned are considered to have notice of the deed whether they saw it or not.
18. The escrow agent or attorney at the close of escrow will file which tax form to be sent to the IRS? a. 1099 – misc. b. 1099 – s c. 1040 d. 360	b. 1099 – s A form 1099-S is a tax document used to ensure that the full amount received for a real estate sale of some kind is accurately reported. When real estate is sold, the seller is often subject to a capital gains tax.
19. When a valid grant deed is prepared, title passes when it is? a. Acknowledged b. Delivered c. Signed d. Recorded	a. Acknowledged Voluntary delivery and acceptance of a valid deed make it enforceable unless fraud can be proven. Recording presumes voluntary delivery and acceptance.
20. Why would an investor purchase real estate in the name of a land trust? a. To save on taxes. b. To add family members to the deed later. c. To homestead the property. d. To hide his identity.	d. To hide his identity. Also, a straw man. A layman or straw man is a figure not intended to have a genuine beneficial interest in a property, to whom such property is nevertheless conveyed to facilitate a transaction.

Definitions Module Nine

Abstract and Opinion
An attorney providing a short summary of the title report.

Abstract of Title
An abstract of title is a report of what was found in a title search, searching virtually all public records related to the property's title, such as previous deeds and liens.

Accrued Expense
An accrued expense is an accounting expense recognized in the books before it is paid for.

Administrator/Administratrix
Male/female executors

Bargain and Sale Deed
A buyer gets no protection from encumbrances whatsoever with a bargain and sale deed. This deed merely states that the grantor holds title to the property, but it doesn't assert that it's also free of liens.
This type of deed has very specialized uses. It's most frequently found in tax sales and foreclosure actions when the history of a property might be a bit murky.

Certificate of Title
A statement of opinion prepared by a title company, licensed abstractor, or attorney on the status of title to a parcel of real property, based on an examination of public records.

Chain of Title
A historical "chain" linked from the first recorded title of a property down through each subsequent conveyance.

Cloud on Title
A cloud is something that casts doubts on the grantor's ownership of the property.
A defect that may adversely affect the marketability of a title, such as an unreleased lien.

Closing Statement - Settlement Statement
A detailed breakdown of all cash received, all charges and credits made, and all costs incurred.

Codicil
A change in a will.

Color of Title
Seller appears to have a good title but does not; property appears to possess good title but after title search is found to be defective; to fix it you need a new deed (confirmatory).

Contract for Deed
The seller passes possession but retains legal title until the total of the purchase price is paid. Seller Financing. The seller is called the vendor and buyer is the vendee.

Decedent
A person who has died.

Deficiency Judgment

A deficiency judgment is an unsecured money judgment against a borrower whose mortgage foreclosure sale did not produce sufficient funds to pay the underlying promissory note, or loan, in full.

Deed

A document that contains the agreement between the grantor and grantee to transfer property interests.

Deed in Lieu of Foreclosure

Friendly foreclosure - Voluntary surrender.

Defective Title

Title that is void due to an improper transfer such as error, fraud, signature flaw, or failure of delivery of consideration.

Escheat

The reverting of property to the State when there are no heirs capable of inheriting.

Escrow Instructions

Instructions, signed by a buyer and seller, that detail the procedures necessary to close a transaction and direct the escrow agent what needs to be done.

Equitable Right of Redemption

The borrower can stop the foreclosure by repaying what he owes up to the moment of sale.

Executor's Deeds, Administrator's Deeds, Sheriff's Deeds

A deed executed pursuant to a court order.
It is used to convey title to the property transferred by court order or by will.
An executor's deed in the case of a deceased person's estate.
A sheriff's deed in the case of a sale of property seized by a local unit of government, town or the bank are two examples such court-ordered deeds.

Gift Deed

A deed for which the only consideration is "love and affection".

Good Consideration

Love and affection; something of value given as consideration to secure property transfer; someone buys property for $1.

Grantor(s)

The seller(s)

Grantee(s)

The buyer(s)

Granting Clause (Habendum Clause)

To have and to hold.
"I grant (convey, bargain, or sell) the property to you."

General Warranty Deed

The deed that gives the most protection to the buyer.
It has five covenants.
1. Covenant of Seisen
2. Covenant of quiet enjoyment
3. Covenant against encumbrances
4. Covenant of further assurance
5. Covenant of warranty forever

Heirs
Individuals who are scheduled to inherit property.

Holographic Will
A holographic will is one that has been written and signed by the testator.

Intestate
Die with NO WILL.
Administrator's Deed is used to convey property to heirs.
Transfer of title by descent.
The laws of the state determine to whom ownership passes when a person dies intestate.
The laws of intestate succession vary from state to state.

Intestate Succession
Statutory method of distribution of property that belonged to someone who died intestate

Insurable Title
The property may have a known defect or defects in the chain of title.
However, with an insurable title, a title insurance company has agreed in advance to provide insurance against the defects ever affecting the ownership or value of the property.

Judicial Foreclosure
The lender seeks to foreclose by filing a civil lawsuit against the borrower and serving the borrower with a formal summons and foreclosure complaint.

Legacy
A disposition of money or personal property by will.

Marketable Title
The chain of ownership (title) to a particular property piece is clear and free from defects.
It can be marketed for sale without additional effort by the seller or potential buyer.

Non-judicial Foreclosure
In the event of a power of sale clause in the mortgage or trust deed, the trustee may initiate foreclosure proceedings.
In deeds of trust and mortgages, power of sale clauses provides the trustee with the authority to begin foreclosure proceedings. Upon default, the trustee gives the county clerk notice (NOD).

Nuncupative Will
The Oral Will.

Prepaid Expenses

A prepaid item is an accounting expense recognized in the books after it is paid for.
A credit

Probate
The property goes through Probate to verify the validity of the will and probate determines the precise assets of the deceased person.
Probate is conducted in the county of the deceased person.

Proration
A proration is an agreement between the buyer and seller that divides various property expenses so that each party only pays for the days they own the property. Several expenses are prorated at closing, including property taxes, homeowner's insurance, HOA dues, and mortgage interest.

Public Records
Public records are documents or pieces of information that are not considered confidential.

Quit Claim Deed
Contains no warranties and gives no implication of how much or how good the grantor's title to the property is.
Usually transferred between people who know each other.
Least protection.

Reconveyance Deed
Executed by the Trustee to return (reconvey) title to property held in trust.
A trust deed conveys ownership by a trustor to a trustee for the benefit of a beneficiary as security for a debt.

Settlement the time at which the property is formally sold and transferred from the seller to the buyer. It is currently that the borrower takes on the loan obligation, pays all closing costs and receives title from the seller.

Settlement/Closing Agent
A settlement agent, or closing agent, handles the real estate transaction when you buy or sell a home. It may also be an attorney or a title agent. He or she oversees all legal documents, fee payments, and other details of transferring the property to ensure that the conditions of the contract have been met and appropriate real estate taxes have been paid.

Short sale
In a short sale, the property is sold for less than what is owed on the owner's mortgage, hence the term" short."

Special Warranty Deed
Likely to be encountered if the property is being acquired through a bank, a tax or foreclosure sale.to be encountered if the property is being acquired through a bank, a tax or foreclosure sale.
Because of the limited warranties, sometimes third parties will use special warranty deeds.
An executor of an estate uses a special warranty deed to transfer property owned by the estate or trust.

Statutory Right of Redemption
The borrower is given time after the property sells to redeem the property.

Strict Foreclosure
Only Connecticut and Vermont have laws that permit a strict foreclosure.

Suit to Quiet Title
A court action to establish property ownership when the title is clouded.
A court action to remove a cloud on title and determine one's right to an ownership interest.

Tax certificate
Official proof of payment of taxes due provided at the time of transfer of property title by the state or local government.

Tax deed
An instrument, like a certificate of sale, given to a purchaser at a tax sale.

Testate
Executor's Deed
Transfer by Will
Passes by Devise

Testate - Wills
A testamentary instrument that becomes effective only after the death of its maker.

Testamentary Will
A testamentary will is the most common type of will.
A testamentary will is the most frequently used will. The rules are clear, so it is less likely to be challenged or questioned.

Title Search
A title search is an examination of all the public records to determine whether any defects exist in the chain of title.

Transferability
A characteristic of value indicating that a property has a good title and marketable title.

Trust Deed
There are three parties in a deed of trust.
Used with Seller Financing.
Trust deeds are easy to foreclose.
The trustee is a third party who plays the role of intermediary in the real estate transaction.
The trust deed represents an agreement between the borrower and a lender to have the property held in trust by a neutral and independent third party until the loan is paid off.

Unmarketable title
Title that can still be transferred, but its defects may limit or restrict its ownership.

Valuable Consideration
Money exchanged for purchase of a property or other item; price paid for unit (sometimes named in the deed/otherwise states "for consideration paid".

Vendor(s)

Seller(s)
Legal Title

Vendee(s)
Buyer(s)
Equitable Title

Vesting
The way title will be taken.

MODULE TEN: PRACTICE OF REAL ESTATE

Tax Aspects of Transfer Real Property

Capital Gains Exclusion

- Personal Residences.
- Occupied as primary residence for 2 of the last 5 years.
- Gains are the difference between the adjusted basis of property and selling price.
- **The Taxpayer Relief Act of 1997.**

Passed by Congress to greatly reduce the tax on the gain to be realized on the sale of real estate, especially for residential real estate.

With the passage of the Act, individuals can exclude up to $250,000 of capital gains from taxation, while married couples can exclude up to $500,000. (Personal residence).

Deductible Home Related Expenses

- Loan originated fees
- Some Interest paid on mortgages
- Real estate taxes
- Discount points
- Pre-payment penalties

1031 Tax Deferred Exchange

- Allows an investor to sell a property, reinvest the proceeds in a new property, and defer capital gain taxes. IRC Section 1031 (a)(1) states:
- "No gain or loss shall be recognized on the exchange of real property held for productive use in a **trade or business or investment** if such real property is exchanged solely for real property of *like-kind* which is to be held either for productive use in a trade or business or investment."
- Parties may defer any capital gains tax due.

Basic 1031 exchange terminology

- **Identification Period**
- A maximum of 45 calendar days from the relinquished property closing to correctly identify potential replacement property or properties.
- **Exchange Period**

Maximum of 180 calendar days after the relinquished property to close.

- **Boot:** "Non-like-kind" property received (usually cash); "Boot" is taxable to the extent there is a capital gain.
- **Like-Kind Property:** Any real property held for productive use in a trade or business or held for investment; both the relinquished and replacement properties must be considered like-kind to qualify for tax deferral.
- **Qualified Intermediary**

The entity which facilitates the exchange; defined as follows:
(1) Not a related party (i.e., agent, attorney, broker, etc.)
(2) Receives a fee
(3) Receives the relinquished property from the taxpayer and sells to the buyer
(4) Purchases the replacement property from the seller and transfers it to the taxpayer
(5) Is a qualified intermediary

- **Relinquished Property:** Property given up by the taxpayer, referred to as the sale, exchange, down leg, or Phase I property.
- **Replacement Property:** Property received by the taxpayer, also referred to as the purchase, target, up leg, or Phase II property.

Meet George

George purchased his home and primary residence for $150,000.
The home was in very extreme disrepair.
George did extensive repairs and upgrades during the time he lived there.
George sold his property 2 years later.
George sold the home for $400,000.
He has a profit on his primary residence of $250,000.

The capital gains exclusion erases taxes on that profit.
George's selling price
minus
George's buying price
equals
Capital Gains

Insert Your Photo Here to be a George.

Depreciation – Straight-Line Method

- Determines the equal annual depreciation allowed in a straight line from the adjusted basis to zero and computed by dividing the adjusted basis by the estimated years remaining of economic life.
- Recovery of an investor's property cost down to zero over 27.5 years (residential) or 39 years (non-residential). Divide the value of an income property by 27.5 (or 39), then deduct that amount on income tax each year.
- Depreciation also reduces the adjusted basis of the building.

Transfer of Title Quiz

1. What protects real estate owners from challenges to their property titles? a. Property insurance b. Title insurance c. Land insurance d. Escrow insurance	b. Title insurance Before issuing title insurance, there is a title search of public records to determine and confirm a property's legal ownership and to find out whether there are any claims are on the property.
2. Title Insurance insures? a. up to the date the insurance is issued. b. into the future up to three title transfers. c. ten years into the future. d. personal property financed.	a. up to the date the insurance is issued. Title insurance issuers up to the date it is issued.
3. The policyholder of a standard title insurance policy is protected against loss resulting from? a. Encumbrances and liens unrecorded. b. Rights of parties in possession. c. Recorded title forgery. d. A defect in the chain of title previously known to the insured.	d. A defect in the chain of title previously known to the insured. Standard policies cover fraud; extended policies cover unrecorded liens and rights in possession. No policy covers known defects.
4. A deed states that the grantors are conveying all their rights and interests to the grantees and to have and to hold. This statement is communicated in? a. The acknowledgment clause. b. The restriction clause. c. The covenant of seisin. d. The habendum clause.	d. The habendum clause Habendum clauses define or explain the ownership to be enjoyed by the grantee, and their provisions must match the grants. It begins with the words to have and to hold.
5. A clause in a mortgage that conveys title to a borrower once the loan is paid in full? a. Reconveyance b. Refinance c. re-neg d. reappraise	a. Reconveyance Reconveyance deeds are issued by mortgage holders when borrowers are free from mortgage obligations. (Paid in full)
6. Which one of the following deeds contains the most covenants? a. Bargain & Sale b. General Warranty c. Quit claim d. Special Warranty	b. General Warranty General Warranty Deed gives the most protection to the Grantee.
7. Which type of deed merely implies but does NOT specifically warrant that the grantor holds good title to the property? a. Special warranty b. Bargain and sale c. Quitclaim d. Trust deed	b. Bargain and sale Grantors are implying that they own and possess the property, but there are no express warranties against encumbrances.
8. Every deed must be signed by? a. The grantor(s)	a. The grantor(s)

b. The grantee(s) c. The grantor and grantee d. The devisee	Every deed must be executed (signed) by either the grantor(s), or someone acting under the grantor's authority.
9. A deed that makes no express or implied warranties that the grantor owns any interest in a property is? a. a warranty deed b. a trust deed c. a grant deed d. a quitclaim deed	d. a Quitclaim Deed A quitclaim deed gives the least protection to the buyer.
10. The owner of a property wishes to convey all interests in it to the next owner without encumbrances, liens, or other title defects. What type of deed would this party most likely use? a. A quitclaim deed b. A general warranty deed c. A deed in lieu of a warranty d. A guardian's deed	b. A General Warranty Deed A General Warranty provides the greatest potential to the buyer.
11. The grantee receives the greatest protection with what type of deed? a. Quitclaim b. General warranty c. Bargain and sale with the covenant d. Executor's e. Incorrect	b. General Warranty There are more covenants between the grantor and grantee in a general warranty deed than in any other deed.
12. If a buyer wants to be sure that he is buying a property with good title, he should rely on the following? a. an attorney's opinion of title. b. a title insurance policy. c. a general warranty deed. d. a title commitment based on the abstract of title from the title company.	c. a General Warranty Deed. The buyer is most protected with this type of deed.
13. A deed states the title conveyed is good, as well as a promise to obtain and deliver any required documents. Which covenant does this deed illustrate? a. Further assurances b. Seisin c. Quiet enjoyment d. Warranty forever	a. Further assurances The covenant of further assurance is a promise to obtain documents to make the title good.
14. Who is usually in the weakest position when facing a claim of title by an outsider? a. Property owner who rents out their property. b. A certificate of title issued by a title company. c. Owner of an unrecorded deed who occupies the property. d. Owners of unrecorded quitclaim deeds who do not occupy the property.	Owners of unrecorded quitclaim deeds who do not occupy the property. Quitclaim deeds simply relinquish any claim the grantor may have to the property.
15. Who signs the deed? a. vendee b. grantee	c. grantor Only the grantor(s) sign the deed.

c. grantor d. vendor	
16. Homeowners are frantic because they want to sell their property and the deed is missing. Which of the following is TRUE? a. They may need to sue for quiet title. b. They must buy title insurance. c. They do not need the original deed if it has been recorded. d. They should execute a replacement deed to themselves.	d. They should execute a replacement deed to themselves. After the deed is recorded, copies of the deed can be found in the county where the property is located.
17. A deed has been properly recorded. Any subsequent purchasers, whether they have examined the record or not, have been given? a. bilateral notice. b. written notice. c. constructive notice. d. executory notice.	c. constructive notice. A properly recorded deed provides constructive notice of its contents, which means that all parties concerned are considered to have notice of the deed whether they saw it or not.
18. The escrow agent or attorney at the close of escrow will file which tax form to be sent to the IRS? a. 1099 – misc b. 1099 – s c. 1040 d. 360	b. 1099 – s A form 1099-S is a tax document used to ensure that the full amount received for a real estate sale of some kind is accurately reported. When real estate is sold, the seller is often subject to a capital gains tax.
19. When a valid grant deed is prepared, title passes when it is? a. Acknowledged b. Delivered c. Signed d. Recorded	a. Acknowledged Voluntary delivery and acceptance of a valid deed make it enforceable unless fraud can be proven. Recording presumes voluntary delivery and acceptance.
20. Why would an investor purchase real estate in the name of a land trust? a. To save on taxes. b. To add family members to the deed later. c. To homestead the property. d. To hide his identity.	d. To hide his identity. Also, a straw man. A layman or straw man is a figure not intended to have a genuine beneficial interest in a property, to whom such property is nevertheless conveyed to facilitate a transaction.
21. To be eligible for a homeowner's capital gains exclusion, in the last five years the homeowners must? a. Own a secondary residence. b. The homeowner must not have previously taken the exclusion. c. Have a five-year occupancy. d. Have a two-year occupancy.	d. Have a two-year occupancy. Two-year occupancy is required. – And it can be taken every two years.
22. Which of the following homeownership costs and expenses may be deducted on Federal Income Taxes? a. Repairs to the exterior building, assessments, and purchasing fees.	c. Mortgage loan origination fees, mortgage loan interest, and local property taxes. More deductions:

b. Cost of purchase-including commissions paid premiums on title insurance and deed encumbrances. c. Mortgage loan origination fees, mortgage loan interest, and local property taxes. d. Repairs, insurance premiums, and interest.	Mortgage fees, interest, points. pre-payment penalties, taxes, mortgage insurance premiums can be deducted.
23. In a 1031 exchange, an escrow agent? a. certifies that the escrow qualifies for a 1031 tax-free exchange. b. deals with foreign currency. c. prepares duplicate settlement statements. d. contacts the IRS.	a. certifies that the escrow qualifies for a 1031 tax-free exchange. Allows an investor to "defer" paying capital gains taxes on an investment property when it is sold, as long another "like-kind property" is purchased with the profit gained by the sale of the first property.
24. To conduct a like-kind exchange, you must use a "Qualified Intermediary" to facilitate the transaction. This person can be: a. A certified public accountant who works with either party in the exchange. b. A real estate licensee representing either party in the exchange. c. Your real estate lawyer. d. An independent third party recognized by the IRS as facilitators of 1031 exchanges.	d. An independent third party recognized by the IRS as facilitators of 1031 exchanges. Qualified Intermediaries facilitate tax-deferred exchanges and should have a thorough understanding of 1031 regulations. Section 1031 says the Qualified Intermediary must be completely independent from the people doing the exchange. This excludes the lawyer, real estate practitioner, CPA, or anyone else who has been an agent or employee in the past two years of the people doing the exchange.
25. What is the most common type of 1031 exchange? a. Simultaneous Exchange b. Construction Exchange c. Forward Delayed Exchange d. Reverse Exchange	c. Forward Delayed Exchange The most common type of exchange is the Forward Delayed Exchange, in which one property is sold and another property is purchased within 180 days. Other less common types include: Simultaneous Exchange, in which two properties are swapped or exchanged simultaneously; Construction Exchange, also known as a Build-to-Suit Exchange, in which funds from the sale of a property are used to construct improvements on the replacement property; and a Reverse Exchange, in which the replacement property is purchased before the sale of the relinquished property.
26. How many days from the closing date of your property's sale do you have to purchase a replacement property? a. 250 days b. 45 days c. 180 days	c. 180 days You have 180 days from the closing date of your sale to purchase a replacement property. Even if the 180th day falls on a Saturday, Sunday, or holiday, the closing

d. 365 days	still must occur no later than the 180th day; the closing will have to be moved to the preceding business day. There also are no exceptions to the 45-day requirement for identifying replacement properties.
27. Which of the following purchases would qualify for a 1031 exchange? a. A $100,000 savings bond. b. 20 percent interest in a business partnership that owns real estate. c. 300 shares of IBM stock. d. 50 percent undivided interest as a tenant-in-common in real estate.	d. 50 percent undivided interest as a tenant-in-common in real estate. A "tenancy-in-common" is a direct ownership interest in real estate. Each owner is considered to have an individual, undivided interest in a property. Therefore, owners can buy, sell, or place their property in a 1031 exchange without regard to the actions of the others. The other answer choices — bonds, stocks, and business partnerships — are not allowed under Section 1031 regulations.
28. In a 1031 exchange, the term "boot" usually refers to a. The exchange of one property for another simultaneously. b. The full market value of both properties combined. c. Whatever personal items are left behind in a property after the seller moves out. d. Any cash proceeds not spent on the purchase of a replacement property during an exchange.	d. Any cash proceeds not spent on the purchase of a replacement property during an exchange. Cash not spent on the purchase of a replacement property during an exchange, called boot, is fully taxable, regardless of the client's adjusted basis on the property. Boot also can be property the taxpayer receives in the exchange that does not qualify as "like-kind." Boot is taxed at federal capital-gains tax rates.
29. Which of the following purchases would not qualify as a like-kind exchange? a. A one-half usage of a duplex when used for your personal residence. b. An office property used for business. c. A vacation home held as an investment. d. Farmland held as an investment.	a. A one-half usage of a duplex when used for your personal residence. Properties sold and purchased in a like-kind exchange must be held for investment or business use — neither can be your personal residence. A vacation home can qualify as an investment property if it's noted as an investment property on your income tax return. However, vacation homes that are classified as second homes are usually excluded. (Property is considered a second home if it's used for personal purposes more than 14 days per year or for more than 10 percent of the time the property is rented at market rate, whichever figure is greater.)
30. To defer capital gains taxes, the replacement property you choose must:	b. Be of equal or greater value than the property you sold

a. Be of any value; no reinvestment requirement exists to defer taxes. b. Be of equal or greater value than the property you sold. c. Be worth no greater than 5 percent more than the property you sold. d. Be worth less than the property you sold.	If you purchase a replacement property worth less than the relinquished property, you'll have to pay a capital gains tax on the difference. You also are required to reinvest all cash proceeds from the sale of your relinquished property on the purchase of your replacement property. Otherwise, you'll have to pay taxes on the difference.
31. How many days from the closing date of your property's sale do you have to identify replacement property? a. 30 days b. 45 days c. 180 days d. 365 days	b. 45 days You have 45 days from the closing of the sale of a property to identify a replacement property or property.
32. For properties to qualify for a "like-kind" exchange, they must be: a. Any type of real estate, except for raw land. b. The same category of real estate, such as commercial or residential. c. Any type of real estate, if it's used as an investment or for business. d. Located within the same state.	c. Any type of real estate, if it's used as an investment or for business. The IRS considers virtually all real estate in the United States to be "like-kind." Thus, you could swap a farm for an apartment building, raw land for a motel, or a store for a single-family rental. However, the property you are selling and the property you are buying both must be held as an investment or for productive use in a trade or business.

Inside the brokerage

Employing Broker

The broker for whom the salesperson works is called the employing broker, and both will be subject to the terms of an **employment agreement**, even when the salesperson is an independent contractor.
Relationship of Broker and Sales Associate
- A real estate salesperson is licensed to perform real estate activities on behalf of a licensed real estate broker.

Employment or Work Contract

- The Broker needs to have an agreement with all licensees affiliated with the broker whether that relationship is as an employee or independent contractor.
- This agreement spells out various terms of the relationship.

Responsibilities of the Broker

- A licensed individual Broker has daily duties that include writing contracts and overseeing transactions for sales and purchasing activities on homes, land, and commercial properties.
- A broker has attained a higher-level license than a real estate agent and can hire real estate agents to work under their supervision.
- A Broker is responsible for the direct supervision of a brokerage firm.
- A broker is responsible for the real estate activities of his salespeople.
- ☐ A broker is not responsible for everything his salespeople do in their day-to-day lives.
- It shall be the duty of the responsible broker to instruct the licensees licensed under that broker in the: fundamentals of real estate practice, ethics of the profession and License Law.

Independent Contractor vs. Employee

Independent Contractor 1099misc.	Employee W-2
Brokers hold no taxes for the salesperson. The salesperson is responsible for their own taxes.	Broker is required to withhold social security, income taxes and other applicable federal and state taxes from earnings.
Broker cannot dictate to salespersons how to do their job. The responsibility is to teach the salespersons ethics, real estate contracts and law and do real estate successfully.	Broker can tell salespeople exactly how to do their job. Time clocks. Mandatory meetings
Salespersons are responsible for their own benefits like health insurance, retirement plan, business cards, signs, and other expenses.	Employees can be offered benefits and retirement plans.
IRS Statutes for Independent Contractors 1. Services must be performed under a written contract providing	90% of income comes from salary or wages.

that they will not be treated as employees for federal tax purposes. 2. 90% of their payments must be directly related to sales or other output, rather than the number of hours worked; and 3. The individual must be a licensed real estate professional.	

Statutory Nonemployees

- Licensed real estate agents are statutory nonemployees and are treated as self-employed for all federal tax purposes, including income and employment taxes.
- The independent contractor receives a "1099 misc." from his broker yearly with the amount of commission received from the broker.
- It is illegal for a broker to supply health insurance or a retirement plan to an independent contractor.
- **1099 MISC.**

☐ Salespersons should practice within their area of competency.
☐ A first year agent should stay away from particularly challenging transactions.
☐ Real Estate Brokers own all listings, transactions, contracts, and clients. When a salesperson changes offices, all listings, transactions, contracts, and clients stay with the broker.

Sales Associate's Compensation

- Commission splits are negotiated between the broker and the sales associate.
- No matter how the sales associate's compensation is structured, only the employing real estate broker can pay it.

Real Estate Assistants may be licensed or unlicensed.

Unlicensed Assistants MAY

- Provide "general" information about listed properties such as location, availability, and address (without any solicitation on behalf of the assistant).
- Perform clerical duties, which may include answering the telephone and forwarding calls.
- Complete and submit listings and changes to a multiple listing service, type contract forms for approval by the licensee and the principal broker, pick-up and deliver paperwork to other brokers and salespersons, obtain status reports on a loan's progress, assemble closing documents, and obtain required public information from governmental entities.
- ☐ Unlicensed Assistants can refer buyers and sellers to her/his broker. Think about it. They answer the phone and may greet people coming to their office.

Office Policy Manual

- The broker must ensure that there is an adequate level of supervision for licensees, licensee assistants, employees and others who perform duties on behalf of the brokerage.
- The broker must take steps to deal with any conduct that may constitute a breach of the licensing requirements to include Code of Ethics violations, if applicable.
- The written office policies may assist in this regard, and should include the following information:

a. Identify what activities require a license (and what does not) and develop policy to display in office.
b. Must possess an active license prior to performing licensed activity.
c. Prohibited from splitting a fee with an unlicensed person.
d. Unlicensed assistants activities.
e. Report individuals who perform licensed activity without a license to licensing authority immediately.

Conveyancer Activities

- A **conveyancer** is an attorney who assists buyers on how to take title.
- It is legal advice.
- Real Estate Professionals cannot act as an attorney or other professional.

Errors and Omissions Insurance

Insurance that covers unintentional activities by an agent. E and O Insurance will not cover an agent who makes a deliberate falsehood or tries to deceive someone on purpose.

A Desk Fee/Cost

- A charge to salespersons in an office to offset the expenses of the office. It is charged per person.
- Some offices will charge a monthly desk fee.
- **Desk Cost**
- An office with a Desk Fee is most likely to be found in a 100% commission office.

A 100% commission plan will likely have a high desk fee (Landlord Brokers).

Company dollar

- Gross income minus all commissions.
- (Basically, it's what's left over after the agents are paid.)
- After finding the Company Dollar, then the bills are paid.

IRS Form 8300

File Form IRS 8300 is delivered to the IRS for cash transfers of $10,000 or over.

Notary

- the most significant thing for a notary to do is make sure the person is who they say they are and that the signing is not under duress or undue influence. (Voluntary)

- the death of an associated broker does not cancel a contract. Associated brokers are broker agents (subagents).

Realtor vs. Realtist

- You are not a REALTOR (Trademarked) until you join the National Association of Realtors.
- It's trademarked. The National Association of Realtors subscribes to a Code of Ethics.
- Realtists are a parallel organization who also subscribes to a code of ethics.

Uniform Commercial Code (UCC)

- A set of laws that established unified and comprehensive regulations for security transactions of personal property and that superseded existing laws in that field.
- In real estate, when buying a business, the personal property transfers with the bill of sale under the UCC.

Accounting For Client Funds

Trust/Escrow Accounts

- The broker is responsible for all trust monies.
- Trust accounts are regulated by the jurisdiction's regulatory authority and subject to audit.
- If a broker accepts funds or items of others, the broker must maintain a trust account that is styled in the name of the broker or registered trade name and the broker must be a signor on the account.
- The broker may authorize additional persons to have signature authority on the account.
- The funds held in a trust account must never be commingled with funds of the broker.
- Monies or items of others shall not be placed in the broker's operating account.
- Trust accounts cannot be sub-accounts.

Deposit Timing

- Earnest money must be deposited in a timely manner, according to state law.
- The broker is Responsible for trust monies, including commingling/conversion.

Responsibility of Funds

Commingling	Conversion
<ul><li>Commingling is the act of mixing the client's funds with the broker's money.</li><li>Generally, a licensee or broker found guilty of commingling his client's funds with his own business account can have his license suspended or revoked.</li></ul>	<ul><li>Conversion is taking client funds and converting them into personal funds.</li></ul>

No sub-accounts

- The broker may maintain several accounts in the same bank or in different banks; however, the broker may not have a ☐ SUB-account under another one of their accounts as a Trust Account.

Bank fees

- Bank fees are not to be deducted from monies of others that are held in trust by the broker, but rather must be paid for by the broker.
- Standing Accounting Practices must be used to maintain client trust accounts.

Property Management Trust Accounts

- Trust accounts for property managers are typically used to keep tenant deposits and rent payments separate from operating capital.

Antitrust Laws

Antitrust laws prohibit business practices that unreasonably deprive consumers of the benefits of competition, resulting in higher prices for products and services.

☐ Antitrust laws protect competition and benefit the consumers.

Purpose
<ul><li>Free and open competition benefits consumers by ensuring lower prices and new and better products.</li><li>Competition brings businesses to find new, innovative, and more efficient methods of production.</li><li>When competitors agree to fix prices, rig bids, or allocate (divide up) customers, consumers lose the benefits of competition.</li></ul>

The Sherman Antitrust Act
The most common violations in real estate are:

Price Fixing	Group Boycotting	Bid Rigging
Price fixing occurs when two or more competing Brokers agree on what commission or other broker fees to charge.	People, real estate boards or companies getting together to boycott a competitor.	Bid rigging most commonly occurs when two or more person or firms agree to bid in such a way that a designated person or firm submits the winning bid.

Allocation of Markets	A Tie In – Tying Arrangement (tie-in)
<ul><li>Customer- allocation agreements involve some arrangement between competitors to split up customers, such as by geographic area, to reduce or eliminate competition.</li><li>Brokers cannot get together and break up a market area. (You take the north side, and my company will take the south side.</li></ul>	The agent tied in the sale of a listing client' home if the client also turns around and buys swampland the agent is selling.

Penalties

Individuals	Corporations
Up to one million dollars and ten years in jail.	Up to one million dollars.

Fair Housing Laws

The Civil Rights Act of 1866

- Prohibits discrimination based on race.
- Gave all citizens the same rights as those previously only enjoyed by whites to inherit, purchase, and sell real and personal property.
- In the wake if the Civil War the Civil Rights Act of 1866 was enacted to protect the civil rights of persons of African descent born or brought to the United States.

Complaints
- Complaints under the Civil Rights Act of 1866 go directly to Federal Court.

Today's Protected Classes

1. race
2. color
3. religion
4. national origin
5. sex
6. familial status
7. handicap

EHO Poster - the Equal Housing Opportunity Poster

Title VIII of the Civil Rights Act of 1968 (Fair Housing Act, TITLE VIII), as amended, prohibits discrimination in the sale, rental, and financing of dwellings, and in other housing-related transactions, because of;

1. race
2. color
3. religion
4. national origin

Jones v. Alfred H. Mayer Co., 1968

- Upheld the Civil Rights Act of 1866 and removed all exceptions.
- Significance: This case was not filed under the Fair Housing Act but under 42 U.S.C. § 1982, which was part of the Civil Rights Act of 1866. This statute was intended to prohibit all race and color discrimination in the sale and rental of property, including governmental and private discrimination.
- ☐ This case removed all exceptions to fair housing.
- ☐ The Civil Rights Act of 1866 was largely ignored until 1968, when the Supreme Court upheld the Act in Jones v. Mayer.

Housing and Community Development Act of 1974

Added gender

1988 Added handicap and familial status.

Familial Status Restrictions

1. Charging higher rents for people with children.
2. Segregating families within areas or buildings.
3. Maintaining an "Adults Only" complex.

1988

Familial Status

Familial status covers:
- families with children under the age of 18
- pregnant persons
- any person in the process of securing legal custody of a minor child (including adoptive or foster parents)
- persons with written permission of the parent or legal guardian

1988 Defined handicapped as a physical or mental impairment.

- Does not include current illegal drug user, or addiction to a controlled substance.
- Modification to rental allowed by persons.
- It is legitimate for a landlord to deny a family based on honest square footage.

- Accessibility and usability requirements for new construction.
- ☐A licensee may not disclose to an owner that an applicant is a member of a protected class.
- Alcohol and drug addicted persons seeking help or have not used for some times are protected.
- People deemed mentally ill do not have to be receiving current treatment.
- A Mentally ill tenant cause issues or behaving inappropriately and actions to correct behavior does not help, that person can be evicted.

1988 (Property Management)

Housing for Older Persons Act (HOPA)

- Restricts Familial Status for building 62 years and older and 55 plus communities.
- To qualify for a 55+ community the neighborhood or complex must have at least 80 percent of their residents be 55 or older.
- ☐ At least 80% of occupied units have one-person age 55 or older living in them.
- An exemption to familial status is provided to housing protections afforded to age and familial classes intended for older people. Housing may be restricted to people 62, or older or 55 or older in cases where at least one occupant per unit is 55 and at least 80 percent of the units are occupied by people ages 55 or older. In these cases, children may be excluded.
- In a 62 or older complex, all occupants must be 62 or over.

1988 (Property Management)

Housing does not have to be made available to persons who would constitute a direct threat to the health and safety of other individuals or the substantial physical damage to the property.
Individual convicted of selling drugs can be denied housing.

1988

- HUD hears the complaints.
- There is one-year time to file a complaint. If a year expires, **"laches"** under the Statute of Limitations applies. Basically, inaction has caused the action to void.
- Awards can be economic and noneconomic damages, injunctive relief, and attorney fees.

Penalties for Violations

- A maximum civil penalty of $21,410 for the first violation. Respondents who had violated the Fair Housing Act in the previous 5 years could be fined a maximum of $53,524, and respondents who had violated the Act two or more times in the previous 7 years could be fined a maximum of $107,050.
- These civil penalty amounts are in addition to actual damages and attorney's fees and costs that may be awarded to someone who has experienced housing discrimination.
- Prior to this adjustment, the penalty amounts were $21,039 for a first violation, $52,596 for a second violation, and $105,194 for a third violation.

Prohibitions for the Sale or Rental of Housing

Prohibitions in Fair Housing
- It is illegal discrimination to take any of the following actions because of race, color, religion, sex,

disability, familial status, or national origin:

1. Refuse to rent or sell housing.
2. Refuse to negotiate for housing.
3. Otherwise make housing unavailable.
4. Set different terms, conditions or privileges for sale or rental of a dwelling.
5. Provide a person different housing services or facilities.
6. Falsely deny that housing is available for inspection, sale, or rental.
7. Make, print, or publish any notice, statement, or advertisement with respect to the sale or rental of a dwelling that indicates any preference, limitation, or discrimination.
8. Impose different sales prices or rental charges for the sale or rental of a dwelling.
9. Use different qualification criteria or applications, or sale or rental standards or procedures, such as income standards, application requirements, application fees, credit analyses, sale or rental approval procedures or other requirements.
10. Evict a tenant or a tenant's guest.
11. Harass a person.
12. Fail or delay performance of maintenance or repairs.
13. Limit privileges, services, or facilities of a dwelling.
14. Discourage the purchase or rental of a dwelling.
15. Assign a person to a particular building or neighborhood or section of a building or neighborhood.
16. For profit, persuade, or try to persuade, homeowners to sell their homes by suggesting that people of a particular protected characteristic are about to move into the neighborhood (blockbusting).
17. Refuse to provide or discriminate in the terms or conditions of homeowners insurance because of the race, color, religion, sex, disability, familial status, or national origin of the owner and/or occupants of a dwelling.
18. Deny access to or membership in any multiple listing service or real estate brokers' organization.

What Types of Housing Are Covered?

The Fair Housing Act covers most housing. (80%)

Exemptions
In very limited circumstances, the Act exempts owner-occupied buildings with no more than four units, single-family houses sold or rented by the owner without the use of an agent, and housing operated by religious organizations and private clubs that limit occupancy to members.

- ☐ Religious organizations and private clubs may be allowed to discriminate under certain circumstances.

These organizations CAN NOT commercially advertise nor involve a real estate broker.

Single-family Housing Exemptions

- The sale or rental of a single-family house is exempted from the rules of the Fair Housing Act ☐ if the owner doesn't own more than three units at one time, and neither a broker nor discriminatory advertising is used.
- ☐ If such a property is sold, no more than one house can be sold during every two-year period.

Discriminatory Restrictive Covenants

- Discriminatory covenants were once common in deeds, but in 1948 the Supreme Court held that such covenants were unenforceable.
- These covenants may still appear in deeds; they are unenforceable, but it does not affect the validity of the conveyance.

Blockbusting/Panic Peddling

- The illegal act of inducing owners to sell now because property value will decrease due to real or rumored group or persons of a protected group are moving into the neighborhood.
- A man going door-to-door in an older neighborhood and telling the residents that children or families from a protected class will be moving into their quiet neighborhood is guilty of blockbusting/panic peddling.

Steering

- This practice is specifically prohibited and recognized as illegal by the Supreme Court.
- The discriminatory practice of directing homebuyers to (or away from) specific areas based on a protected class to maintain homogeneity.
- Steering is when an agent shows buyer properties only in neighborhoods where the agent believes the buyer should live.

Steering Is a Form of Discrimination
John, who is an Asian man, meets with a real estate broker to discuss purchasing a house for his family. When John names the neighborhood that he is interested in, the broker asks John if he is sure that his family will feel comfortable there. The broker tells John that she has a wonderful listing in another neighborhood where there are more "people like them." When the broker takes John to see the house, John notices that the residents of the neighborhood appear to be mostly Asian. John files a complaint with HUD because steering someone to a certain neighborhood because of his race is a form of race discrimination.

Exclusionary Zoning

- The "Not in My Back Yard" (NIMBY) factor is an unfortunate reality.
- Zoning that operates to exclude a class protected under the law may be illegal.

Financial and Brokerage Service Discrimination

- Any type of discrimination in the lending of money for home mortgages is illegal under the Fair Housing Act.
- Discrimination may also take the form of a refusal to take or process an individual loan application or it may be in the form of "redlining," a practice where loans or mortgages are refused based upon the character of the neighborhood.
- **Predatory practices** that single out a protected class are illegal.

Redlining

- Redlining is a discriminatory practice that puts services (financial and otherwise) out of reach for residents of certain areas based on race or ethnicity. It can be seen in the systematic denial of mortgages, insurance, loans, and other financial services based on location (and that area's default history) rather than on an individual's qualifications and creditworthiness. Notably, the policy of redlining is felt the most by residents of minority neighborhoods.
- ☐ Redlining cases are often very difficult to prove because the courts recognize that lenders must be free to consider legitimate business interests by making investments that are economically sound.

American with Disabilities Act

The Americans with Disabilities Act (ADA) prohibits discrimination against people with disabilities in several areas, including employment, transportation, public accommodations, communications and access to state and local government' programs and services.

Public Accommodations (Title III)

Public accommodations include facilities such as restaurants, hotels, grocery stores, retail stores, etc., as well as privately owned transportation systems.

Title III requires that all new construction and modifications must be accessible to individuals with disabilities. For existing facilities, barriers to services must be removed if readily achievable.

Equal Access to Facilities

- No one can be discriminated against based on disability in any place of public accommodation (a private entity with facilities open to the public).
- Architectural (Architectural Barriers) and communication barriers must be removed if it is "readily achievable" to do so.
- All companies with ☐ **15 or more employees** must abide to ADA.

Department of Justice (DOJ) - ADA Enforcement

Federal agency that has the authority to enforce all provisions of the Americans with Disabilities Act (ADA).

Advertising and Technology

> The Fair Housing Act makes it unlawful to make, print, or publish, or cause to be made, printed, or published, any notice, statement, or advertisement, with respect to the sale or rental of a dwelling, that indicates any preference, limitation, or discrimination because of race, color, religion, sex, handicap, familial status, or national origin, or an intention to make any such preference, limitation, or discrimination.

Descriptive Words

> **Words descriptive of dwelling, landlord, and tenants.**
> White private home, Colored home, Jewish home, Hispanic residence, adult building.

> Word's indicative of race, color, religion, sex, handicap, familial status, or national origin.

Sex	Handicap
<ul><li>Stating, or tending to imply that the housing being advertised is available to persons of only one sex and not the other, except where the sharing of living areas is involved.</li><li>Exclusions for dormitory facilities by educational institutions.</li></ul>	<ul><li>Crippled, blind, deaf, mentally ill, retarded, impaired, handicapped, physically fit.</li></ul>

Familial status	Catch words
<ul><li>Adults, children, singles, mature persons.</li><li>Exclusion for housing for older persons.</li></ul>	<ul><li>Words and phrases used in a discriminatory context *should be* avoided, e.g., restricted, exclusive, private, integrated, traditional, board approval or membership approval.</li></ul>

Colloquialisms

Words or phrases used regionally or locally which imply or suggest race, color, religion, sex, handicap, familial status, or national origin.

These provisions would include pamphlets, letters, and electronic communications, and would also cover press releases about real estate deals and even references in letters to matters pertaining to properties.

Directions to real estate for sale or rent (use of maps or written instructions)

- Directions can imply a discriminatory preference, limitation, or exclusion.
- For example, references to real estate location made in terms of racial or national origin significant landmarks, such as an existing black development (signal to blacks) or an existing development known for its exclusion of minorities (signal to whites).
- Specific directions which refer to a racial or national origin significant area may indicate a preference.

- References to a synagogue, congregation or parish may also indicate a religious preference.

Area (location) description

Names of facilities which cater to a particular racial, national origin or religious group, such as country club or private school designations, or names of facilities which are used exclusively by one sex may indicate a preference.

Examples of the selective use of advertisements which may be discriminatory:

Selective geographic advertisements

Such selective use may involve the strategic placement of billboards; brochure advertisements distributed within a limited geographic area by hand or in the mail; advertising in particular geographic coverage editions of major metropolitan newspapers or in newspapers of limited circulation which are mainly advertising vehicles for reaching a particular segment of the community; or displays or announcements available only in selected sales offices.

Selective use of equal opportunity slogan or logo

When placing advertisements, such selective use may involve placing the equal housing opportunity slogan or logo in advertising reaching some geographic areas, but not others, or with respect to some properties but not others.

Use of Equal Housing Opportunity logotype, statement, or slogan

All advertising of residential real estate for sale, rent, or financing should contain an equal housing opportunity logotype, statement, or slogan as a means of educating the home seeking public that the property is available to all persons regardless of race, color, religion, sex, handicap, familial status, or national origin.

Symbols or logotypes

Symbols or logotypes which imply or suggest race, color, religion, sex, handicap, familial status, or national origin.

Human Models

- The selective use of human models in advertisements may have discriminatory impact.
- Human models in photographs, drawings, or other graphic techniques may not be used to indicate exclusiveness because of race, color, religion, sex, handicap, familial status, or national origin.
- If models are used in display advertising campaigns, the models should be clearly definable as reasonably representing majority and minority groups in the metropolitan area, both sexes, and, when appropriate, families with children.

- Models, if used, should portray persons in an equal social setting and indicate to the public that the housing is open to all without regard to race, color, religion, sex, handicap, familial status, or national origin, and is not for the exclusive use of one such group.
- Selective advertising may involve an advertising campaign using human models primarily in media that cater to one racial or national origin segment of the population without a complementary advertising campaign that is directed at other groups.
- Another example may involve use of racially mixed models by a developer to advertise one development and not others.
- Similar care must be exercised in advertising in publications or other media directed at one sex, or at persons without children.
- Such selective advertising may involve the use of human models of members of only one sex, or of adults only, in displays, photographs or drawings to indicate preferences for one sex or the other, or for adults to the exclusion of children.

Other Advertising Issues

Puffery

- An exaggerated opinion, not necessarily based in fact, intended to portray the property in a more favorable light. Example: "This property is one of the best buys in the neighborhood. It is sure to go up in value".
- Puffing could lead to misrepresentation.
- Although not illegal, be careful.
- Puffing is an exaggerated statement.
- This is the best house in the best neighborhood. The buyer knows of nicer houses and nicer neighborhoods, but he buys it anyways.

Blind Ad

An advertisement that disguises the advertiser's identity, i.e., contains a phone number with no other identifying data. Licensed brokers should not use blind ads and must disclose agency.

Fraud

Intentional deception or misrepresentation – a material misstatement of fact.

Use of technology in Advertising

Technology in Real Estate Practice

- Smartphones
- Email/Texting
- Social Media
- Internet Advertising

The Telephone Consumer Protection Act (TCPA)

- In most cases, FCC rules under the Telephone Consumer Protection Act and Junk Fax Prevention Act prohibit sending junk faxes.
- Restricts the use of the facsimile machine to deliver unsolicited advertisements.

CAN- SPAM Act – The unsubscribe button in emails.

A law that sets the rules for commercial email, establishes requirements for commercial messages, □ gives recipients the right to have you **stop emailing** them, and spells out tough penalties for violations.

The Telephone Consumer Protection Act (TCPA)

The Do Not Call Registry
- The Registry does not apply to **political calls or calls from non-profits and charities and legitimate survey calls.**
- Fines up to $40,654 per call.

18 months follow-up
Calls are permitted from companies with which you have done or sought to do business. Specifically, a company can call you up to 18 months after you last did business with it.

IDX Technology

The technology used by real estate professionals to put the MLS on their website.

Electronic Contracting

1. Uniform Electronic Transaction Act (UETA)
2. Electronic Signatures in Global and National Commerce Act (E-Sign)
- Electronic signatures are valid even if state laws conflict.
- □ A consent process is required if persons would like to substitute electronic documents for written documents.

Module Ten: Practice of Real Estate Quiz

1. Being a fiduciary requires an agent to always act in good faith to the benefit of the principal. Which is an example of a principal's request that the agent may disobey? a. Do not hold an open house previously agreed to be held open. b. WITHOUT EXCEPTION, do not show the property without a 48-hour notice. c. Do not use a yard sign to indicate the property is for sale. d. Do not show the seller client's home to a person of a certain religion if the request is placed in writing and signed by the client.	d. Do not show the seller client's home to a person of a certain religion if the request is placed in writing and signed by the client. An agent does not have to follow illegal or unethical orders.
2. When acting as an employee rather than an independent contractor, a salesperson is obligated to? a. list properties in his or her own name. b. advertise property on his or her own behalf. c. assume responsibilities assigned by the broker. d. accept a commission from another broker.	c. assume responsibilities assigned by the broker. The salesperson's acts as a sub agent.
3. What are the requirements for independent contractor status used by the Internal Revenue Service? a. 90% or more of the individual's income is based on sales production rather than hours worked b. a written agreement that specifies that the individual will not be treated as an employee for tax purposes c. a current real estate license d. All of these.	d. All three of these are needed.
4. All the following are true of an independent contractor's written agreement EXCEPT? a. the contractor must have the employer withhold Social Security taxes. b. the contractor is expected to pay for her own vacation. c. the contractor may set her own hours. d. the contractor must pay her own withholding and Social Security taxes.	a. the contractor must have the employer withhold Social Security taxes. Independent contractors are not employees, so the employer will not withhold taxes. Independent contractors must have a written agreement stating that they set their own schedule and they must pay their own taxes, expenses, and vacations.
5. Whether a salesperson is associated with a broker as an employee or as an independent contractor is important? a. for income tax purposes. b. when applying for a license c. when listing property, as an independent contractor may list in his or her own name. d. when representing property managers.	a. for income tax purposes. Employees are W9 filers and Independent Contractors receive a 1099misc.
6. For federal tax purposes, the form a broker will give an agent to file their taxes is a? a. 5024 – misc. b. 1099 misc.	b. 1099 misc. 1099 misc. indicates the amount of money your broker has given you within

c. 1099 – s. d. 940	a specific year.
7. Determining whether a broker/agent needs an employee or independent contractor should largely be based upon the type of work the assistant would be doing, and the extent of supervision the broker/agent desires to have over the assistant. a. true b. false	a. true Determining whether a broker/agent needs an employee or independent contractor should largely be based upon the type of work the assistant would be doing, and the extent of supervision the broker/agent desires to have over the assistant is true.
8. All the following are characteristics of an independent contractor relationship with a broker EXCEPT? a. you do not need a license b. 90% or more of your compensation must come from sales productivity c. you must have a written contract with the broker defining the relationship d. you assume responsibility for paying your own income tax	a. you do not need a license Employees for the developer or owner of the property do not need licenses.
9. A licensee who is paid in a lump sum and who is personally responsible for paying his or her own taxes is probably a(n)? a. transactional broker. b. buyer's agent. c. independent contractor. d. employee.	c. independent contractor. independent contractors are responsible for paying their own taxes.
10. For many people being an employee is far more familiar and instinctive than being an independent contractor. a. true b. false	a. true Most people are employees.
11. A salesperson leaves her current broker to join a new brokerage firm. The listings the salesperson has at the old firm are? a. taken to the new firm. b. renegotiated. c. left with the old firm. d. amended to move to the new firm.	c. left with the old firm. Listings belong to the brokerage firm.
12. A broker has established the following office policy: "All listings taken by any salesperson associated with this real estate brokerage must include compensation based on a 7 percent commission. No lower commission rate is acceptable." If the broker attempts to impose this uniform commission requirement, which of the following statements is true? a. The broker may, as a matter of office policy, legally set the minimum commission rate acceptable for the firm. b. The broker must present the uniform commission	a. The broker may, as a matter of office policy, legally set the minimum commission rate acceptable for the firm. The broker did not conspire with other brokerages to set pricing.

policy to the local professional association for approval. c. The salespersons associated with the brokerage will not be bound by the requirement and may negotiate any commission rate they choose. d. None are true.	
13. A real estate broker must keep on file following its consummation complete records relating to any real estate transaction for? a. one year. b. five years. c. six years d. three years.	d. three years. Keep all records for three years. They can be kept electronically.
14. Brokers are covered by errors and omissions insurance for? a. unintentional misrepresentations. b. intentional misrepresentations. c. ignorance of fair housing, d. fraud	a. unintentional misrepresentations. Errors and omissions insurance (E&O) is a type of liability insurance that protects companies and their workers or individuals against claims.
15. A real estate broker must be attentive to "desk cost" to run a competitive, yet profitable business. Which of the following represents the correct method of calculating desk cost? a. Add the total of all the furniture for each salesperson. b. Calculate the gross annual profit for the firm, less the expenses, divided by the number of salespersons. c. Divide the total cost of rent, utilities, and advertising by the number of salespersons. d. Divide the total operating expenses of the firm, including salaries, rent, insurance, etc., by the number of salespersons.	c. Divide the total cost of rent, utilities, and advertising by the number of salespersons. Desk cost is the total of the operating expenses of the firm, divided by the number of salespersons employed by that firm. These brokers may be considered "landlord" brokers. Desk cost companies can be found in a 100% commission office.
16. Three properties are managed by a broker for three different owners. Emergency repairs are needed at one property, but the owner lacks enough money in his escrow account. The broker used funds from another owner's account for the repairs, then reimburses the first owner with a check. Which of the following statements is true? a. The broker has acted properly by safeguarding the client's interest. b. Such action is proper when the management account balance is high. c. The broker is in violation for improperly handling escrow funds. d. The broker must use personal funds for repair if there is not enough money in the management account.	c. The broker is in violation of regulations for improperly handling escrow funds. You cannot mix client funds. The broker is in violation of regulations for improperly handling escrow funds. The broker could go to jail and have his license suspended.
17. MATCH: money paid by a buyer to a seller at the time of entering a contract to indicate intent and ability of the buyer to carry out the contract? a. Earnest money	a. Earnest money Earnest money is a deposit made to a seller that represents a buyer's good

b. Equity c. Discount point d. Escrow	intentions.
18. Broker Dean employs Martha as his bookkeeper. Martha is responsible for maintaining the brokerage's accounting ledgers. She also prepares and signs all checks disbursed from Dean's escrow and operating accounts. Which of the following statements is true of this situation? a. Martha may not prepare, and sign commission checks unless she is a licensed real estate salesperson. b. Dean could be charged with culpable negligence for allowing his bookkeeper to withdraw funds from the escrow account. c. Dean does not need to sign the checks; however, he must be an authorized signatory on the account. d. Dean must countersign all checks disbursed from the escrow account.	c. Dean does not need to sign the checks; however, he must be an authorized signatory on the account. A manager can be a signer on the brokers trust account
19. Which of the following describes money belonging to others? a. money a broker would keep in a trust or escrow account. b. future commissions to be earned. c. buyer's source of funds for a down payment. d. the profits to come from a real estate transaction.	a. money a broker would keep in a trust or escrow account. Client and customer funds are the money a broker would keep in a trust or escrow account.
20. The main purpose and function of state laws requiring brokerage firms to have trust accounts is? a. to have a safe place to keep commissions belonging to salespeople and funds from buyers and sellers. b. so, the state can audit the firm at any time. c. to have a safe place and additional protection for funds that don't belong to the firm. d. to enable the brokerage to keep operations and funds from buyers and sellers in the same account.	c. to have a safe place and additional protection for funds that don't belong to the firm. Trust accounts hold money from the public and are not allowed to hold the firm's operations funds or earned commissions.
21. MATCH: The illegal practice of mixing a buyer's, seller's, tenant's, or landlord's funds with the broker's money? a. dutiful conversion b. dutiful conversion c. commingle d. statutory embellishment	c. commingle Commingling is illegal!!
22. MATCH: An escrow trust account. a. Is the account where the payroll taxes for withholding is placed. b. Is a separate account established to hold money belonging to others. c. Should have the words "Operating Account" in its account identification.	b. Is a separate account established to hold money belonging to others. Trust accounts are separate accounts established to hold money belonging to clients or customers.
23. Today is April 1. Salesperson Rebecca has just received investor Teresa's earnest money check dated April 7th.	b. Receipt is hereby acknowledged of the sum of $5,000 dated April 7 payable to

Furthermore, the check is made payable to Bob Wilson, Attorney Trust Account. Which of the following is the best wording to include in the Contract to Purchase and Sell Real Estate? a. Receipt is hereby acknowledged of a promise to pledge $5,000 as an earnest money deposit on or before April 7. b. Receipt is hereby acknowledged of the sum of $5,000 dated April 7 payable to Bob Wilson, Attorney Trust Account (by check) as an earnest money deposit c. Receipt is hereby acknowledged of the sum of $5,000 as an earnest money deposit. d. Receipt is hereby acknowledged of a check for $5,000 as an earnest money deposit to be held in escrow.	Bob Wilson, Attorney Trust Account (by check) as an earnest money deposit All prudent information on the home to be purchase and escrow account should be present on the earnest money check.
24. The purpose of collecting an earnest money deposit is to? a. display the buyer has the intention to carry out the deal. b. ensure a commission will be paid. c. set aside funds for prorated taxes. d. All the above.	a. display the buyer has the intention to carry out the deal. An earnest money deposit is not mandatory in an offer. Nonetheless, it does display the intent of the buyer to complete the transaction.
25. What is the purpose of trust or escrow, accounts? a. to provide an account that is separate from operational or personal accounts. b. to make interest on client funds. c. to comingle easily. d. all the above.	a. to provide an account that is separate from operational or personal accounts. Client funds are held separately from all other funds.
26. The money in the broker's escrow account can? a. Be withdrawn for personal reasons. b. Be held the earnest money deposits of the buyer. c. Be held the commission amounts to be paid the broker. d. Be comingled with other client escrow accounts in case the money is held for property management accounts.	b. Be held the earnest money deposits of the buyer. Earnest money shows the buyer's true intentions. The broker is always responsible for earnest money.
27. Earnest money submitted with an offer for a sales contract is _____. a. good business. b. not allowed. c. mandatory.	a. good business Earnest money shows the buyer's true intentions.
28. Brokerage firm trust accounts must be a? a. demand account. b. mutual fund account. c. savings account.	a. demand account. Demand accounts allow the broker to deposit and withdraw funds without restrictions. (A basic noninterest bearing checking account is most common.)
29. A salesperson finds a buyer for a home he has listed. The buyer gives the salesperson an earnest money cashier's check for $2,000. What should the salesperson do with the check? a. deposit it into the broker's trust account.	d. Immediately give it to his broker An earnest money deposit is generally held in the broker's trust account.

b. take a picture of it and give it back. c. staple it to the offer. d. Immediately give it to his broker.	
30. Which of the following forms of payment would be considered good funds? a. Savings and Loan teller's check b. Electronic transfer of funds c. Cashier's check d. all of these are correct.	d. all of these are correct. All are acceptable funds.
31. A buyer made an offer on a property and refused to present an earnest money deposit. a. The seller should not accept the offer. b. The Listing agent should not present the offer. c. Earnest money deposits are not required. d. The selling agent should not present the offer.	c. earnest money deposits are not required. Unless both parties have agreed in writing, earnest money is not required.
32. Earnest money deposits should be? a. deposited into a personal account. b. deposited into a safe deposit box.. c. deposited into an escrow/trust account. d. deposited into the broker's business account.	c. deposited into an escrow/trust account. All earnest money checks are deposited into an escrow the next business day after an accepted offer.
33. An example of conversion could be? a. Using earnest money to pay for any personal use. b. Keeping client money separate from other accounts. c. Releasing trust accounts as specified by contract. d. Returning client funds when both parties agree in writing.	a. Using earnest money to pay for any personal use. Converting client funds to personal funds.
34. Jim and Ruth are both salespersons who work for NMN Realty. One afternoon, they agree to divide their town into a northern region and a southern region. Jim will handle listings in the northern region, and Ruth will handle listings in the southern region. Which of the following statements is true regarding this agreement? a. The agreement between Jim and Ruth does not violate antitrust laws. b. The agreement between Jim and Ruth constitutes illegal price-fixing. c. Jim and Ruth have violated the Sherman Antitrust Act and are liable for triple damages. d. They will be in violation of licensing laws.	a. The agreement between Jim and Ruth does not violate antitrust laws. Jim and Ruth are at the same brokerage. Their actions would be in violation if they were at two separate companies.
35. What is the FTC's competition mission? a. To enforce the rules of the competitive marketplace. b. To enforce free trade. c. To enforce open borders. d. All of these.	a. To enforce the rules of the competitive marketplace. THE FEDERAL TRADE COMMISSION'S (FTC) MISSION: To prevent business practices that are anticompetitive or deceptive or unfair to consumers; to enhance informed consumer choice and public
36. The Sherman Act imposes criminal penalties of up to	a. 100 million – $1 million – 10 years

_____ for a corporation and _____ for an individual, along with up to _____ in prison. a. $100 million – $1 million – 10 years b. $10 million – $5 million – 8 years c. $ 1 million – $500 thousand – 5 years d. $150 million – 100 thousand – 2 years	The Sherman Act imposes criminal penalties of up to $100 million for a corporation and $1 million for an individual, along with up to 10 years in prison.
37. The basic objectives of the antitrust laws are to? a. All of these. b. to protect the process of competition for the benefit of consumers. c. making sure there are strong incentives for businesses to operate efficiently. d. keep prices down. e. keep quality up.	a. All of these. The antitrust law's objective is to protect the competition for the benefit of consumers, making sure there are strong incentives for businesses to operate efficiently, keep prices down, and keep quality up.
38. MATCH: US laws enacted to curb anti-competitive business, industry, and professional behavior? a. Antitrust Laws b. Sherman Act c. Landmark Laws d. Equity Act	a. Antitrust Laws Antitrust laws protect consumers from predatory business practices. They ensure that fair competition exists in an open-market economy.
39. Certain acts are considered so harmful to competition that they are almost always illegal. These include all the following except; a. only using one broker for transactions. b. plain arrangements among competing individuals or businesses to fix prices. c. divide markets. d. rig bids.	a. only using one broker for transactions. Certain acts are considered so harmful to competition that they are almost always illegal. These include plain arrangements among competing individuals or businesses to fix prices, divide markets, or rig bids.
40. _____ occurs whenever two or more competitors agree to take actions that have the effect of raising, lowering, or stabilizing the price of any product or service without any legitimate justification. a. Illegal price fixing b. Illegal boycotting c. illegal group boycotting d. all of these.	a. Illegal price fixing Illegal price fixing occurs whenever two or more competitors agree to take actions that have the effect of raising, lowering, or stabilizing the price of any product or service without any legitimate justification.
41. MATCH: Act or practice that causes or is likely to cause substantial injury to consumers which is not reasonably avoidable by consumers themselves and not outweighed by countervailing benefits to consumers or competition. a. All of these are examples of unfairness. b. Coercion or fraud c. Keeping info from consumers d. Targeting vulnerable consumers	a. All of these are examples of unfairness. An act or practice is unfair when it causes or is likely to cause substantial injury to consumers.
42. Antitrust violations include all the following except? a. individual decision to use one closing attorney b. price fixing (no going rate)	a. individual decision to use one closing attorney

c. group boycotting (conspiracy) d. allocation of customers (geographical) e. allocation of markets (do not compete) f. tie-in agreements	Antitrust violations include: price fixing (no going rate) group boycotting (conspiracy) allocation of customers (geographical) allocation of markets (do not compete) tie-in agreements
43. The _____ require that each company establish prices and other terms on its own, without agreeing with a competitor. a. Antitrust Laws b. SEC Laws c. FBI Laws d. DOJ Laws	a. antitrust laws The antitrust laws require that each company establish prices and other terms on its own, without agreeing with a competitor.
44. Which violation would it be if Bob required his buyer to purchase swamp land for the buyer to buy the property he really wants? a. Tying contract b. Clayton Act c. Wheeler-Lea Act d. Interlocking directorates	a. Tying contract An agreement in which the seller conditions the sale of one product (the "tying" product) on the buyer's agreement to purchase a separate product (the "tied" product) from the seller.
45. Along with a financial penalty, abusers of competitive practices can get up to how many years in jail? a. 10 b. 20 c. 5 d. 7	a. 10 Penalties for violating antitrust laws include criminal and civil penalties: Violations of the Sherman Act individuals can be fined up to $350,000 and sentenced to up to 10 years in prison. Companies can be fined up to $10 million.
46. Plain agreements among competitors to divide sales territories or assign customers are almost always? a. Illegal b. Legal c. not a violation. d. not an illegal activity.	a. Illegal Plain agreements among competitors to divide sales territories or assign customers are almost always illegal.
47. All the following are prohibited by antitrust laws, except? a. boycotting other brokers in the marketplace. b. dividing the market to restrict competition. c. agreeing to set sales commissions and management rates. d. receiving compensation from both the buyer and the seller.	d. receiving compensation from both the buyer and the seller. Compensation can be from either the client, the customer, or both.
48. The federal antitrust laws are enforced by: a. the Department of Justice. b. the Treasury Department. c. the Office of the Mint. d. The Office of Budget and Management.	a. the Department of Justice. The United States Department of Justice Antitrust Division is a law enforcement agency that enforces the U.S. antitrust

	laws.
49. The following is considered prima facie evidence of discrimination by a broker. a. Failure for a customer to qualify for a loan. b. Failure of the lender not to grant. c. Failure to display an equal opportunity poster at the broker's office. d. Failure to keep appointments.	c. Failure to display an equal opportunity poster at the broker's office. Prima Facie meaning IN YOU FACE discrimination.
50. Federal Fair housing laws prohibit discrimination based on? a. Sex b. Political beliefs c. College affiliation d. Education	a. Sex Discrimination against an individual because of gender identity, including transgender status, or because of sexual orientation is discrimination because of sex in violation of Title VII.
51. The Civil Rights Act of 1866 prohibited discrimination based on? a. National Origin b. Familial Status c. Race d. Pregnancy	c. Race The Civil Rights Act of 1866, declared that all people born in the United States were U.S. citizens and had certain inalienable rights, including the right to make contracts, to own property, to sue in court, and to enjoy the full protection of federal law.
52. Which of the following statements is true of complaints relating to the Civil Rights Act of 1866? a. They are handled by HUD. b. They must be taken directly to federal courts. c. They are no longer reviewed in the courts. d. They are handled by state enforcement agencies.	b. They must be taken directly to federal courts. Violations are the Fair Housing Act of 1866 are taken to the federal government.t
53. What states do the provisions of the 1968 Federal Fair Housing Act apply; a. in all states. b. only in states that have substantially equivalent laws. c. only states that do not have substantially equivalent laws. d. only in states that have ratified the act.	a. in all states. The Civil Rights Act of 1866 rests on the 13th amendment abolishing slavery. Since these are federal laws and statues they apply in all states.
54. MATCH: The federal law (often referred to as the Fair Housing Act) that prohibited discrimination in housing based on race, creed, or national origin. a. Civil Rights Act of 1968 b. Civil Rights Act of 1866 c. The Sherman Act d. The Housing Act	a. Civil Rights Act of 1968 The Civil Rights Act signed into law in April 1968–popularly known as the Fair Housing Act–prohibited discrimination with the sale, rental and financing of housing based on race, religion, national origin, and sex
55. Brokers receive listings of houses for sale, and the sellers specify that they won't sell to any Russian families. Which of the following should the broker do? a. Require that the owner sign a separate legal document.	b. Explain to the owner that the instruction violates federal law and that the broker cannot comply with it.

b. Explain to the owner that the instruction violates federal law and that the broker cannot comply with it. c. Abide by the principal's directions even though they conflict with the fair housing laws. d. Advertise the property exclusively in Asian-language newspapers.	Never violate fair housing laws.
56. The federal Fair Housing Act protects all the following EXCEPT? a. familial status b. retirement age c. handicap status d. national origin	b. retirement age Federal fair housing laws do not protect age.
57. The Fair Housing Act of 1968 was meant as a follow-up to the Civil Rights Act of 1964. It is called the? a. Fair Act b. Fair Housing Act c. Fair Housing Enactment d. Fair Rental Housing Act	b. Fair Housing Act Also known as Title VIII of 1968.
58. Who is protected under the Federal Fair Housing Law's familial status? a. Children under the age of 18 and pregnant women. b. Seniors over the age of 55. c. Persons under the age of 21. d. People 18 years of age and younger.	a. Children under the age of 18 and pregnant women. Familial status means the makeup of your family. The FHA prohibits discrimination including children under the age of 18 living with parents/guardians, pregnant women, and people seeking custody of children under 18.
59. Federal fair housing laws protect all the following people against discrimination EXCEPT? a. Homosexuals b. Children c. Baptists d. Russians	a. homosexuals The answer is homosexuals. Homosexuality (sexual orientation) is protected by some city and state laws but is not a part of federal fair housing laws.
60. A real estate broker who specializes in selling residential property in a specific area may refuse to accept a listing on a property in that area for which of the following reasons? a. Because of the minority status of any of the residents in that area. b. Because of the minority status of the owner of the residence. c. Because the owner's required price is substantially above the market price around the residences. d. For any of the reasons.	c. Because the owner's required price is substantially above the market price in the residences. A broker should refuse to take a listing if the owner's price is substantially above the market value of the property. If he refused because of the minority status of anyone, then he would be discriminating based on race.
61. If a person wishes to seek intervention from discrimination, they must? a. file a written complaint with HUD within 1 year. b. file a complaint with the Real Estate Commission. c. file a written complaint with HUD within 2 years.	a. file a written complaint with HUD within 1 year. A person seeking intervention must file a written complaint with the Office of Fair

d. file a written complaint with the State of Mississippi.	Housing within one year.
62. Ignorance of the law is? a. not a legal defense for discrimination. b. an acceptable legal defense for a charge of discrimination. c. a cause of dismissal since there was no intent. d. a clause in the Fair Housing Act that excludes illegality.	a. not a legal defense for discrimination. "Ignorance of the law" is not an excuse for violating the law.
63. A charge of violation of Federal Fair Housing laws can be heard by an administrative law judge within the Department of Housing and Urban Development (HUD) or by a federal district court judge in Federal court. The advantage of a federal court hearing to the complaining party is that? a. there is no dollar limit on damages paid. b. the federal district court is faster. c. there is no benefit. d. federal district court allows for the complaints to be heard locally.	a. there is no dollar limit on damages paid. If any party elects to have a federal civil trial, HUD must refer your case to the U.S. Department of Justice for enforcement. The U.S. Department of Justice will file a civil lawsuit on your behalf in the U.S.
64. Violating Fair Housing practices, an agent? a. will lose their license only b. will get probation. c. will get arrested immediately. d. will have his license revoked and will be criminally prosecuted.	d. will have his license revoked and will be criminally prosecuted. Licensees are held to a higher standard than the public. Violating a fair housing condition is serious.
65. You cannot _____ against (punish) an applicant, employee, or former employee for reporting discrimination. a. retaliate b. demote c. give a pay raise to d. any of these	a. retaliate Participating in a discrimination investigation or lawsuit or opposing discrimination (for example, threatening to file a charge or complaint of discrimination).
66. Congress established a national policy of fair housing throughout the United States. Which of the following properties does this law apply to? a. Single-family residences that are individually owned and that are offered for sale through a real estate broker. b. Single-family residences owned by private individuals who own more than three such residences. c. All type family dwellings of six units where the owner occupies one of the units. d. All of these are correct.	d. All of these are correct This act applies to all these situations.
67. The single mother with two young children applied to rent a condominium in a resort-like development designed for those over 55, The development is 90% occupied by adults over 55. The mother was denied based on the age of her children. The Federal Fair Housing Act protects? a. the condo owner from being forced to rent to the	a. the condo owner from being forced to rent to the family because of the age of over 80% of the occupants of the development. A senior living community may be

family because of the age of over 80% of the occupants of the development. b. the condo owner only. the community must find housing for the family. c. the condo owner and the community because the condo, based on honest square footage, is too small. d. the single parent of two preschool children. THERE ARE NO EXCEPTIONS	lawfully exempt from the FHA's familial status protections if: every occupant is 62 years of age or older 80% of the housing units are occupied by at least one person over the age of 55.
68. A new real estate salesperson made substantial efforts to obtain listings in a non-integrated community. He found success by insinuating to property owners that minorities move into the area; the value of their homes would decrease. Which of the following terms best describes the activities of the Salesperson? a. Steering b. Panic peddling c. Blockbusting d. Both Panic Peddling and Blockbusting	d. Both Panic Peddling and Blockbusting This illegal activity is both panic peddling and blockbusting.
69. An agent told homeowners that according to him, the entry of different minority groups into the neighborhood would reduce the value of property. The following are the practices of the salesman? a. Permissible if the representations are true b. Grounds for disciplinary action c. Unethical, but beyond the jurisdiction of the Real Estate Commissioner d. Justified if his activities do not decrease property values for neighboring properties.	b. Grounds for disciplinary action Such activities would be defined as promoting panic selling (blockbusting) which is against the fair housing laws. Therefore, the salesman could have his license suspended or revoked by the Real Estate Commissioner.
70. An Eastern European couple buys a home from a broker. Afterwards the broker sends out a flyer stating: "Property values will fall.". "I can help you find a new home in a better neighborhood." This is an example of? a. redlining. b. steering. c. blockbusting. d. nothing.	c. blockbusting. Essentially, blockbusting is moving a group of people into an area and advertising that property values are going to drop in that area.
71. Blockbusting is an acceptable practice? a. under no circumstance b. only under the supervision of the real estate licensees c. only when approved by either HUD or the Justice Department d. only if the seller and buyer mutually agree	a. under no circumstance By claiming that minority influx will lower property values, Blockbusting is an illegal and discriminatory practice by which some people attempt to mislead a property owner into entering a real estate transaction for their own financial gain.
72. A broker induces an owner to sell by telling him that Muslims are moving into the neighborhood. This broker is guilty of...? a. Greenlining b. Conversion	d. Blockbusting It involves inciting homeowners to sell by making representations about minority entry into the neighborhood.

c. Testing d. Blockbusting	
73. A minority couple asked a salesperson to find them a property worth around $500,000. The salesperson showed the couple lower-priced property in integrated neighborhoods only. This may be an example of? a. blockbusting. b. redlining. c. steering. d. puffing.	c. steering. It appears the salesperson was driving their clients into the neighborhoods the salesperson believes the clients belonged in.
74. Realtors are quite worried about racial segregation. The broker has drawn out a map for each racial or ethnic group. Racial balance in residential housing is the aim of this policy. Which statement about this broker's policy is true? a. The broker's policy constitutes illegal steering because it is discriminatory regardless of broker's intentions. b. While the broker's policy may appear to constitute blockbusting, application of the effects test proves its legality. c. The broker's policy clearly shows the intent to discriminate. d. While the broker's policy may appear to constitute steering, application of the intent test proves its legality.	a. The broker's policy constitutes illegal steering because it is discriminatory regardless of broker's intentions. Steering is illegal regardless of intent.
75. A minority couple came to a salesperson looking for a house. The salesperson has some properties for which the couple qualify but avoids showing or mentioning these listings. Instead, the salesperson shows only properties in low priced and integrated neighborhoods. This practice may be? a. redlining b. steering and redlining c. blockbusting d. steering.	d. steering. The practice of racially steering potential home buyers toward or away from certain neighborhoods is called racial steering.
76. Actions that are illegal by federal and state fair housing laws include. a. offering advantageous loan terms b. offering advantageous loan terms to first time home buyers c. refusing to show the certain residential property to non-English speaking home seekers d. showing all residential properties to a non-English speaking home seeker	c. refusing to show the certain residential property to non-English speaking home seekers Steering and redlining are both illegal practices.
77. The act of directing home seekers toward or away from areas either to maintain or to change the neighborhood is considered? a. Blockbusting. b. Redlining. c. Steering.	c. Steering. The practice of racially steering potential home buyers toward or away from certain neighborhoods is called racial steering.

d. Ignoring.	
78. Denial of a mortgage would be allowed if the denial was based on? a. Sex b. Age c. Race d. Lack of income	d. Lack of income The applicant must have a source of income to qualify for a loan.
79. The Americans with Disabilities Act (ADA) provides protection to those who? a. are age 55 or older. b. have been convicted of selling drugs. c. are receiving treatment for alcoholism. d. have suffered financial hardship because of health costs.	c. is receiving treatment for alcoholism. Those who are receiving treatment for alcoholism are protected under ADA.
80. This federal act that prohibits discrimination against persons with disabilities, where disability is defined as a physical or mental impairment that substantially limits a major life activity. a. Blockbusting b. Americans with Disabilities Act c. Redlining Act d. Title VI	b. Americans with Disabilities Act The Americans with Disabilities Act of 1990 is a law that prohibits unjustified discrimination based on disability.
81. Converting the format of a leasing contract to large print is a response to? a. Regulation Z b. HUD1 c. Truth in Lending Act d. ADA	d. ADA Blind, visually impaired, or deaf-blind individuals may require a qualified reader; information in Braille, large print, or electronically for use with a computer screen-reading program; or audio recordings of printed materials. Someone who is a "qualified" reader is one who can read effectively and accurately, without bias.
82. A mentally disabled person that was declared incompetent can't enter a contract unless? a. A person appointed by the court may enter the contract on the disabled person's behalf. b. A person appointed by a parent can sign legal contracts for the disabled person. c. A disabled person can under no circumstances enter a contract without the written certification acquired while in school. d. A disabled person can correctly spell his/her name.	a. A person appointed by the court may enter the contract on the disabled person's behalf. When a person is mentally incapacitated and is unaware that he or she entered a contract, it is voidable.
83. An accommodation that is not made in a way that offers equal opportunity for a particular individual to use and benefit from a dwelling may be characterized as? a. discrimination b. blockbusting c. steering	a. discrimination As a broad term, discrimination encompasses all types of discriminatory acts. It can be discriminatory if you

d. redlining	violate fair housing laws; or if you violate ADA laws.
84. Which laws provide guidance for making public facilities accessible? a. ADA b. FNME c. RESPA d. FDIC	a. ADA The Americans with Disabilities Act of 1990 or ADA is a civil rights law that prohibits discrimination based on disability.
85. Which of the following would NOT be a requirement under ADA or fair housing laws? a. A landlord must allow disabled tenants to make changes to the property and may not charge the tenants or force them to move. b. The owner of a commercial building could refuse to make changes to the "first come first serve" parking to accommodate a disabled tenant. c. A building with a no-pets policy would have to allow service animals without an additional charge. d. A tenant who makes changes to an apartment to accommodate a disability can be required to return the unit to its original condition upon lease expiration.	b. The owner of a commercial building could refuse to make changes to the "first come first serve" parking to accommodate a disabled tenant. A commercial landlord is expected to provide a disabled tenant with a parking space under reasonable accommodations.
86. In compliance with the ADA, all architectural barriers in existing facilities must be removed: a. even if at great expense b. only if someone complains c. when you hire disabled persons d. if removal is "readily achievable"	d. if removal is "readily achievable" "Readily achievable" means, able to be carried out without much expense.
87. A rental agent has allowed a person dependent on a wheelchair to make necessary, minor changes to a rental property, these changes are referred to as? a. Disability accommodations b. reasonable modifications c. Trade fixtures modification d. Replacement fixtures	b. reasonable modifications An accommodation is a change, exception, or adjustment to a policy, practice, or service on the property. A reasonable modification is a structural change.
88. The ADA required all the following alterations to a public facility except? a. Lowered drinking fountains. b. Grab bars in handicapped bathroom stalls. c. Automatic open doors. d. Automatic sprinkler systems.	d. Automatic sprinkler systems. Automatic sprinkler systems are not required.
89. The law requires an employer to provide reasonable accommodation to an employee or job applicant with a disability unless doing so would cause significant difficulty or expense for the employer. a. true b. false	a. true Law requires employers to provide reasonable accommodations to employees and job applicants with disabilities unless it would cause the employer significant difficulty or expense ("undue hardship").
90. For a brokerage firm to show it is following fair	b. prominently display the equal

housing laws, the firm must? a. make sure all brokers and salespersons take an annual fair housing course. b. prominently display the equal opportunity poster in the office. c. survey all its licensees to make sure they are not steering. d. establish territories for all its licensees to prove equal treatment to all areas of the city.	opportunity poster in the office. The brokerage would be guilty of Prima Facie discrimination if the poster is not displayed.
91. It would be a violation to post an advertisement that states? a. Source of income must be verified b. Section 8 not accepted c. Criminal background checks will be done d. Allowable occupancy based on square footage, family size and make up.	b. Section 8 not accepted Discriminatory advertising does not allow advertising that states "Section 8 not accepted".
92. All the following are violations of fair housing in advertising except? a. Small two bedroom with one bath. b. Christian housing c. English speakers only d. No kids	a. Small two bedroom with one bath. Discriminatory Advertising Examples include statements such as "no kids," "Christian housing," and "English speakers only."
93. If you are advertising online, understand that? a. including or excluding certain audiences or neighborhoods in the settings of your advertisements could be discriminatory. b. advertising in general terms is discriminatory. c. advertising a home in a single-family zoned neighborhood is a violation of fair housing. d. advertising a "smoke free" is a discriminatory practice.	a. including or excluding certain audiences or neighborhoods in the settings of your advertisements could be discriminatory. Using phrases like "no kids" and "Christian housing" is illegal. Also, marketing techniques with more sophistication can exclude populations based on the racial or ethnic composition of certain protected classes and certain neighborhoods. A statement that "Section 8 not accepted" is illegal in jurisdictions that forbid discrimination by income.
94. Discrimination based on the source of income. It would be a violation to post an advertisement that states? a. Source of income must be verified b. Section 8 not accepted c. Criminal background checks will be done d. Allowable occupancy based on square footage, family size and make up.	b. Section 8 not accepted Examples of Discriminatory Advertising In jurisdictions that prohibit discrimination based on source of income, it would be a violation to post an advertisement that states "Section 8 not accepted."
95. A new salesperson showing a property has made several statements to her buyers. All the following statements by the salesperson would be considered puffing EXCEPT? a. "The best views in the city are in this neighborhood."	c. "This neighborhood has the highest SAT scores." The answer is "This neighborhood has the highest SAT scores." Puffing is

b. "The finest lake and mountain views in the state are in this neighborhood." c. "This neighborhood has the highest SAT scores." d. "This is the best house in the neighborhood."	making a statement that is clearly an exaggeration of fact. SAT scores are fact; so, if this statement is made, then it must be true, or it is fraudulent and not considered to be puffing.
96. Which of the following describes a statement obviously exaggerated claims or statements that reasonable consumers would not take seriously? a. puffery b. misrepresentation c. duress marketing d. unfair misleading	a. puffery Puffery usually isn't considered misleading because it's an obvious exaggeration.
97. A salesperson told a customer that his listing has the best view of the ocean. The customer noticed that the property has a peek a boo view of the ocean. This is an example of? a. blockbusting. b. intentional fraud. c. negligent misrepresentation. d. puffing.	d. puffing. Puffing is an exaggerated statement.
98. 60 Oak Road has 5 acres of open pasture and a large home. The home has 5 bedrooms and 4 bathrooms. Call 555-555-5555 now for information! What is missing from this advertisement that makes it a blind ad? a. A legal description of the property. b. Broker's information. c. Salesperson Name. d. Square footage of the home.	b. Broker's information. An ad in which a broker attempts to. advertise a property for sale without disclosing. the fact she is a licensed real estate broker, or. when a broker attempts to mislead the public.
99. MATCH: Fraud a. The intentional misrepresentation of a material fact to harm or take advantage of another person. b. Laws designed to preserve the free enterprise of the open marketplace by making illegal certain private conspiracies and combinations formed to minimize competition. c. Representing both parties to a transaction; while this practice is illegal in many states, in other states it is legal if disclosed and agreed to by the parties. d. Negligent Misrepresentation	a. The intentional misrepresentation of a material fact to harm or take advantage of another person. The intentional misrepresentation of a material fact to harm or take advantage of another person.
100. Under do not call regulations which call would be improper? a. A call on a for sale by owner ad to solicit a sale listing b. calling for survey purposes c. call to a specific business phone d. a call within 3 months of an inquiry	a. A call on a for sale by owner ad to solicit a sale listing If the FSBO owner is on the Do Not Call List, you could obtain a fine
101. A population's detailed characteristics, including its age, education, and other characteristics, is called? a. Population analysis b. Demographics	b. Demographics Demographics is the study of a population-based on factors such as age,

c. Family lifestyles d. Household data	race, and sex. Demographic data refers to socio-economic information expressed statistically, also including employment, education, income, marriage rates, birth and death rates and more factors.
102. All the following are categories of the uses of real property EXCEPT? a. Residential b. Developmental c. Agricultural d. Industrial	b. Developmental There are five main categories of real estate: residential, commercial, industrial, raw land, and special use.
103. People in the real estate business who primarily focus on creating new properties are? a. brokers. b. developers. c. zoning administrators. d. excavators.	b. developers. Developers create communities.
104. All the following are considered commercial property EXCEPT? a. an apartment building. b. a parking lot. c. a shopping center. d. a business opportunity.	a. an apartment building. The answer is an apartment building. Apartments are residential, not commercial.

Definitions Module Ten

1031 Tax Deferred Exchange
Allows an investor to sell a property, reinvest the proceeds in a new property, and defer capital gain taxes.

Allocation of Markets
Customer- allocation agreements involve some arrangement between competitors to split up customers, such as by geographic area, to reduce or eliminate competition.

American with Disabilities Act
The Americans with Disabilities Act (ADA) prohibits discrimination against people with disabilities in several areas, including employment, transportation, public accommodations, communications and access to state and local government' programs and services.

Antitrust Laws
Antitrust laws prohibit business practices that unreasonably deprive consumers of the benefits of competition, resulting in higher prices for inferior products and services.

Architectural barriers
Obstacles or other features in the built environment that impede individuals with disabilities from gaining full and complete access.

Bid Rigging
Bid rigging most commonly occurs when two or more person or firms agree to bid in such a way that a designated person or firm submits the winning bid.

Blind Ad
An advertisement that disguises the advertiser's identity, i.e., contains a phone number with no other identifying data. Licensed brokers should not use blind ads and must disclose agency.

Blockbusting/Panic Peddling
The illegal act of inducing owners to sell now because property value will decrease due to real or rumored group or persons of a protected group are moving into the neighborhood
A man going door-to-door in an older neighborhood and telling the residents that children or families from another country will be moving into their quiet neighborhood is guilty of blockbusting/panic peddling.

CAN- SPAM Act
A law that sets the rules for commercial email, establishes requirements for commercial messages, ☐ gives recipients the right to have you stop emailing them, and spells out tough penalties for violations.

Capital Gains Exclusion
Personal Residences.
Occupied as primary residence for 2 of the last 5 years.
The difference between the adjusted basis of property and selling price.
1. The Taxpayer Relief Act of 1997.
    a. Passed by Congress to greatly reduce the tax on the gain to be realized on the sale of real estate, especially for residential real estate.
    b. With the passage of the Act, individuals can exclude up to☐ $250,000 of capital gains from taxation, while married couples can exclude up to ☐ $500,000. (Personal residence).

Civil Rights Act of 1866
Prohibits discrimination based on race.

Commingling
Commingling is the act of mixing the client's funds with the broker's money.

Company dollar
Gross income minus all commissions.

Conversion
Conversion is taking client funds and converting them into personal funds

Conveyancer Activities
A conveyancer is an attorney who assists buyers on how to take title.
It is legal advice.

Department of Justice (DOJ) - ADA Enforcement
Federal agency that has the authority to enforce all provisions of the Americans with Disabilities Act (ADA) but focuses primarily on ADA Title II (public services by State and local government) and ADA Title III (public accommodations).

Depreciation – Straight-Line Method
Determines the equal annual depreciation allowed in a straight line from the adjusted basis to zero and computed by dividing the adjusted basis by the estimated years remaining of economic life.

Desk Fee/Cost
A charge to salespersons in an office to offset the expenses of the office. It is charged per person.

Discriminatory Restrictive Covenants
Discriminatory covenants were once common in deeds, but in 1948 the Supreme Court held that such covenants were unenforceable.
These covenants may still appear in deeds; they are unenforceable, but it does not affect the validity of the conveyance.

Employing Broker
The broker for whom the salesperson works is called the employing broker, and both will be subject to the terms of an employment agreement, even when the salesperson is an independent contractor.

Errors and Omissions Insurance
Insurance that covers unintentional activities by an agent. E and O Insurance will not cover an agent who makes a deliberate falsehood or tries to deceive someone on purpose.

Exclusionary Zoning
The "Not in My Back Yard" (NIMBY) factor is an unfortunate reality.
Zoning that operates to exclude a class protected under the law may be illegal.
If the attack is grounded on the Constitution, the plaintiff will have the burden of proving purposeful discrimination as defined in the Supreme Court's opinion.

Financial and Brokerage Service Discrimination

Any type of discrimination in the lending of money for home mortgages is illegal under the Fair Housing Act.

Discrimination may also take the form of a refusal to take or process an individual loan application or it may be in the form of "redlining," a practice where loans or mortgages are refused based upon the character of the neighborhood.

Fraud
Intentional deception or misrepresentation – a material misstatement of fact.

Group Boycotting
People, real estate boards or companies getting together to boycott a competitor.

IDX Technology
The technology used by real estate professionals to put the MLS on their website

IRS Form 8300
File Form IRS 8300 is delivered to the IRS for cash transfers of $10,000 or over.

Jones v. Alfred H. Mayer Co., 1968
Upheld the Civil Rights Act of 1866 and removed all exceptions.
Significance: This case was not filed under the Fair Housing Act but under 42 U.S.C. § 1982, which was part of the Civil Rights Act of 1866. This statute was intended to prohibit all race and color discrimination in the sale and rental of property, including governmental and private discrimination.
This case removed all exceptions to fair housing.

Price Fixing
Price fixing occurs when two or more competing Brokers agree on what commission or other broker fees to charge.

Puffery
An exaggerated opinion, not necessarily based in fact, intended to portray the property in a more favorable light. Example: "This property is one of the best buys in the neighborhood. It is sure to go up in value".

Redlining
Redlining is a discriminatory practice that puts services (financial and otherwise) out of reach for residents of certain areas based on race or ethnicity. It can be seen in the systematic denial of mortgages, insurance, loans, and other financial services based on location (and that area's default history) rather than on an individual's qualifications and creditworthiness. Notably, the policy of redlining is felt the most by residents of minority neighborhoods.

Steering
This practice is specifically prohibited and recognized as illegal by the Supreme Court.
The discriminatory practice of directing homebuyers to (or away from) specific areas based on a protected class to maintain homogeneity
Steering is when an agent shows buyer properties only in neighborhoods where the agent believes the buyer should live.

Tie In – Tying Arrangement (tie-in)
The agent tied in the sale of a listing client' home if the client also turns around and buys swampland the agent is selling.

Title VIII of the Civil Rights Act of 1968 (Fair Housing Act, TITLE VIII), as amended, prohibits discrimination in the sale, rental, and financing of dwellings, and in other housing-related transactions, because of
race
color
religion
national origin

Uniform Commercial Code (UCC)
A set of laws that established unified and comprehensive regulations for security transactions of personal property and that superseded existing laws in that field.

MODULE ELEVEN: Basic Math Concepts

Math Used in Real Estate

- As a real estate agent, you might not have to use math every day, but you should be prepared for when a real estate math question arises. Real estate agents should know these math concepts:
  1. Not that Challenging.
  2. Math is not challenging and there are only a few concepts in real estate math that you need to learn. You'll have a better chance of getting through the exam and throughout your career if you practice and understand math problems.

Loan to Value Ratios

The percentage of value of the property that can be borrowed is called the loan to value ratio (LTV). An acceptable loan to value ratio is set by the bank.

Value: $400,000
Loan: $320,000 * The amount to be financed
Loan to Value Ratio is 80%
400,000 – 320,000 equals $80,000 down payment

☐ When financing a property, loan to value is based on appraised value, not sales price.

Equity

The difference between a property's value and the debt on the property is a good definition of Equity
Value: $400,000
Loan: $320,000

Down Payment: $80,000 is the equity

Discount Points

A point equals 1 percent of the loan amount. *a common math question.

A point is not 1 percent of the sale price of the house, but 1 percent of the loan amount.

Sales Price: $200,000
Down payment: 20%
If 2 points are paid, how much is that?

200,000 x .80 equals loan amount of 160,000
160,000 x .02 equals $3200
2 points is $3200

Property Tax

Property tax is an ad valorem tax, which means it is based on value.
Mill rate is also known as the millage rate.
Your home's value is determined by your local tax assessor's office.
Property taxes are critical to funding the operations of municipal and other local government entities.

For example, if the mill rate is 7 and a taxpayer's personal residence has a taxable value of $150,000, then, using the calculation formula, the homeowner's property tax bill for his residence is $1,050.

So that means that for every $1,000 of assessed value, $7 is owed in property taxes.
The assessment is based on the tax assessor's estimation of the market value of your property.

Prorations

- Prorate means "to divide proportionately." In real estate we prorate the buyer's and seller's income and expenses, which include items like interest on loans, property taxes, homeowner fees, and rents collected.
- Prorations are either between the Buyer and Seller or Buyer and Broker or Seller and Broker. Prorations are posted as Debits (taking money from a person) and Credits (giving money to a person).
- When prorating, calculate the number of days owed for the expense, interest, or rents.
- The days are based on either a banker's year (also called a statutory year) which consists of 30 days in every month (360 days on the National part of the exam) or a calendar year (365 days on the State part of the exam).
- Calendar Leap Year would be 366 days. When you are given a proration problem, you will be told which calendar to use.

Assumption of Loan

Debit Seller and Credit Buyer
(Take that loan away from the seller and give it to the buyer. ☐)

Seller Agrees to Selling Price of $250,000		
Commission Agrees to pay 8% (negotiable)		
4% to you	Multiple Listing Service	4% to cooperating broker

Seller	Meeting of the Minds at $250,000 Purchase Agreement	Buyer
	The Purchase Agreement is the contract between the Seller and Buyer	

Example: the property sold for $250,000

Your Broker gets 4% of $250,000 = $10,000	Some other Broker
(250,000x .04 = 10,000)	Don't care.
$10,000 commission to Broker	Who cares?
Your employment agreement is 50/50.	

50% of $10,000 is $5,000.	
You get $5,000	

PITI (Principal, Interest, Taxes, and Insurance) payments
1. Principle
2. Interest
3. Taxes
4. Insurance

QUESTION

The Situation
1. Sale Price: $300,000.00
2. Down Payment: 20%
3. Interest Rate: 6.5%
4. Terms: 30 years
5. Homeowner's Insurance: $1850.00 per year
6. Property Tax: Assessed at 70% of its purchase price and $2.84 per $100.00. (Mill rate)
7. What is the monthly payment?

Principle Interest and Terms
Sale Price: $300,000.00
Down Payment: 20%
Interest Rate: 6.5%
Terms: 30 years

Step One: Find the loan amount.
Down payment: 300,000 x .20 = 60,000
Loan amount: 300,000 x .80 = 240,000
80 + 20 = 100% of the money.
Loan Amount: $240,000
Interest Rate: 6.5%
Terms: 30 years

Amortization Table

AMORTIZATION TABLE

Monthly Payment per $1,000 of Loan

Interest Rate: 6.5 for the term of 30 years

Interest Rate per Year	Life of the Loan							
	5 years	10 years	15 years	20 years	25 years	30 years	35 years	40 years
5	$18.88	$10.61	$7.91	$6.60	$5.85	■■	$5.05	$4.83
5½	19.11	10.86	8.18	6.88	6.15	■■	5.38	5.16
6	19.34	11.11	8.44	7.17	6.45	■■	5.71	5.51
6½	■■	■■	■■	■■	■■	6.32	6.05	5.86
7	19.81	11.62	8.99	7.76	7.07	6.66	6.39	6.22
7½	20.04	11.88	9.28	8.06	7.39	7.00	6.75	6.59

AMORTIZATION TABLE

Monthly Payment per $1,000 of Loan

Interest Rate per Year	Life of the Loan							
	5 years	10 years	15 years	20 years	25 years	30 years	35 years	40 years
5	$18.88	$10.61	$7.91	$6.60	$5.85	$5.37	$5.05	$4.83
5½	19.11	10.86	8.18	6.88	6.15	5.68	5.38	5.16
6	19.34	11.11	8.44	7.17	6.45	6.00	5.71	5.51
6½	19.57	11.36	8.72	7.46	6.76	6.32	6.05	5.86
7	19.81	11.62	8.99	7.76	7.07	6.66	6.39	6.22
7½	20.04	11.88	9.28	8.06	7.39	7.00	6.75	6.59
8	20.28	12.14	9.56	8.37	7.72	7.34	7.11	6.96
8½	20.52	12.40	9.85	8.68	8.06	7.69	7.47	7.34
9	20.76	12.67	10.15	9.00	8.40	8.05	7.84	7.72
9½	21.01	12.94	10.45	9.33	8.74	8.41	8.22	8.11
10	21.25	13.22	10.75	9.66	9.09	8.78	8.60	8.50
10½	21.50	13.50	11.06	9.99	9.45	9.15	8.99	8.89
11	21.75	13.78	11.37	10.33	9.81	9.53	9.37	9.29
11½	22.00	14.06	11.69	10.67	10.17	9.91	9.77	9.69
12	22.25	14.35	12.01	11.02	10.54	10.29	10.16	10.09
12½	22.50	14.64	12.33	11.37	10.91	10.68	10.56	10.49
13	22.76	14.94	12.66	11.72	11.28	11.07	10.96	10.90
13½	23.01	15.23	12.99	12.08	11.66	11.46	11.36	11.31
14	23.27	15.53	13.32	12.44	12.04	11.85	11.76	11.72
14½	23.53	15.83	13.66	12.80	12.43	12.25	12.17	12.13
15	23.79	16.14	14.00	13.17	12.81	12.65	12.57	12.54
15½	24.06	16.45	14.34	13.54	13.20	13.05	12.98	12.95
16	24.32	16.76	14.69	13.92	13.59	13.45	13.39	13.36

240,000 divided by 1000 = 240
6.32
(Meet 6.5 and 20 years)
240,000 divided by 1000 = 240
6.32
240 x 6.32 = <u>1516.80</u>

Principal and Interest Payment
1. <u>Sale Price: $300,000.00</u>
2. <u>Down Payment: 20%.</u>
3. <u>Interest Rate: 6.5%.</u>
4. <u>Terms: 30 years</u>
5. Homeowner's Insurance: $1850.00 per year
6. Property Tax: Assessed at 70% of its purchase price and $2.84 per $100.00. (Mill rate)
7. What is the monthly payment?

Insurance
Homeowner's Insurance: $1850.00 per year
1850 divided by 12 months = <u>154.16</u>

Homeowners Insurance
1. <u>Sale Price: $300,000.00</u>
2. <u>Down Payment: 20%. DONE</u>
3. <u>Interest Rate: 6.5%. DONE</u>
4. <u>Terms: 30 years DONE</u>
5. <u>Homeowner's Insurance: $1850.00 per year. DONE</u>
6. Property Tax: Assessed at 70% of its purchase price and $2.84 per $100.00. (Mill rate) DONE
7. What is the monthly payment?

Taxes
Property Tax: Assessed at
70% of its purchase price and
$2.84 per $100.00. (Mill rate)
70% of its purchase price

Purchase price of 300,000 x .70 (70 percent) = 210,000
$2.84 per $100.00. (Mill rate)
210,000 divided by 100 = 2100
2100 times 2.84 = 5964
5964 divided by 12 months = <u>497</u>
1. <u>Sale Price: $300,000.00. DONE</u>
2. <u>Down Payment: 20%. DONE</u>
3. <u>Interest Rate: 6.5%. DONE</u>
4. <u>Terms: 30 years DONE</u>
5. <u>Homeowner's Insurance: $1850.00 per year. DONE</u>
6. <u>Property Tax: Assessed at 70% of its purchase price and $2.84 per $100.00. (Mill rate) DONE</u>
7. What is the monthly payment?

What is the monthly payment?

240 x 6.32 = <u>1516.80</u>
1516.80
Principal and Interest Payment
1850 divided by 12 months = <u>154.16</u>

Homeowners Insurance
154.16
Homeowner's Insurance
210,000 divided by 100 = 2100
2100 times 2.84 = 5964
5964 divided by 12 months = <u>497</u>
497

Property Tax
Total MONTHLY Payment
$2167.96

Module Eleven: Math Quiz

1. Ana, John, and Jim bought together a property worth $675,000. John put up $337,500, Ana put up 25%. How much money did Jim have to come up with? a. $172,564. b. $158,943. c. $168,750. d. $89,500.	c. $168,750. $675,000. John put up $337,500, Ana put up 25%. How much money did Jim have to come up with? 675,000 times .25 equals ($168,750 Ana) Johns = 337,500 Ana= 168,750 John plus Ana equal = 506,250 for them $675,000 minus 506,250 = 168,750
2. John bought a rental apartment building for $215,000. The assessed value is $205,000. The tax rate is $1.50 per 100 of assessed value. What is the monthly tax? a. $307.75 b. $256.25 c. $3075 d. None of the above	b. $256.25 The Assessed Value is $205,000. The tax rate is $1.50 per 100 of assessed value. $205,000 divided by 100 equals 2050 times $1.50 equals $3,075 divided by twelve (12 months.) equals 256.25.
3. Ana bought a home for $165,000. Her assessed value is $160,000. She is taxed 2.25 for every 100 of assessed value. What is her monthly tax due? a. $301.25 b. $295.87 c. $303.65 d. None of the above.	d. None of the above. Assessed value is $160,000. She is taxed 2.25 for every 100 of assessed value. What is her monthly tax due? $160,000 divided by 100 equals 1600 times 2.25 equals 3600 divided by 12 months equals 300.
4. A broker received a commission of 6% of the selling price from his client. The commission was $9720. The sales price of the property was? a. $160,000. b. $158,000.	c. $162,000. 6% of the selling price from his client. The commission was $9720. 162,000 times .06 equals 9720.

c. $162,000. d. None of the above.	

U. S. Department of Housing and Urban Development

**EQUAL HOUSING
OPPORTUNITY**

Thank you for trusting the Real Estate Training Institute.

Made in the USA
Columbia, SC
17 May 2023

16826922R00213